D1807287

A COSMOPOLITAN JURISPRUDENCE

H Patrick Glenn (1940–2014), Professor of Law and former Director of the Institute of Comparative Law at McGill University, was a key figure in the global discourse on comparative law. This collection is intended to honour Professor Glenn's intellectual legacy by engaging critically with his ideas, especially focusing on his visions of a 'cosmopolitan state' and of law conceptualized as 'tradition'. The book explores the intellectual history of comparative law as a discipline, its attempts to push the objects of its study beyond the positive law of the nation state, and both its potential and the challenges it must confront in the face of the complex phenomena of globalization and the internationalization of law. An international group of leading scholars in comparative law, legal philosophy, legal sociology, and legal history takes stock of the field of comparative law and where it is headed.

Helge Dedek is Professor of Law at McGill University and former Director of the McGill Institute of Comparative Law. Since 2014, he serves as Co-Editor-in-Chief of the *American Journal of Comparative Law*.

ASCL STUDIES IN COMPARATIVE LAW

ASCL Studies in Comparative Law publishes monographs and collections that broaden theoretical and practical knowledge of the world's many legal systems. Published under the direction of the American Society of Comparative Law, the *ASCL Studies* examine legal problems in a comparative light to advance legal science, develop technical insights, and promote greater cooperation across jurisdictional and cultural boundaries. This book series serves legal practitioners and those seeking to improve law and justice by publishing in-depth comparative studies of specific legal problems in every area of law.

The series has two general editors. David Gerber is Distinguished Professor of Law and Co-Director of the Program in International and Comparative Law at Chicago-Kent College of Law, Illinois Institute of Technology. He is past President of the American Society of Comparative Law. Mortimer Sellers is Regents Professor of the University System of Maryland and Director of the Baltimore Center for International and Comparative Law. He is past President of the Internationale Vereinigung für Rechts- und Sozialphilosophie.

A Cosmopolitan Jurisprudence

ESSAYS IN MEMORY OF H. PATRICK GLENN

Edited by

HELGE DEDEK

McGill University

CAMBRIDGE
UNIVERSITY PRESS

University Printing House, Cambridge CB2 8BS, United Kingdom

One Liberty Plaza, 20th Floor, New York, NY 10006, USA

477 Williamstown Road, Port Melbourne, VIC 3207, Australia

314–321, 3rd Floor, Plot 3, Splendor Forum, Jasola District Centre, New Delhi – 110025, India

103 Penang Road, #05–06/07, Visioncrest Commercial, Singapore 238467

Cambridge University Press is part of the University of Cambridge.

It furthers the University's mission by disseminating knowledge in the pursuit of education, learning, and research at the highest international levels of excellence.

www.cambridge.org
Information on this title: www.cambridge.org/9781108841726
DOI: 10.1017/9781108894760

First published 2022

A catalogue record for this publication is available from the British Library.

Library of Congress Cataloging-in-Publication Data
NAMES: Dedek, Helge, 1973– editor. | Glenn, H. Patrick, honouree.
TITLE: A cosmopolitan jurisprudence : essays in memory of H. Patrick Glenn / edited by Helge Dedek, McGill University, Faculty of Law.
DESCRIPTION: Cambridge, United Kingdom ; New York, NY : Cambridge University Press, 2022. | Series: Ascl studies in comparative law | Includes bibliographical references and index.
IDENTIFIERS: LCCN 2021026911 (print) | LCCN 2021026912 (ebook) | ISBN 9781108841726 (hardback) | ISBN 9781108795258 (paperback) | ISBN 9781108894760 (ebook)
SUBJECTS: LCSH: Law lcsh | LCGFT: Festschriften.
CLASSIFICATION: LCC K561 .C67 2022 (print) | LCC K561 (ebook) | DDC 340/.2–dc23
LC record available at https://lccn.loc.gov/2021026911
LC ebook record available at https://lccn.loc.gov/2021026912

ISBN 978-1-108-84172-6 Hardback

The perspective of the cosmopolitan must entail relationships to a plurality of cultures understood as distinctive entities. (And the more the better; cosmopolitans should ideally be foxes rather than hedgehogs.) But furthermore, cosmopolitanism in a stricter sense includes a stance toward diversity itself, toward the coexistence of cultures in the individual experience. A more genuine cosmopolitanism is first of all an orientation, a willingness to engage with the Other.

Ulf Hannerz[*]

[*] Ulf Hannerz, 'Cosmopolitans and Locals in World Culture' (1990) 7 *Theory, Culture & Society* 237, 239.

Contents

Foreword

William Twining

Patrick Glenn died unexpectedly in 2014. This book was put together in his honour. Patrick would not have wanted a conventional *festschrift* or *liber amicorum*. He preferred dialogue, conversations, even criticism. The contributors have proceeded in the same spirit. The result is a series of responses to his writings in the form of extensions, applications, refinements, queries, and dissents, which combine to augment his legacy in a number of directions. All of the chapters exhibit great respect for him as a person, thinker, and scholar, but all engage with him critically.

Glenn is now famous as the author of *Legal Traditions of the World*, which was published in 2000, having already been awarded the Grand Prize of the International Academy of Comparative Law two years prior. It is already in its fifth edition. For comparatists, he was already well known as an erudite, thoughtful, and highly original scholar who was given to challenging orthodoxies within the sub-discipline. What was surprising to almost everyone is that *Legal Traditions of the World* also turned out to be an audacious, radical, and provocative contribution to general jurisprudence. On publication, this work attracted a great deal of attention. Taken on its own, it has given Glenn the image of an *agent provocateur*, but it has to be set in the context of his later writings, which, although highly original, are more nuanced, reflective, and narrowly focused. As the authors of the subsequent chapters make clear, his later writings refine, amplify, and develop the bold theses of *Legal Traditions of the World*.

I first met Patrick in 2003 during his stay in Oxford. We became friends, had some enthralling conversations, and stayed in touch, but I have regretted that we never had much closer contact. Stimulated by the second edition of *Legal Traditions of the World* (2004), a group of us held a seminar at the School of Oriental and African Studies in 2005, and I helped to coordinate the publication of a symposium in the first volume of the *Journal of Comparative Law*.[1] Praise and criticism were evenly distributed and Patrick responded with characteristic grace and verve.[2]

[1] Nicholas HD Foster (ed), 'A Fresh Start for Comparative Legal Studies?' (2006) 1 *JCL* 100.

[2] H Patrick Glenn, 'Legal Traditions and *Legal Traditions*' (2007) 2 *JCL* 69.

As soon as I read *Legal Traditions of the World*, I realized that this was an important book, but it required several readings before I realized how important it was. It is worth spelling out the main reasons for its significance for both legal theory and the discipline of law.

First, it adopts a genuinely global perspective without the tendencies to reductionism of most globalization theory and inflated 'globababble'.[3] Glenn takes on all law, broadly conceived, in the whole world, but his message is one of complexity. Legal phenomena are varied, fluid, constantly changing, and interacting. They cannot be captured by simple static snapshots of 'momentary legal systems'.

Second, *Legal Traditions of the World* shows how macro-comparative law, often dismissed as not intellectually respectable, can be central to developing a vision of legal phenomena that no longer treats sovereign nation states and Western municipal legal systems as the 'essence' of law. By moving beyond Western perspectives, it contributes significantly to the decolonization of comparative law and legal theory.

Third, by choosing tradition as his central concept in preference to legal systems, culture, civilizations, or legal families, Glenn reinserts history and pastness at the core, while rejecting dichotomies between past and present. *Legal Traditions of the World* can be seen as reviving the dormant tradition of historical jurisprudence of Vico, Montesquieu, Maine, and Vinogradoff and joins forces with contemporary jurists like Brian Tamanaha in re-establishing sociohistorical perspectives as the third, often missing, pillar of theoretical understandings of law.[4] Although Glenn did not develop this very far, he has also provided an important bridge to world history, which is again becoming a respectable pursuit.[5] However, I share the feelings of Martin Krygier and David Nelken (expounded in this volume) that Patrick was over-optimistic in suggesting that traditions are inherently benign and supportive of his hopes for 'sustainable diversity'.

Glenn's particular conception of tradition in terms of 'flows of normative information' has provoked much criticism and discussion. Clearly, there are conceptual difficulties, but in my view it suits his purposes very well. He gives the concept sufficient analytical purchase to enable comparison of traditions in terms of four aspects: information as the core that constitutes the identity of a tradition, its underlying justification, its concept of change, and how the tradition relates to other traditions.[6] Moreover, as he pointed out to me in conversation, the concept of culture combines both ideas and actual practices while downplaying the past,[7] whereas by confining the idea of tradition to information (ideas in a broad sense), he

3 William Twining, *Jurist in Context* (CUP 2019) 234.

4 Brian Z Tamanaha, A *Realistic Theory of Law* (CUP 2017).

5 See, for example, the work of Jürgen Osterhammel and colleagues.

6 H Patrick Glenn, *Legal Traditions of the World: Sustainable Diversity in Law* (5th edn, OUP 2014) xxvi.

7 On culture as a concept, see H Patrick Glenn, 'Legal Cultures and Legal Traditions' in Mark van Hoecke (ed), *Epistemology and Methodology in Comparative Law* (Bloomsbury 2004) 7, 11ff.

had made his project more manageable while treating the past as part of the present. These intriguing claims are explored in depth in the ensuing chapters.

Fourth, comparative law as a distinct sub-discipline has tended to focus on a rather narrow range of issues. Glenn, on the other hand, opens up the field by linking it directly to such topical ideas as corruption, fundamentalism, multivalent logic, 'clash of civilizations', and even chaos theory.

This volume neatly sets the ideas of Glenn the *agent provocateur* in the context of more nuanced and careful reflections of an immensely erudite and original scholar, and as John Bell suggests, he undermines any sharp dichotomy between macro- and micro-comparative studies. It brings out clearly why Patrick Glenn's work deserves the attention of legal theorists and colleagues in other disciplines in addition to giving new directions to comparative law.

Acknowledgements

The publication of this volume concludes a long journey, throughout which a debt of gratitude has accumulated. First, I wish to thank Jane Glenn for kindly offering advice and, especially, for giving this project her blessing. Jane Glenn also suggested that I reach out to William Twining, whose participation in this project has been of pivotal importance. Besides contributing the Foreword, William Twining has accompanied this undertaking from its inception, has read the manuscript, and has offered feedback, guidance, and assistance throughout.

I also wish to express my gratitude to all the authors who have contributed to this volume for making this tribute possible. I am grateful to Vivian Curran, in particular, for organizing a panel in memory of Patrick Glenn at the 2018 World Congress of Comparative Law at Fukuoka, where several contributors to this book had a chance to present their homage to Patrick Glenn and to workshop their ideas.

I am grateful to Matt Gallaway of the Cambridge University Press for his stewardship, and to two anonymous peer reviewers for their constructive criticism. Richard Kay and Mortimer Sellers have kindly welcomed this volume into the *ASCL Studies in Comparative Law Book Series*. My McGill colleague Lysanne Larose graciously allowed me to use the beautiful portrait she took of Patrick Glenn in 2012. The *Archives de la Ville de Montréal* gave their permission to make use of an archival image of Buckminster Fuller's Expo 67 American Pavilion. Special thanks are owed to Montreal artist Michel de Broin, who generously agreed to images of his artwork 'Black Whole Conference' being used in this book and as its cover image.

Jennifer Anderson and Amber Lynch have offered feedback and overseen the logistics of the editing process, both aptly drawing on their ample experience (inter alia) as Article Editors of the *American Journal of Comparative Law*. Cora Madden assisted in the editing process and created the index. Finally, I am grateful to the Eddie Look and Winnie Wing Yin Chan Fund and the Law & You Fund for financial support.

Helge Dedek

Notes on Contributors

John Bell is Emeritus Professor of Law at the University of Cambridge. He has written extensively on French law, comparative legal method, and German law. His major works include *European Legal Development: The Case of Tort* (with David Ibbetson, Cambridge University Press, 2012) and *Markesinis's German Law of Torts* (5th ed., edited with André Janssen, Bloomsbury, 2019). Previous publications have included *Judiciaries within Europe* (Cambridge University Press, 2006), and books on French constitutional and administrative law. Until 2019 he was editor of the *Cambridge Law Journal*. He taught previously in England at the University of Oxford (1980–89) and the University of Leeds (1989–2001), as well as at the Universities of Paris 1 and 2 (1974–75 and 1985–86).

Mauro Bussani is Professor of Comparative Law at the University of Trieste, Adjunct Professor at the University of Macao, and Member of the Faculty of the Católica Global School of Law (Lisbon). He has a PhD Honoris Causa from the University of Fribourg. He has been a visiting professor in Brazil, Canada, China, France, Hungary, Israel, Peru, Portugal, Serbia, Switzerland, the United Kingdom, and the United States. He is a member of the American Law Institute, the Société de législation comparée (France), and a Titular Member of the International Academy of Comparative Law. He coedits three comparative law series, one for Intersentia, one for Brill and one for Oxford University Press. His principal publications include 29 books (of which eighteen are edited) and more than 160 essays, written in English, French, and Italian. Many of his works have been translated into Chinese, Japanese, Korean, Portuguese, Serbian, Spanish, and Turkish.

Vivian Grosswald Curran is Distinguished Professor of Law and Vice President of the International Academy of Comparative Law as well as past President of the American Society of Comparative Law. She also is correspondante étrangère of the Institut des sciences juridique et philosophique de la Sorbonne, Centre de droit comparé et internationalisation du droit. She serves on the Board of Advisors of the Max Planck Institute for Comparative and International Private Law, Hamburg, and the Luxembourg Max Planck Institute for Procedural Law's Comparative Procedural Law and Justice Project. Her writing is in the area of comparative and transnational law and her most recent book is *Porosités du droit/Law's Porosities* (Société de législation comparée, Paris, 2020).

Helge Dedek is a Full Professor of Law at McGill University. He is interested and has published in comparative and transnational legal history, legal theory, and private law. He is a Titular Member of the International Academy of Comparative Law and has held appointments as Professor of Transnational Law and Foreign Legislations at Lausanne University and as Director of the McGill Institute of Comparative Law. Since 2014, he has been serving (together with Franz Werro) as the Editor-in-Chief of the *American Journal of Comparative Law*.

Thomas Duve is Director of the Max Planck Institute for Legal History and Legal Theory and Professor of Comparative Legal History at Goethe University Frankfurt. His work focuses on the legal history of the imperial spaces of the Iberian monarchies in the early modern period and modernity. He is particularly interested in the history of canon law and moral theology, especially that of the School of Salamanca, and in the history of knowledge creation in the field of law and other modes of normativity. Further fields of interest include the history and methodology of the discipline of legal history.

Michele Graziadei is Professor of Comparative Private Law at the University of Torino and Fellow at the Collegio Carlo Alberto, in Torino. His research focuses on the methodology of comparative law, comparative legal history, legal pluralism, legal translation, and other theoretical problems relating to the comparison of laws. He is a Titular Member of the International Academy of Comparative Law, and President of the Italian Society for Research in Comparative Law (SIRD). He is the author of over a hundred publications in several languages.

Ko Hasegawa is Professor Emeritus of Legal Philosophy and a Visiting Fellow and Adjunct Lecturer at the Advanced Institute of Law and Politics at the School of Law, Hokkaido University, Sapporo, Japan. His academic interests are broadly the structure of legal thinking, rights and justice, and the concept of law. He has published three books and many papers on various issues in legal philosophy. He has also co-edited a book for an introduction to legal philosophy and edited a collection of collaborative essays on the problem of the interaction of different legal systems. Further, as he developed a comparative interest in law, he communicated with H Patrick Glenn for several years until his untimely death, in particular, concerning the problem of the confluence of *Legal Traditions*. Professor Hasegawa is currently working on the logic of confluence in law, especially through considering the reception problem in modern Japanese law, for bridging between the explorations of legal philosophy and the ones of comparative law and legal history.

Ahmed Fekry Ibrahim is a researcher in Islamic law and Islamic studies. He holds a BA from Al-Azhar University, an MA from the American University in Cairo, and a PhD in Islamic studies from Georgetown University (2011). His research interests cover juristic discourse and court practice in both the formative period of Islamic law and the post-classical Mamluk and Ottoman periods. He is the author of *Pragmatism in Islamic Law: A Social and Intellectual History* (Syracuse University Press 2015), and *Child Custody in Islamic Law: Theory and Practice in Egypt since the Sixteenth Century* (Cambridge University Press 2018). His research has been supported with research grants from the Fonds de recherche du Québec–Société et culture (FRQSC) and the Social Sciences and Humanities Research Council of Canada (SSHRC). He can be reached at afi@georgetown.edu.

Marie Seong-Hak Kim is Professor of History at St Cloud State University (USA), and attorney at law. She specializes in comparative legal history with emphasis on Korea, Japan, and France. She is the author of *Custom, Law, and Monarchy: A Legal History of Early Modern France* (Oxford University Press 2021), *Constitutional Transition and the Travail of Judges: The Courts of South Korea* (Cambridge University Press 2019), *Law and Custom in Korea: Comparative Legal History* (Cambridge University Press 2012), and *Michel de L'Hôpital: The Vision of a Reformist Chancellor during the French Religious Wars* (Truman State University Press 1997), and the editor of *The Spirit of Korean Law: Korean Legal History in Context* (Brill Nijhoff 2016).

Martin Krygier is Gordon Samuels Professor of Law and Social Theory at the University of New South Wales, Australia; Honorary Professor, RegNet, Australian National University, and Senior Research Fellow, Central European University Democracy Institute. He is a fellow of the Academy of Social Sciences in Australia. His works include *Philip Selznick: Ideals in the World*; *Between Fear and Hope*; *Civil Passions*, and (as editor) *Spreading Democracy and the Rule of Law?*; *Rethinking the Rule of Law After Communism*; *Community and Legality*; *The Rule of Law After Communism*; *Marxism and Communism*; and *Bureaucracy*. He writes on the conditions and nature of the rule of law, and the challenges involved in developing and sustaining it, particularly in politically scarred societies, more particularly those of post-communist Europe. He has a particular interest in the implications of populism for the rule of law and constitutional democracy. His writings seek to meld politically engaged legal and political theory with social theory, observation, and experience. In 2016, he was awarded the Dennis Leslie Mahoney Prize in Legal Theory, for his book on Philip Selznick and his writings on the rule of law.

David Nelken, PhD, LLD (Cambridge), has been Professor of Comparative and Transnational Law at the Dickson Poon School of Law, King's College, London, since 2013 (and was Vice Dean and Head of Research, 2013–16). From 1976 to 1989 he taught at Cambridge, Edinburgh, and University College, London, before moving to Italy in 1990 as Distinguished Professor of Legal Institutions and Social Change at the University of Macerata. From 1995 to 2013 he was also Distinguished Research Professor of Law at Cardiff University, and from 2010 to 2014 Visiting Professor of Criminology at Oxford University. Professor Nelken's research involves theoretical enquiry and empirical investigation in the areas of comparative sociology of law and legal and social theory and criminology, and awards received include the American Sociological Association Distinguished Scholar Award (1985), the Sellin-Glueck International Award of the American Criminological Society (2009), the Podgorecki Distinguished Senior Scholar Award from the International Sociological Association (2011), and the (United States) Law and Society Association's International Scholar Award (2013). In comparative law, he has been mainly interested in discussions of legal culture and legal transplants; see, for example, *Adapting Legal Cultures* (edited with Johannes Feest, Hart/Bloomsbury 2001) and *Comparative Law: A Handbook* (edited with Esin Örücü, Hart/Bloomsbury 2007).

Esin Örücü started her academic career at the University of Istanbul and then joined the University of Glasgow in 1976, where she is now Professor Emerita of Comparative Law. Professor Örücü is also Professor Emerita of Comparative Law, Erasmus University, Rotterdam, and a Visiting Professor at Okan University, Istanbul. She holds an honorary doctorate from the University of Uppsala and is a Titular Member of the International Academy of Comparative Law. She also served as Vice Chair of the Scottish Association of Comparative Law. Professor Örücü has authored and edited many prominent books, articles, and book chapters, dealing with comparative law, in general, mixed jurisdictions, multiple aspects of Turkish law, including family law, constitutional law, and historical aspects of the Ottoman Empire.

Giorgio Resta, PhD University of Pisa (1999), is Full Professor of Comparative Law at the University of Roma Tre. Senior Wainwright Fellow at McGill Law School (2015), he taught courses as a visiting professor at McGill, EHESS, and Nagoya, among other universities. Associate Member of the International Academy of Comparative Law, ELI fellow, Honorary Member of the Italian Civil Law Association, and co-founder of the Italian Academy for the Internet Code, he served as a member of two Legislative Reform Committees appointed by the Italian Ministry of Justice. He is the author of books and essays in the fields of comparative law, law and technology, law and history, and general private law.

Gunnar Folke Schuppert is Professor Emeritus of Public Law and Administrative Science at Humboldt University Berlin. He led a research project on rule of law at the Collaborative Research Centre 700 (SFB) titled 'Governance in Areas of Limited Statehood' until 2017 and is a fellow at the Max-Weber-Kolleg Erfurt.

From 2003 to 2011, he held a research professorship on 'New Forms of Governance' at the Berlin Social Science Centre (WZB) and was Managing Director of the WZB Rule of Law Centre. He has authored over 200 academic publications. Most recent publications include *Eine globale Ideengeschichte in der Sprache des Rechts* (*A Global History of Ideas in the Language of Law*) (Max Planck Institute for European Legal History Research Paper Series No. 2019–02) (English translation forthcoming); *The World of Rules: A Somewhat Different Measurement of the World. Global Perspectives on Legal History* (Max Planck Institute for European Legal History No. 10, 2017); and *Governance of Diversity: Zum Umgang mit kultureller und religiöser Pluralität in säkularen Gesellschaften* (2017).

William Twining is the Emeritus Quain Professor of Jurisprudence at University College London, having held the post until 1996. He is a leading member of the Law in Context movement, and has contributed especially to jurisprudence, intellectual history, and the legal theory of 'globalization'. Publications include *General Jurisprudence: Understanding* Law *from a Global Perspective* (Cambridge University Press 2009) and *Globalisation and Legal Theory* (Cambridge University Press 2000).

Catherine Valcke is Full Professor, Faculty of Law, at the University of Toronto. She has taught, lectured, and published on comparative law and comparative law theory worldwide, including in such journals as *Nomos*, the *American Journal of Comparative Law, Harvard Journal of Law and Public Policy, Yale Journal of International Law*, and the *European Review of Private Law*. Her work on English and French contract law was recently cited as 'illuminating' by the English House of Lords. An elected member of the International Academy of Comparative Law, she has acted as National Reporter for Canada to the Congress of the Academy on several occasions. Her book *Comparing Law* (Cambridge University Press 2018) bridges comparative law and legal theory in developing an analytic framework for comparative law that is consistent with the traditional literature accumulated to date and will guide future work in the field.

Neil Walker holds the Regius Chair of Public Law and the Law of Nature and Nations at the University of Edinburgh. His main area of expertise is constitutional theory. He has published extensively on the constitutional dimension of legal order at sub-state, state, supranational, and global levels, and on the relationship between security, legal order, and political community. Previously, he was Professor of Legal and Constitutional Theory at the University of Aberdeen (1996–2000) and Professor of European Law at the European University Institute, Florence (2000–08). He has held various visiting appointments, including Eugene Einaudi Chair of European Studies, University of Cornell (2007), Distinguished Visiting Professor of Law, University of Toronto (2007), Global Professor of Law, New York University (2011–12), Sidley Austin-Robert D McLean Visiting Professor of Law, Yale University (2014–15), and International Francqui Chair, University of Leuven, (2017). He has an LLD (Honoris Causa) from the University of Uppsala, is a fellow of the British Academy, and is also a fellow of the Royal Society of Edinburgh. His most recent books are the monograph, *Intimations of Global Law* (Cambridge University Press, 2015) and the edited collections, *The Scottish Independence Referendum: Constitutional and Political Implications* (co-editor, Oxford University Press, 2016), and *Sovereignty in Action* (co-editor, Cambridge University Press, 2019). He is presently completing a study of the EU as an 'experimental project'.

Images

INTRODUCTION

Where the 'Real Action' Is: From Comparative Law to Cosmopolitan Jurisprudence

Helge Dedek[*]

I A COSMOPOLITAN JURISPRUDENCE

In his 2005 work *Black Whole Conference* (Image 1), Montreal artist Michel de Broin arranges chairs into an austere and solemn black sphere. Chairs, especially conference chairs, art critic Bernard Schütze writes about this piece, insinuate communication, collective discussion; the shape of the sphere, without beginning and end, and with each chair positioned equidistant from the centre, appears to create a 'public sphere' and conditions allowing for an ideal speech situation: '[H]ierarchy is abolished and central authority is evacuated.'[1] The centre cannot hold? Here, the centre is empty, and yet nothing falls apart.

Can law be imagined thus, de-centred, as an organic, self-sustaining yet open discourse without beginnings and ends, without borders? Can it be theorized successfully without the central concepts of authority, power, force – and should it be? Patrick Glenn was one of the scholars who had the ambition and courage to try. His belief in the possibility of dialogue and in the potential to negotiate conflict crystallized in his concept of 'tradition'. He believed in the possibility of a peaceful coexistence in which traditions engage in perpetual exchange and yet maintain their distinctive identities – a vision, without notions of hierarchy and dominance, of a global 'sustainable diversity' of traditions (in the plural) in which the division between centre and periphery has collapsed.

Understanding law as 'tradition(s)', however, allowed Patrick to take another step. Himself a participant in the discursive tradition of comparative law, he meant to free this troubled sub-discipline from the conventional, self-imposed limitation of using the legal 'systems' of nation states as 'units of comparison' and thus the nation state as

* Some of the reflections offered here were presented on the occasion of a plenary panel in memory of H Patrick Glenn at the 2018 Congress of the International Academy of Comparative Law in Fukuoka; I am grateful to the Academy for the invitation and to Vivian Curran for initiating this event. For comments, research, and editing assistance I am grateful to Jennifer Anderson, Alicia Krausewitz, Amber Lynch, Alex McPhail, and Shona Musimbe.

1 Bernard Schütze, 'On Michel de Broin's "Black Whole Conference"' <https://micheldebroin.org/en/works/black-whole-conference-i-2>.

IMAGE 1 Michel de Broin, *Black Whole Conference* (2005). Collection du Musée d'art contemporain du Val-de-Marne, France

its foremost reference point. Yet this fixation on the nation state and its positive law, he found, did not only unduly limit the understanding of 'comparative law'; it held back Western thought about law in its entirety. As William Twining also points out in his foreword,[2] Patrick's suggestion to conceptualize law without relying on the nation state as its reference point had the jurisprudential ambition to offer a theory about law, and not just about 'comparative law', especially as an alternative to positivist theories.

Patrick's target was a tradition of methodological nationalism in law. This aspect of his work, in particular, showed a remarkable sensitivity to the theoretical developments that had begun to question methodological nationalism across disciplines in the preceding decades; and this aspect is also, I believe, a theoretical reflection of a genuine optimism and belief in the possibility of a peaceful coexistence through 'sustainable diversity' that characterized Patrick as a person. Hence this book's substantive focus on these theoretical aspects of Patrick's work, and on his ambition to which the book owes its title: daring to conceive of his own *Cosmopolitan Jurisprudence*. In the historical process of slowly overcoming the Westphalian matrix of statehood factually and theoretically, 'cosmopolitan legal theory', as he called it in his very last article

[2] William Twining, 'Foreword', in this volume.

(posthumously published in 2016), would 'play the role of a "critical theory" in presenting alternatives to current forms of normativity, whatever their forms.'[3]

From an anthropological perspective, Ulf Hannerz once described cosmopolitanism, in a now often-cited definition, as 'first of all an orientation, a willingness to engage with the Other' that is premised on an intellectual openness to diversity itself.[4] This definition beautifully captures what to me seems to be animating Patrick Glenn's cosmopolitan aspirations; it also hands us the key to a better understanding of the role that 'comparative law' plays in this vision. For Patrick, the practice of 'comparative law', or maybe more accurately, of *being* a comparative thinker indeed is pivotal in that it defines the epistemological starting point of his intellectual enterprise: to never think in terms of only one national tradition, of only one methodological framework, of only one belief or value system. Thus embracing, *absolutely*, the relativity of perspective would open up the possibility of recognizing oneself in the other and would pave the way to an understanding of 'comparison' far beyond traditional 'comparative' analysis. As Patrick put it:

> Why was comparative law a distinct, marginal and boring discipline for the nineteenth and twentieth centuries? It was distinct because it was constructed as separate from the law itself, and as something which followed it (like the cigarette after sex, in the old movies). *It was marginal because people are more interested in the real action than what follows it.* It was boring for all of the above.[5]

Patrick wanted to make 'comparative law' sexy again. And he wanted to bring it where the 'real action' is: he wanted to demonstrate its foundational role for the very concept of law itself and change, in the process, our understanding of what 'comparative law' is and could be.[6] 'Comparative law' would thus no longer be relegated to the role of the 'boring afterthought' but could actualize its potential to contribute to the discourses on 'globalization' and 'multiculturalism' which, in the last decades of the twentieth century, had shown that the prevailing methodological nationalism was simply inadequate to meet the challenges of the 'cosmopolitan condition' (Ulrich Beck).[7] Patrick hoped that grasping this potential of a 'comparative' (ie, a not stationary and static) perspective would prepare the ground for nothing less than a new cosmopolitan understanding of law. Thinking in terms of 'sustainable diversity', 'conciliation', *convivencia* was his

[3] H Patrick Glenn, 'Differential Cosmopolitanism' (2016) 7 *TLT* 57, 69.

[4] Ulf Hannerz, 'Cosmopolitans and Locals in World Culture' (1990) 7 *Theory, Culture & Society* 237, 239. Of course, for Hannerz, the 'unit' of reference is 'culture'.

[5] H Patrick Glenn, 'Com-paring' in Esin Örücü and David Nelken (eds), *Comparative Law: A Handbook* (Hart 2007) 91 (my italics).

[6] Cf Richard Janda, 'Cosmopolitan Normative Information: Patrick Glenn's Legal Theory' (Intergentes 2016) <http://intergentes.com/es/tag/richard-janda-es>.

[7] Cf Ulrich Beck, 'The Cosmopolitan Condition: Why Methodological Nationalism Fails' (2007) 24 *Theory, Culture & Society* 286. See also Helge Dedek, 'Out of Site: Transnational Legal Culture(s)' in Peer Zumbansen (ed), *Oxford Handbook of Transnational Law* (OUP 2021) 89 <https://ssrn.com/abstract=3678046>.

alternative to the pessimistic essentialism that had gained currency in the 1990s, epitomized in the trope of the 'clash of civilizations'.[8] In this vision, the incessant flow of information is not contained by national borders and the demarcation lines that are said to separate 'cultures' are blurry at best.

In contrast to the confrontative imagery of the 'clash', the sphere of *Black Whole Conference* may be interpreted as symbolizing the ideal of an unrestricted global discourse and of an indeed 'cosmopolitan' conversation. Yet, the sculpture prompts many more associations and interpretations. Its stark symmetrical arrangement is reminiscent of those wondrous geometrical structures that occur in nature yet only reveal themselves under the microscope: a diatom, perhaps? With the pandemic, our world has changed and our collective reference systems have shifted; and the legs of the chairs pointed outwards like spikes, *crown-like*, will most strongly stir the association of a virus – *the* virus. The reference to viruses, diatoms, or single-celled organisms trigger connotations of autopoietic self-assemblage in the borderland between life and inanimate matter, of systems differentiating themselves from their environment. The sculpture's title also hints to something that is complete in itself, even impenetrable, something the insides of which are unknowable from the outside. In *Black Whole Conference*, the delineation between the inside and outside of the system and its environment seems sharper than in the case of the tradition-concept as imagined by Patrick, where borders were always porous, and lines always fuzzy.

That living through a global pandemic inevitably brings to the fore, in the perception of the beholder, the connotation of the virus, also throws into relief the amplified challenges to a discursive, borderless, post-national view of the law in such difficult times. Never has our planet seemed smaller than during the pandemic; and never in recent memory have national borders been so hermetically closed and national authority so strongly reasserted on the entire planet as during the pandemic.

But it is not only national borders that keep the uninvited out. This cosmopolitan theory of law, this idealistic vision of inclusion, was being developed, critiqued, applauded, and disparaged within its own context of another microcosm: academia and its disciplinary sub-systems of 'law' and 'comparative law'. It is academics who enjoy the scholarly leisure to think and reflect about law without direct involvement in violence and conflict, and to produce theories and discuss them at their global conferences – themselves forming a system that clearly defines inside and outside, with gatekeeper mechanisms that jealously guard the access points of speaker authorization and qualification.

We take another look at the imposing chair leg-spikes, evocative of a biological defence mechanism: the *Black Whole Conference* proceeds *à huis clos*. One cannot help but see the irony of a global class of tenured professors who are enamoured with

8 Samuel P Huntington, 'The Clash of Civilizations' (1993) 72(3) *Foreign Aff* 22; Samuel P Huntington, 'If Not Civilizations, What? Paradigms of the Post-Cold War World' (1993) 72(5) *Foreign Aff* 186.

the language of inclusion and diversity yet rarely reflect the mechanisms that regulate the access to this rarefied group. It is an irony the thought of which Patrick Glenn, always open to critical self-reflection, would have, I hope, appreciated.

The sphere of interlocking conference chairs of the *Black Whole Conference* transposes into the realm of scholarly discourse a structure reminiscent[9] of the geodesic dome pictured on the cover of Patrick Glenn's *On Common Laws*[10]: R Buckminster Fuller's spherical US Pavilion (see Image 2),[11] designed for the 1967 Montreal world exposition 'Expo 67' that was held under the motto of 'Terre des Hommes'.[12]

Buckminster Fuller was (not unlike Patrick Glenn) an unabashed idealist; and he was (also in this regard, as some might say, not without similarities with Patrick) [13] a brilliant tinkerer and in many respects an autodidact.[14] A systems theorist of sorts,[15] he believed that 'the material world consisted of information patterns made manifest', and that by channelling and controlling this flow of information (through information technology and design) human agency was therefore instrumental in shaping the future of humanity.[16] As Fuller himself expressed it in his curious neologisms, he believed in the potential of human ingenuity to be redirected from 'killingry to advanced livingry – adequate for all humanity'.[17] Thus intended to contribute to 'transforming warfare to welfare',[18] Fuller's designs were

9 On the piece evoking associations of 'the utopian geometry and spaceship dreams of a Buckminster Fuller' see also Schütze (n 1).

10 The cover image can be viewed on the OUP website: <https://global.oup.com/academic/product/on-common-laws-9780199287543?lang=en&cc=us>.

11 Rebecca Dalvesco, 'R Buckminster Fuller, the Expo '67 Pavilion and the Atoms for Peace Program' (2017) 50(5) *Leonardo* 486.

12 The motto drew inspiration from Antoine de Saint-Exupéry's story *Terre des Hommes* and, in particular, the quote: 'To be a man is to feel that by carrying one stone you contribute to building the world'; see Gabrielle Roy and Guy Robert, *Terres des Hommes/Man and His World* (Canadian Corporation for the World Exhibition 1967) 20ff.

13 In his (as far as I know, unpublished) contribution to the Fukuoka panel in Patrick's honour, Ralf Michaels drew a connection between Patrick's work and the concept of 'amateurism' as expounded by Annalise Riles as a fruitful space of scholarly creation, see Annalise Riles, 'Legal Amateurism' Cornell Legal Studies Research Paper No. 16–41 <https://ssrn.com/abstract=2859017>.

14 But see Fred Turner, 'A Technocrat for the Counterculture' in Hsiao-Yun Chu and Roberto G Trujillo (eds), *New Views on R Buckminster Fuller* (Stanford University Press 2009) 147, offering a critical perspective on how Fuller also exaggerated his position as an outsider to enhance his aura of non-conformity.

15 Joachim Krausse, 'Thinking and Building: The Formation of R Buckminster Fuller's Key Concepts in "Lightful Houses"' in Chu and Trujillo (n 14) 73.

16 Turner (n 14) 152. On Patrick Glenn's early fascination with the potential of information technology, see eg, H Patrick Glenn, 'The Use of Computers: Quantitative Case Law Analysis in Civil and Common Law' (1987) 36 *ICLQ* 360.

17 R Buckminster Fuller, *Ideas and Integrities: A Spontaneous Autobiographical Disclosure* (Prentice Hall 1963) 249.

18 Cf Junzi Huang, 'Science as Utopia: Infrastructures, Pedagogies, and the Prophecy of Design' in Thomas S Popkewitz and others (eds), *The International Emergence of Educational Sciences in the Post-World War Two Years* (Routledge 2021) 80ff.

IMAGE 2 R Buckminster Fuller, US Pavilion, Expo 67, Montreal – Archives de la Ville de Montréal, VM94-EX136-779

part of a grand utopian vision of a peaceful human coexistence. Intended or not, the choice of the Expo 67 Pavilion for the cover of *On Common Laws* was thus one of a weighty symbolism – also in light of the fact that Fuller's designs, at a time of an emerging peace movement and evolving social and ecological awareness, became counter-culture icons of a hopeful alternative modernism.[19] Patrick's project was *modern* in the same way – despite his sense of humour and irony, there was no trace of 'post-modern' ironic detachment in his work; he was serious in his hope and optimism and in his belief in the constructive, real-world potential of a 'cosmopolitan' open-mindedness in legal thought.

However, if we look a little closer, we also notice that the cover image Patrick chose for *On Common Laws* shows Fuller's American Expo 67 Pavilion not in its original but in its different current appearance. In 1976, the acrylic panels that constituted the outer skin of the dome were destroyed in a fire, and, against Fuller's wishes, never restored.[20] What remains today (see Image 3) is the structure's delicate steel latticework, the lack of the opaque solid border shell giving the dome an even heightened air of levity and transparency. With light passing through the structure unrefracted and air circulating freely between the inside and outside, the sphere's boundary and has dissolved into a paradoxic – and thus very Glennian – borderline that has ceased to separate and to exclude.

[19] Felicity de Scott, *Architecture or Techno-Utopia: Politics After Modernism* (MIT Press 2007) 10.

[20] 'History of the Biosphere' (*Government of Canada*, 14 March 2017) <www.canada.ca/en/environment-climate-change/services/biosphere/about/history.html>.

IMAGE 3 The US Expo 67 Pavilion, now called the 'Biosphere' and housing an environment museum (Photo: Guilherme Duarte Garcia, 2013)

The structure, as pictured on the cover of *On Common Laws*, is now called 'Biosphere' and houses an ecology museum run by Environment Canada: a federal institution that under the transparent, opened-up dome of the former US Pavilion now flies the Canadian flag.[21] I have always thought that Patrick's 'willingness to engage with the Other' was not only animated by the cosmopolitanism of the globetrotting comparatist but also by the specifically Canadian approach to diversity *within* that is so very much part of a certain Canadian self-image[22]; a diversity embraced by an approach to 'multiculturalism'[23] (implemented as an official 'policy' as early as 1971)[24] which envisioned a plurality of cultural identities within one Canadian identity and thus aspired to the ideal of the 'mosaic' – as opposed to a 'melting pot' of assimilation.[25] It is striking that the political architect of the policy of multiculturalism, Pierre Elliott Trudeau, imagined as the vessel for this diverse

21 'The Biosphere' (*Government of Canada*, 5 June 2020) <www.canada.ca/en/environment-climate-change/services/biosphere.html>.

22 See, from a critical perspective, David Austin, 'Narratives of Power: Historical Mythologies in Contemporary Québec and Canada' (2010) 52 *Race & Class* 19.

23 On the specifically Quebecois alternative vision of 'interculturalism' see Gérard Bouchard, 'What Is Interculturalism?' (2011) 56 *McGill LJ* 435; Gérard Bouchard, *Interculturalism: A View from Quebec* (University of Toronto Press 2015); Charles Taylor, 'Interculturalism or Multiculturalism?' (2012) 38 *Philosophy and Social Criticism* 413.

24 Cf the 'Announcement of Implementation of Policy of Multiculturalism within Biligual Framework' by Prime Minister Pierre Elliott Trudeau on 8 October 1971, Canada, Parliament, House of Commons, Debates, 28th Parliament, 3rd sess, vol VIII (1971) 8545. See eg, Will Kymlicka, 'Canadian Multiculturalism in Historical and Comparative Perspective: Is Canada Unique?' (2003) 13 *Const Forum* 1.

25 For a critical assessment of this vision from various disciplinary perspectives, see: Keith Banting and Will Kymlicka, 'Canadian Multiculturalism: Global Anxieties and Local Debates' (2010) 23 *British Journal of Canadian Studies* 43; Howard Palmer, 'Mosaic Versus Melting Pot? Immigration and

and 'just'[26] society a Canadian state that transcended traditional notions of the nation state and national sovereignty[27] – indeed a *cosmopolitan* state.

Montreal, where the geodesic dome is a well-established landmark, is an exceptional environment to experience the urban reality of an 'internal cosmopolitanism' not as an idealistic vision or top-down policy but as a social fact: a 'cosmopolitanism by default', as it has been called.[28] Patrick had a connection to this city that spanned more than four decades; both he and his wife Jane Glenn taught at McGill's Faculty of Law in Montreal beginning in 1971. It is also in the light of this connection that I hope that Patrick would have appreciated the link with a work of artist Michel de Broin, whose pieces have a major presence in Montreal's public space – pieces whose 'dizzy logic'[29] would have been a good fit, I think, for Patrick's knack and passion for exploring unconventional ideas and non-traditional logics.

Patrick Glenn, unexpectedly, far too early, passed away on 1 October, 2014. This collection of essays aims to honour him as a colleague, interlocutor and friend, and to reflect upon his intellectual achievements.

II CRITICAL ENGAGEMENT

Patrick's work has been widely praised, won awards, made its way into the 'mainstream' of comparative law, and also caught the attention of neighbouring disciplines such as legal history and legal theory. It has also given rise to (at times harsh) criticism, for obvious reasons: his project was extremely – maybe too – ambitious. With respect to their thrust and ambition, Patrick's writings are admirable in their coherence and consistency. At the same time, Patrick was, as a theorist, unrestricted by the allegiance to a singular disciplinary perspective or school of thought, and his reflections drew eclectically from many disciplines and literatures. Consider, for example, the publisher's description of his last book, *The Cosmopolitan State*[30]: '[The] interdisciplinary approach combines constitutional law, history, political

Ethnicity in Canada and the United States' (1976) 31 *International Journal* 488; Ceri Peach, 'The Mosaic Versus the Melting Pot: Canada and the USA' (2005) 121 *Scottish Geographical Journal* 3. In his critical analysis, Cecil Foster has described the 'mosaic' thus: 'Canada would be recognized as a conceptual barbarian that is a composite: a unity with many different parts, with, in the Hegelian sense, the official recognition of different darknesses that come together – not to occlude the light – but to synchronize it into a single beam that is miraculously pure White light' – Cecil Foster, *Blackness and Modernity. The Colour of Humanity and the Quest for Freedom* (McGill-Queen's UP 2007) 344.

26 For a contemporaneous critical perspective on Trudeau's political slogan/vision of a 'Just Society', see only the famous response by Cree writer Harold Cardinal, *The Unjust Society* (Douglas & McIntyre 1969).

27 Cf Pierre Elliott Trudeau, *The Essential Trudeau* (Ron Graham ed, McClelland & Stewart 1998) 112.

28 Annick Germain and Martha Radice, 'Cosmopolitanism by Default: Public Sociability in Montréal' in Jon Binnie and others (eds), *Cosmopolitan Urbanism* (Routledge 2005) 112, 125.

29 Byrne McLaughlin, 'Review: Michel de Broin, Montreal, at Musée d'art contemporain' (*Art in America*, 27 November 2013) <www.artnews.com/art-in-america/aia-reviews/michel-de-broin-61583>.

30 H Patrick Glenn, *The Cosmopolitan State* (OUP 2013) (hereafter Glenn, *TCS*).

theory, international relations, and new logics to provide a clear picture of current thought.'[31] Even more challenging was his attempt to reconcile his ideas on law as 'tradition' with an overwhelming mass of empirical data about the laws grouped together into traditions.[32] This indefatigable curiosity in how others are doing and thinking law brings to mind Ulf Hannerz's observation that, indeed, 'cosmopolitans should ideally be foxes rather than hedgehogs'.[33]

William Twining opined that given the scope of such an endeavour, errors seem inevitable, and that, in light of the project's intellectual courage, '[t]here is also room for some, but not too much, charity in interpretation.'[34] Others have not been so kind. In an academic world characterized by increasing specialization and professionalization, it is unsurprising that critics have even gone so far as to call into question the quality of Patrick Glenn's work as 'serious' scholarship.[35]

There is no way around it: Patrick's work strongly polarized readers. It is, I believe, indeed almost impossible to read Glenn without objections, without at least being slightly irritated: not only with regard to his work on specific traditions but also, and, in particular, with respect to the theoretical basis of his work. Yet, I submit that it is precisely this irritating and disruptive quality that has been critical in jolting a self-referential discourse out of a cycle of replicating identical language games; and I would suggest that one of the most important aspects of Patrick's legacy will be that his work has helped to start, and has contributed to, important and necessary conversations – and that it has the potential to keep doing so. The starting point might be disagreement; however, the process of clearly formulating what started out as a visceral response of dissent not only makes the reader appreciate Patrick's creativity and acute sensitivity to pressing issues, but it almost inevitably prompts further insight and opens doors for new ideas, even if the initial motivation was to contradict and refute a specific statement or claim. Andrew Halpin, writing about Patrick's work, said it best: 'The process of disagreeing with him always left one feeling that what had been learned by engaging with his work far exceeded the particular contribution offered in making a criticism of it.'[36]

Professor Halpin made this remark in his contribution to a book on *The New Logics*. Begun as a project by Patrick and finished posthumously by my colleague Lionel Smith, this collection is one of the expeditions into a theoretical thicket – law

31 See the promotional text available on OUP's website: <https://global.oup.com/academic/product/the-cosmopolitan-state-9780199682423?q=Cosmopolitan%20state&lang=en&cc=us>.

32 H Patrick Glenn, *Legal Traditions of the World* (5th edn, OUP 2014) (hereafter Glenn, *LTW*).

33 Hannerz (n 4).

34 William Twining, 'Glenn on Tradition: An Overview' (2006) 1 *JCL* 107, 109.

35 Cf James Q Whitman, '"A Simple Story", Review of *Legal Traditions of the World*' (2004) 4 *Rechtsgeschichte/Legal Hist* 206 – a criticism that Professor Whitman has – in an admirable display of frankness, tact, and character – by now withdrawn, see James Q Whitman, 'The Hunt for Truth in Comparative Law' in Helge Dedek and Franz Werro (eds), *What We Write About When We Write About Comparative Law, an AJCL Special Issue* (Supp 2017) 65 *Am J Comp L* 181.

36 Andrew Halpin, 'The Application of Bivalent Logic, and the Misapplication of Multivalent Logic to Law' in H Patrick Glenn and Lionel D Smith (eds), *Law and the New Logics* (CUP 2017) 208.

in its relationship to non-classical logic – not everyone will be willing to enter. Professor Halpin had explicitly criticized Patrick several times in his publications, and he recalled:

> One of the delights of engaging in academic debate with Patrick Glenn was meeting up with him some time after the disagreement had appeared in print to be greeted with a warm smile and an enthusiasm to continue the discussion, with a genuine expectation that each side had something worthwhile to contribute. Generosity and openness characterized Patrick as a person and as a scholar.[37]

Since Patrick appreciated genuine reflection on his work and embraced and welcomed the criticism such reflection brought about, inviting *critical engagement* with Patrick's writings has thus been the leitmotif of this collection. This approach is a more fitting tribute to him, I believe, than a hagiographical flattery *in memoriam* could ever be. The book wants to celebrate him as I hope he would have wanted: by engaging critically and thus honestly with his ideas and attempting to move the conversation forward.

III PATRICK GLENN AND THE DISCIPLINE OF COMPARATIVE LAW

Patrick Glenn contributed to the discourse in 'comparative law' for four decades. He was himself very much rooted in this discursive tradition, and his work kept shaping the conventions of this discourse even at a time when his chosen topics began to transcend the traditional boundaries of the discipline. Yet Patrick always remained embedded and present, first and foremost, in the disciplinary structures, institutions, and networks of 'comparative law'.

Patrick Glenn's publishing career began in international and comparative private law and civil procedure. His first monograph was *La capacité de la personne en droit international privé français et anglais*,[38] based on his Strasbourg doctoral thesis. We can glean from his long list of publications[39] how Patrick subsequently became increasingly interested in foundational questions, leading to the publication of the first edition of his treatise *Legal Traditions of the World* in 2000. Underlying this work is an attempt to conceptualize law without relying on the nation state as its sole reference point.

Based on this theoretical foundation laid by his work on 'tradition(s)', Patrick engaged in further projects that aimed to show the misguidedness of fixating on the positive law of the nation state. In the monograph *On Common Laws* (2006),[40] he argued that the 'classic concept of common law is a means of reconciling the law of

37 Ibid.

38 H Patrick Glenn, *La capacité de la personne en droit international privé français et anglais* (Dalloz – Bibliothèque de droit international privé 1975).

39 'H Patrick Glenn: Publications', in this volume.

40 H Patrick Glenn, *On Common Laws* (OUP 2006).

the state and the many forms of transnational law which may complement it.' In his last completed monograph *The Cosmopolitan State* (2013),[41] he took the position that the state is indeed best understood *as* tradition. He made this latter point pronouncedly in the very last journal article published in his lifetime, entitled 'The State as Legal Tradition'.[42] Finally, in a posthumously published article, he argued that states could only be successful to the degree that they 'discovered a means of dealing with [their] own necessarily cosmopolitan character'.[43]

It is difficult to imagine that a project such as Patrick Glenn's, taking as many methodological liberties as it did, could have been successfully undertaken in any other academic discipline, be it in the social or the 'hard' sciences. His work thus serves as an indicator of the state of the discipline of 'comparative law', in particular, and even of law as a university discipline, in general. Not only is Patrick's trajectory as a scholar best understood against the backdrop of the development of 'comparative law' as an academic discipline in recent decades, but it can also be read as paradigmatic of the struggle of 'comparative law' to break free from its self-limiting tradition, which was engendered in the twentieth century. 'Comparative law' had become separated from its earlier 'ethnological' foundations located in the works of thinkers such as Maine, Vinogradoff, Kohler, and Post, and had reduced itself to a positivist and functionalist undertaking with a heavy private law bias.[44] Particularly from the 1980s onwards, this paradigm of 'comparative law' began to face criticism from within the discipline, leading up to a moment of crisis characterized by 'febrile introspection', as William Twining has called it.[45]

Patrick's oeuvre thus stands as a synecdoche for the development of the entire discipline: starting from relatively conventional roots in the 'classical' areas of research of the comparative private lawyer, Patrick Glenn – equipped with a doctorate in law and a curious mind – tried to break the constraining disciplinary mould by branching out into other disciplines. His *Legal Traditions* bears witness to this path, in displaying theoretical and interdisciplinary ambition while still remaining rooted in the more traditional (and more private law-heavy) scholarship of René David and Zweigert/Kötz.

In its endeavour – which some might call courageous, and others quixotic – to give brief outlines of *all* the major *Legal Traditions* of the world (to the extent of conceptualizing traditions as abstract ideal types, as in the case of Patrick Glenn's image of the 'chthonic' tradition), *Legal Traditions* is also reminiscent of the older, universalist school of comparative law and the attempts by scholars such as Paul Vinogradoff to map a global overview of legal development.[46] Eventually, Patrick found his way to a theoretical approach that concentrates on constitutionalism and

[41] Glenn, *TCS* (n 30).

[42] H Patrick Glenn, 'The State as Legal Tradition' (2013) 2 *CJICL* 704, 713ff.

[43] Glenn, 'Differential Cosmopolitanism' (n 3) 59.

[44] See Giorgio Resta, Chapter 2 in this volume; Helge Dedek, 'Kindred Not by Choice: "Legal Families" and the History of Comparative Law' (2022) 70 *Am J Comp L* (forthcoming).

[45] Twining (n 34) 108.

[46] Eg, Paul Vinogradoff, *Outlines of Legal History*, vols 1–2 (OUP 1920/1922).

the state (and its transcendence) as the logical capstone and focal point of all his previous endeavours (cf *The Cosmopolitan State*).

His work stands out in another way: while the discipline of comparative law was mired in decades of paralyzing self-doubt and methodological navel-gazing, he had the courage to suggest a reconstructive project of grand – perhaps too grand – proportions. Insofar as he may be considered to have succeeded, we could either read this success as a 'fresh start for comparative law' or simply assume that by breaking its traditional methodological rules, Patrick Glenn left the discipline behind him; in other words, perhaps his project had ceased to be a project of 'comparative law' in the sense that is usually accepted today.[47] Insofar as he may be considered to have failed, on the other hand, he nevertheless showed that the initiative of venturing beyond the traditional boundaries of the discipline was inevitable – and in so doing, his work gave rise to the question of how alternative visions of that initiative could look.

IV TRADITION

This trajectory is exemplified by Patrick's thought on tradition. His project of writing about the *Legal Traditions of the World* seems, at first sight, to reproduce other well-known categories of macro-comparative law such as 'families', 'cultures', or 'circles' (*Rechtskreise*). In this respect, the description of macro-units of comparison, his work remains within the well-accepted conventions of the genre. At first sight, Patrick only uses a different taxonomy, its main distinctive feature – in the context of the classical, European macro-comparative literature – being the introduction of a 'chthonic tradition'. This taxonomic addition, first found in the first edition of *Legal Traditions* in 2000, epitomizes the disciplinary embeddedness and thus relativity of Patrick's work. How problematic this degree of generalization and stereotyping was, has always been obvious at least from an Indigenous or Post/De-Colonial studies perspective – and is even more clearly visible nowadays, in light of the level that general public awareness has reached, beyond the scholarly discourse in specialized disciplines. Yet, read in the context of the 'legal families' genre in the discipline of 'comparative law', which is deeply conditioned by its own, mostly unreflected-upon colonial history,[48] Indigenous legalities had traditionally not been considered as crossing the threshold from 'custom' to 'law'. Including Indigenous legalities in what was to become a standard treatise in 'comparative law' could thus be considered almost pioneering work at least *within* a discipline that is slow to come to terms with its own colonial past.

Yet 'tradition' was to become much more than simply a new label for both well-known and (according to the conventions of the genre) newly added macro-comparative units or categories. 'Tradition' also was the cornerstone of Patrick's theoretical project. To him,

47 See Janda (n 6).
48 Cf Dedek, 'Kindred Not by Choice' (n 44).

thinking about law in terms of 'tradition' meant something fundamentally different than understanding law in terms of national 'legal systems', of law as an 'ought' whose 'validity' depends on being somehow 'given' by a (national) legislator. He imagined law as a discourse, as a flow of information, unrestrained by spatial or temporal borders. 'Tradition' seemed to capture this fluidity, and, to borrow from Martin Krygier, the 'pastness', the authoritative presence of the past so typical of legal discourse.[49]

In accordance with this central role the concept played in Patrick's thought, he spent great energy and effort on devising a theory of tradition. The word 'tradition' had, of course, been used before in legal scholarship. Harold Berman's *Law and Revolution*[50] with its focus on the 'formation of the Western Legal Tradition' is a prominent example. In the 1980s, Martin Krygier had then made serious efforts to theorize law *as* tradition.[51] Reflecting on Patrick's efforts and revisiting his own work on 'tradition' in this volume, Martin Krygier likens the theoretical purchase of 'tradition' in Patrick's contribution to comparative law to what 'class' became for Marx, 'bureaucracy' for Weber, or 'rules' for Hart. Whether one deems such an attempt successful or not, whether the theory built around such keywords can be refuted or not, it remains the case that once such intellectual weight has been attached to it, the word indeed loses, as Krygier puts it, its 'weightlessness'.[52] Given that much theoretical gravitas, it cannot be bandied about as if it weighed nothing. With respect to 'tradition' this means that, whether we agree with Glenn or not, 'tradition' must not be used lightly, in a similar way as 'culture' cannot be used, as jurists have been known to do,[53] in a strictly commonsensical manner, as an amorphous stand-in for something we cannot quite express, as if the insights from sociology, anthropology, philosophy, and so on were not available.

If we, in this vein, were to reflect for a moment on the further theoretical implications of, and connotations triggered by, the use of 'tradition', one starting point might be to recall that our brief introductory reflection on *Black Whole Conference* and its evoking Habermasian associations of authority-free discourse in a global setting invited the comparison with Patrick's tradition-concept as capturing the discursive nature of law. To a theory that thus imagines law as an unending, perpetual flow of information, the definition of law as an 'ought' backed up by sanction is necessarily anathema. The 'positivists' – especially Hart and Kelsen who only feature in Patrick's work as broad-stroked sketches bordering on caricatures – are therefore its obvious theoretical antagonists. 'Tradition' operates in a twofold manner: it shifts the focus away from law as a machinery of coercion, and from the identification of this machinery with the state. 'Traditions' are not, in Patrick's thought, coextensive with the nation state and its positive law.

49 Martin Krygier, 'Law as Tradition' (1986) 5 *Law & Phil* 237, 240.

50 Harold J Berman, *Law and Revolution: The Formation of the Western Legal Tradition* (Harvard University Press 1983).

51 See the overview in Martin Krygier, Chapter 6 in this volume, n 2.

52 Ibid.

53 See Dedek, 'Out of Site' (n 7).

In its discursive, anti-statist, anti-positivist thrust this theory mostly tunes out the dimension of law as power, force, and violence. Here, then, another aspect of Patrick's concept of tradition steps to the fore. Patrick's theory is not just concerned with observing and describing traditions but has a peculiar yet prominent normative twist. In this dimension, it emphasizes what seems to be the possibility of overcoming conflict through communication – or, if you will, through communicative action – opening the door to an 'epistemology of conciliation'. This potential is somehow seen as an inherent propensity of the concept of 'tradition' itself, which is why conceptualizing law through 'tradition' is supposed to help uncover this conciliatory potential.

In its discursive bend, Patrick's perception of law as tradition gravitates towards meta-narratives: law not in its application to the non-initiated, to the outsider that culminates in the use of force, but law as a conversation *about* law. The depictions of real-life traditions that seem to epitomize such a discursive nature therefore figure prominently in Patrick's narration: traditions of elegant erudition in the exchange and reconciliation of legal arguments such as the scholarly disputes and exchanges in Jewish law or Islamic law, or the Learned Law of the *ius commune*.

Such legal conversations or conversations about law have surely a prominent part to play in the social practice of law, especially in its overlaps and interactions with other social – academic, religious, and so on – fields (or systems, if you will). But these phenomena hardly stand *pars pro toto*. To model a general theory of law on such discursive traditions deliberately tunes out the dimension of law in which the word *is* violence, where the dispute on meaning takes place in the (by now proverbial) field of pain and death.

The tradition-concept aims to create an epistemological framework for the (re-)conciliation of and between traditions. 'Commensurability' is thus the foundation for the process of 'com-paring' in the sense of a 'bringing together' of traditions.[54] Yet in a global order characterized by a post-colonial hegemonic hierarchy, the challenge of (re-)conciliation presents itself specifically against the backdrop of a history of injustice and violence, and in the context of conditions of inequality in which recognition of the non-hegemonic tradition is never fully realized. The bias against acknowledging the role and presence of violence in all of legal discourse ultimately manifests itself in a lack of sensitivity towards the *epistemic* violence inevitably implied in the assumption of commensurability – as long as it is not acknowledged and or indeed questioned that the 'common measures' upon which 'commensurability' is predicated, that is, the 'universal' language and the concepts that determine the framework of commensurability, typically are those imposed by the hegemonic tradition.[55] Such undoubtedly

54 Glenn, 'Com-paring' (n 5) 92ff.

55 Compare eg, James Tully, *Strange Multiplicity: Constitutionalism in an Age of Diversity* (Columbia University Press 1995) 39. This is obviously a complex and laden subject; Canadian Indigenous scholars have, for example, concretely reflected on this in the context of applying the concept of 'sovereignty' – see only John Borrows, 'Sovereignty's Alchemy: An Analysis of *Delgamuukw v British Columbia*' (1999) 37 *Osgoode Hall LJ* 537; Taiaiake Alfred, 'Sovereignty' in Philip J Deloria and Neal Salisbury (eds), *A Companion to American Indian History* (Blackwell 2002) 460. For an explicit

IMAGE 4 Michel de Broin, *Black Whole Conference* (2005)

well-intentioned universalism is also the function of a not reflected-upon privilege which takes for granted that one's own 'measures' are the ones universally applied.

The way in which the Glennian tradition-concept focuses on communication (referred to as passing on of 'normative information'[56]) and highlights the self-referentiality of legal discourse (exemplified especially by its 'pastness'), invites comparison with systems theory, especially in the Luhmannian vein. If the conference chairs of the *Black Whole Conference* (Image 4) are a metaphor of communication, the shell they form (reminiscent of a virus or a single-celled organism) and the never-ending feedback loop of self-referential information and autopoiesis are the places where our associative process takes us next. Firmly linking the chairs to a rigid border-shell, legs turned outside in a gesture hostile to the sphere's environment, the structure seems to epitomize (if not almost caricaturize) systemic closure as one of the tenets of systems theory.

rejection of Glenn's assumption of commensurability, see Aaron J Mills, *Miinigowiziwin: All that Has Been Given for Living Well Together: One Vision of Anishinaabe Constitutionalism* (PhD thesis, University of Victoria 2019) 45 <http://dspace.library.uvic.ca/bitstream/handle/1828/10985/Mills_Aaron_PhD_2019.pdf>.

56 See eg, H Patrick Glenn, 'A Concept of Legal Tradition' (2008) 34 *QLJ* 427.

However, despite certain similarities regarding the focus on self-referential cycles of communication, when it comes to 'closure', the parallels abruptly come to an end. Of course, Luhmann's 'systems' are not solipsistic either; just as 'traditions' supposedly exchange 'normative information' with each other, 'systems' communicate through various structural 'couplings'. Yet, the respective starting points of both approaches are diametrically opposed. Luhmann's theory starts out from the claim that a system *is* difference – and therefore must necessarily focus on the operational significance of the line dividing inside and outside, on differentiation and distinction as a premise of even the possibility of exchange with the environment while maintaining the identifiability of a given system.[57] The Glennian tradition-concept, by contrast, is all about the erasure of binaries and hard boundary lines: '[C]losure is inherently problematic, and remains vulnerable to surrounding texture and the challenge of new and different forms of closure.'[58] Closures and borders are, from this perspective, not phenomena to be diagnosed in order to better understand social structures. They are rather seen as concepts that inherently carry the risk of limiting our imagination and should thus be avoided in the conceptualization of law. Since lawyers have thought for too long in terms of borderlines – be they national, territorial, or doctrinal – a theory that avoided this imagery would liberate jurisprudence from these self-imposed limitations.

The significance attached to the postulate of the inherent fluidity of the tradition-concept in Patrick's thought can hardly be overestimated. This property of the tradition-concept is, for example, what supposedly sets apart 'tradition' as a 'unit of comparison' from conventional categories of macro-comparison such as 'families'. In a chapter published in 2006,[59] Patrick commented on the custom in comparative law scholarship of grouping together the 'laws of the world' in such macro-comparative units. Posing the question, 'Why should one taxonomize the laws of the world?', he gave the clear answer *that one should not*. Targeting especially the 'legal families' literature, he conjectured that it was born out of a nineteenth-century scientism and claimed that such legal taxonomization unduly assumes that law is 'static' and that it 'reifies' the object of the taxonomic exercise.

Yet of course, when we look at *Legal Traditions of the World*, it would seem that we find a replication of exactly such groupings, the well-known 'families' (common, civil, Islamic, Jewish law, etc.), relabelled as 'traditions'. However, in Patrick's thought, applying the lens of 'tradition' was an entirely different exercise than a mere relabelling of 'families' or 'legal circles'. Because of the specific understanding of tradition as inherently fluid and protean, a tradition-based understanding of

57 For an accessible introduction to this aspect of his theory, see Niklas Luhmann, 'System as Difference' (2006) 13(1) *Organization* 37 (translation of a 1991 lecture, Peter Gilgen trs). See also Catherine Valcke, Chapter 7 in this volume.

58 Glenn, *TCS* (n 30) 291.

59 H Patrick Glenn, 'Legal Tradition' in Mathias Reimann and Reinhard Zimmermann (eds), *The Oxford Handbook of Comparative Law* (OUP 2006) 422.

the laws of the world could never amount to an exercise of 'taxonomizing' in the first place. While the conventional view presented the laws of the world as lifeless objects, dead, impaled on pins in a showcase, the tradition-based view worked from the built-in premise that traditions are constantly evolving and not only interact but are entangled in a way that makes clear separation impossible.

Patrick's tradition-concept dissolves hard contrasts between here and there and now and then, and paints a picture of simultaneous distinctness and likeness. The reconceptualization of law as tradition, goes the claim, makes sure that distinguishing between single traditions does not *separate* and *demarcate borders* in a way that conventional taxonomies do. Traditions, in a peculiar ambivalence, have, on the one hand, a concrete existence; cognition of empirical traditions is possible. At the same time, they seem to be concretizations of a larger, one might say Platonic idea of 'tradition', which allows even for the remarkable assessment that an individual, empirically observable tradition does not qualify as the *proper* expression of this larger idea of 'tradition', as reflected, for example, in Glenn's statement on the corruption of tradition: 'Fundamentalism, and ensuing efforts of domination, emerge not as corruption of particular traditions – they faithfully reflect major elements of teaching of their particular tradition – but as corruption of what we understand as tradition, the gathering together into larger, still coherent, identity.'[60]

These ideal traditions are not simply static snapshots of a certain state of affairs at the certain point in time; rather, the distinction of past and present is dissolved into process. By way of the perpetual 'authoritative presence of the past' the binary is resolved into different stages of continuous flow of information; traditions are in a permanent state of *becoming*. Stasis and reification, by contrast, are the hallmarks of a positivistic approach that focuses on a concrete legal system and 'validity of norms' – 'artificial petrification' being the inevitable consequence.

Such a focus on historical process; on binaries and apparent contrast reconceived as complementary moments of concretizations of totalities, contradictions thus not denied yet transcended; and on concepts that are becoming, through different stages of development throughout history, 'true' expressions of themselves: is all of this not the semantic register of Hegelian (and Marxian) dialectics? The similarities regarding central tenets such as motion, process, change, flux, and the aversion to anything static might make it more relatable why Patrick would gravitate towards inquiries into non-classical logics. Whether and to what degree Hegel's and Marx's dialectics can be reconciled with formal logic is a notorious problem tackled by many an expert;[61] the (possible) conflict of dialectics with the law of non-contradiction, for example, has inspired logicians to push beyond classical logics and to attempt to

60 Glenn, *LTW* (n 32) 51.

61 See eg, Kazumi Inoue, 'Dialectical Contradictions and Classical Formal Logic' (2014) 28(2) *Int'l Stud Phil Sci* 113. Famous is Karl Popper, 'What Is Dialectic?' (1940) 49 *Mind* 403 (emphatically emphasizing the irreconcilability and claiming that accepting the premises of Hegelian dialectics would mean 'one would have to give up all scientific activity'. Ibid, 317).

formulate broader, more flexible dialectical logics that relegates the law of non-contradiction and formal logic to a 'limited and well-defined area (notably the static and the changeless)'.[62]

However, as far as I can tell, Patrick never named this literature as a source of inspiration, nor did he reflect on this parallel. His forays into non-traditional logic were inspired by other sources, and when, in the concluding remarks of *The Cosmopolitan State*,[63] he cited Deleuze and Guatteri ('no-one has ever died of contradictions'[64]), he seems to have placed himself, consciously or not, in a different intellectual tradition.[65] And yet, even though the parallel might not be the result of an actual inspiration, it might help us better understand what appears to me to be one of the main reasons why Patrick Glenn's work has been so controversial. Just as is the case with Hegelian thought, buying into Patrick's way of seeing the world and the role of law in it requires a leap of faith.

It might be helpful, for a moment at least, to consider thinking about his ideas less as a theory and rather as a belief system, or maybe even better as a kind of worldview or *Weltanschauung*.[66] Incommensurability, abominable to Patrick's approach to 'com-paring', here looms large: if one does not share the same worldview, communication and mutual understanding face almost insurmountable obstacles. For example, from the perspective of Patrick's tradition-based understanding of law, it is well-nigh impossible to find a common language to engage theorists like Hart or Kelsen. The Glennian worldview must perceive them and their theories as examples of the rationalist tradition gone awry, or, to invoke a different register: products of a false consciousness. The ease with which Patrick's thought transitions between 'is' and 'ought', between how *Legal Traditions* are, how we ought to see them to better understand the law, and how law and traditions themselves ought to be, sweeps us up, carries us away, and leaves us mystified, not unlike the eternally enigmatic 'only the rational is real, and the real is rational'. The Hegelian dialectic, as one observer once put it, 'furnishes a pattern to which *Weltanschauung* dances'.[67] That is how I like to think of Patrick's work: an invitation to a dance, its appeal not only intellectual but also visceral – joyful and full of hope. You can enjoy it for its own sake and for the inspiration it may bring, even without becoming a believer. But not everybody likes to dance.

62 See Graham Priest, 'Dialectic and Dialetheic' (1989/1990) 53 *Sci & Soc'y* 388, 391.

63 Glenn, *TCS* (n 30) 292.

64 Gilles Deleuze and Felix Guatteri, *Anti-Oedipus* (Robert Hurley and others trs, reprint, Continuum 2004) 166.

65 Compare, exploring this theme, Karen Houle and Jim Vernon (eds), *Hegel and Deleuze: Together Again for the First Time* (Northwestern University Press 2013).

66 It is not by accident that Lenin turned to Hegel when he was forging the 'scientific socialism' of the nineteenth century into a *Weltanschauung*: see eg, Iring Fetscher, 'Die Entstehung des dialektischen Materialismus als metaphysischer Weltanschaung' (1953) 50(2) *Zeitschrift für Theologie und Kirche* 184.

67 Jerome Ashmore, 'Three Aspects of Weltanschauung' (1966) 7(2) *The Sociological Quarterly* 215, 227.

V THE CONTRIBUTIONS TO THIS BOOK

The contributors to this book, fortunately, have accepted the invitation to dance (and despite their dance cards, without exception, being abundantly full). The international group of authors represents a diverse spectrum of methodologies, schools, and styles of scholarship; the authors engage critically with Patrick's ideas and use them as an entry point to push the conversation further. I have grouped their fifteen essays into three sections each centred on one theme; but in light of Patrick's own path as a scholar, the disciplinary framing of his work, and the interconnectedness of its main themes, it goes without saying that these sections should not be thought of as thematically exclusive silos. Borderlines, here, are fuzzy as well; any given essay may touch not only on one, but on two or all three themes that are the main foci of the book.

The first section, entitled 'The Tradition of Comparative Law: Context, History, Promise' takes as a jumping-off point the theme of Patrick Glenn's disciplinary embeddedness and the trajectory of his work vis-à-vis the development, history, and future of 'comparative law'. In his opening chapter 'How to Do Comparative Law: Some Lessons to Be Learned',[68] *Mauro Bussani* reflects on how Patrick Glenn's scholarly legacy has contributed to our understanding of (comparative) law, focusing on the central notions of law, tradition, and conciliation. *Giorgio Resta*'s contribution, 'The "Comparative Method" at the Roots of Comparative Law',[69] then enquires into the intellectual history of 'comparative law' by revisiting some distinctive traits of the original discourse on the 'comparative method' and highlighting, in particular, the importance of the 'scientific paradigm' for the acceptance of comparative law as a subject of legal research, and how the loss of foundational assumptions such as taxonomic essentialism and evolutionary determinism precipitated the loss of belief in the 'comparative method'. In the aftermath of this paradigm shift developed a tradition of private law-heavy micro-comparison – it is Patrick Glenn's criticism of this tradition and Patrick's own macro-comparativism that inspire *John Bell*'s reflections on the 'The Value of Micro-Comparison':[70] it is, in his opinion, the careful and thorough analysis of specific problems that tells us how legal systems *really* work, and that is, therefore, also capable of bringing about valuable general insights into the operation of law.

In Chapter 4, *Esin Örücü* contemplates another way in which mainstream comparative law responds to sociocultural change, especially with regard to the complexities that comparative scholarship encounters in the context of mixed legal systems.[71] *Michele Graziadei* then appraises Patrick Glenn's role in advancing the conversation on comparative law, and shifting its research paradigm through

[68] Mauro Bussani, Chapter 1 in this volume.
[69] Giorgio Resta, Chapter 2 in this volume.
[70] John Bell, Chapter 3 in this volume.
[71] Esin Örücü, Chapter 4 in this volume.

exploring what pluralism entails both at the national and at the transnational level for comparative law studies. His assessment of Patrick's contribution is summed up in the title of his chapter: 'Breaking Barriers in Comparative Law'.[72]

The second part of the collection, entitled 'The Concept of Tradition: Potential and Challenges' zeroes in on Patrick Glenn's conceptual framework. In this part of the book, the goal of the contributing authors is to provide their perspectives on the concept of 'tradition' and its role in and potential for legal discourse. In Chapter 6, *Martin Krygier* revisits the topic of 'tradition' that he first considered in the 1980s.[73] He applauds Patrick Glenn's decision to emphasize the concept's significance for the understanding of law. Yet, writes Krygier in his chapter 'Too Much Information',[74] while we should acknowledge that even complex legal orders typically are traditions, it is more difficult to agree with Glenn that acknowledging this fact could have real-life implications for the coexistence of, and mutual accommodation among, legal and social orders.

As we have seen, Patrick Glenn contrasted the two ways of conceptualizing law as 'tradition' and as 'system', whereby, in his opinion, the latter heuristic lens unduly promoted a static, reified, and state-centred understanding of law. In her chapter 'Legal Systems as Legal Traditions',[75] *Catherine Valcke* seeks to dispel the notion that both perspectives are irreconcilable; rather, she advances a definition of national legal systems as traditions, characterized by fluid borderlines yet still consistent with the Westphalian conception of the nation state.

David Nelken's chapter 'Learning from Patrick Glenn: Tradition, Change, and Innovation'[76] then takes a closer look at the relationship between tradition and change, and aims to better explain this relationship by focusing on how tradition is produced and reproduced. He scrutinizes, in particular, the Rabbinical innovation of the *Prozbul* within the Talmudic law tradition and comes to the conclusion that in order for change to be effected within a tradition, change has to be explicable not as a deviation from the tradition but rather as embodying the best efforts to maintain and uphold it.

Similar themes with respect to the emergence and the (re-)production of a legal tradition are explored by *Ahmed Fekry Ibrahim* in his chapter 'The Sunni Legal Tradition: An Overview of Pluralism, Formalism, and Reform'.[77] To better understand the Islamic law tradition, he advocates a 'realist' approach that goes beyond the 'law in the books', the exchanges of learned jurists, and consciously incorporates judicial practice, thus also opening up new avenues for legal change. In the concluding contribution in this part, 'Commensurability, Comparative Law, and

[72] Michele Graziadei, Chapter 5 in this volume.
[73] See Krygier (n 49).
[74] Martin Krygier, Chapter 6 in this volume.
[75] Catherine Valcke (n 57) .
[76] David Nelken, Chapter 8 in this volume.
[77] Ahmed Fekry Ibrahim, Chapter 9 in this volume.

Confucian Legal Tradition',[78] *Marie Seong-Hak Kim* uses an examination of the concepts and practices of lineage property in historical Confucianism to discuss and gain perspective on Patrick Glenn's thought on tradition and, specifically, the commensurability of traditions.

The last part of the collection, entitled 'Crossing Boundaries: Cultural Transfer, Legal Cosmopolitanism, and the Dissolution of the State' brings together essays focusing on themes that are connected to Patrick Glenn's interest in the concept of 'stateless' common laws, in mechanisms of diffusion of legal knowledge and transfer of information, and eventually the possibility of rendering the concept of the state itself dispensable.

In the first contribution to this last part of the collection, entitled 'The School of Salamanca: A Common Law?',[79] *Thomas Duve* reflects on the fact that Patrick Glenn developed his ideas on traditions, common laws, and the cosmopolitan state through the observation of historical processes – but to what extent, asks the author, could his ideas inform and benefit research in legal history, and especially a *global* legal history? The example of the School of Salamanca, which Glenn once described as Hispanic common law, Duve explains, shows the opportunities but also the limits of his approach.

In her chapter 'The Un-Common Law',[80] *Vivian Grosswald Curran* approaches the history of another common law, and from another angle: she examines the development of the English common law, its origins, and its contrast with the civilian systems of Continental Europe, and enquires whether the history of this common law could lead to differences that would create insurmountable obstacles to a future European common law. While Curran points to a growing mutual understanding between traditions, *Ko Hasegawa*, in the next chapter, homes in on exactly this moment of interaction, the process of 'normative information' passing from one tradition to the other. In his chapter 'The Fabric of Normative Translation',[81] Hasegawa demonstrates the need for a theory of 'normative translation', a process he sees exemplified by the Japanese appropriation and re-creation of the Western concept of 'right'.

The two final chapters of the collection focus, in particular, on Patrick Glenn's ideas with respect to statehood, sovereignty, and cosmopolitanism. In his contribution 'Statehood as Process: The Modern State Between Closure and Openness',[82] *Gunnar Folke Schuppert* turns to the tensions between 'elements of closure' and 'the cosmopolitan way' in the conceptualization of the state and specifically examines a sequence of processes that restricts the cosmopolitan opening-up of states.

The final word belongs to *Neil Walker*. Walker points out Glenn's trajectory as an unconventional comparatist, making his enquiry into the apparent oxymoron of the

78 Marie Seong-Hak Kim, Chapter 10 in this volume.

79 Thomas Duve, Chapter 11 in this volume.

80 Vivian Grosswald Curran, Chapter 12 in this volume.

81 Ko Hasegawa, Chapter 13 in this volume.

82 Gunnar Folke Schuppert, Chapter 14 in this volume.

'cosmopolitan state' not a departure from but a plausible continuation of his comparativism. Glenn's investigation, writes Walker in his chapter 'Cosmopolitan Attachments',[83] paints a powerful picture of a global cosmopolitan practice that, against the vision of stronger versions of cosmopolitanism, is not itself globally located but rather rooted in different state 'subsoils'.

VI A COSMOPOLITAN CONVERSATION

Yet how would Patrick Glenn have responded, Walker wonders, to the challenge of a nativist populism that counts 'cosmopolitanism' among its favourite targets? Neil Walker himself offers a nuanced answer to this question:

> If he were still with us, I am sure he would have much to say about how, in such hostile circumstances, we defend and refine the cosmopolitan way and prevent it from coming adrift from its moorings while seeking to do justice to the real concerns on which such hostility feeds.[84]

Indeed, cosmopolitanism is hit hard by the global 'great regression'.[85] To the springtide of resurging nationalism, nativism, xenophobia, and racism, the 'cosmopolitan' is anathema, and, of course, often used, combined with the accusation of 'rootlessness', as a specifically anti-semitic trope.[86] Such anti-cosmopolitanism is not only born out of hatred and ignorance but also spawned by a cult of the irrational. When we see enlightenment ideals thus pitted against the destructive thrust of a dark counter enlightenment,[87] there can be no doubt whatsoever as to which side to pick – a choice that will mirror the spirit of Patrick's work and its central theme of *convivencia*, a living together in peace on a basis of recognition and tolerance.

It is also clear that a 'critical cosmopolitan theory' of the kind to which Patrick aspired must go further; it must widen its scope beyond only seeing Western ideologies locked in battle, beyond the conceptualization of this tension as an antagonism between enlightenment and counter-enlightenment. It has to embrace cosmopolitanisms 'from below' that are not 'rooted' in variants of liberal citizenship and do not spring from enlightenment values of universality and

83 Neil Walker, Chapter 15 in this volume.

84 Ibid.

85 Cf Heinrich Geiselberger (ed), *The Great Regression* (Polity 2017).

86 On this, see, for example, Lars Rensmann, 'The Politics of Paranoia: How – and Why – the European Radical Right Mobilizes Antisemitism, Xenophobia, and Counter-Cosmopolitanism' in Charles A Small (ed), *Global Antisemitism: A Crisis of Modernity* (Martinus Nijhoff 2013) 223 and the collection Lars Rensmann and Julius H Schoeps (eds), *Politics and Resentment: Examining Antisemitism and Counter-Cosmopolitanism in the European Union and Beyond* (Brill 2011); Michael L Miller and Scott Ury, 'Dangerous Liaisons[.] Jews and Cosmopolitanism in Modern Times' in Gerard Delanty (ed), *Routledge Handbook of Cosmopolitan Studies* (Routledge 2012) 554.

87 Vincenzo Cicchelli and Sylvie Mesure, 'Introduction: Splendors and Miseries of Cosmopolitanism' in Vincenzo Cicchelli and Sylvie Mesure (eds), *Cosmopolitanism in Hard Times* (Brill 2020) 10ff.

progress.[88] But going even further, it has to acknowledge that there are forms of 'rootedness', especially Indigenous 'rootedness',[89] that entirely elude Western imagination and verbalization – and it therefore must acknowledge that in this context, *pace* Patrick Glenn,[90] an assumption not of universalizing commensurability, but of radical incommensurability might be the truest form of recognition.[91]

Thinking about such urgent questions, with and beyond Patrick's ideas – this is, undoubtedly, where the 'real action' is. Not only did Patrick Glenn succeed in demonstrating the relevance of 'comparative law' in linking it (albeit in his own idiosyncratic version) to this discourse, but 'comparative law' served him as a perfect platform to launch an assault on the methodological nationalism in which law is mired more deeply than almost any other discipline. Packaged as 'comparative law' – unassuming and inconspicuous, a Trojan horse of sorts – his surprisingly subversive ideas reached much deeper into the mainstream than progressive scholarship from the margins commonly dares hope. His 'cosmopolitan jurisprudence' itself thus contributed to the *cosmopolitanization* of legal discourse writ large; and in this, he has nudged the entire discipline a little bit closer to where the 'real action' is.

This collection hopes to make a modest contribution to this project. With this endeavour in mind, we return to the beginning of this introductory chapter, and to the artwork that, just as thoughtful academic work, invited a variety of interpretations, none of which can 'take up exclusive and extensive lodgings here'.[92] As we have seen, *Black Whole Conference* can be read as a hermetically closed sphere, spikes pointed outwards defensively to keep the uninvited out. At the same time, as was our first observation, it can also be interpreted as a sphere that is open and free from a dominating central authority, a 'public sphere', enabling the free exchange and mutual recognition of ideas. Although it is necessarily a small number of scholars who contribute to this book, it is not meant to establish a closed, exclusive circle; this book does not lay claim to an exclusive continuation of a 'legacy'. Rather, it seeks to continue a conversation that resonates with the theme with which we started, the theme of an inclusive discourse and the 'willingness to engage with the Other'[93]: in that sense, a 'cosmopolitan' conversation.

[88] See only Pheng Cheah, 'Cosmopolitanism' (2006) 23 *Theory, Culture & Society* 486, 491ff; Sheldon Pollack and others, 'Cosmopolitanisms' in Carole Breckenridge and others (eds), *Cosmopolitanism* (Duke University Press 2002) 6; Homi Bhabha, 'Unsatisfied: Notes on Vernacular Cosmopolitanism' in Laura Garcia-Morena and Peter Pfeifer (eds), *Text and Nation* (Camden House 1996) 191ff.

[89] Aaron J Mills, 'The Lifeworlds of Law: On Revitalizing Indigenous Legal Orders Today' (2016) 61 *McGill LJ* 847, 860ff.

[90] See also Kim, Chapter 10 in this volume.

[91] Once more Mills, *Miinigowiziwin* (n 55) 45.

[92] Schütze (n 1).

[93] Hannerz (n 4).

PART I

The Tradition of Comparative Law

Context, History, Promise

1

How to Do Comparative Law: Some Lessons to Be Learned

Mauro Bussani

I A PERSON AS A SCHOLAR

I have always thought that Patrick Glenn's personal features – his modest and unassuming way of communicating and his persistent open-mindedness to new and others' arguments – also lie at the core of his scholarly work. In the following pages, I will try to show this connection by putting in context and in perspective his legacy as a scholar.

Notwithstanding his impressive production, there is no doubt that Patrick Glenn will be long remembered for his *opus magnum* and for the debates it triggered. In my view, *Legal Traditions of the World*[1] is grounded upon three key notions: Law, Tradition, and Conciliation. I will address these notions critically and sequentially, as if they were strands of a thread through which Patrick Glenn's personality and scholarship are woven.

II WHAT LAW?

Glenn does not introduce a 'concept of law' or explicitly criticize the concepts of others. Yet, he relies on the findings of a long line of legal anthropologists (and a shorter one of comparative law scholars) showing that, in non-Western traditions, there is no distinct line between legal and non-legal forms of normativity.[2] Glenn's recognition of legal traditions that do not sharply divide legal from non-legal norms, or that do not gain legality from their relation to state authority, reminds all of us that

[1] H Patrick Glenn, *Legal Traditions of the World: Sustainable Diversity in Law* (5th edn, OUP 2014) (hereafter Glenn, *LTW*).

[2] Ibid, 60–94, 98–129, 180–215, 287–315, 319–56. See also, among many others, Masaji Chiba, 'Legal Pluralism in Mind: A Non-Western View' in Hanne Petersen and Henrik Zahle (eds), *Legal Polycentricity: Consequences of Pluralism in Law* (Dartmouth 1995) 71–83; Masaji Chiba, 'Three Dichotomies of Law: An Analytical Scheme of Legal Culture' (1987) 1 *Tokai L Rev* 279; Michel Alliot, 'Les transferts du droit ou la double illusion' in Michel Alliot (ed), *Le droit et le service public au miroir de l'anthropologie* (Karthala 2003); Franz von Benda-Beckmann, 'Who's Afraid of Legal Pluralism?' (2002) 47 *J Leg Plur* 37, 48–52; Jorge L Esquirol, 'The Failed Law of Latin America' (2008) 56 *Am J Comp L* 75. See also Michele Graziadei, Chapter 5 in this volume; Ahmed Fekry Ibrahim, Chapter 9 in this volume.

there is no transcendent reason for which law has to be positive (ie, established by the state and its organs) or flow from the exercise of state coercion.[3] From this perspective, Glenn breaks away from the almost exclusive emphasis that mainstream scholarship puts on state law as the lodestar of any given legal system or effort to understand law.[4] This is an issue that deserves to be looked into at some length. I will do so now by recalling some data on others' experiences, and then by focusing on the Western landscape.

Glenn is right in pointing out that positive law (as we mean it) is not necessarily the core of legal systems outside the West. Out there, positive law is constantly challenged by the relevance that each society assigns to other legal layers. These layers may come from what Glenn calls the chthonic legal tradition of the given society. But they may also be of religious origin (Christianity, Islam, etc.), or they may come from the European colonial or postcolonial legacy – both the latter sources may have been added alongside, or superimposed on, local traditional law. Some of the religious and colonial layers are still effective producers of legal order, and some are not. But the point is, traditional layers have never disappeared. On the contrary, they have always impinged upon and affected the enforcement of 'transplanted' legal rules.[5] From the Western positivistic viewpoint, these phenomena are not clearly visible because although history has bequeathed the Western part of the world a multifarious

[3] The latter assumption is still widespread outside comparative law circles. An excellent example of this assumption is Frederick Schauer, *The Force of Law* (CUP 2015). On this point, see also Martin Krygier, Chapter 6 in this volume.

[4] On the connected views that overlap the notion of state with that of nation state, it may be worth recalling that

> contemporary legal and political theory largely assumes the existence of 'nation-states' which would represent the confluence of a nation (a people homogeneous in religion, language and ethnicity) with the legal and political structures of a state. In reality there never has been, and there never will be, a nation-state. Even the smallest state in the world today, Tuvalu, has a diverse population.

H Patrick Glenn, 'International and Foreign Factors in Legal Reform: Risk and Opportunities' in Mauro Bussani and Lukas Heckendorn Urscheler (eds), *Comparisons in Legal Development: The Impact of Foreign and International Law on National Legal Systems* (Schulthess 2016) 224. See also H Patrick Glenn, *The Cosmopolitan State* (OUP 2013) 86–92, 98–101.

[5] Cf Michel Doucet and Jacques Vanderlinden (eds), *La réception des systèmes juridiques: Implantation et destin* (Bruylant 1994); William Graham Sumner, *Folkways: A Study of the Sociological Importance of Usages, Manners, Customs, Mores, and Morals* (Ginn 1906); Lon L Fuller, 'Human Interaction and the Law' in Robert Paul Wolff (ed), *The Rule of Law* (Simon & Schuster 1971); Masaji Chiba, 'Introduction' in Masaji Chiba (ed), *Asian Indigenous Law in Interaction with Received Law* (KPI 1986); Masaji Chiba, 'Conclusion' in Chiba, *Asian Indigenous Law*; von Benda-Beckmann, 'Who's Afraid of Legal Pluralism?' (n 2) 48–52; Werner Menski, 'The Uniform Civil Code Debate in Indian Law: New Developments and Changing Agenda' (2008) 9 *Germ LJ* 211, 216–44; Rodolfo Sacco, 'The Sub-Saharan Legal Tradition' in Mauro Bussani and Ugo Mattei (eds), *The Cambridge Companion to Comparative Law* (CUP 2012) 314–21. Cf Eugen Ehrlich, *Grundlegung der Soziologie des Rechts* (reprinted from 1st edn 1913, Duncker & Humblot 1929) 49–54, 315–19; Santi Romano, *The Legal Order* (Mariano Croce tr, Routledge 2017), translated from Santi Romano, *L'ordinamento giuridico* (E. Spoerri 1918).

background,[6] mainstream legal discourse of the last two centuries has always seen law as the creation of the state. Consequently, the popular view – which has also shaped the way we look outside the Western *koiné* – is that rules cannot be law as we generally understand it when they come from sources other than the state. It should be further noted, according to Patrick Glenn,[7] that this view is nothing but the fruit of European ethnocentrism and that it is mainly due to the way European legal thought has systematized the reality with which it was faced. To the European rulers (and lawyers) of the past few centuries, it has been only too convenient to imagine that the law and the state coincide because both have long appeared to be their own.[8]

Yet, even if different societies rely on different sources, or combine state and non-state law, all societies live by law and manage to make their rules effective. Actually, it is easy to acknowledge that whatever its source, the law of any society has basic functional and structural features in common with the state law that we know: it preserves a social order through obedience to rules. It is still law because it is society's response to the need for social order.[9] This is why, for the study of any legal system to be accurate, it is necessary to distinguish and analyse the roles played by the official and the unofficial sources of law, the traditional layers and the layers of different origin, as well as the ways in which they interact and affect each other. This is a cognitive pathway that can be kept open only (it is worth emphasizing again) if one gets rid of the positivistic posture that does not allow one to consider a rule that does not stem from the state's authority as properly 'legal'.

III . . . POSITED BY WHOM?

To be sure, these caveats – thanks also to Patrick Glenn's scholarship – are today well known and usually taken into consideration in the most advanced comparative law debates, as well as by legal historians, legal pluralists, legal anthropologists, and sociologists, when they deal with non-Western realities.[10] What still remains under-noticed or

6 For an analysis revealing how some of the intimate and long-standing features of the Western legal tradition may work as the most reliable criteria to understand what is, and what is not, the 'West', see Mauro Bussani, *El derecho de Occidente: Geopolítica de las reglas globales* (rev edn, Marcial Pons 2018) chs 10–13, translated from Mauro Bussani, *Il diritto dell'Occidente: Geopolitica delle regole globali* (Maria Elena Sánchez Jordán tr, Einaudi 2010) 60, 69–72; Mauro Bussani, 'Deglobalizing Rule of Law and Democracy: Hunting Down Rhetoric Through Comparative Law' (2019) 67 *Am J Comp L* 701, 704–739.

7 Glenn, *LTW* (n 1) 142–47, 159–61, 272–79.

8 See also Wolfgang J Mommsen and Jaap A de Moor (eds), *European Expansion and Law: The Encounter of European and Indigenous Law in 19th- and 20th-Century Africa and Asia* (Berg 1992); Chiba, *Asian Indigenous Law* (n 5); Tom W Bennett, 'Comparative Law and African Customary Law' in Mathias Reimann and Reinhard Zimmermann (eds), *Oxford Handbook of Comparative Law* (2nd edn, OUP 2019).

9 On the role that non-official rules play in achieving social order, see the authors cited in note 5.

10 Eg, Rodolfo Sacco, 'Mute Law' (1995) 43 *Am J Comp L* 455; Doucet and Vanderlinden (n 5); Norbert Rouland, *Anthropologie juridique* (Presses Universitaires de France 1988); Oscar G Chase, *Law, Culture and Ritual: Disputing Systems in Cross-Cultural Context* (NYU Press 2005) 30–46, 94–124; Richard L Abel (ed), *The Politics of Informal Justice* (Academic Press 1982); Werner Menski,

peripheral in comparative law debates, however, is that these caveats apply to Western settings as well. I will try to show why these caveats should be taken seriously by juxtaposing the positivist attitude of accepting as legal only that which comes from the state with two phenomena, which are of a different mould and origin but converge to shape a legal landscape that is very different from the one mainstream scholarship usually refers to. These are (1) the erosion of the West(phalian) state and (2) the thriving of unofficial sites of production of legal order in wide areas of Western social and economic relations.

Notwithstanding that the developmental paths of these two phenomena overlap in some areas, I will address them separately.

1 *The State as a Habit*

As to the dynamics affecting the role of the state, the data to be considered is well known. Fields such as commerce, maritime and aerial navigation, fishing, agriculture, food, telecommunications, intellectual property, the value of currencies and mortgages, the environment, the exploitation of sea resources, and the use of space and energy resources, on top of, obviously, finance, have long been the objects of a discipline that is largely denationalized – that is, they are not determined or exclusively dependent on the state but on centres of rule production that are based in regional and global arenas. The so-called global orders have been and are ever more shaping (especially as far as the economic turf is concerned) the choices of state actors and disaggregating the latter's traditional functions on a spectrum of different agendas and interests[11] – sometimes deeply puzzling local grassroots and ruling classes unable to make sense out of these developments.[12]

To be sure, the weakening of an autonomous capacity of economic government is not bound to make the state disappear in the short term.[13] Rather, that process assigns to the state a new role: that of an agency, public and local, to transcend the legal,

Comparative Law in the Global Context: The Legal Systems of Asia and Africa (2nd edn, CUP 2006) 3; Chiba, 'Introduction' (n 5); Chiba, 'Conclusion' (n 5); von Benda-Beckmann, 'Who's Afraid of Legal Pluralism?' (n 2); Roger Cotterrell, *Law, Culture and Society: Legal Ideas in the Mirror of Social Theory* (Ashgate 2006) 112–16, 155–59.

11 For example, among many others, Sabino Cassese, 'Introduction' in Sabino Cassesse (ed), *Research Handbook on Global Administrative Law* (Edward Elgar 2016) 4–11; Jan H Dalhuisen, *Dalhuisen on Transnational and Comparative Commercial, Financial and Trade Law* (3rd edn, Hart 2007) ix; José E Alvarez, *International Organizations as Law-Makers* (OUP 2005) 217–68, 608–20; Benedict W Kingsbury, 'The International Legal Order' (2005) *NYU Public Law and Legal Theory Working Papers* 14 <https://pdfs.semanticscholar.org/a097/5c987a43d3a1c7efc0ec002091e475b16db8.pdf>; Francis G Snyder, 'Governing Globalization' in Michael B Likosky (ed), *Transnational Legal Processes: Globalization and Power Disparities* (Butterworths 2002) 71–97; John Braithwaite and Peter Drahos, *Global Business Regulation* (CUP 2000) 488; Gunther Teubner, '"Global Bukowina": Legal Pluralism in the World Society' in Gunther Teubner (ed), *Global Law without a State* (Dartmouth 1997).

12 See also Neil Walker, Chapter 15 in this volume.

13 'The state, as frozen accident, is beginning to melt, though the process may be a very long one': Glenn, *LTW* (n 1) 53.

economic (and financial) order. Thanks to its domestic monopoly of the normative sanctioning power, the state is called on to monitor the implementation of values and principles coming from regional, international, global, and public and private centres of production of a legal order. It is a model of organization that reminds us of the indirect rule through which the British Empire administered its colonies, relying on indigenous governors or intermediaries. But the point remains that the internal dynamics of the state government are destined to increasingly suffer the stiletto of legal, economic, and financial globalizations, to wear less the clothes of the rule-maker and ever more those of the rule-taker.[14]

The specific modalities of development (and the geographical distribution) of this phenomenon obviously deserve extensive discussion.[15] For the limited purposes of this chapter, however, let me only note how the aforementioned phenomenon makes clear that studying legal systems cannot be any longer (if it could ever be) an exegetic exercise of worship of state law. The tradition of positivism has, among many other things, relied on and forged the classical distinctions between comparative law, foreign law, and international law. These are distinctions that nowadays account for only a piece of the legal reality – their relevance is particularly emphasized in those debates where domestic and international law specialists aim to construct a disciplinary wall to protect self-determined interests. From a comparative law point of view, the remaining (large) part of legal reality should instead push scholars to compare an array of law-producing entities – either among themselves or with the structures of domestic state law. These entities often defy being squeezed, or cannot be squeezed at all, into the mainstream positivistic account of the sources of law (national and international), both because they are supra- and transnational in nature, and because they produce thriving legality at levels different from those controlled by the state and international law instruments.[16]

14 All in all, the state risks revealing itself as a valuable structure, but only if understood in terms of path dependency. On the one hand, the state works as an entity that is useful for the implementation and the protection of global orders; on the other hand, it appears to be a structure that is far less costly to keep as is (if necessary, eroding its borders from the outside) rather than substituting it in the short term.

15 See, eg, Sabino Cassese, *The Global Polity: Global Dimensions of Democracy and the Rule of Law* (Global Law Press 2012) 15–22; Anne-Marie Slaughter, *A New World Order* (Princeton University Press 2004) 12–15, 266–69; Donald B King, 'The Unknown World Government: Some Very Recent Commercial Law Developments and Gaps' (2005) 23 *Pa St Int'l L Rev* 535; Achim Hurrelmann and others, 'Is There a Legitimation Crisis of the Nation-State?' in Stephan Leibfried and Michael Zürn (eds), *Transformations of the State?* (CUP 2005); Martin van Creveld, *The Rise and Decline of the State* (CUP 1999) 336–415; Charles Tilly, *Coercion, Capital, and European States, A.D. 990–1992* (Blackwell 1990). See also Stanley Aronowitz and Peter Bratsis (eds), *Paradigm Lost: State Theory Reconsidered* (University of Minnesota Press 2002); Susan Marks, 'Empire's Law' (2003) 10 *Ind J Glob Leg Stud* 449; Antonio Negri, 'Postmodern Global Governance and the Critical Legal Project' (2005) 16 *Law & Crit* 27, 30–32.

16 On the different 'levels of law' – global, international, regional, transnational, inter-communal, territorial state, sub-state, and non-state – see the classification offered in William Twining, *Globalisation and Legal Theory* (Butterworths 2000) 139.

Yet, establishing distance from the most transient elements and/or from the elements that can change with just the stroke of a legislator's pen does not always prove to be an easy task. It did to Patrick Glenn but not to just anyone. The cultural sway of mainstream legal positivism may often drive the comparative law scholar off track, in search of what is most glimmering, most practically useful, or more understandable to the audience that she targets as her own.[17] In the latter perspective, the core study of comparing legal data introducing change, or expressing permanence or resistance, unavoidably ends up being conducted as if these were phenomena stemming only from national authoritative sources. What underpins this working method is the idea that all legal actors operate via a one-to-one correspondence with the values and legal culture of the whole, or the vast majority, of the members of the societies concerned. Consequently, the arrangement of similarities and differences across legal systems, and even the classification of these systems, may be safely shaped according to what is said and done by the 'official' legal actors. Needless to say, the aforementioned method and its results may be seen as useful to spread and enhance comparative legal knowledge in many Western scholarly and public debates. But these debates are not the only ones, not even in the West, and they do not cover the whole spectrum of legal reality that comparative law is called upon to understand.

2 *A Challenge from Within*

The failure of legal positivism can also be appreciated from a different and, as I said, interconnected perspective – which, once again, goes under-debated in mainstream discourses. The presence of a stratified multilevel legal system is discernible, not only outside the West but also within our own societies. I refer to the survival (or sometimes the rebirth) of different legal 'layers' in which rules flourish indifferent to, or even in contrast with, the official law of the state, and disputes are settled outside the official circuits of adjudication.[18]

Even though incidentally, I have to stress that in speaking of these layers, I am not taking into account the pan-Western debate (and its positivistic inspiration) that concerns the role performed by so-called social norms as something different from what is strictly understood to be law. At the basis of the current analysis there is, as

17 Jürgen Basedow, 'Comparative Law and Its Clients' (2014) 62 *Am J Comp L* 821, 835–36.

18 A thorough analysis of the issues dealt with in this section can be found in Mauro Bussani, 'Strangers in the Law: Lawyers' Law and the Other Legal Dimensions' (2019) 40 *Cardozo L Rev* 3125. For the purposes of this chapter, one can see, on the presence, in the West, of multiple normative orders that push litigation to the periphery of dispute processing, eg, Stewart Macaulay, 'Elegant Models, Empirical Pictures and the Complexities of Contract' (1977) 11 *L & Soc'y Rev* 507; Sally Engle Merry, *Getting Justice and Getting Even: Legal Consciousness among Working Class Americans* (University of Chicago Press 1990) 37–63, 88–109; Norbert Rouland, *Aux confins du droit* (Odile Jacob 1991); Herbert Jacob, 'The Elusive Shadow of the Law' (1992) 26 *L & Soc'y Rev* 565. Cf W Michael Reisman, *Law in Brief Encounters* (Yale University Press 1999); Daniel Jutras, 'The Legal Dimensions of Everyday Life' (2001) 16 *Can JL & Soc'y* 45.

previously stated, the assumption that the law is the whole of the rules that a given community (regardless of its size and social or economic sophistication) adopts to govern itself. Once this definition of the legal phenomenon is taken, any distinction between legal and social rules disappears as long as the rules at issue correspond to the above-mentioned requisites.[19]

For the purposes of this chapter, the existing legal stratification in the West can be roughly introduced by taking into consideration four layers of rules. One, and only one, of our legal horizons is contained in what can be named as the 'ordinary official layer', to which Western legal discourse and legal education usually refer. It is the stratum where we encounter positive, or would-be positive (as is the case for most soft law initiatives) legal rules – that is, the rules enacted, or intended to be acknowledged, by an officially recognized authority and usually carved into national and local regulations, treaties, or other international law instruments, and worked out in judicial decisions derived from the same texts. It is only here that behaviours, entitlements, and disputes are controlled by official law and official circuits of adjudication. The other levels of legal experience are grounded in different rules. Under the legal skies where the lodestar is not state law, a layer that regulates common situations is the one relying on rules and tools of dispute settlement that have a customary origin and that are inspired by the principle of 'personal authority'. This is the layer to which most Western family and kinship relationships belong.[20] Another layer is also given order by the 'unofficial' rules and 'unofficial' adjudication devices, but these rules and devices have, at least in part, a different nature and origin. They are rooted in communitarian customs and their enforcement is guaranteed by extra-kinship factors.[21] This is something that in the West can be observed

[19] Compare the distinction between 'law' and 'legislation' made in Friedrich A Hayek, *Law, Legislation and Liberty, Vol 1: Rules and Order* (University of Chicago Press 1973) 35–51, 72–74, 124–26. According to Hayek, 'law' belongs to the category of endogenous orders growing or originating from within a given society – ie, growing spontaneously through rules which people live in accordance with – because of mutual expectations, whereas 'legislation' belongs to the category of exogenous orders imposed from the outside or from above, with a view of influencing the endogenous rules when they evolve in a direction which is regarded to be wrong or one-sided by a democratically elected legislature.

[20] Eg, Robert C Ellickson, *The Household: Informal Order around the Hearth* (Princeton University Press 2008); Lawrence M Friedman and Grant M Hayden, *American Law: An Introduction* (3rd edn, OUP 2017) 20; Elizabeth S Scott, 'Social Norms and the Legal Regulation of Marriage' (2000) 86 *Va L Rev* 1901, 1903; Eric A Posner, *Law and Social Norms* (Harvard University Press 2000) 72–76. See also Eric A Feldman, *The Ritual of Rights in Japan* (CUP 2000) 357; Boaventura de Sousa Santos, *Toward a New Common Sense: Law, Globalization, and Emancipation* (2nd edn, CUP 2002) 426–34; Jutras (n 18) 45–51.

[21] In both this and the aforementioned 'kinship' layer, one can easily observe that rewards usually amount to goods, services, or obligations to which a person would assign a positive (economic or non-economic) value. Likewise, punishments actualize in goods, services, and obligations to which a person would assign a negative (economic or non-economic) value. See Gillian K Hadfield and Barry R Weingast, 'Law without the State: Legal Attributes and the Coordination of Decentralized Collective Punishment' (2013) 1 *JL & Courts* 3–5; Barak D Richman, 'Norms and Law: Putting the Horse before the Cart' (2012) 62 *Duke LJ* 739, 747; Lisa Bernstein, 'Private Commercial Law in the

largely in the exercise of property rights (especially outside urban contexts),[22] in the settlement of small disputes arising in everyday life,[23] and in the management of small businesses[24] – even though the 'small value' cap seems irrelevant to many.[25] The last layer that deserves mention here is the one occupied by transnational business and financial law fields – where the rules applied are mostly provided by private or semi-private international bodies, or are the result of customs developed over time by commercial and financial practices. This is a layer where business actors may not only operate by their own rules but also adopt 'home-made' regimes for settling disputes, establishing their own courts and nominating their own judges.[26]

Cotton Industry: Creating Cooperation through Rules, Norms, and Institutions' (2001) 99 *Mich L Rev* 1724, 1776.

22 Robert C Ellickson, *Order without Law: How Neighbors Settle Disputes* (Harvard University Press 1991); Antonio Gambaro, 'Perspectives on the Codification of the Law of Property: An Overview' (1997) 5 *ERPL* 497. See also Hernando de Soto, *The Mystery of Capital: Why Capitalism Triumphs in the West and Fails Everywhere Else* (Basic Books 2000).

23 Ellickson, *Order without Law* (n 22) 50, 87, 185, 209. See also Mauro Bussani and Marta Infantino, 'Tort Law and Legal Cultures' (2015) 63 *Am J Comp L* 77, 83–90.

24 Stewart Macaulay, 'Non-Contractual Relations in Business: A Preliminary Study' (1963) 28 *Am Soc Rev* 55. See also Commission on Legal Empowerment of the Poor, *Making the Law Work for Everyone: Working Group Reports*, vol 2 (Toppan Printing 2008) 196–267; Janet Tai Landa, *Trust, Ethnicity, and Identity: Beyond the New Institutional Economics of Ethnic Trading Networks, Contract Law, and Gift-Exchange* (University of Michigan Press 1994).

25 In many fields, the 'small value' cap is actually irrelevant. A good example is the huge amount of money involved in daily transactions that are fully controlled by the unofficial rules worked out by the cotton and diamond industries in the United States and elsewhere. See Barak D Richman, *Stateless Commerce: The Diamond Network and the Persistence of Relational Exchange* (Harvard University Press 2017); Lisa Bernstein, 'Opting Out of the Legal System: Extralegal Contractual Relations in the Diamond Industry' (1992) 21 *JLS* 115; Bernstein, 'Private Commercial Law in the Cotton Industry' (n 21) 1724. '[E]mpirical studies have called attention to the relative insignificance of formal contracts and enforcement mechanisms in the interaction of business partners': Jutras (n 18) 55. It is worth recalling that the same kind of allegiance to extra-kinship, customary, and unofficial rules may be found in the 'global law' arenas and in the body of the state itself – in the latter case they may be termed praxis or constitutional conventions. See the references in Bussani, *El derecho de Occidente* (n 6) 93–109, 123–40. See also David J Bederman, *Custom as a Source of Law* (CUP 2010) 90ff (on the survival and flourishing of customary unofficial practices in US separation-of-powers constitutional law); Robert M Cover, 'Nomos and Narrative' (1983) 97 *Harv L Rev* 4, 31 (discussing communities committed to different 'constitutional visions'); Peter M Blau, *The Dynamics of Bureaucracy: Study of Interpersonal Relations in Two Government Agencies* (2nd edn, University of Chicago Press 1963) 183–206 (for a field study of bureaucratic institutions, and their formal and informal mechanisms of control, adaptation, and change).

26 Jan H Dalhuisen, 'Legal Orders and Their Manifestation: The Operation of the International Commercial and Financial Legal Order and Its Lex Mercatoria' (2006) 24 *Berk J Int'l L* 129; Chris Brummer, *Soft Law and the Global Financial System: Rule-Making in the 21st Century* (2nd edn, CUP 2015); Anne-Marie Slaughter, 'Governing the Global Economy through Government Networks' in Michael Byers (ed), *The Role of Law in International Politics, Essays in International Law* (OUP 2000) 202. For a historical overview (from the mid-thirteenth to the mid-twentieth century), see Mary Elizabeth Basile and others (eds), *Lex Mercatoria and Legal Pluralism: A Late Thirteen Century Treatise and Its Afterlife* (Ames Foundation 1998).

While this is not the place to discuss either the internal fabric of all these layers[27] or the (variable) degree of consistency between unofficial rules and state law, one has to note that unofficial legal layers have always existed in the West.[28] It is only the long-standing positivistic attitude of legal education and scholarship that has largely obscured the phenomenon in its treatises and books, as well as in its teaching methods and programmes, and consequently, in judicial culture and decisions.[29] These layers exist and persist for many reasons. The most popular of these reasons centres on the notions of functionalism and rationalism, although there is no real contrast between the two. The former is grounded in the idea that people respect unofficial rules because of reciprocity and the expectation of social gain.[30] The latter is embraced by those who wish to highlight how compliance with unofficial rules is in direct relation to their utility, rationality, and efficiency.[31]

27 See the works cited in notes 20–26.

28 Eg, Esin Örücü, 'What Is a Mixed Legal System: Exclusion or Expansion?' in Esin Örücü (ed), *Mixed Legal Systems at New Frontiers* (Wildy, Simmonds & Hill 2010); Roderick A Macdonald, 'Metaphors of Multiplicity: Civil Society, Regimes and Legal Pluralism' (1998) 15 *Ariz J Int'l & Comp L* 69; Avner Greif, *Institutions and the Path to the Modern Economy: Lessons from Medieval Trade* (CUP 2006).

29 See also Helge Dedek, 'Stating Boundaries: The Law, Disciplined' in Helge Dedek and Shauna Van Praagh (eds), *Stateless Law: Evolving Boundaries of a Discipline* (Ashgate 2015) 9, 21; Gillian K Hadfield and Barry R Weingast, 'Microfoundations of the Rule of Law' (2014) 17 *Ann Rev Pol Sci* 21.

30 Eg, Marc Galanter, 'Reading the Landscape of Disputes: What We Know and Don't Know (and Think We Know) About Our Allegedly Contentious and Litigious Society' (1983) 31 *UCLA L Rev* 4; Posner (n 20) 171–77; Bronislaw Malinowski, *Crime and Custom in Savage Society* (first published 1926, Routledge 1982) 46–49; see also Jeremy Bentham, A *Comment on the Commentaries* (JH Burns and HLA Hart eds, University of London Press 1977) 231–34, as well as the end of note 31.

31 Ellickson, *Order without Law* (n 22) 283; John McMillan and Christopher Woodruff, 'Dispute Prevention without Courts in Vietnam' (1999) 15 *JL Econ & Org* 637; Lewis A Kornhauser, 'Are There Cracks in the Foundation of Spontaneous Order?' (1992) 67 *NYU L Rev* 647; Anthony T Kronman, 'Contract Law and the State of Nature' (1985) 1 *JL Econ & Org* 5; Avinash K Dixit, *Lawlessness and Economics: Alternative Modes of Governance* (Princeton University Press 2004) 10–11; Oliver E Williamson, 'Calculativeness, Trust, and Economic Organization' (1993) 36 *JL & Econ* 453, 471–72. See also Cass R Sunstein, 'Social Norms and Social Roles' (1996) 96 *Colum L Rev* 903, 930.

On the top of different utilitarian reasons, general notions of reciprocal fairness and cooperation, mutual trust, common values, expectations, and beliefs may and actually do motivate participants in these groups. The legal upshot is the compliance with sets of rules that are grounded on the credibility of each one's commitments to her self-interest and/or self-perceived identity as a member of a personal, business, professional community, or of a defined socio-demographic group with which one shares what matters in the given life setting. Abiding by their own law allows people to be loyal to their notions of honour and to their views of what they are and are doing, and assures them that they will preserve the opportunity to engage in future transactions, maintain a trustworthy reputation, and remain in good community standing with no, or very limited, need to resort to official law devices. See, eg, Barak D Richman, 'How Community Institutions Create Economic Advantage: Jewish Diamond Merchant in New York' (2006) 31 *L & Soc Inq* 383, 393–94, 409; Bederman (n 25) passim, 179ff; Barbara Yngvesson, 'Re-Examining Continuing Relations and the Law' 1985 (1985) *Wis L Rev* 623; Elinor Ostrom, *Governing the Commons: The Evolutions of Institutions for Collective Action* (CUP 1990) 184; Tom R Tyler, *Why People Obey the Law* (Princeton University Press 1990; republished 2006) 173. See also Bernstein, 'Private Commercial Law in the Cotton Industry' (n 21) 1745.

IV AN UNASSUMING LESSON

What is certain is that taking into account the stratification of the law proves to be extremely fruitful for acquiring the necessary awareness about the legal relationships to be understood and dealt with, whatever the perspective – domestic, international, or comparative. Thus, from the specific comparative law viewpoint, the final question becomes the following: Given that a legal system is not a monolithic institution but a dynamic entity, and that each of its layers stands in a different relation to the pressure (due to prestige or other driving factors) coming from the other layers – domestic, foreign, or international[32] – what cognitive dimension is left if we overlook the relevant phenomena, which, in addition to 'official' law, deeply affect the living law of different societies? The answer lies in the need for a multilayered, pluralistic, and comparative perspective.[33] Such a perspective would help call into question traditional understandings of the legal dimension(s), connect mainstream visions with the broader social contexts producing them, and unveil the cultural assumptions that underlie and support the operations of law mechanisms. To delve beyond conventional wisdom into the cultural and operational frameworks in which all law operates and is embedded would be both promising and challenging for this perspective. But carrying on this perspective requires legal scholars to be equipped with far-sighted views, cultural tolerance, and a modest sense of self-worth, precisely the qualities for which Glenn's personality and scholarship are remarkable.

V LEGAL TRADITION: A LESSON OF OPEN-MINDEDNESS

Potentially less controversial, but definitely crucial in Patrick Glenn's *Weltanschauung*, is the notion of tradition. He sees it as a 'bran-tub' of information,[34] available to individuals, communities, and societies as they make choices for themselves. In Glenn's view, historically the legal traditions have always exchanged information, to the point that sometimes it can be difficult to identify a given piece of information with just one tradition,[35] even though it is easy for a person who identifies with any given tradition to retrieve and use information from another tradition[36] – and scholarly findings show how often people live astride traditions and identities, and retrieve, enjoy, and exploit information coming from their multifarious backgrounds.[37]

32 De Sousa Santos (n 20). See also Keebet von Benda-Beckmann, 'Why Bother About Legal Pluralism? Analytical and Policy Questions: An Introductory Address' in Keebet von Benda-Beckmann and Harald W Finkler (eds), *Folk Law and Legal Pluralism: Societies in Transformation: Papers of the XIth International Congress* (Department of Circumpolar Affairs 1999). See also the works cited in notes 25–26.

33 See also Jutras (n 18) 60–63.

34 Glenn, *LTW* (n 1) 13. See also Martin Krygier, Chapter 6 in this volume.

35 Glenn, *LTW* (n 1) 34–41.

36 Ibid, 13–16.

37 Eg, Thomas W Pogge, 'Group Rights and Ethnicity' in Ian Shapiro and Will Kymlicka (eds), *Ethnicity and Group Rights* (NYU Press 1997); Will Kymlicka, *Liberalism, Community and Culture*

If one takes seriously the idea of tradition as a relentless flow of information, and that the way this flow arranges itself in a given society forges the latter through the dynamics of individuals' mindsets and preferences, then three important consequences follow.

First, in any society, the strength of identitarian forces of all groupings, such as those based on language, religion, and family ties, should be seen as contingent and dependent upon the kind of information available in the given tradition and to the different groupings. Second, one should acknowledge that every time the flow of a tradition comes into contact with another, they both exchange information and grow to challenge and/or incorporate one another. Glenn goes as far as to underline that '[t]he conclusion that tradition is the controlling element in determining social identity means that there are no fundamentally different, totally irreconcilable social identities in the world.'[38] This is an issue which I will come back to later, but a broad notion of tradition is crucial to Glenn's way of understanding law, because it captures elements that tend to be missed by legal theorists who analyse law in abstract terms (such as command, norms, rules, and principles). What they particularly miss, in Glenn's view,[39] is the sway of the past and its relentless dynamics.[40] The third consequence is that isolation of a legal tradition is wholly exceptional. Most diffusion has been informal rather than formal; most influence involves exchange or reciprocity rather than movement in one direction only; the main agents of change are not always governments but can equally well be individuals and groups such as merchants, jurists, and emigrants (including colonizers). From this perspective – it should go without saying, *mais cela va peut-être mieux en le disant* – one can

(Clarendon 1989) 186; Seyla Benhabib, Ian Shapiro, and Danilo Petranoviç, 'Editor's Introduction' in Seyla Benhabib, Ian Shapiro, and Danilo Petranovic (eds), *Identities, Affiliations, and Allegiances* (CUP 2007); David Nelken, 'Eugen Ehrlich, Living Law, and Plural Legalities' (2008) 9(2) *Theo Inq L* 443. See also Seth Godin, *Tribes: We Need You to Lead Us* (Penguin 2008). Indeed, in the majority of known societies, Western and otherwise, individual identities are spread over different layers of affiliation dictated, for example, by religion, family, the local-national-transnational idiom, professional and economic choices (abstract and ideal or concrete and investment oriented), food choices, political options, and belonging to an ethnic or territorial community (the latter being obviously less common for those states whose borders were hetero-established, and thus are ethnically 'imaginative'). These 'affiliations', though with varying intensity and range of action, express needs, orient the choices of individuals and groups, demand or postulate representativeness, require rules respectful of their identities, and circulate information about those needs and choices and about expected representation and rules. See Philip Selznick (with the collaboration of Philippe Nonet and Howard M Vollmer), *Law, Society, and Industrial Justice* (Russell Sage Foundation 1969) 271–73; Bernard Gert, 'Loyalty and Morality' in Sanford V Levinson, Joel Parker, and Paul Woodruff (eds), *Nomos LIV. Loyalty* (NYU Press 2013) 3, 6ff; Derek Parfit, *Reasons and Persons* (Clarendon 1984) 199ff; Bussani, 'Strangers in the Law' (n 18). More generally, see Amartya Sen, *Identity and Value: The Illusion of Destiny* (Norton 2006); Martha C Nussbaum, *Women and Human Development: The Capabilities Approach* (CUP 2001).

38 Glenn, *LTW* (n 1) 39.

39 But see also John Henry Merryman, *The Civil Law Tradition: An Introduction to the Legal Systems of Western Europe and Latin America* (2nd edn, Stanford University Press 1995) 2.

40 Glenn, *LTW* (n 1) 23–27.

smoothly appreciate how common law and civil law traditions are only one part of the story in the context of world history, but also acknowledge that these are traditions that have been as much importers as exporters of each other[41] and of other traditions.[42]

Further, Glenn points out that no tradition can exercise full control over what information is preserved and captured in the future, therefore implicitly but straightforwardly rejecting the post-Enlightenment tendency to treat tradition and change as antinomies.[43] This is a valuable lesson in assessing the mainstream representation of legal globalization phenomena, that is, the view according to which legal globalization-[s] should be seen as a progressive march towards the uniformity of legal institutions and rules, thereby discarding history and geography, because the past is given and the future is (common, and) given too.[44] Patrick Glenn's open-mindedness, the capacity of including and composing apparent antinomies in a breathing vision of the reality to come, is a(nother) fundamental lesson to be learned by everyone.

VI LEGAL CONCILIATION

As I have mentioned, according to Glenn, there are 'no fundamentally different, totally irreconcilable social identities in the world'.[45] At the same time, he is well aware that the imposition of rules and institutions from above or outside the given legal system often reveals itself to be a lose–lose game.[46] This is why he prefers discussing the problem from the perspective of a possible reconciliation of laws, a process Glenn sees as grounded in 'accepting (not tolerating) the major, complex legal traditions of the world (all of them)', and in 'seeing all traditions as one's own, in some measure, since each is dependent on the others'.[47] As to this sort of cultural (messianic?) revolution, I am both more sceptical and pessimistic than Patrick Glenn. Beyond being unavoidably selective and asymmetrical (we cannot pretend these 'reconciling' attitudes could develop with the same modalities, at the same time, across all 'major' legal traditions), I think legal reconciliation's value and desirability depend, among many other things, on the way it is carried out and on the potential scores (and qualities) of the winners and losers.

Three remarks are in order here. First, anthropologists teach us that the majority of societies develop their own expansive ethnocentrism, to be understood as the tendency to consider one's form of civilization better than others, and therefore to try

41 Nicholas Kasirer, 'Legal Education as Métissage' (2003) 78 *Tul L Rev* 500.
42 Glenn, *LTW* (n 1) 134–36, 165–70, 175–76, 236–41.
43 In these terms, see William Twining, 'Glenn on Tradition: An Overview' (2006) 1 *J Comp L* 107, 111, in the wake of Martin Krygier, 'Law as Tradition' (1986) 5 *Law & Phil* 237, 239. See also Chapter 8 in this volume.
44 See the criticism of this view in Glenn, *LTW* (n 1) 272–79, 372–76.
45 Ibid, 39.
46 Ibid, 275–83.
47 Ibid, 378.

to spread it as much as possible and expand and strengthen one's own interests.[48] The West was, is, and will be no exception. Second, lessons from the past and the present show us how often initiatives targeting from outside the transformation of others' laws lack the support of adequate comparative law means, required to meet the basic needs of contextualization for the solutions to be applied in the new, or newly shaped settings. Third, in assessing these endeavours, one should differentiate the various possible levels of analysis. The evaluation of the cultural aspects is one thing, the evaluation of the applicative aspects is, or may be, another.

On a cultural level, those who, like Glenn,[49] pay due attention to the teachings of history know how colonization, one of the most evident phenomena of the compression of legal diversity, first determined a process of propagation of the European model within the colonies, albeit with limited effectiveness and ultimately a critical reaction to that forced diffusion (although not necessarily to the whole of its contents). Moreover, in the language of the students of traditional models, the superimposition of foreign models – irrespective of the wishes of the local elites, who often have been and still are educated in the West – is mostly seen as a tool of de-culturalization, of trampling on the weaker identity, and of destruction of possible meanings.[50]

On the operative level, other evaluations are needed. Here, it is critical to recognize – in the wake of Glenn and many others[51] – that not all differences from the Western paradigms are to be celebrated, (1) because many of them could be the result of customary rules that a large part of the involved society would well do without (one can think of the developments taking place in relation to female genital mutilation or polygamy in (some of) the concerned societies[52]); and/or (2) because

48 See, eg, Serena Nanda and Richard L Warms, *Cultural Anthropology* (10th edn, Cengage Learning 2011) 10ff; Michael Herzfeld, *Anthropology Through the Looking-Glass: Critical Ethnography in the Margins of Europe* (CUP 1989) 78, 97; Christoffel AO van Nieuwenhuijze, *Culture and Development: The Prospects of an Afterthought* (Institute of Social Studies 1983) passim and esp 3, 21, 24ff, 48; Edmund R Leach, 'Etnocentrismi' in Ruggiero Romano and others (eds), *Enciclopedia Einaudi*, vol 5 (Einaudi 1978); Edmund R Leach, 'The Nature of War' in Stephen Hugh-Jones and James Laidlaw (eds), *The Essential Edmund Leach: Anthropology and Society* (Yale University Press 1965) 354–56; Claude Lévi-Strauss, *Race et histoire* (Pouillon 1952); Tzvetan Todorov, *Nous et les autres: La réflexion française sur la diversité humaine* (Seuil 1989); Ernesto De Martino, *La fine del mondo: Contributo all'analisi delle apocalissi culturali* (Einaudi 2002) 394–98; Sumner (n 5) – Sumner is credited with coining the term 'ethnocentrism'.

49 Glenn, *LTW* (n 1) 376–79.

50 See Rodolfo Sacco, 'Diversity and Uniformity in the Law' (2001) 49 *Am J Comp L* 171, 178–79; Étienne Le Roy, 'Quels projets de société pour les africains du XXIe siècle?' in Camille Kuyu (ed), *À la recherche du droit africain du XXIe siècle* (Connaissances et Savoirs 2005); Steven Wilf, 'The Invention of Legal Primitivism' (2008) 10(2) *Theo Inq L* 485, 491. 'It may be recalled that since the 16th century the development of capitalism has called for the destruction of differences in laws, standards, currencies, weights and measures, taxes, customs duties at the level of nation state': Bhupinder S Chimni, 'International Institutions Today: An Imperial Global State in the Making' (2004) 15 *EJIL* 1, 7. See also Antony Anghie, *Imperialism, Sovereignty and the Making of International Law* (CUP 2004) 5.

51 Glenn, *LTW* (n 1) 28–30.

52 Eg, Bussani, *El derecho de Occidente* (n 6) 55–56, 197–201; Radhika Coomaraswamy, 'The Contemporary Challenges to International Human Rights' in Scott Sheeran and Sir Nigel Rodley (eds), *Routledge Handbook of International Human Rights Law* (Routledge 2014) 132–33.

keeping in place those differences can be very costly in terms of Western-style economic development (assuming the latter is the model to be pursued): It suffices to think of patterns of distributing land and other entitlements according to religious, clannish, gendered, or political criteria.[53] Further, one has to acknowledge that legal uniformity processes can be carried out through the spontaneous acceptance of the same body of rules by different groups of law users, producing effective and widespread transnational compliance without imposition from above or outside[54] – the '*lex mercatoria*',[55] the rules regulating international diamond traffic,[56] or the international water policy agreements,[57] are good examples in this respect.

VII THE LESSON OF OPTIMISM

What the foregoing observations allow one to better understand is the reason for which the circulation of Western legal models has so often been ineffective and inefficient outside the Western world. On the one hand, one should be aware that the needs to be met and the tools to be used when transplanting or 'importing' any rule are factors that vary considerably, depending on the area of the law in question, and on the area of the world one targets – finance is not welfare, healthcare is not commerce, and what is necessary to make any reform in the matter of procedural law effective is quite different if one considers the case of, for example, France as compared to Burundi.[58] On the other hand, the lack of a common cultural background shared by law-makers and law-takers,[59]

53 See the references to the vivid debate in Bussani, *El derecho de Occidente* (n 6) 104–09, 250–56.

54 Eg, David A Westbrook, 'Theorizing the Diffusion of Law: Conceptual Difficulties, Unstable Imaginations, and the Effort to Think Gracefully Nonetheless' (2006) 47 *Harv Int'l LJ* 489.

55 Karl Kroeschell, 'Universales und partikulares Recht in der europäischen Rechtsgeschichte' in Karl Kroeschell and Albrecht Cordes (eds), *Vom nationalen zum transnationalen Recht* (CF Müller 1995) 273; Helmut Coing, *Europäisches Privatrecht, I: Älteres Gemeines Recht 1500 bis 1800* (CH Beck 1985) 519–23. See also Basile and others (n 26).

56 See note 25.

57 Eg, Philippe Cullet, 'International Water Norms and Principles – Impacts on Law and Policy Development in India' in Bussani and Heckendorn Urscheler (n 4).

58 Rather, what is evident is a paradox. Trade – which is based on exchanges and interests that may be closely entwined with local culture, rules, and needs – is largely controlled by a uniform official law adjudicated by a global official institution (the WTO) in the shadow of which a few powerful actors (the United States, the EU, China, the WB, the IMF, and the biggest multinationals) maintain an unofficial but extensive ability to manoeuvre. Finance, which thrives on exchanges, interests, and technical matrices broadly common to all the operators on the planet, has been governed to date by an unofficial law made and shared by the global financial actors, and by official laws largely depending on the local (national/regional) regulations – whose possible 'capture' by big business actors is a phenomenon that deserves extensive discussion. Eg, Marver J Bernstein, *Regulating Business by Independent Commission* (Princeton University Press 1955); Jean-Jacques Laffont and Jean Tirole, 'The Politics of Government Decision-Making: A Theory of Regulatory Capture' (1991) 106 *QJ Econ* 1089; Chris Brummer, 'Why Soft Law Dominates International Finance – And Not Trade' (2010) 13 *J Int'l Econ L* 623.

59 As now realized even by the World Bank in its programs for legal and judicial reforms: see Hassane Cissé, 'Justice Reform: The Experience of the World Bank' in Bussani and Heckendorn Urscheler (n 4) 24–26.

and the neglect of the essential involvement of the local law-users – what Patrick Glenn would call the lack of a critical mass of information exchange – may make any transplantation process an exercise in mere wishful thinking, or may have its implementation on the ground costing (economically, politically, and socially) an excessive price in terms of time, money, and energy.[60]

Patrick Glenn would subscribe to the abovementioned remarks, perhaps. Yet, his attitude is more 'optimistic'. He is not overly concerned with expansive ethnocentrism;[61] in his view, conflictual, oppressive, and violent encounters between legal traditions appear to be nothing but an unavoidable moment of legal traditions' everlasting cohabitation and interchange. Seen this way, dominance efforts are a perennial 'form of corruption' affecting all major legal traditions in their relentless survival dynamics – dynamics in which the winner of today might well be the loser of tomorrow. This is why Glenn invites the readers to see 'the major, complex legal traditions of the world . . . as mutually interdependent, such that the loss of any of them would be a loss to all the others, which would then lose a major source of support, or at least of self-interrogation'.[62] This would be the first step for 'acting positively to sustain diversity in law':[63] a process that could 'improve communication between lawyers of the world . . . enhance the prospect for peaceful settlement of disputes' but also 'enhance the legal mission.'[64]

It may be that Glenn's optimism stems once more from his 'human-friendly' and bright personality, or from growing up within a culture (the Canadian one) that has maintained over time the values of diversity and coherence, holding together diverse viewpoints while striving for a common identity. It may also be that this kind of culture – what Glenn would right away call 'tradition'[65] – have something to teach everyone about how to cope with the legal challenges of an increasingly transnational world. Certainly, Patrick Glenn taught us a lot about how to try to understand all of this. *Merci*, Patrick!

60 Eg, Stephen Golub, 'The Legal Empowerment Alternative' in Thomas Carothers (ed), *Promoting the Rule of Law Abroad: In Search of Knowledge* (Carnegie Endowment for International Peace 2006); Mary McClymont and Stephen Golub (eds), *Many Roads to Justice: The Law Related Work of the Ford Foundation Grantees Around the World* (Ford Foundation 2000); Michael R Anderson, 'Access to Justice and Legal Process: Making Legal Institutions Responsive to Poor People in LDCs' (2003) *IDS Working Paper* 178 <www.ids.ac.uk/files/dmfile/Wp178.pdf>; Julia Eckert and others (eds), *Law against the State: Ethnographic Forays into Law's Transformations* (CUP 2012).

61 See note 50 and corresponding text.

62 Glenn, *LTW* (n 1) 378.

63 Ibid.

64 Ibid.

65 Ibid, 73, 163. See also Esin Örücü, Chapter 4 in this volume.

2

The 'Comparative Method' at the Roots of Comparative Law

Giorgio Resta

I THE CONTEMPORARY DEBATE ON THE METHODS OF COMPARATIVE LAW

In the past two decades comparative law scholars have rediscovered the importance of the debate on method. Left for a long time in the background as a by-product of the old controversy on the epistemic status of the discipline (comparative law as 'method' or 'science'),[1] the 'struggle for the methods' – as François Gény once defined it[2] – has experienced a sudden revival.

Not only articles and collections of essays[3] but also monographs and handbooks[4] have increasingly dealt with the theoretical framework of comparative law teaching and scholarship. If only a few years ago Günther Frankenberg noted 'the marginal role of theory and method in comparative legal studies',[5] nowadays answering the

[1] For the latest on this, see Uwe Kischel, *Rechtsvergleichung* (CH Beck 2015) 28.

[2] François Gény, *Science et technique en droit privé positif: Nouvelle contribution à la critique de la méthode juridique* (Recueil Sirey 1914) 2 (translated by author).

[3] See, eg, Esin Örücü, 'Methodology of Comparative Law' in Jan M Smits (ed), *Elgar Encyclopedia of Comparative Law* (2nd edn, Edward Elgar 2012); Mark Tushnet, 'Some Reflections on Method in Comparative Constitutional Law' in Sujit Choudhry (ed), *The Migration of Constitutional Ideas* (CUP 2007); Geoffrey Samuel, 'Taking Methods Seriously (Part One)' (2007) 2 *J Comp L* 94; Geoffrey Samuel, 'Taking Methods Seriously (Part Two)' (2007) 2 *J Comp L* 210; Jaakko Husa, 'Methodology of Comparative Law Today: From Paradoxes to Flexibility?' (2006) 58 *RIDC* 1095; Béatrice Jaluzot, 'Méthodologie du droit comparé: Bilan et perspective' (2005) 57 *RIDC* 29; Vernon Valentine Palmer, 'From Lerotholi to Lando: Some Examples of Comparative Law Methodology' (2005) 53 *Am J Comp L* 261; Otto Pfersmann, 'Le droit comparé comme interprétation et comme théorie du droit' (2001) 53 *RIDC* 275.

[4] Among others, see Günter Frankenberg, *Comparative Law as Critique* (Edward Elgar 2016); Maurice Adams and Dirk Heirbaut (eds), *The Method and Culture of Comparative Law: Essays in Honour of Mark Van Hoecke* (Hart 2014); Geoffrey Samuel, *An Introduction to Comparative Law Theory and Method* (Hart 2014); Pier Giuseppe Monateri (ed), *Methods of Comparative Law* (Edward Elgar 2012); Maurice Adams and Jacco Bomhoff (eds), *Practice and Theory in Comparative Law* (CUP 2012).

[5] Günter Frankenberg, 'Critical Comparisons: Re-Thinking Comparative Law' (1985) 26 *Harv Int'l LJ* 411, 416. See also Ralf Michaels, 'Im Westen nichts Neues? 100 Jahre Pariser Kongreß für Rechtsvergleichung – Gedanken anläßlich einer Jubiläumskonferenz in New Orleans' (2002) 66 *RabelsZ* 97.

question of 'how to compare' seems to have become more important, or academically valuable, than the carrying out of comparative enquiries themselves.

Such a renewed fascination with methodological issues might be taken as evidence of the strength and intellectual vivacity of a discipline too quickly accused in the past of oversimplifying the serious theoretical issues involved in the process of 'comparing' or 'understanding the other'. But it might also be regarded as a sign of the serious challenges faced by comparative law, as an academic discipline, in a post-national environment. Comparative law seems to be at a turning point for the simple reason that the overall cultural, political, and institutional framework that surrounded its emergence and development is gradually fading.

As Patrick Glenn has repeatedly pointed out, comparative law, as an autonomous subject, is the product of the nineteenth century.[6] It is, more specifically, the logical outcome of a series of factors, such as state legal positivism, a territorially based notion of jurisdiction, and a 'scientific' paradigm of legal research.[7] The collapse of the Westphalian order has deeply transformed, and largely overcome, the material basis of legal nationalism;[8] legal artefacts are no more considered the exclusive product of the political state;[9] the faith in a neutral and detached description of the legal reality has lost much of its appeal.[10] Comparative law scholars have perceived the challenges as having derived from the crisis of the conception of normativity that developed during the epoch of legal positivism. Most of the critiques raised against the 'conventional model' of comparative law are rooted in the acknowledgement of the 'decline of state law'[11] as well as of the dissolution of the theoretical framework that surrounded it.

Given this background, the debate on methodology should be considered a precious occasion to critically reflect on the whole theoretical framework of comparative law in a changing global scenario.[12] The risk that has to be carefully avoided, however, is to reduce the whole discussion to a sort of contest concerning the best 'cookbook recipe',[13] that is, the 'right method of comparative research'. So conceived, this would be a meaningless question, if for no other reason than that it is not possible to assess the effectiveness of any method without having previously

6 H Patrick Glenn, 'The Aims of Comparative Law' in Smits, *Elgar Encyclopedia of Comparative Law* (n 3) 67–68.

7 See in particular Ralf Michaels, 'Transnationalizing Comparative Law' (2016) 23 *MJ* 352.

8 See generally H Patrick Glenn, *The Cosmopolitan State* (OUP 2013); on this point, see Gunnar Folke Schuppert, Chapter 14 in this volume.

9 Roderick Macdonald and Kathy Glover, 'Implicit Comparative Law' (2013) 43 *RDUS* 123; Ralf Michaels, 'Was ist nichtstaatliches Recht? Eine Einführung' in Gralf-Peter Calliess (ed), *Transnationales Recht: Stand und Perspektiven* (Mohr 2014); on this, see also Michele Graziadei, Chapter 5 in this volume.

10 H Patrick Glenn, 'Quel droit comparé?' (2013) 43 *RDUS* 23, 30–31; Frankenberg, 'Critical Comparisons' (n 5) 77.

11 Glenn, 'Quel droit comparé?' (n 10) 27 (translated by author); on this, see also Mauro Bussani, Chapter 1 in this volume.

12 Ibid, 32–43; Michaels, 'Transnationalizing Comparative Law' (n 7) 355–57.

13 Kischel (n 1) 93.

clarified what the specific aims of the enquiry are – comparative law having multiple, heterogeneous uses.[14] And indeed, as Patrick Glenn observed, 'the history of comparative law is not one of adherence to a methodological norm but rather one of deviation and variety. There is no comparative method'.[15]

Indeed, this is a very thoughtful and important remark, which should always be taken into account whenever one embarks into similar debates. However, it might be useful to note that 'eclecticism' as a theoretical perspective is itself the sign of the times and the logical outcome of the abandonment of the paradigm – to recall Frankenberg's terminology – of 'cognitive control'.[16] Looking back at the history of comparative law, one cannot but be struck by the circumstance that throughout the formative era, the idea that obtained most credit in European intellectual circles was the opposite one – namely that there was indeed *a* comparative method.

In this chapter I focus on the rise of legal comparativism, with the aim of bringing back to light some distinctive traits of the original discourse on the 'comparative method' and highlighting the importance of the 'scientific paradigm' for the acceptance of comparative law as an autonomous subject of legal research.

The literature on legal comparativism before the Paris Conference of 1900 is quite sparse and certainly not abundant, perhaps because the association between comparative law and evolutionary jurisprudence makes legal comparativism obsolete and uninteresting for contemporary scholars. Rereading today some of the early contributions on the characters and aims of comparative studies is nonetheless an instructive exercise. Indeed, not only does it show that, since the beginning, the endorsement of extra-legal sciences – like biology and philology – has played an important role, both as an analytical tool to understand reality and as a rhetoric instrument to achieve the legitimization of a new 'discipline'. It also shows that the trust in the existence of a standard method, shared by many prominent scholars in the nineteenth century, suddenly disappeared as soon as the theoretical meta-framework that sustained the original discourse of comparative law – characterized, as Patrick Glenn repeatedly pointed out, by taxonomic essentialism and evolutionary determinism – lost its intellectual legitimization and its material basis.

Catching a glimpse of the theory of comparative law before the 1900 Paris Conference, therefore, might be a fruitful exercise to add historical depth to the contemporary debate on method and to better understand the nature of the challenges faced by the 'conventional model' of comparative law today.

14 Jürgen Basedow, 'Comparative Law and Its Clients' (2014) 62 *Am J Comp L* 821; Robert Leckey, 'Review of Comparative Law' (2017) 26 *S & LS* 3; Esin Örücü, 'Developing Comparative Law' in Esin Örücü and David Nelken (eds), *Comparative Law: A Handbook* (Hart 2007) 48–49.

15 H Patrick Glenn, 'Against Method?' in Adams and Heirbaut (n 4) 17.

16 Frankenberg, 'Critical Comparisons' (n 5) 416.

II THE RISE OF COMPARATIVISM

As noted by Francis Goyet,

> the expression *comparaison n'est pas raison* (comparison is not reason) reminds us both that comparison is an instrument for producing intelligibility and that this instrument works well, almost too well: from here comes the need to be prudent in using the extremely fertile method of *comparatisme* (comparative studies).[17]

Indeed, it is useful to keep in mind a distinction between *comparison* as a practical tool in the quest for human understanding and *comparativism* as a theoretical framework, a 'methodological guarantee of cognitive discovery',[18] and an autonomous field of research.[19]

Comparison is long established as one of the main techniques of discovery and reasoning in the field of natural sciences.[20] In the social sciences, likewise, comparisons have been frequently resorted to as an effective instrument to produce intelligibility. To say it with Alexis de Tocqueville: 'Quiconque n'a étudié et vu que la France, ne comprendra jamais rien, j'ose le dire, à la révolution française.'[21] Comparisons belong as well to the traditional patrimony of legal reasoning and judicial practice, as it is paradigmatically shown by the medieval experience of *ius commune*, characterized by the systematic comparison and hybridization of different branches of the law.[22]

By contrast, comparativism as a mentality, and more specifically as an autonomous field of research, is a much more recent and culturally situated phenomenon. The rise of comparative disciplines dates to (the end of the eighteenth century and) the beginning of the nineteenth century and is a typically European phenomenon.[23] An observer of intellectual trends as acute as Friedrich Nietzsche personally witnessed such a phenomenon, referring to his own century as the 'age of comparison'.[24] An age,

17 Francis Goyet, 'Comparison' in Barbara Cassin (ed), *Dictionary of Untraslatables: A Philosophical Lexicon* (Princeton University Press 2014) 160.

18 WJT Mitchell, 'Why Comparisons Are Odious' (1996) 70 *World Literature Today* 321, 323.

19 On this distinction, see Pier Giuseppe Monateri, 'Methods in Comparative Law: An Intellectual Overview' in Monateri, *Methods of Comparative Law* (n 4) 10–15.

20 See Jonathon W Moses and Torbjørn L Knutsen, *Ways of Knowing: Competing Methodologies in Social and Political Research* (2nd edn, Palgrave Macmillan 2012) 52, 95.

21 Alexis de Tocqueville, *L'ancien régime et la révolution* (7th edn, Lévy Frères 1866) 27. On Tocqueville's comparative approach, see Neil J Smelser, 'Alexis de Tocqueville as Comparative Analyst' in Ivan Vallier (ed), *Comparative Methods in Sociology: Essays on Trends and Applications* (University of California Press 1971).

22 See, for further details, Paolo Napoli, 'Le droit, l'histoire, la comparaison' in Olivier Remaud, Jean Frédéric Schaub, and Isabelle Thireau (eds), *Faire des sciences sociales: Comparer* (EHESS 2012) 127–34; H Patrick Glenn, *On Common Laws* (OUP 2005) 12–43.

23 See Guy Jucquois, *Le comparatisme: Généalogie d'une méthode*, vol 1 (Peeters 1989) 21; Guy Juquois, *Le comparatisme: Émergence d'une méthode*, vol 2 (Peeters 1993) 9; Guy Jucquois and Pierre Swiggers, 'Comparatisme: Contours d'une visée' in Guy Jucquois and Pierre Swiggers (eds), *Le comparatisme devant le miroir* (Peeters 1991); Goyet (n 17) 162.

24 Friedrich Nietzsche, *Human, All Too Human* (first published 1878, RJ Hollingdale tr, CUP 1996) 24 (aphorism in n 23). On this, see Erik Jayme, 'Das Zeitalter der Vergleichung: Emerico Amari und

he wrote, in which men felt less 'bound by their tradition', the 'fermentation of motivations within them' was greater, 'and the greater in consequence their outward restlessness, their mingling together with one another, the polyphony of their endeavors'.[25] Distinctive features of this time were the distrust of traditional answers provided by religion and metaphysics, the discovery of the temporal dimension, the faith in modern sciences, and the systematic confrontation of natural and cultural patterns.[26] As Nietzsche observed,

> [j]ust as in the arts all the genres are imitated side by side, so are all the stages and genres of morality, custom, culture. Such an age acquires its significance through the fact that the various different philosophies of life, customs, cultures can be compared and experienced side by side; which in earlier ages, when, just as all artistic genres were attached to a particular place and time, so every culture still enjoyed only a localized domination, was not possible. Now an enhanced aesthetic sensibility will come to a definitive decision between all these forms offering themselves for comparison: most of them – namely all those rejected by his sensibility – it will allow to die out. There is likewise now taking place a selecting out among the forms and customs of higher morality, whose objective can only be the elimination of the lower moralities. This is the age of comparison![27]

Natural sciences were at the forefront of such experimentation, and it is in this field that the comparative approach was first developed and systematically applied.[28] Whereas in the eighteenth century the main concern was classificatory, taxonomic essentialism (being the dominant attitude of 'naturalists' like Linné and Buffon), at the end of the century the effort towards the explanations superseded the mere classification of biological varieties.[29] Scientific nomenclatures were previously based on the assumption of an unchanging natural order and the continuity of species. The attention gradually shifted to discontinuities, to the irregularities breaking up the graduation of species.[30] Explaining such gaps and anomalies became the natural scientist's main task, and the efforts spent at providing such explanations eventually led to the theory of the evolution of organisms.[31] A critical role was played in this context by the advent of new disciplines, such as comparative anatomy, paleontology, and comparative embryology. Georges Cuvier's scholarship, in particular, decisively contributed to the emergence of comparative anatomy, by

Friedrich Nietzsche' in Aldo Mazzacane and Reiner Schulze (eds), *Die deutsche und die italienische Rechtskultur im 'Zeitalter der Vergleichung'* (Duncker & Humblot 1995).

25 Nietzsche (n 24) 24.

26 See Jucquois, *Le comparatisme*, vol 2 (n 23) 60–72.

27 Nietzsche (n 24) 24.

28 On comparison as a fundamental method in biology, see Ernst Mayr, *The Growth of Biological Thought: Diversity, Evolution, and Inheritance* (Belknap Press 1982) 31.

29 Ibid, 183; Jucquois, *Le comparatisme*, vol 2 (n 23) 17.

30 Jucquois, *Le comparatisme*, vol 2 (n 23) 22.

31 Mayr (n 28) 343, 360.

postulating the preponderance of the organs' function (functional activities) over their structure (physical features).[32]

By linking every organ to its functions, it became possible to identify similarities among species, which went beyond the realm of the 'visible'.[33] According to Cuvier, scientific comparisons are an essential tool in the field of natural sciences, supplementing the lack of experimental evidence; it is through this method that the so-called general laws of observation may be discovered:

> Mere observation will, however, avail but little without comparison, we must observe attentively the same body in the various positions in which it is at different times placed by nature; and we must compare different bodies with each other, until we can recognise any invariable relations, which may exist between their structure and the phenomena which they exhibit. Thus may such bodies, when diligently observed and carefully compared with each other, be considered as experiments ready prepared by the hand of nature, who may be supposed to add to or subtract from each in the manner the experimentalist does in his laboratory with the inert materials subject to his control, and herself to present us with the result of such additions or subtractions.
>
> By these means we may arrive at a knowledge of the laws which regulate the phenomena of natural history, strictly speaking, subject to our observation, and which are employed by the great Governor of the universe with the same determinate precision as those which are opened to our view by the general sciences.[34]

The adoption of a 'comparativist' mentality went along with the abandonment of a creationist and anthropocentric vision of the world.[35] Indeed, as noted by Guy Jucquois, whereas for the classic world, entities are composed of inventories of morphological traits, similar or identical, mirroring pre-existing and eternal hierarchies, traits are now regarded as subservient to a specific task, implying a general functional homogeneity.[36] The advent of Darwinian evolutionism eventually displaced the vision of the universe as an immutable cosmos, as well as of man's centrality within such universe.[37]

Systematic comparison affirmed itself as an instrument of critical reasoning, and as such it led to a deep renewal of the scientific discourse in many fields.[38] Modern humanities, in particular, were starkly influenced by the rise of comparative

32 Michel Foucault, *Le parole e le cose: Un'archeologia delle scienze umane* (Biblioteca Universale Rizzoli 1978) 286.

33 Ibid, 292. As explained by Jucquois, *Le comparatisme*, vol 2 (n 23) 67, 'if the gills resemble the lungs, it is only because one postulates that both carry out the same task, namely breathing' (translated by author).

34 Georges Cuvier, *The Animal Kingdom Arranged in Conformity with Its Organization*, vol 1 (E Griffith ed and tr, first published in French 1817, GB Whittaker 1827) 5–6.

35 Norbert Rouland, *Anthropologie juridique* (Presses Universitaires de France 1988) 36.

36 Jucquois, *Le comparatisme*, vol 2 (n 23) 67.

37 Mayr (n 28) 394.

38 On the convergence between biology and philology, see Foucault (n 32) 303; Edward W Said, *Orientalism* (Penguin 2003) 142.

disciplines, and especially by comparative linguistics (or 'philology', as it was called in the nineteenth century).[39] Favoured by colonial conquests, namely by the British colonization of India, which prompted the discovery of the affinities between Sanskrit and the old European languages,[40] as well as by the development of a scientific approach to the study of 'family of languages' within German universities, this discipline had a sudden and enormous success.[41] Indeed, biologists and linguists cited each other quite frequently.[42] Among the basic assumptions of comparative philology were the following:

> Languages are organisms that live, develop, and die. Brought by the migration of peoples, they change place and extend themselves through the globe. Like living species, they may be regrouped in branches, families, and subfamilies. As is the case for natural species, linguistic evolution follows a trend of growing complexity. The comparison of lexicon of sister languages provides a demonstration of the filiation and leads to the discovery of the mother language, even when there are no traces of it left.[43]

The achievements of comparative linguistics proved very influential, if for no other reason than because they helped answer the pressing question of the 'origins' of human life and spiritual forms.[44] In particular, the demonstration of the grammatical and lexical affinity among Indo-European languages, with Sanskrit being the primeval one,[45] brought immediately to light the convergence between the genealogical problem and the historical problem.[46] When nineteenth-century linguists compared languages, as John Lyons reminds us, they did so 'primarily if not exclusively, from a diachronic, or historical point of view and for the very specific purpose of demonstrating that the languages in question either did or did not belong to the same so-called family of languages – that they were or were not genetically related'.[47] The comparative method was functional to the reconstruction of parent languages and proto languages. Its ability to provide a 'scientific' explanation – albeit

39 Pier Giuseppe Monateri, 'Éléments de comparaison des études comparatives' in Pierre Legrand (ed), *Comparer les droits, résolument* (Presses Universitaires de France 2009) 69–76.

40 On the famous address delivered by Sir William Jones to the Royal Asiatic Society of Bengal, see James Turner, *Philology: The Forgotten Origins of Modern Humanities* (Princeton University Press 2014) 97.

41 Foucault (n 32) 305–18; Turner (n 40) 91.

42 See John W Burrow, *Evolution and Society: A Study in Victorian Social Theory* (CUP 1966) 109 (noting that Darwin referred to philology to illustrate the concept of rudimentary organs. Legal scholars, as it is well known (see Franz Wieacker, *Storia del diritto privato moderno*, vol 2 (Giuffrè 1980) 315–16), were also much influenced by biological paradigms, as it is clearly shown, among other examples, by Emerico Amari's book on comparative legislation (see below n 73).

43 Bernard Laks, 'Le comparatisme: De la généalogie à la génétique' (2002) 36 *Langages* 19, 21 (emphasis omitted) (translated by author).

44 Mircea Eliade, *La nostalgie des origines: Méthodologie et histoire des religions* (Gallimard 1971) 77.

45 Turner (n 40) 92.

46 Monateri, 'Éléments de comparaison des études comparatives' (n 39) 73; Foucault (n 32) 316–18.

47 John Lyons, 'Linguistics and Law: The Legacy of Sir Henry Maine' in Alan Diamond (ed), *The Victorian Achievement of Sir Henry Maine: A Centennial Reappraisal* (CUP 1991) 297.

based on inferential evidence – of the patterns of development of various societies explains the enormous prestige obtained by the 'Comparative Method':

> The establishment of the Comparative Method of study has been the greatest intellectual achievement of our time. It has carried light and order into whole branches of human knowledge which before were shrouded in darkness and confusion. It has brought a line of argument which reaches moral certainty into a region which before was given over to random guess-work. Into matters which are for the most part incapable of strictly external proof it has brought a form of strictly internal proof which is more convincing, more unerring. In one department, the first, perhaps the greatest, to which it has been applied, the victory of the Comparative Method may now be said to be assured. The Science of Language has been placed on a firm basis, from which it is impossible to believe that it can ever be dislodged.
>
> ....
>
> On us a new light has come. I do not for a moment hesitate to say that the discovery of the Comparative method in philology, in mythology – let me add in politics and history and the whole range of human thought – marks a stage in the progress of the human mind at least as great and memorable as the revival of Greek and Latin learning.[48]

As the preceding excerpt makes clear, for the contemporary observers, there is a single comparative method – indeed, the use of capital letters in most of the literature of the time is significant – and this is the one developed and fruitfully applied by comparative linguistics. It is no wonder, therefore, that the 'genealogic' approach typical of early comparative linguistics was soon extended to other branches of the social sciences and the humanities concerned with providing evolutionary accounts of the origin of cultural forms and social institutions.[49] The comparative method became the most common tool to construct inferential histories of societies.[50]

Among the institutions whose development was a matter for debate were of course the legal institutions. However, it was not uncontroverted that the approach followed in comparative linguistics could be automatically transposed to legal studies. The 'comparative method' presupposed the extension of the enquiry to various phenomena, but always on the assumption of their functional homogeneity. This element appeared to be problematic in the field of legal research. In a context in which 'romantic nationalism' was at its peak,[51] jurists were inclined to assert the unique and

48 Edward A Freeman, *Comparative Politics* (Macmillan 1873) 1, 301–2.

49 On the early discourses on comparative mythology, see ibid, 6–8; Eliade (n 44) 81.

50 See EA Hammel, 'The Comparative Method in Anthropological Perspective' (1980) 22 *Comp Stud Soc'y & Hist* 145.

51 On this, see, in particular, Helge Dedek, 'When Law Became Cultivated' in Geneviève Helleringer and Kai Purnhagen (eds), *Towards a European Legal Culture* (CH Beck 2014) 367–90. See also James Q Whitman, *The Legacy of Roman Law in the German Romantic Era* (Princeton University Press 2014) 99–112.

incommensurable character of the entities their science dealt with. The law was regarded as an isolated product of a specific culture, deeply rooted in local traditions. Therefore, the study of different experiences, which was the basis for a comparison, was not considered a pressing concern.[52]

III COMPARING LAWS?

Among the most influential voices raised against the comparative reasoning there was that of Friedrich Karl von Savigny.[53] Despite the emphasis put on the law as a specific historical product, and as such capable of critical knowledge,[54] Savigny was at best sceptical about the usefulness of legal research having a broad scope, extending far beyond one's own tradition. In particular, his critical stance on comparative law (and more specifically comparative legal history) was manifested in the occasion of the polemical exchange of ideas with Anton Friedrich Thibaut about the possibility of adopting a civil code for Germany. However, the matter for debate was not simply the use of the comparative enquiry as a source of inspiration for local law reforms (and indeed, Savigny's opposition to the idea of a civil code for Germany was based on a detailed and insightful analysis of the *code Napoléon*), but rather for the aims of legal education and scholarship. Indeed, Thibaut embraced the call for a universal history (and theory) of law, which was a recurring theme within the German philosophical culture,[55] and which found a first outline in the work of Anselm Feuerbach,[56] before being further developed by Eduard Gans.[57] Thibaut put the emphasis on the necessity of looking at the experience of other traditions and namely at those of the non-European civilizations in order to achieve a deeper knowledge of the law. To understand her own culture, he wrote, any European traveller has to leave Europe, and this is true for the law as well.[58] Ten enriching lectures on the Persian or Chinese legal system, he

52 A similar resistance to the use of the comparative method would characterize, in the long run, disciplines like anthropology, history, and history of religions: see Robert A Segal, 'In Defense of the Comparative Method' (2001) 48 *Numen* 339; Cécile Vigour, *La comparaison dans les sciences sociales: Pratiques et méthodes* (La Découverte 2005) 44–62.

53 On the attitude of the German Historical School towards comparative reasoning, see Gábor Hamza, *Comparative Law and Antiquity* (Akadémiai Kiadó 1991) 34.

54 On this, see Léontin Jean Constantinesco, *Traité de droit comparé: Introduction au droit comparé*, vol 1 (Librairie générale de droit et de jurisprudence 1972) 70–71.

55 See Mario G Losano, *Sistema e struttura nel diritto: Dalle origini alla scuola storica*, vol 1 (Giuffrè 2002) 108; Giorgio Del Vecchio, 'Sull'idea di una scienza del diritto universale comparato' (1909) *Rivista italiana per le scienze giuridiche* 173.

56 See Heinz Mohnhaupt, 'Universalgeschichte, Universal-Jurisprudenz und rechtsvergleichende Methode im Werk P.J.A. Feuerbachs' in Heinz Mohnhaupt (ed), *Rechtsgeschichte in den beiden deutschen Staaten (1988–1990): Beispiele, Parallele, Positionen* (Klostermann 1991) 119–21.

57 Eduard Gans, *Das Erbrecht in weltgeschichtlicher Entwicklung. Eine Abhandlung der Universalrechtsgeschichte* (Maurer 1824–1835).

58 Anton Friedrich Justus Thibaut, 'Über die Nothwendigkeit eines allgemeinen bürgerlichen Rechts' in Anton Friedrich Justus Thibaut (ed), *Civilistische Abhandlungen* (Mohr u Zimmer 1814) 433.

went on, may foster in our students a more profound sense of the law than the study of the minute details of the succession *ab intestato* from Augustus to Justinian.[59] Savigny bitterly replied that the interest in studying foreign legal traditions is strictly dependent on their inherent 'value',[60] and from this point of view no other system of law was comparable to the prestigious tradition of Roman law. Furthermore, since 'the essence of the law is to be inferred from the whole past of a nation',[61] and it is inextricably bound to the history of its spiritual forms, it is hardly instructive to survey the experience of different civilizations, and namely of those not belonging to the 'Christian-European nations'.[62] As a result, only the Roman–Germanic legal tradition appeared to Savigny worthy of consideration and study,[63] having also regard to the practical necessity of building a legal infrastructure for the unification of Germany. Such a restrictive stance was taken by a whole generation of jurists, sharing an almost religious respect for a territorially based notion of jurisdiction and for a 'romantic' vision of the relationship between the law and the 'culture' of a nation.[64]

Outside of the mainstream, though, the interest for the dimension of 'otherness' in the law remained alive. The development of comparative studies took two main directions: one pragmatic, the other more theoretical.[65] The former is more frequently recalled within the descriptions of the history of comparative law: it consists of the study of 'foreign laws' of countries placed at a 'similar level of development' (according to the terminology adopted by Edouard Lambert and the various contributors to the Paris Conference of 1900) and is functional – mainly although not uniquely – to the aims of law reform, including supranational harmonization. The latter tends nowadays to be forgotten, but it gave rise to the first veritable 'theory' of comparative law, one that was extremely influential at the time of the Paris Conference. Its main features were the integration of historical and comparative approaches, taxonomic essentialism, an interest in the legal institutions, beliefs, and ideas of all societies (included ancient and 'primitive' societies), and a concern for a positivist explanation of the development of the law. Comparative law was hardly distinguishable, at this stage, from anthropology and sociology, and the convergence between different sociolegal perspectives inspired

59 Ibid.

60 Friedrich Karl von Savigny, 'Stimmen für und wider neue Gesetzbücher' (1817) 3 *Zeitschrift für geschichtliche Rechtswissenschaft* 1, 6.

61 Friedrich Karl von Savigny, 'Über den Zweck dieser Zeitschrift' (1815) 1 *Zeitschrift für geschichtliche Rechtswissenschaft* 1, 6.

62 Von Savigny, 'Stimmen für und wider neue Gesetzbücher' (n 60) 6–7.

63 In particular, von Savigny underlined the importance of studying the history of German law, Roman law, and Canon law. See ibid, 5–7.

64 See generally James Q Whitman, 'The Neo-Romantic Turn' in Pierre Legrand and Roderick Munday (eds), *Comparative Legal Studies: Traditions and Transitions* (CUP 2003) 312, 316. See also Dedek (n 51) 362.

65 See, lastly, Stefan Vogenauer, 'Rechtsgeschichte und Rechtsvergleichung um 1900: Die Geschichte einer anderen "Emanzipation durch Auseinanderdenken"' (2012) 76 *RabelsZ* 1122, 1125–41.

an impressive stream of studies, which defined a counter-model in relationship to the orthodox legal science.[66]

It is worth noting that the earlier confrontation with the issue of methodology of comparative legal research took place within this latter strand of studies. Indeed, as early as 1810 Anselm Feuerbach raised an important question, which was not only rhetorically effective, but went to the core of an issue strongly debated at the time, namely the relationship between the legal science and the natural sciences.

He asked, 'Why does the anatomist have its comparative anatomy, whereas the jurist has not yet its comparative science of law?'[67] He then went on to note that

> [c]omparison and combination are the richest sources of discovery for empirical sciences. Only on the basis of several contrasts one may really understand what is contrasted; only by considering similarities and differences, as well as their grounds, one may bring to light the distinctive features and the intimate essence of each object. Just like the philosophy of language is based on the comparison of languages, the substance of the universal theory of law, of the science of legislation, has to be grounded on the comparison of laws and customs of nations (the nearest and the farthest ones) of all time and places.[68]

The question raised by Feuerbach is an interesting one because it shows that already at the beginning of the century, legal scholars regarded the achievements obtained in the fields of anatomy and philology as a model to be followed by the legal science as well.[69] Such a dialogue was not interrupted: jurists continued to look at such disciplines not only for inspiration but also with the aim of gaining scientific legitimization for new theoretical frameworks – as is exemplified by Julius von Kirchmann's invective against the unfruitfulness of traditional jurisprudence[70] – or innovative methods of research. A transdisciplinary theorem was mobilized, in other words, within the struggle for the acceptance of a counter-model. And such a theorem proved particularly powerful, since it was in line with the scientific bent, the 'urge to classify, order, abstract and generalize',[71] which was characteristic of the epoch. The early discourses on comparative law – as well as the later elaboration on legal transplants[72] – show particularly well this attitude

66 See Alba Negri, *Il giurista dell'area romanista di fronte all'etnologia giuridica* (Giuffrè 1983) 3, 105.

67 Anselm Feuerbach, 'Blick auf die deutsche Rechtswissenschaft. Vorrede zu Unterholzners juristischen Abhandlungen (1810)' in Anselm Feuerbach, *Kleine Schriften vermischten Inhalts* (Otto 1833) 152, 163 (translated by author).

68 Ibid.

69 With particular regard to the influence of natural sciences, see Rainer M Kiesow, 'Science naturelle et droit dans la deuxième moitié du XIXe siècle en Allemagne' in Paul Amselek (ed), *Théorie du droit et science* (Presse Universitaires de France 1994) 187.

70 On von Kirchmann's approach, see Kiesow (n 69) 187.

71 Burrow, *Evolution and Society* (n 42) 145.

72 H Patrick Glenn, 'On the Use of Biological Metaphors in Law: The Case of Legal Transplants' (2006) 1 *J Comp L* 358.

and offer a clear description of what was meant at that time by the notion of 'comparative method'.[73]

IV THE 'COMPARATIVE METHOD'

Among the most illustrative examples are the later works of the great English legal historian and comparativist Henry Sumner Maine. Whereas methodological reflections play a marginal role in *Ancient Law*, in the later part of his scientific production Maine openly reflected on the theoretical and methodological basis of the new science of 'comparative jurisprudence'.[74] This follows Maine's formative experience in India as Legal Member of the Governor General's Council,[75] when he had the occasion to test 'in the field' the hypotheses about legal progress advanced in *Ancient Law* and became acquainted with the local rules, customs, and institutions. Leaving aside the important point concerning the relationship between high culture and imperialism,[76] it is worth noting that he developed a coherent approach to comparative legal history which was mainly exposed in the introductory pages of his famous research on the *Village-Communities in the East and West*:

> The enquiry upon which we are engaged can only be said to belong to Comparative Jurisprudence, if the word 'comparative' be used as it is used in such expressions as 'Comparative Philology' and 'Comparative Mythology'. We shall examine a number of parallel phenomena with the view of establishing, if possible, that some of them are related to one another in the order of historical succession.
>
> . . . .
>
> I should, however, be making a very idle pretension if I held out a prospect of obtaining, by the application of the Comparative Method to jurisprudence, any results which, in point of interest or trustworthiness, are to be placed on a level with those which, for example, have been accomplished in Comparative Philology. To give only one reason, the phenomena of human society, laws and legal ideas, opinions and usages, are vastly more affected by external circumstances than language.[77]

73 As regards the influence of comparative anatomy and physiology on the definition of a 'comparative method', see LA Warnkoenig, 'Ueber Vergleichende Staats- und Rechtsgeschichte' (1856) 28 *Kritische Zeitschrift für Rechtswissenschaft und Gesetzgebung des Auslandes* 386. For a significant example of the influence of biology on early comparative law, see Emerico Amari, *Critica di una scienza delle legislazioni comparate* (Tip de RI de Sordo-Muti 1857), and on Amari, see Jayme (n 24) 21.

74 See Raymond CJ Cocks, *Sir Henry Maine: A Study in Victorian Jurisprudence* (CUP 1988) 203. On the differences between John Austin's and Henry Maine's perspectives on 'comparative jurisprudence', see Frederick Pollock, 'The History of Comparative Jurisprudence' (1903) 5 *J Soc'y Comp Leg* 74, 86. See also William Twining, 'Maine and Legal Education: A Comment' in Diamond (n 47) 215.

75 See Gordon Johnson, 'India and Henry Maine' in Diamond (n 47); Katharina S Schmidt, 'Henry Maine's "Modern Law": From Status to Contract and Back Again?' (2017) 65 *Am J Comp L* 147.

76 On this, see Edward W Said, *Culture & Imperialism* (Chatto & Windus 1993) 198–99, who openly refers to Maine's scholarship and biography.

77 Henry S Maine, *Village-Communities in the East and West: With Other Lectures, Addresses, and Essays* (first published 1871, 7th edn, John Murray 1895) 6, 8.

In *Ancient Law*, Maine drew a parallel between law and geology;[78] now it is philology – and in particular comparative philology – which is at centre stage. The reputation that this discipline had achieved in England in the 1860s explains the importance that the discipline assumed in Maine's later writings.[79] Maine's analysis is aimed at carrying further the achievements of the comparative study of language (and mythology), namely transposing to the study of legal institutions the basic idea that establishing a connection between languages belonging to the same 'family', enables us to fill the gaps in the history of particular members of such family.[80] In his lecture, *The Effect of the Observation of India on Modern European Thought*, he wrote:

> India has given to the world Comparative Philology and Comparative Mythology; it may yet give us a new science not less valuable than the sciences of language and of folk-lore. I hesitate to call it Comparative Jurisprudence because, if it ever exists, its area will be so much wider than the field of law. For India not only contains (or to speak more accurately, did contain) an Aryan language older than any other descendant of the common mother-tongue, and a variety of names of natural objects less perfectly crystallised than elsewhere into fabulous personages, but it includes a whole world of Aryan institutions, Aryan customs, Aryan laws, Aryan ideas, Aryan beliefs, in a far earlier stage of growth and development than any which survive beyond its borders. There are undoubtedly in it the materials for a new science, possibly including many branches.[81]

Comparative linguistics, then, is taken by Maine as a reference model in order to develop such a 'new science' of comparative jurisprudence. The scientific element is particularly important, because it marks a significant innovation for the development of English jurisprudence and adds a peculiar variant to the traditional historical approach.[82] As noted by Paul Vinogradoff, 'Maine brings into the field of enquiry a new element, the element of *science* in the English sense of the world, that is of exact knowledge based on observation and aiming at the formulation of laws.'[83] In accordance with such a scientific attitude, he accepts the 'Indo-European

78 Henry S Maine, *Ancient Law: Its Connection with the Early History of Society and Its Relation to Modern Ideas* (first published 1861, John Murray 1908) 2–3 ('If by any means we can determine the early forms of jural conceptions, they will be invaluable to us. These rudimentary ideas are to the jurist what the primary crusts of the earth are to the geologist. They contain, potentially, all the forms in which law has subsequently exhibited itself'; he then goes on to say that 'the Inquiries of the jurist are in truth prosecuted before observation had taken the place of assumption.'). On this point, see Peter Stein, *Legal Evolution: The Story of an Idea* (CUP 1980) 88.

79 Burrow, *Evolution and Society* (n 42) 148–53.

80 Bernard S Jackson, 'Law and Language: A Metaphor in Maine, a Model for His Successors?' in Diamond (n 47) 262. See also Stein (n 78) 91–92.

81 Henry S Maine, 'The Effect of Observation of India on Modern European Thought' in Maine, *Village-Communities* (n 77) 210–11.

82 The same concern for a scientific treatment of the history of societies will characterize the early anthropological discourse on the comparative method, see Edward B Tylor, 'On a Method of Investigating the Development of Institutions: Applied to Laws of Marriage and Descent' (1889) 18 *J Anthropological Inst Great Brit & Ireland* 245.

83 Paul Vinogradoff, *The Teaching of Sir Henry Maine: Inaugural Lecture* (Henry Frowde 1904) 10–11.

parameters'[84] of comparative linguistics. 'Modern philology', as he noted, 'has suggested a grouping of peoples quite unlike anything that had been thought of before.'[85] Hence his research focuses only on the laws, customs, and institutions of the 'Aryan' societies, which had common descent, according to the philological canons. By contrast, he left in the background, as unfruitful and speculative, the study of other chthonic traditions.[86]

The 'Comparative Method' is regarded by Maine as an analytic tool infrequently used by jurists, but nonetheless extremely promising. '[I]f the Comparative Method', he wrote, 'applied to laws, institutions, customs, ideas, and social forces should ever give results resembling those given by Comparative Philology and Comparative Mythology, it is impossible that the consequences should be insignificant'.[87] However, having direct knowledge of the differences existing among the phenomena observed by each discipline, Maine is conscious that within the study of law, the 'comparative method' cannot be employed as the 'absolutely universal solvent'.[88] Whereas Savigny emphasized the similarities between law and language, both seen as a natural offspring of a peculiar 'culture' and not amenable to top-down modification,[89] Maine is more cautious. As the Danish linguist Rasmus Rask observed, language is much more stable (and therefore more recognizable in the long term) than laws and institutions, which may change dramatically.[90] Maine had direct experience of this circumstance and openly acknowledged that 'law and legal ideas . . . are vastly more affected by external circumstances than language'.[91] Affinities among legal institutions and customs, in other words, are not proof of common origin and derivation, but may be ascribed to different causes, such as direct transmission and imitation, or independent invention.[92] This suggests a non-mechanical implementation of the technique of 'scientific comparison', which has to be adapted in order to take account of the multiplicity of factors implied in the workings of the law. The main amendment suggested by Maine consists of the integration of the comparative method with the historical method.[93] The former is essentially synchronic in its applications, whereas the latter is essentially diachronic.

84 Roslyn Jolly, 'Robert Louis Stevenson, Henry Maine, and the Anthropology of Comparative Law' (2006) 45 *J Brit Stud* 556, 571.

85 Maine, 'Effect of Observation of India on Modern European Thought' (n 81) 209.

86 Stein (n 78) 92; Alan DJ Macfarlane, 'Some Contributions of Maine to History and Anthropology' in Diamond (n 47) 141. On the notion of 'chthonic legal traditions', see H Patrick Glenn, *Legal Traditions of the World: Sustainable Diversity in Law* (5th edn, OUP 2014) 60–94.

87 Maine, 'Effect of Observation of India on Modern European Thought' (n 81) 230.

88 On this notion, see Freeman (n 48) 7, 15.

89 Friedrich Karl von Savigny, *Von Beruf unsrer Zeit für Gesetzgebung und Rechtswissenschaft* (Mohr u Zimmer 1814) 9, 11.

90 On this point, see Jackson (n 80) 264.

91 Maine, *Village-Communities* (n 77) 8.

92 Freeman (n 48) 17–22.

93 According to Pollock and several other scholars, Maine's historical approach was influenced by the German historical school, and namely by von Savigny. See Burrow, *Evolution and Society* (n 42) 142–44.

However, it is only through a synergic implementation of the two approaches that, according to Maine, one may achieve deeper knowledge about the content and meaning of legal institutions[94]:

> I think I may venture to affirm that the Comparative Method, which has already been fruitful of such wonderful results, is not distinguishable in some of its applications from the Historical Method. We take a number of contemporary facts, ideas, and customs, and we infer the past form of those facts, ideas, and customs not only from historical records of that past form, but from examples of it which have not yet died out of the world, and are still to be found in it. When in truth we have to some extent succeeded in freeing ourselves from that limited conception of the world and mankind, beyond which the most civilised societies and (I will add) some of the greatest thinkers do not always rise; when we gain something like an adequate idea of the vastness and variety of the phenomena of human society; when in particular we have learned not to exclude from our view of earth and man those great and unexplored regions which we vaguely term the East, we find it to be not wholly a conceit or a paradox to say that the distinction between the Present and the Past disappears. Sometimes the Past *is* the Present; much more often it is removed from it by varying distances, which, however, cannot be estimated or expressed chronologically. Direct observation comes thus to the aid of historical enquiry, and historical enquiry to the help of direct observation. The characteristic difficulty of the historian is that of recorded evidence, however sagaciously it may be examined and re-examined, can very rarely be added to; the characteristic error of the direct observer of unfamiliar social or juridical phenomena is to compare them too hastily with familiar phenomena apparently of the same kind. But the best contemporary historians, both of England and of Germany, are evidently striving to increase their resources through the agency of the Comparative Method; and nobody can have been long in the East without perceiving and regretting that a great many conclusions, founded on patient personal study of Oriental usage and idea, are vitiated through the observer's want of acquaintance with some elementary facts of Western legal history.[95]

The integration of the historical and the comparative approach has a critical importance in Maine's analysis.[96] It led to a revision of many a priori assumptions accepted by modern Western thought, such as the economist's belief in economic motives as the main driving force of human behaviour, or Bentham's utilitarian social philosophy.[97] These were regarded by Maine as unhistorical generalizations inapplicable to societies different from those of modern Europe; deduction from first principles should by contrast be supplanted by an empirically based study of

94 See Pollock (n 74) 76.

95 Maine, *Village-Communities* (n 77) 6–8.

96 Napoli (n 22) 136–39.

97 Maine, 'Effect of Observation of India on Modern European Thought' (n 81) 231–33. The attitude criticized by Maine will be later defined by Karl Polanyi, *The Livelihood of Man* (Academic Press 1977) 6 as 'economistic fallacy'.

formal rules and other various forces, like customs and beliefs, which make for order and social cohesion. At the same time, the integration of the two approaches makes it possible to abandon the economist's meta-framework without falling into 'total relativism'.[98]

Indeed, the most important idea is that it is possible to fill the gaps left by the historical records by looking at comparable institutions in less-advanced societies,[99] which still bear the fossilized relics of the past. The historical method, from this point of view, may be supplanted and even 'corrected'[100] by the Comparative Method, as Maine argues, with regard to the history of property rights and institutions.[101] Indirect (diachronic) evidence is obtained through direct (synchronic) observation. In this way, the understanding of the early legal history of Europe could be deepened by studying the institutions of other societies (namely India) that share a common parentage.

This method of enquiry, which paralleled comparative philology, obviously rests on one basic assumption, namely that 'the law of civilized societies was the product of the development through a series of identifiable stages related to, but distinct from, the development of society itself.'[102] Only under a model of 'staged legal development', in which the order of stages is constant and not subject to variations, is it possible to make meaningful inferences from one society (eg contemporary India) to another (eg early Europe), however variable their rate of progress.[103] Although he had no sympathy for rigid evolutionary determinism, it can be hardly disputed that Maine believed in a 'law of progress', underpinning the gradual development of society from its infancy to its mature stages, according to a process of growing complexity.[104] And of course, such a law of progress was not the result of a neutral scientific preference, but it was inherently coherent with the Victorian zeitgeist, and in particular with the idea that the history of 'progressive societies' started with Greece and culminated in the British Empire.[105]

98 See also Burrow, *Evolution and Society* (n 42) 155.

99 In this case: India in relation to ancient European societies. See Maine, *Village-Communities* (n 77) 13 ('If an ancient society be conceived as a society in which are found existing phenomena of usage and legal thought which, if not identical with, wear a strong resemblance to certain other phenomena of the same kind which the Western world may be shown to have exhibited at periods here belonging chronologically to the Past, the East is certainly full of fragments of ancient society.').

100 Maine, Effect of Observation of India on Modern European Thought' (n 81) 224.

101 Ibid, 220–26.

102 Stein (n 78) 99; Maine, *Village-Communities* (n 77) 15.

103 In these terms, see Jolly (n 84) 569.

104 Henry S Maine, *Lectures on the Early History of Institutions* (John Murray 1875) 225–26. On Maine's theory of progress, see John W Burrow, 'Henry Maine and Mid-Victorian Ideas of Progress' in Diamond (n 47) 55.

105 Maine, 'Effect of Observation of India on Modern European Thought' (n 81) 238–39 ('To one small people, covering in its original seat no more than a handsbreath of territory, it was given to create the principle of Progress. . . . That people was the Greek. Except the blind forces of Nature, nature moves in this world which is not Greek in its origin. A ferment spreading from that source has vitalised all the great progressive races of mankind, penetrating from one to another, and producing results

On the one hand, Maine's scholarship was highly innovative: not only did he adopt a notion of 'law' which was radically different from the positivist paradigm diffused in England by John Austin, and much 'thicker' than that,[106] but he also freed legal-historical research from its nationalist character and narrow scope of observation (which was the legacy of the German historical school)[107] and opened it to the study of other cultures and traditions. On the other hand, he stood under the influence of his own time, attributing great value to the ideal of a 'scientific treatment of the problems of social life'.[108] On this basis, he diligently followed the path of comparative linguistics and limited his historical-comparative enquiry to the so-called Indo-European family, not unlike a wide range of continental scholars, whose reflections were inspired by what has been recently defined – following the path opened by Martin Bernal's seminal book *Black Athena* – the 'Aryan model of the Western legal tradition'.[109]

Such a limitation was overcome by later research, in particular by the German scholars grouped around the *Zeitschrift für Vergleichende Rechtswissenschaft*, and among them especially Franz Bernhöft, Joseph Kohler, and Albert Hermann Post. They focused their attention on the laws and customs of all societies, including the so-called primitive societies, with the aim of developing a new science of 'ethnological jurisprudence'.[110] The 'Comparative Method' was accordingly attributed an even stronger importance.[111] As soon as the analysis encompassed oral traditions – societies 'without history' as they were then frequently defined – the historical approach proved impracticable.

Since none of these German scholars had ever done any fieldwork and had to rely on the data of early amateur ethnographers and of colonial administrations, the comparative method was resorted to as a necessary tool to build generalizations and construct general laws of development of societies. Among the various examples of

accordant with its hidden and latent genius, and results of course often far greater than any exhibited in Greece itself. It is this principle of progress which we Englishmen are communicating to India. We did not create it. We deserve no special credit for it. It came to us filtered through many different media. But we have received it; and as we have received it, so we pass it on.').

106 As seen earlier, the comparative study of law encompasses 'ideas, beliefs and customs'. On this, see Jolly (n 84) 563.

107 Constantinesco (n 54) 70–74.

108 Vinogradoff (n 83) 11.

109 Monateri, 'Methods in Comparative Law' (n 19) 11 (internal quotation marks omitted) (meaning 'a theory of the strong cross-cultural links among different peoples traceable back to a past common Indo-European period, producing a framework of similarities of their various institutions'). See also PG Monateri, 'Black Gaius: A Quest for the Multicultural Origins of the "Western Legal Tradition"' (2000) 51 *Hastings LJ* 479, 493; Paul Koschaker, 'L'Histoire du droit et le droit comparé surtout en Allemagne' in *Introduction à l'étude du droit comparé: Recueil d'études en l'honneur de Edouard Lambert* (Sirey: Librairie générale de droit et de jurisprudence 1938) 275–76.

110 Kaius Tuori, *Lawyers and Savages: Ancient History and Legal Realism in the Making of Legal Anthropology* (Routledge 2015) 57; Vogenauer (n 65) 1141–43; Negri (n 66) 18.

111 Koschaker (n 109) 280–81.

such an approach, one of the clearest is represented by a short manifesto on ethnological jurisprudence by Albert Hermann Post.[112]

Moving from the assumption that one of the main tasks of the jurist is to collect the 'jural customs and notions of all the nations of the earth' and then provide a causal explanation of the regularities observable even among unrelated societies, Post maintains that since a historical treatment of oral traditions would be impossible, the comparison is 'the only aid at the disposal of the science'. However, the practicability of such a method cannot be evaluated in the abstract, but only at the end of the analysis:

> The scientific possibility of a purely comparative method depends upon facts, the existence or non-existence of which can only be determined by the application of the method itself. The question is whether in the development of human law definite legal customs and conceptions exist and regularly occur even among unrelated peoples, or whether the law of every people, at least of every kindred group of peoples, is an isolated product standing in no relation whatever to the law of other peoples. If there be rules of legal conduct which recur everywhere on the globe and which pass through a stated course of development, the method by comparison is applicable: to explain a given legal custom of one nation we may avail ourselves of the corresponding legal customs of another. If such be not the case, a purely comparative method is a scientific chimera.[113]

CONCLUSION

The resort to the comparative method as a tool to fill the gaps left by historical records and to reconstruct uniform patterns of development was bitterly criticized by the later generation of anthropologists as a baseless work leading only to 'artificial and sterile constructions'.[114] Franz Boas, in particular, denounced the epistemological flaws of the 'grand theories' of early comparativists (and legal primitivists). He criticized, in particular, the faith in the existence of uniform 'laws that govern the growth of society', whose discovery was considered to be 'a means of understanding the causes furthering and retarding civilization'.[115] At the same time, Boas urged scholars to abandon the deductive method and derive 'by truly inductive processes

[112] Albert H Post, 'An Introduction to the Study of Ethnological Jurisprudence' (1897) 11 *The Open Court* 718, 720–21 (TJ McCormack tr). By the same author, see also *Der Ursprung des Rechts: Prolegomena zu einer allgemeinen vergleichenden Rechtswissenschaft* (Schulzesche 1876); *Einleitung in die Naturwissenschaft des Rechts* (Schulzesche 1879); *Bausteine für eine allgemeine Rechtswissenschaft auf vergleichend-ethnologischer Basis*, vols 1–2 (Schulzesche 1880–1881); *Einleitung in das Studium der ethnologischen Jurisprudenz* (Schulzesche 1886); *Grundriss der ethnologischen Jurisprudenz*, vols 1–2 (Schulzesche Schwartz 1894–1895); 'Ethnological Jurisprudence' (1891) 2 *The Monist* 31 (TJ McCormack tr).

[113] Post 'Introduction to the Study of Ethnological Jurisprudence' (n 112) 720–21.

[114] Bronislaw Malinowski, *Crime and Custom in Savage Society* (Kegan Paul, Trench, Trubner 1926) 4.

[115] Franz Boas, 'The Limitations of the Comparative Method of Anthropology' (1896) 4 *Science* 901.

the actual history of definite phenomena', leaving the comparison to a second stage of the enquiry.[116]

The 'realist' turn in anthropology was paralleled by a similar evolution in the legal debate.[117] After the Paris Conference, the ethnological jurisprudence was marginalized and comparative law took another direction.[118] Comparative law scholars abandoned the idea of building global histories of society and, even though the taxonomic project continued to appear fashionable, the efforts were not anymore directed towards the explanation of diversity by means of universal laws of development. The scope of comparative analyses became narrower, being mostly limited to the law of modern capitalist societies, and induction gradually replaced deduction as a general method of research.[119] New paradigms of comparative law emerged, leading to the diffusion of new methods (the functional method being the most famous example) and contributing to the actual eclecticism of the comparative project.

The early discourses on comparative law, embedded as they were in a Eurocentric and colonialist framework,[120] have lost any interest and appeal for the contemporary observer. Still, they are instructive because they highlight some general trends in comparative law research which tend to be replicated, although in different forms. Patrick Glenn, among others, has put the emphasis on taxonomic essentialism and scientific positivism as two distinctive features of the 'orthodox' approach to comparative law,[121] an approach nowadays challenged on many grounds, but still counting on various adepts and sympathizers. There is another element, which emerges from the previous analysis and which is worth underlying, and this is the peculiar attitude of comparativists to rely on transdisciplinary theorems. The 'Comparative Method', as we have seen, represented a generalization of the approach developed within (comparative anatomy and) comparative philology. But the endorsement of extra-legal sciences to orient the theoretical framework of comparative legal research is a constant that is still at work.

Whereas in the past the scientific 'canon' was represented by biology and philology, nowadays economics has obtained a privileged position. Comparative law scholars tend to be particularly sensitive to the change in the overall intellectual trends, probably because they constantly strive to find a coherent theoretical framework, which might aid in the difficult task of understanding legal variety and its

116 Ibid, 905.

117 On this, see the remarkable research by Tuori (n 110) 1–12. It would also be interesting to follow the development in the historical sciences, where the rise of the comparative method dates to the contribution by (Pirenne and) Bloch: see Marc Bloch, 'Pour une histoire comparée des sociétés européennes' (1928) 46 *Revue de synthèse historique* 15.

118 On such a paradigm shift, see Vogenauer (n 65) 1148–53.

119 On the rise of empiricism and especially on Ernst Rabel's contribution, see Giorgio Resta, 'Les luttes de clocher en droit comparé' (2017) 62 *McGill LJ* 1153.

120 Tuori (n 110) 3, 8–9.

121 Glenn, 'Quel droit comparé?' (n 10) 27–31.

relationship with different societies. Comparative law is 'naturally' open to interdisciplinary research,[122] but it should not lose the perception of the specificity of legal phenomena (whatever their sources and their distinctive features in the various traditions). As Guido Calabresi has recently argued, extra-disciplinary theorems might be extremely useful, insofar as they do not force the process of understanding into rigid schemes, thereby narrowing instead of enriching the observer's perspective.[123] The risk pointed out by Franz Boas is still actual, although the grand theories of today, leading to an holistic reconstruction of the 'laws that govern the growth of society' and the 'causes furthering or retarding civilization',[124] are probably not rooted in biology anymore, but rather mostly in economics, as the recent debate on the 'ranking' of legal systems according to their efficiency has unequivocally shown.[125] Such exercises in 'numerical comparative law' are undoubtedly interesting, as they reflect the overall trend towards the generalization of quantitative methods of research, of indicators and rankings of performance, which perfectly fit the contemporary model of a 'scored society'. However, a deeper analysis of the epistemological foundations of the so-called new comparative law and economics easily unveils – as observed by Patrick Glenn – that 'it is concentrated exclusively on state laws and generally economic indicators, and is a by-product of contemporary capitalism'.[126] As such, it suffers from the same weaknesses of the orthodox model, which the most advanced comparative legal scholarship in the last fifty years strived to overcome. From this point of view, Patrick Glenn's lesson is invaluable, and not only for his emphasis on a richer notion of both 'law' and 'tradition',[127] but also for his constant plea for methodological pluralism.

122 See generally Jan M Smits, 'Law and Interdisciplinarity: On the Inevitable Normativity of Legal Studies' (2014) 1 *Crit Analysis of L* 75, 83.

123 Guido Calabresi, *The Future of Law & Economics* (Yale University Press 2016) 2–16 (contrasting 'Economic Analysis of Law' and 'Law & Economics' as two opposite approaches of interdisciplinary research).

124 Boas (n 115) 905.

125 The reference is mainly to the legal origins hypothesis and the further projects which sprang out of the law and finance movement: see, among many others, Ralf Michaels, 'Comparative Law by Numbers? Legal Origins Thesis, Doing Business Reports, and the Silence of Traditional Comparative Law' (2009) 57 *Am J Comp L* 765.

126 Glenn, 'Against Method?' (n 15) 17.

127 See Mauro Bussani, Chapter 1 in this volume.

3

The Value of Micro-Comparison

John Bell[*]

Micro-comparison is the traditional approach of many comparative lawyers. We take a very specific social issue, such as same-sex marriage, and then look at how it is regulated by a number of different legal systems. We look at similarities and differences and try to draw conclusions from them. Those conclusions might be about whether the problem is really the same in different countries, whether the approach of the different legal systems is similar, or it might be about the place of law in different societies. William Twining has usefully made two points about the place of micro-comparison.[1] First, micro-comparison is not the only kind of comparative law research. As Patrick Glenn's work demonstrates, there is also macro-comparison, which takes as its subject matter the way broadly defined topics, such as the rule of law, operate across a broad range of different parts of the world. Twining remarks,

> There are good reasons for taking seriously the enterprise of constructing total pictures or maps of law in the world. Setting the local in the context of the global serves the values of any form of contextual study –for example, maintaining a sense of scale and proportion; avoiding the dangers of parochialism; establishing the subject of study to others. Furthermore, micro-comparison presupposes macro-comparison; they are complementary rather than alternatives.[2]

It is true that micro-comparison can be undertaken in ways that accentuate the significance of rather narrow differences within Western European countries. For example, an emphasis can be placed on the differences between English law and French or German law as if these are indicative of more general differences between legal traditions. Indeed, the distinctive ways in which English and French legal systems have developed, particularly between the late eighteenth century and the First World War, become characterized as the *summa divisio*

* I am grateful to William Twining for his insights.

1 William Twining, *Globalisation and Legal Theory* (Butterworths 2000).

2 Ibid, 184.

between legal systems.[3] Secondly, there are dangers in the traditional emphasis on micro-comparisons in the way they are often practised. There can be too narrow a focus by looking mainly at comparison of legal rules within Western Europe, on state law, and on the relationship to parent common law or civil law systems. This is only one example of the comparative tradition, but its prevalence has a potentially distorting effect on the secondary literature of comparative law:

> The result is that much of the secondary literature about comparative law as a field is narrowly focused, overlooks some examples of best practice, and underestimates the richness, diversity and unevenness of transnational and cosmopolitan legal studies .... The Country and Western model has four main weaknesses: it is narrowly conceived; it has been artificially isolated from cognate fields; it is out of date; and it is under-theorised.[4]

This is not the place to worry about whether comparative law is under-theorized. I would merely remark that it has a lot more theoretical discussion on methodology than the most common form of legal research, doctrinal legal scholarship. Twining is essentially making two comments. The first is that there is too high a density of comparative law scholarship concentrated on comparisons within Western Europe, especially in private law. The result can be that secondary literature draws heavily on these studies in order to develop its general theories.[5] Furthermore, the classic secondary literature tends to divide up European legal traditions in very detailed ways and then produce broad-brush groupings for other legal systems. The second is that the agenda of work should not be detailed comparisons of aspects of the law of obligations, while other topics are less well covered. For example, Twining makes valuable criticism of the comparators used by the World Bank and other bodies to assess the performance of countries in terms of 'human rights', 'the rule of law', 'good governance', and 'democracy'.[6] There is a concern that legal scholarship should make a significant difference to less advantaged people and that is not reflected in the agenda of comparative law and its conferences.

Both the critique of Twining and the example of Glenn offer a chance to think about the place of micro-comparison. This chapter suggests that, although the work of Patrick Glenn demonstrates the importance of the kind of macro-comparison that Twining encourages, there remains an important place for traditional micro-comparison, both as a grounding for macro-comparisons and as a way of developing a sensibility for the complexity of the way in which legal systems actually work.

[3] Contrast this with the more careful and subtle approach of Thomas Lundmark, *Charting the Divide between Common Law and Civil Law* (OUP 2012).

[4] Twining (n 1) 187, 189.

[5] Eg, Ugo Mattei, *Comparative Law and Economics* (University of Michigan Press 1997).

[6] Twining (n 1) 192.

I GLENN'S MACRO-COMPARISON

In this volume, we celebrate the achievements of Patrick Glenn. Much of Patrick Glenn's work illustrates the broader agenda that Twining identifies with macro-comparison. Although he was very good at undertaking micro-comparison, Glenn's intellectual energies were mainly directed towards developing more sophisticated macro-comparative analyses. His *Legal Traditions of the World*[7] came out after Twining's book. Rather than classify particular legal systems within a Procrustean bed of a particular category of legal system, Glenn sought to illuminate a variety of systems in which the past experience of dealing with social problems in an ordered way built up into a tradition. His focus was deliberately not on nation states and their legal systems. Many of these are recent and most are contingent. He was concerned much more to look at approaches to resolving legal problems that are connected with particular social or ideological viewpoints. These are associated with some legal systems, but are neither confined to particular nation states nor operate exclusively over a whole legal system. There may be more than one tradition in operation within the same legal system.

In Glenn's analysis, law is one mechanism by which a group of people enable themselves to manage the problems of living together in a predictable and cohesive manner. A tradition involves doing things today in a way that is coherent with the past, so there is not just a *de novo* reaction to a situation, but a more measured and predictable approach. So that the core of a tradition is bringing the past to bear on the solution to a present problem. A tradition involves both a process of transmission (the *traditio*)[8] and the material handed on (described by Glenn as a 'bran-tub of information'[9]) from which inspiration is drawn for the solution. The tradition is a common resource on which individuals can draw and which helps to create a common identity (even where people may often draw on more than one tradition).[10] The tradition is grounded in values other than the law. Many of the traditions he mentions (Talmud, Islamic, and Hindu) are religious in character. Others (civil law, common law, and Chinese law) are ideological in the way they treat the law. The core of Glenn's analysis is that there are distinct approaches to resolving legal problems that are handed on by these traditions within particular communities. Traditions are by no means homogeneous. Based on past experience and often as the result of different communities living together, particular traditions emerge as blends of approaches. Given this analysis, it is not surprising that, in his final edition, Glenn made it clear that he did not rely on the concept of state law, but had a more cosmopolitan perspective to embrace mercantile and other types of

7 H Patrick Glenn, *Legal Traditions of the World: Sustainable Diversity in Law* (OUP 2000).

8 Here I would not only add the process, but also the methodology of tradition. See further, Catherine Valcke, Chapter 7 in this volume.

9 See H Patrick Glenn, *Legal Traditions of the World: Sustainable Diversity in Law* (5th edn, OUP 2014) 13–16 (hereafter Glenn, *LTW*).

10 Ibid, ch 1.

law.[11] It fits naturally with an account of traditions based on religious tradition. That fits with the idea that there are distinct approaches to resolving legal problems, which are often blended in specific contexts.

Presenting legal traditions can give rise to contestable results. Glenn focused principally on private law and on commercial law in the examples he gave and in the construction of the legal traditions he described. He did not give a lot of space to an account of public law within the traditions he described. Of course, they are recent, and they owe relatively little to Roman law or religious law, other than a broad conceptual distinction between public and private law and a few specific concepts. In the Western common law and civil law traditions, public law owes much to canon law, the law of the first great European public administration. But national administrative laws developed in their own way. If concepts such as fundamental individual rights rightly find their place in Glenn's account of the civil law tradition, as it now exists,[12] then the values of the *Rechtsstaat* or *l'État de droit* also are essential parts of it. The submission of the state to law is a deeply embedded value these days, even if it was a product of nineteenth-century liberalism. For many civilian countries, there is a deep cleavage between the rules and principles of public law and those of private law, but there is also a way of living with these two sets of norms. Few legal systems have distinct courts to reinforce this distinction in the norms that are applicable to public and private persons. Yet both of these features are important aspects of the civil law tradition today in contrast to the common law, and even more so in contrast to the other traditions that Glenn identified.

If a belief in individual rights rooted in the Enlightenment forms part of the Western civil law tradition, then the modern manifestations of this in constitutional justice and the transnational legal instruments and institutions on human rights deserve to be part of an account of contemporary legal traditions. As Louis Favoreu pointed out, there is a tradition of constitutional justice now found in the countries of the civil law tradition, which is distinct from common law and Scandinavian countries, but which has nothing to do with the heritage of Roman or canon law.[13] Since the creation of the Austrian Constitutional Court in 1920, there has been a development of constitutional courts as distinct from ordinary courts. These courts have helped to develop a distinct constitutional law that has facilitated the protection of rights, as well as enforce more domestic concerns about the division of powers either among federated entities or between the executive and the parliament. Members of these courts have regular links, and it would seem strange to omit this feature from a description of the modern civil tradition. One can recognize, as do Konrad Zweigert and Hein Kötz,[14] that the division into 'legal families' or 'legal

11 Ibid, 274–75.

12 Ibid, 147–51.

13 Louis Favoreu, *Les cours constitutionnelles* (3rd edn, Presse Universitaire de France 1996) 16–27.

14 Konrad Zweigert and Hein Kötz, *An Introduction to Comparative Law* (3rd edn, Tony Weir tr, OUP 1998) 65.

traditions' is different depending on whether one looks at public law or private law. All the same, there is sufficient in common between the public and criminal law heritages of the civil law countries to give this a place in any account of the modern continental European tradition (which might be a better label than 'civil law'). My point is that we can see legal traditions as divided up in different ways. Glenn was fully aware of the diversity of the underpinning reality of the 'traditions' that he identified.[15] The groupings are there to provide structure and insight. The structure enables one to see the interaction of different features. The insight focuses on common themes. Now these themes are necessarily selective and, in a short book, limited. The cartography of legal traditions depends on the broad themes that one wants to accentuate.

Glenn's principal focus in dividing legal traditions was on the power of ideas. These seem to shape the division between the different legal traditions he describes. Hindu and Islamic laws are based on religious ideas and values. Civil law and common law are based on different approaches to law, even if they share much in common. The organizing ideas or values are significant features of Glenn's account. But for him, the major organizing ideas are change, rationality, and humanism. He is right to identify the importance of legal positivism. One major idea that gets less prominence is the rule of law, the idea that the law provides an overriding scheme for evaluating social reality. Glenn does have the idea that law expands its empire and provides a mechanism for social bindingness.[16] Equally, the constitutional tradition of modern times provides a content of substantive rights to the rule of law. The rule of law is connected with another Kelsenian idea of power, the monopoly of force by the state. The idea that law controls the use of force is not original, but the institutionalization and monopolization of force is perhaps distinctive in the West. Law in many ways goes beyond simply recognizing private power: it legitimates and limits it, if not also replacing it.

But, as Glenn also pointed out, processes of making rules and applying them to concrete situations are important. Different legal systems have distinctive processes for resolving disputes. For example, the classical Roman law system had some similarities to the chthonic systems (the use of the lay *iudex*), but had special features, such as the role of the praetor as a kind of professional gatekeeper of the way a lay person would judge the case. But these Roman features have changed as the role of judging has been professionalized. The distinctive feature of the Western legal tradition inherited from Roman law is the discrete character of the legal dispute: the problem is only seen from the legal point of view, rather than allowing the parties to present a holistic approach to a problem (as would happen in mediation or in chthonic law). Processes beget *institutions*, such as courts and legal professions. Law is also begotten within the institution of the state, which is separate

15 Glenn, *LTW* (n 9) 361–65.
16 Ibid, 145.

from society. Canon law and the Renaissance state have created varieties of legal professions, and later periods have formalized their role and education. The importance of universities alongside the professions in the process of induction has increased since the Middle Ages, but takes different forms. Legal education is as much shaped by understandings of national education policy, as by the civilian heritage. Finally, and importantly, the law is by nature normative, and so there are *norms* that lay down what should happen. But, by contrast with religious systems, law is seen as normative independently of the way individuals judge its moral rightness. Glenn rightly considers the common law to be an ethic of adjudication, but one which is not necessarily transposable to other systems.[17] The relationship of ideas to the operation of institutions and legal professions as factors in legal change is important. This was a feature that was studied as part of the project on European legal development that David Ibbetson and I led. Our research colleagues did identify social and political ideas as shaping the development of the law.[18] But they also pointed to the way in which professions and institutions had an influence on the way that the law of tort developed over the nineteenth and twentieth centuries.[19] In both of these analyses, it is possible to see the way in which influences cut across legal traditions.[20] This reinforces the view expressed by Glenn that there can be many cross-cutting themes, which are illuminating and which are not captured in his groupings of traditions.[21]

What emerges from the book is a picture of law as a pragmatic exercise. It is about lawyers drawing on a variety of traditions and materials in a particular social setting to solve problems. Similar to René David's legal families,[22] Glenn's traditions are not pure. He explains how they are the product of different layers of sedimentation over the years – blending different experiences into a functioning system that has built up over time. Geography and history have played their part in giving rise to a distinctive mix over time in particular regions, and it is these experiences that give rise to the traditions he identifies. For example, in chapter 8 of *Legal Traditions of the World*, he discusses Hindu tradition in terms of the coming together of different ideas over many centuries.[23] At the same time, there is the instantiation of Hindu law within a particular country, such as India, which is a mix of different legal traditions.[24] The history of colonization, by Muslim rulers and then by the British, has shaped the current law. Such an analysis sees pluralism as a key feature of legal development. For Glenn, '[d]iversity is here not just a way of managing resistance and local

17 Ibid, 273–82.

18 See Michael Lobban and Julia Moses (eds), *The Impact of Ideas* (CUP 2012).

19 See Paul Mitchell (ed), *The Impact of Legal Institutions and Professions* (CUP 2012).

20 See John Bell and David Ibbetson, *European Legal Development: The Case of Tort* (CUP 2012) 42–45.

21 See Glenn, *LTW* (n 9) 364–65.

22 René David, *Les grands systems de droit contemporains* (11th edn, C Jauffret-Spinozi ed, Dalloz 2002) 15.

23 Glenn, *LTW* (n 9) 289–96.

24 Ibid, 310–14.

circumstance; it is fundamental'.[25] This approach fits the more detailed study by Werner Menski, which also stresses plurality in personal laws, among other features, as the way in which Hindu law has coped with contemporary social developments. For Menski, by going back to Hindu roots, Indian law has needed to draw less on the Western legal traditions for transplants.[26] Both Glenn and Menski give a picture of lawyers and legislators drawing on features of tradition and modernity to help society adapt. In this collection, Ahmed Fekry Ibrahim provides us with a different account of pluralism – this time within a so-called single Islamic 'tradition'.[27]

Although the characterization of traditions could have been presented differently, there are important lessons that can be learned. The analysis leads to conclusions about general issues such as the rule of law. Bodies such as the World Bank have created governance indicators to measure the effectiveness of individual states. Rule of law is one such indicator.[28] The World Bank has a particular perspective on how a justice system should work and effectively compares countries to that standard. The results are contestable.[29] It is based largely on putting together data from other databases and surveys, rather than any careful attempt to understand how the legal system in question actually works. In that sense, it is extremely formalist, rather than substantive. One feature is that the distinctiveness of legal traditions is not respected. The approach is narrow and does not explore the features that make a legal system robust in terms of the rule of law. There is a real sense that everything is being fitted into a single framework for no other reason than ease of measurement.

Glenn offers a different perspective. He suggests that the rule of law can allow a much greater sense of diversity. Glenn's approach to the diversity of legal traditions is well expressed in chapter 10 of *Legal Traditions of the World*. He recognizes the complexity of the individual traditions that the book identifies. The traditions as ideas and practices have operated in different periods and with different interpretations. They consist of numerous sub-traditions among particular legal actors and on particular topics. There is an internal diversity, if not conflict, as part of the everyday operation of a tradition. Yet, overall, there is some form of coherence that still provides a family resemblance among the diverging parts of the tradition. Two types of thinking are attached to this way of living the law. The first is multivalent thinking. Rather than legal rules being 'all or nothing' in producing prescriptive results, there is the approach of acknowledging the validity of competing principles, perhaps making suggestions of how to handle situations in which they conflict, and then leaving the resolution of the inevitable tensions to a 'situation sense' on the

[25] Ibid, 314.

[26] Werner Menski, *Comparative Law in a Global Context* (2nd edn, CUP 2006) 277–78.

[27] See Ahmed Fekry Ibrahim, Chapter 9 in this volume.

[28] 'Worldwide Governance Indicators' (*World Bank*) <http://info.worldbank.org/governance/wgi/index.aspx#reports>.

[29] See Lorne Neudorf, *The Dynamics of Judicial Independence: A Comparative Study of Courts in Malaysia and Pakistan* (Springer 2017).

particular facts of a case.[30] That can lead to a pluralism in solutions. The second approach is the need to recognize the space for state law and the space for other (private and often collective) ways of regulating affairs. It may be that, from the legal point of view, state law claims exclusive competence to regulate social situations. But from the social point of view, there are problems with expecting the state to deal with every problem that the social media identifies as worrying. Glenn's 'ways of diversity' provide a more humble and sane scope for law and its claims. His demonstration of the diversity of legal traditions encourages a different kind of understanding of the rule of law.

So, from Glenn's work, we see not only how macro-comparison can be undertaken, but how its approach can enrich an understanding of the law that is not confined to drawing on Western European experiences.

II EXAMPLES OF MICRO-COMPARISON: THE WORK OF BERNARD RUDDEN

An alternative approach to comparative law is to look at the work of Bernard Rudden who was, *par excellence*, a person who used the micro detail in order to provide wider lessons. Glenn knew and appreciated his work. But I think Rudden's approach does show the broader value of micro-comparison with its grounding in the reality of the way in which the law operates.

His article 'Torticles' is a splendid piece, which I often use to illustrate the nature of the common law of torts in contrast to other legal systems.[31] The distinctiveness of the work is to ensure that there is enough attention to detail, but also that lessons are drawn out. Essentially, he uses the contrast with the very general civil law formulations in nineteenth-century civil codes to bring out an important feature of the common law – that it has evolved around specific problems with specific rules and without an overarching framework. This is a matter of fact, but the article also brings out the way in which a legal system and its approach have evolved.

Equally, his article in French on efficient breach[32] was specifically about the rules on breach of contract. He analyses rules of the American Uniform Commercial Code and contrasts them with Articles 1142 and 1150 (as they then were) of the French Civil Code of 1804. He notes the original meaning of the French provisions and also the ways in which these had been interpreted by the courts, typically in a form which was in contrast to efficient breach. In one sense, it is narrow; it contrasts two legal systems on a very specific point – the enforcement of contracts. But in an important way, he is using economic theory to challenge a more dominant moralistic value system in France. The article, then, can be read as a debate about the social function of the law within contract. The purpose of the article was essentially

30 Glenn, *LTW* (n 9) 379–84.

31 Bernard Rudden, 'Torticles' (1991) 6 *Tulane Civil LF* 105. In a similar style, see Bernard Rudden, 'Notes Towards a Grammar of Property' [1980] *Conveyancer* 325.

32 Bernard Rudden and Philippe Juilhard, 'La théorie de la violation efficace' (1986) 38 *RIDC* 1015.

educative, to explain the economic analysis to a French legal public that did not know much about it.

In a similar vein, his work on the duty of disclosure takes a very specific aspect of the law of contract in France and England, but develops it into another insight into the economic function of law. He is trying to suggest that the French are too protective of individuals who suffer harm at the expense of the proper functioning of the market.[33] In his view,

> the legal rule can inhibit the economic objective in that, if you pardon the exaggeration, individuals who are deprived on the chance to take advantage of their professional education prefer ignorance. Thus, the economic disincentive of the obligation to disclose can lead them, by a simple analysis of costs and profits, to cease all research for information . . . .[34]

His contribution on 'gentlemen's agreements' connects to an interest he shared with Jean Carbonnier on law and non-law.[35] This was the general report for the Congress of the International Academy of Comparative Law in Bristol in 1998. It thus provides an overview of a series of national reports from Western or Western-influenced countries on the rules governing the law of contract. Rudden examines both the disclaimer of contractual obligation and the disclaimer of legal commitment to make good any loss arising as a consequence of a person's actions. But he draws from the reports not only specific conclusions but also more general conclusions about the attitude of lawyers. They were 'finding it difficult to see why anyone would prefer *vacuum juris* to *vinculum juris*'[36] and '[w]hen confronted with the sweeping exclusion of their universe, the jurists' response seem[s] to be one of dark suspicion, displaying a reluctance to accept that there may be good alternatives to the legal enforcement of contracts.'[37]

Bernard Rudden was not one to engage in grand generalizations. He preferred the well-worked vignette. But the vignette was researched in detail and linked to a non-legal approach based on economic theory about the function of law. He was good at challenging theories by focusing on detail. I remember the work he did on Anglo-French contract law. He found Patrick Atiyah's approach particularly indefensible, namely that the law is about providing remedies for reliance on executed contracts. Rudden imagined a pair of jeans and how its existence depended on promissory, executory contracts, which Atiyah was keen to dismiss as unimportant.[38] It is the eye

33 Bernard Rudden, 'Le juste et l'inefficace: Pour un non-devoir de renseignements' (1985) 84 *RTDCiv* 91, *followed up in* Bernard Rudden, 'The Duty of Disclosure' [1991] *Ins L&P* 45.

34 Rudden, 'Le juste et l'inefficace' (n 33) 93.

35 Bernard Rudden, 'The Gentleman's Agreement in Legal Theory and in Modern Practice' (1999) 7 *ERPL* 199.

36 Ibid, 220.

37 Ibid.

38 See Bernard Rudden, 'The Domain of Contract' in Donald Harris and Denis Tallon (eds), *Contract Law Today* (OUP 1989).

for the telling illustration that was the pedagogically brilliant part of Rudden's scholarship. The micro-comparison is retold in a way that is sufficiently stylized as to bring out the broader implications. But those broader implications are always grounded in solid reality, rather than grand principle or assumption. It is that kind of scholarship that can produce generalization but avoids being simplistic.

The portfolio of Rudden's works[39] shows a scholar grappling with big themes: the role of law in the economic system of Western capitalism, the role of legal rules in legal practice (when does law matter?), and the role of law in socialism and post-socialism in the Soviet Union and Russia. But he did not write grand books or grand articles on those themes. He took specific problems that illustrated the issues and showed how they worked in concrete legal systems. There is no grand rhetoric of the Twining or the Glenn.

So, in Rudden and Glenn we have contrasting ways of conducting primary comparative research. Each is able to address broad questions about the role of law and the way it functions. But they offer insights with limitations. Generalization from micro-comparison is always tentative. Specific conclusions are robust, but extending the insights beyond the evidence that has been carefully gathered is a problem. On the other hand, the ideas that macro-comparison presents are subject to qualification if a significant body of empirical information can be adduced that does not fit.[40] So the struggle is to achieve the right balance between specific information and general theory.

III THE PURPOSE OF MICRO-COMPARISON

Jaakko Husa is correct that there does not need to be any rigid separation between macro-comparison and micro-comparison.[41] As he suggests, those engaging in micro-comparison need to be aware of the general features of the type of legal system with which they are dealing. At the same time, the macro-comparatist might have to study specific individual issues in order to see the significance of the general features of law that she is perceiving and presenting in the macro-comparison.

The work of Patrick Glenn shows the importance of macro-comparison. He is able to integrate not only the legal rules and institutions, but also the social culture and ideology, as well as its history and geography. Law is not treated as an isolated phenomenon, but it is seen as a social process that reflects broader cultural ideas and values. Glenn notes that the traditions he is presenting reflect a 'deep history'.[42] It is that depth of the resonance of the law within a social community that macro-comparison is able to highlight. Bernhard Grossfeld, too, would endorse the study

39 Best summarized in Peter Birks and Arianna Pretto (eds), *Themes in Comparative Law: Essays in Honour of Bernard Rudden* (OUP 2002) 289–96.

40 See Mathias Siems, *Comparative Law* (CUP 2014) 80–93.

41 Jaakko Husa, *A New Introduction to Comparative Law* (Hart 2015) 103–04.

42 Glenn, *LTW* (n 9) 7.

of tradition, but very much as the context for understanding the law of another country: '[I]t is essential for us to understand the social, political and cultural background of the foreign law and comprehend the organic nature of its rules.'[43] Comparative law draws attention to worldwide tendencies exhibited in a foreign system, but perhaps understated in one's own legal system.[44] But for Grossfeld, the broadening of perspective is rooted in micro-comparison.[45]

I too would highlight the importance of the process of micro-comparison. As Glenn pointed out, traditions can be grouped by big ideas in the way he finds most useful, but Grossfeld notes that they can be grouped along different thematic lines, such as casuistry, analogical reasoning, or intergenerational equity.[46] Any person engaging in macro-comparison needs to have a feel for the subject matter with which they are dealing and how best to present its complexity. As Husa implies, you need to have undertaken some specific and detailed comparison of the law of particular legal systems on a topic to be confident that you are drawing out the most helpful elements of the legal systems. There is a necessary interplay between the detailed evidence and the broad theory. For example, it might be thought that the law and its structure would reflect fairly closely the prevalent social ideas in society. But that is not as straightforwardly true. Karl Renner found that, when he was trying to describe the relationship of socialist ideas and the law of his country, there were a number of features that did not match, especially in the law of property.[47] Property concepts and rules continued to be used in law long after the underlying ideology changed. The form of words and the legal rules may formally stay the same, but the underlying function has changed. The legal system enjoys a kind of relative formal autonomy from the underlying ideology, even if the basic function needs eventually to be aligned:

> The organic character of the legal order is the fact that the totality of legal institution existing at a given time must fulfil all general functions. This means that the law is an organised whole determined by the needs of society. Every legal institution as part of it, therefore, is more or less closely related to all others; and it is its function, not the content of its norms, which make for this connection.[48]

This observation led Renner to a more sophisticated understanding of the macro-level relationship between the economic base and the legal superstructure within Marxist thought.[49] Specific attention to an area of law led to a better theory. The point of this example more generally for macro-comparison is that high-level theories about the relationship between ideas and law may need to be adjusted when you

43 Bernhard Grossfeld, *The Strengths and Weaknesses of Comparative Law* (Tony Weir tr, OUP 1990) 45.

44 Ibid, 112.

45 Ibid, 3.

46 Ibid, 364.

47 Karl Renner, *Institutions of Private Law and Their Social Functions* (Otto Kahn-Freund ed, Agnes Schwarzschild tr, Routledge 1976) ch 3.

48 Ibid, 76.

49 See ibid, ch 3.

pay closer attention to the detail. Examples can be multiplied, but the most frequent is the comparison between common law and civil law systems, which is often based on high-level generalization without adequate attention to the way the detail of the operation of the different groups of systems.[50]

Dissatisfaction with broad generalization at a macro-level can produce valuable results. Lorne Neudorf[51] took the concept of 'judicial independence', which is seen by the World Bank and others as a key indicator of adherence to the rule of law. These studies treat common law countries as very similar because of the formal structure and protections for judicial independence. But, on a closer analysis of two countries, which share both a common law legal tradition and Islamic religious traditions, he was able to show that judicial independence was conceived in radically different ways in Malaysia and Pakistan. In Malaysia, there was a much greater deference to the executive. In Pakistan, the judiciary had taken a much more proactive approach and called in matters on their own initiative, much as has been done by the Indian Supreme Court. He proposes therefore a much more 'context sensitive' approach to an idea such as 'judicial independence'.[52] Constitutional conditions differ between countries even when they share many similar general features of their traditions. This can lead to specific changes which attention to the general features of a legal tradition can miss.

So why undertake micro-comparison? My first argument is that you don't get very far in understanding how legal systems work by making broad generalizations about legal families and traditions. Glenn himself relied on at least two bodies of literature in his studies of particular traditions. On the one hand, there are general works, for example, on Islamic law and Islamic thought, which predominate in many discussions of specific traditions, but he also relied on a number of specific micro-studies of aspects of Islamic law in particular countries. In addition, he relied significantly on contacts with scholars in the field as informants. The building of the micro-pictures enables the author to have some solidity in the generalizations which she undertakes. This approach of building of micro-pictures enabled Glenn to see in his conclusion that legal systems often involve a complex mix of traditions. In the first place, boundaries of national laws have often changed several times. As Glenn noted in relation to common laws in Europe, there are special places where the links between traditions intersect. Andrew Harding has made this point in relation to Southeast Asian laws. Countries like Malaysia and Indonesia have a series of different layers of legal traditions influencing not only the past content of the law, but shaping how it works at present.[53] Like Twining, Harding is keen that the jurist

[50] See further my comment on an earlier edition of Glenn's *Legal Traditions of the World*: John Bell, 'Chapter Five: Civil Law Tradition' (2007) 1 *JCL* 130.

[51] Neudorf, *Dynamics of Judicial Independence* (n 29) 10–21.

[52] Ibid, 30–32, 242–47.

[53] Andrew Harding, 'Comparative Public Law: Some Lessons from South-East Asia' in Andrew Harding and Esin Örücü (eds), *Comparative Law in the 21st Century* (Kluwer 2002) 266.

should not just focus on legal rules and concepts, but that she should also immerse herself in the context and understand the way a particular legal system works. The result, he suggests, is that we would discover not only similarities within groupings of legal systems in a region but similarities with other systems.

The 'so what?' question that comes at the end of any micro-comparison research pushes the researcher to explain why the research results might be interesting for others. That encourages generalization beyond the limits of the evidence with the ambition of stimulating further work by people with different expertise. But the robustness of macro-comparison depends on its ability to be verified in the close examination of specific instances of legal systems which it is supposed to explain. Macro-comparison is typically an exercise of seeing patterns in specific instances and developing a theory that continues on that pattern. There is a reciprocal relationship between macro- and micro-levels.

IV COMMON LAWS: AN ILLUSTRATION OF WHY MICRO-COMPARISON MATTERS

An illustration of why it matters to engage in micro-comparative studies can be given by looking at the debate about 'common laws'. One of the perennial quests of many comparative law studies is to discover common principles across different legal systems with a view to enacting common laws.

Glenn wrote extensively on this. He saw common laws as possible vehicles for reconciling peoples. These were not arbitrarily imposed, but part of human collaboration.[54] He saw universalization as a particular vocation of legal traditions, of enabling better relationships as people move in different ways, not limiting themselves to the borders of nation states. At the same time, Glenn recognized that there are a number of common laws around the world whose relationship has to be negotiated by national laws. In his view, common laws in the world have existed in the past and then been influential in shaping national laws. These common laws should shape how the law develops in the future. The resort to comparative law is but one indicator of this mutual relationship between national and common laws.[55] In his concrete examples in his book *On Common Laws*, he drew attention to the way in which the Romanistic *ius commune* and the common law operated as pre-national and then supranational points of reference for national laws. This, he considered, provided a model of how law might respond to the mobility of people and commerce in the modern world where the state is less important.

Stated at such a level of abstraction, this may seem plausible. But there are two issues of significance that closer attention through micro-comparisons would make clear. First, as Jan Smits notes, what is the nature of these 'common' laws? Are they the same kind of sets of rules and principles as national laws? Smits considers that

[54] H Patrick Glenn, *On Common Laws* (OUP 2005) 143.
[55] Ibid, 94.

they are bound to be pitched at a much higher level of generality.[56] Alain Wijffels agrees from the perspective of a legal historian.[57] In his view, the kind of European common law that is needed is unlike the codifications of the nineteenth and twentieth centuries with their detailed rules that are tightly integrated through a common instrument. We are not looking for a tight systematization in relation to particular subject areas and are not seeking to bind supranational and municipal legal orders through positive rules.[58] Rather, the European common law is more like points of orientation for conduct, rather than specific rules that can deliver immediate injunctions to people or solutions to disputes. In part this is because the laws do not emanate from a hierarchical superior with ultimate coercive power to enforce them. Nor do they have democratic authority or legitimacy, which underpins them. They represent an attempt to articulate the kinds of considerations that are usually thought relevant in the resolution of social problems by the law. The important feature for the decision-maker is to know the factors that ought to be taken into account and the reasons why one approach might be more useful than another. National rules are often designed to be more specific. As a result, as Wijffels suggests, they are principles that may direct solutions in particular directions. The result is a different way of thinking. It is not a matter of applying rules in a relatively mechanistic fashion, but of orienting a debate about the right solution. Such an interplay between grand theorizing about the desirability of 'common laws' and the attention to the detail of how they are drafted and work reveals interesting features about the complexity of law and it increases our attention to the different social and other phenomena that law involves. But it also qualifies the apparent claims of macro-comparison.

Concrete analyses of the issues through micro-comparison enable the reality of such issues to be explored. The merit of much comparative work in recent years is that it has tried to see how far the ideas of people like Glenn can be realized in concrete branches of law. The Draft Common Frame of Reference (DCFR)[59] and the Principles of European Tort Law (PETL),[60] to take two examples, are very serious and detailed efforts to produce common laws. The authority or status of the DCFR or the PETL could have been seen as a set of principles that serve as a set of values to orient the application of the law in individual legal system, a kind of regulative ideal to which national laws would look. But, however much conceived initially in this way, they have become

56 Jan M Smits, *The Mind and Method of the Legal Academic* (Edward Elgar 2012) 84–85.

57 Alain Wijffels, 'European Private Law: A New Software Package for an Outdated Operating System' in Mark Van Hoecke and François Ost (eds), *The Harmonisation of European Private Law* (Hart 2000).

58 Ibid, 114–15.

59 Christian Von Bar (ed), *Principles of European Law: Non-Contractual Liability Arising out of Damage Caused to Another* (OUP 2009).

60 European Group on Tort Law, *Principles of European Tort Law: Text and Commentary* (Springer 2005).

constructed in many particulars as a set of interlocking, quite detailed rules. The end product is a code that could be enacted by a number of countries to replace their existing provisions. They would be longer than most European national code provisions on delict, but much shorter than any summary restatement of the English and Irish common laws.[61] These projects are not avowedly political projects of unification of laws, but there is a clear underlying sense that the diverse EU legal systems can be brought together around the principles in such common frameworks. If the texts produced were simply to operate as a regulative ideal, then the detail could be more limited within the provisions and could be left to the commentary. Instead, we really have a model code of rules. The object is not so much to influence decision-makers, but to provide them with a prepared solution for situations that arise. The care with which the scholars have given to provide coherent solutions demonstrates this wish to provide solutions that are capable of being applied in a number of different situations. But, then examining them in some depth, one can see the problems that arise. These 'common laws' really only work if they replace the municipal law in large part, at least with regard to the substance. They are systematic in the classic sense that Wijffels identified, such that problems are resolved by one conceptual structure in the common law, but in a different way in specific national systems.

The code-like ambitions of the DCFR, for example, are evident from the attempt to cover every topic. But, in the end, the authors have to recognize that systems will diverge for policy reasons, and so the DCFR remits the resolution of a number of topics to national laws. There are a range of areas where many countries have special rules, for example, on nuclear installations or motor vehicles, and the desire to include them within common principles on non-contractual liability is rather misguided. For instance, it is not clear that the authors need have included areas such as motor vehicle liability (Article 3:205) within the DCFR. They acknowledge that the special provisions in many national laws have strong social insurance principles and provide compensation typically without proof of fault. There are also often ceilings on the amounts of liability. These provisions are, typically, outside the general principles of delict and have their own justification. It would be better to consider them as *sui generis* and leave the DCFR to concentrate on general principles. The rationale for many of these rules is different from many of the principles of delict law and so they could be left out of consideration. After all, the result of creating a liability for the keeper of a vehicle for the harm it causes is an approach that many systems do not accept in the form the DCFR presented. The debate on such provisions as

[61] Compare the length of Andrew Burrows, *A Restatement of the English Law of Contract* (OUP 2016) (255 pages of provisions and commentary), and Neil Andrews, *Contract Rules: Decoding English Law* (Intersentia 2016) (388 pages of provisions and commentary).

Article 3:205 and following suggests that there will be special national laws on liability alongside the DCFR. That kind of provision suggests that the better way of structuring a 'common law' is to confine it to the general principles of delict and leave the rest to specific uniform laws or national laws as *lex specialis*. Looking at the detail of attempts at common codes in the light of existing municipal laws enables a proper debate on what it means to have 'common laws' that high-level discussion of principles at a macro-level does not foster with enough clarity.

The second issue is that there are genuine disagreements between legal systems as to what is the best resolution to a problem. So any set of common laws has either to set out the alternatives or to make choices between competing solutions. The Chairman of the DCFR states that '[l]ike every other scholarly legal work, they restate the current law and introduce possible models for its further development'.[62] But the work cannot 'restate' the law where there are significant differences between legal systems. It must and does choose the 'best' solution. But the authority for its view of what is 'best' rests with the arguments of the authors. The preface reads as if the work is the product of a technician, presenting in ordered form the existing law. Actually, it provides the product of serious reflection by sophisticated experts, who have made value judgements about how the law should be structured and developed. It is their synthesis and proposal for adjustment, and it cannot simply rely on the authority of existing national laws. Essentially, the authors have developed model answers influenced by the laws of the member states, but not determined by them. The DCFR and the PETL are not a summary of national laws, nor a lowest common denominator. They are deliberately a search for best practice. In doing this, the authors have often departed from particular legal systems. For example, on the need for unlawfulness, the authors of the DCFR and the PETL have departed from German and Austrian laws and made the concept unnecessary. The authors are more willing to allow for the recovery of economic loss than German or English law is. These examples illustrate the necessity to make a principled selection of best practice, which makes the DCFR and the PETL more than just restatements. The systems to be reconciled are much further apart in the conceptual structure and values than in the way the American Restatements are constructed. So the choices of concepts, solutions, and values are genuine choices of policy, rather than technical smoothing of inconsistencies.

A further example of a policy choice is the liability for children. Article 3:103 decides that persons under eighteen years of age should be held liable 'only in so far as that person does not exercise such care as could be expected from a reasonably careful person of the same age in the circumstances of the case'. This age-related test would not trouble Swedish or English or German lawyers, but the test goes firmly against the approach of French law adopted in 1984. Now there are clear merits in

[62] Von Bar (n 59) xi.

some of these proposals. But the important point is that we are not faced in the principles of the DCFR and the PETL with a simple harmonization around agreed points of reference, a lowest common denominator. We are faced with a code, drawn up after serious thought, which adopts 'the best solution', having considered how different solutions would approach a problem. This requires the different systems to change.

Contemporary 'common law' discussion is different from that discussed by Glenn. The *ius commune* and the English common law were national bodies of law developed in a fragmentary way that came to be seen as useful for resolving the problems of other countries or groups of people. Rather like Glenn views legal traditions, the approach of lawyers was to treat this kind of law as an optional pragmatic resource, part of an ongoing collaboration. The more modern common laws are artificial supranational bodies of principles (if not rules) designed to promote convergence. That is why they are offered as 'best practice', drawing on the experience of different countries. Micro-comparison is needed not just to provide the raw material which can be synthesized into common 'codes' or 'restatements'. It can also help to understand the points of resistance and the different contexts in which these principles will have to be applied. It will enable lawyers and others to understand what else has to change, apart from the formal rules or principles for these common laws to work. It is in the attention to the detailed tension between broad statements of common laws and the detail of existing municipal laws that the character of the change that Glenn suggested becomes more apparent.

CONCLUSION

I have argued that micro-comparison is an important aspect of comparative law. It provides the material for macro-comparison to develop and provides a way of checking its robustness. In many senses, macro-analysis cannot be rushed and is a mature scholar's job. First, Glenn shows how much you have to read yourself into an area before you can generalize. You need to have read a lot of micro-analyses before you can be confident that you can say anything meaningful at a macro-level. The richness of the specific data in micro-analyses enables a sophisticated macro-picture to emerge. Twining is right that the lack of density of micro-analyses has hampered the sophistication of macro-analyses. The strong criticism of the 'legal families' literature and its classification of non-European legal systems into over-large and poorly defined groupings bears witness to the lack of underpinning micro-studies. The complaints of people like Harding demonstrate how little substantive knowledge underpinned earlier characterizations of the law in areas of the world such as Southeast Asia.[63] The implication is that those who undertake micro-comparative law today should have

[63] Harding (n 53) 266.

a more diversified range of interests and talents from those, like Rudden (or myself), who have undertaken the task in recent years. Diversified interests, because they need to be interested in grand ideas of governance, rather than just the practical impact of different legal concepts and institutions. Divergent skills, because they basically need a different set of linguistic abilities that will open up Asian and African countries, rather than the local countries easily accessible by short-haul jet or by train, and whose linguistic structure is moderately cognate to that of their mother tongue. Certainly, the Anglo-Saxon arrogance in assuming that materials will be available in English in sufficient quantity has never been well-founded, even in my (limited) experience of Western European legal systems, and was certainly never assumed by scholars like Glenn, Twining, or Rudden. Unfortunately, the range of linguistic competence in many countries is diminishing as English becomes dominant, such that the pool of those able to undertake the wider-ranging research that macro-comparison demands, is shrinking.[64]

Second, training in the comparative method requires the development of a capacity to undertake small-scale studies. A scholar learns the difficulty of undertaking comparison between legal systems and drawing meaningful conclusions about them from working on a small scale. It is easy to put forward grand theories, but it is hard to defend them. Sophisticated attention to a small project enables the serious questions to be tackled in a manageable fashion. Such projects also enable training in spotting questions that are of potentially broader significance. Although the specific question may appear to be narrow and the method is tight in order to produce robust results, the project needs to be potentially fruitful and that will require some pre-understanding of global issues. There is virtue in 'learning by doing' in this way and that is possible in the small micro-comparison. But the encouragement from Twining to follow Glenn and undertake macro-comparison requires a different way of working. It will typically involve collaboration across continental and language groups. First-hand knowledge is blended into the work of a team.

This is borne out by my own personal experience, even in traditional 'Country and Western' research. The European Legal Development project brought together seventy scholars almost entirely from Western Europe to look at the broad question of what are the factors affecting the development of the law. We can typically identify what has changed in the law between two periods, but it is often not clear why there has been change. Is this simply due to factors within the law, or within other aspects of the same socioeconomic community, or is it the result of some other external change? In order to explore this very broad question, it was necessary to

[64] See N Jones and others, 'First European Survey on Language Competences' (*EU Commission*, 2012) esp 35 <www.surveylang.org/media/ExecutivesummaryoftheESLC_210612.pdf> (on the frequency of level B2 achievement in relation to first and second target (European) languages). The Survey also notes that English is the most commonly taught first foreign language except in the United Kingdom and Belgium (a bilingual country). Ibid, 7.

choose a narrower focus. So we took the development of fault liability in tort over the period 1850–2000 in Western Europe. Even within this specific topic, it was necessary to select six major themes: the development of tort doctrine, liability for road accidents, liability for medical treatment, liability for technological change, liability between neighbours, and liability for products. These then allowed us to have two higher-level studies on factors affecting change: social and political ideas, professions, and institutions. Only by making use of the work of these different scholars in written form or in seminar discussion were David Ibbetson and I able to write our overview book[65] where we were able to suggest particular explanations of the changes in the law that we had seen and to generalize from them. But, even as we worked on the generalization, we were forced to go back and undertake a number of small micro-projects triggered by the work that others had already done, but which needed amplifying in the light of the kinds of conclusions we were trying to develop. I do not see this as an unusual comparative law process. By drawing on the work of so many colleagues, we were able to have greater complexity and richness in the data we sought to explain. But it shows clearly the importance of collaboration in micro-comparison as a basis for further work of generalization.

In many ways, Glenn will be a special case. He wrote a single-authored book of macro-range of legal systems, work of this kind is necessarily going to involve the input of a wide variety of individuals. Whilst Glenn was able to undertake the eclectic reading of the work of others and thereby ground his own synthesis, others will find it more efficient to work in collaborative teams where constant interaction with colleagues will refine the basic information and the reliability of the conclusions and generalizations that are being made.

65 Bell and Ibbetson (n 20).

4

Sociocultural Challenges for Comparative Legal Studies in Mixed Legal Systems

Esin Örücü

INTRODUCTION

In *On Common Laws*,[1] H Patrick Glenn demonstrated that universality and particularity, unity and diversity, unity in diversity, and expansion and local sensibility are the defining moments in the history of legal systems. Glenn observed that the concept of common law, not as it lives in the name of the 'Common Law tradition' but in its primary historical sense, is common in relation to law that is not common: it lives as 'relational common law', surviving and functioning in relation to the particular law that has priority over it. It is present only in a manner compatible with the local law, with no obligatory content, and no binding or unifying authority. Thus common laws define themselves in relation to others, and 'they are in a constant dynamic state'.[2] He demonstrated that the 'Common Law', the *ius commune, le droit commun, el derecho comun, il diritto commune*, and *das gemeine Recht*, with their different experiences, all share these characteristics. In addition, multiple, interactive common laws, reflecting the essential diversity of European law, 'each radiating out from major centers of population or influence', variously accommodated '*iure propria* internal to each of them'.[3] This led Glenn to make the point that today, for our understanding of the *ius commune*, the hypothesis of multiple common laws is 'as plausible as that of a single overarching common law'.[4] This point is crucial for a number of projects in different fields that are working towards the creation of common cores for 'European laws'. This point is also fundamental in the search for an understanding of legal traditions in mixed legal systems, which I will discuss later in this chapter.

Tracing the *ius commune*, the common law as originating in England, France, Germany, and Spain, as well as the other common laws of Europe, Glenn dealt with the early expansion of *ius unum* and the common law. He also reminded us that

[1] H Patrick Glenn, *On Common Laws* (OUP 2005) (hereafter Glenn, *OCL*). For a review of Glenn's book, see Esin Örücü, 'Book Review' (2006) 10 *Edinburgh L Rev* 463.

[2] Glenn, *OCL* (n 1) 43.

[3] Ibid, 21.

[4] Ibid, 25.

there are a number of common laws 'free of a territorial base', such as canon law and commercial law.

More importantly, Glenn considered the relations of common laws with each other. His claim was that common laws, tolerant of particular laws, are also tolerant of each other. Rather than being aggressive, they share information. Thus interrelationship and interaction are crucial, and we know that interrelationship breeds convergence. Again, this observation is crucial to my analysis of mixed legal systems in the following pages.

Looking beyond rules, substance, and structure, towards legal tradition and legal culture, what becomes obvious is the interrelationships between legal systems. Though this may sound like the reverse of the usual claim that rules and solutions may look alike while legal cultures and traditions differ, in essence rules and structures may have developed differently and diverged over time, but their legal traditions and cultures overlap and are interrelated. The interaction of common laws with each other and their relationship with particular laws also create overlaps and blends that point to overlaps and blends of socio-cultures. Thus we can detect from these facts that the blending of socio-cultures and the birth of new socio-cultures is not difficult to imagine.

It is also easy to detect elements such as customary or religious laws within what look like simple mono-systems, be they civil law or common law ones. In addition, legal traditions (systems, families, circles) are in constant contact and confluence. One of the results of this is the birth of mixed legal systems, dual systems, hybrids or composites, and legal pluralisms. To study and analyse the working of any legal system requires an understanding of social and cultural contexts, but to study and analyse these hybrids requires an even greater appreciation of social and cultural nuances. Furthermore, all systems are shifting and in transition, and never closed. There is constant diffusion and infusion taking place.[5] Therefore, we must ask whether context and local significance are everything, and how they are to be evaluated in relation to comparative legal studies, especially in mixed legal systems.

Although until recently classical comparative law provided only blunt tools for understanding dynamic systems, multidisciplinary approaches have entered the horizon of modern-day comparative law as it gears itself up for this new task. And it is in the study of mixed legal systems that the two rival approaches can work together, analysing rules as well as analysing the impact of context.

The input of comparative law to the sociolegal is enormous, yet the challenges of socio-culture for comparatists are also vast. This can be demonstrated most fruitfully through an examination of complex mixed legal systems and legal pluralism.[6] This

[5] See the contributions in Sue Farran and others (eds), *The Diffusion of Law: The Movement of Law and Norms Around the World* (Ashgate 2015), and especially Esin Örücü, 'Infusion of the Diffused: Four Circles of Diffusion Infusing the Legal System of Turkey' in Farran and others (n 5).

[6] See generally the contributions in Esin Örücü (ed), *Mixed Legal Systems at New Frontiers* (Wildy, Simmonds, and Hill 2010).

chapter, after considering some of the mainstream and postmodern approaches within comparative law, will address some of these issues and end by asking: Whose laws, whose culture, whose tradition, and whose language? The dominant *hybriditygeist* of our day should help us shed some new light on these questions.[7]

I MAINSTREAM COMPARATIVE LAW FACED WITH SOCIOCULTURAL CHALLENGES

Until the last decades of the twentieth century, classical and mainstream comparative law remained rooted in positivism, legalism, and assumptions about legal centralism and monism, both in law and culture: one law and one culture in one jurisdiction. It also relied heavily on functional equivalence, regarded as the triumphant creation of Zweigert and Kötz.[8] The underlying idea of this approach is that social problems are shared, wherever the legal system is and of whatever colour, because we are all human and face similar problems; legal rules are there to solve these problems. Although various legal systems may provide different institutions and rules to do the same job, these institutions and rules can be regarded as functionally equivalent since they solve the same problem, though in different ways. Thus, the comparative lawyer needs to compare these solutions, whether they are to be found in law or elsewhere.

Simply put, the question to be answered by the functional-institutional approach is: Which institution in system *B* performs an equivalent function to the one under survey in system *A*? From the answer to this question, the concept of 'functional equivalence' emerges. The other side of the same coin is the problem-solving approach. Then the question becomes: How is a specific social or legal problem, encountered both in society A and in society B, resolved? That is, which legal or other institutions have developed to cope with this problem? In this way, the comparative lawyer seeks out institutions having the same role, that is, having 'functional comparability', or solving the same problem. What is undertaken here is also the 'functional juxtaposition' of comparable solutions. Functional enquiry corresponds to the utilitarian approach to comparative law. It is said that 'the fact that the problem is one and the same warrants the comparability'.[9] According to the functionalist-institutionalist approach, the above-mentioned questions, once answered, are in fact translated into functional questions.

7 The concepts of hybrid and hybridity have become popular today. The idea of hybridity marries legal theory, anthropology, sociology, and comparative law, while looking at the fluid complexity of the normative phenomenon, including state and nonstate norms. See Séan Patrick Donlan, 'Remembering: Legal Hybridity and Legal History' (2011) 2 *Comp L Rev* 1; Séan Patrick Donlan, 'To Hybridity and Beyond: Reflections on Legal and Normative Complexity' in Vernon Palmer, Mohamed Y Matter, and Anna Koppel (eds), *Mixed Legal Systems: East and West* (Ashgate 2015).

8 See K Zweigert and H Kötz, *An Introduction to Comparative Law* (Tony Weir tr, 3rd edn, OUP 1998).

9 M Schmitthoff, 'The Science of Comparative Law' (1939) 7 *CLJ* 94, 96 (quoting Max Salomon, *Grundlegung zur Rechtsphilosophie* (2nd edn, Rothschild 1925) 30).

To put the issue another way, we can say that the approach should be factual, that is, to be meaningfully comparable, institutions should be solving the same factual problem.[10] Thus a fact-based, in-depth research methodology needs to be used. Here, comparability benefits from findings of similarity since it can then further develop on *praesumptio similitudinis*. The starting point here is a 'concrete problem', with the focus being on the same facts. If the facts are not the same, then there is no comparability.

However, when institutional facts encountered in one legal system have no counterpart in the other legal system, problems start to arise, and the functional approach may not be satisfactory. If the countries under comparison have social orders, legal traditions, and cultures that are entirely different from one another, then the legal rules that regulate situations specific to only one of the societies must be separated from the legal rules that regulate shared situations. Once we accept this, then it can be claimed that comparative lawyers can only work in systems that are in some way related or similar.

The usefulness of the functional approach cannot be denied if what is meant by 'law' is a body of rules only, and if a micro-level comparison is directed at these rules, since a body of rules is created for the purpose of solving human problems most of which are indeed shared.[11] For instance, in the context of the European Union, where comparative law is a driving force with a decisive role in the harmonization process, the 'functional comparative analysis method' shifts the focus from the 'vertical' to the 'horizontal' and provides the potential for convergence of both the legal systems and the legal methods of the member states. This process leads to gradual and eventual legal integration, and therefore to build on similarities may be not only decisive, but also desirable. Within the EU, the legal systems concerned are either civil law or common law legal systems – or, we should say, predominantly so, since no legal system is purely homemade, and contamination is always present. Even if we accept that they are predominantly so, we have to remember that the new entrants to the Union come from another background and context, that is, the socialist legal family.

The functionalist approach, though harshly criticized by many contemporary comparatists, cannot be discarded in its entirety and is still of some use. Indeed, the 'functionalist method', in any of its forms, has recently gained a special place in common core studies in Europe, notwithstanding the fact that we know it is not the sole approach available to comparative law research.

II THE PLACE OF SOCIO-CULTURE IN COMPARATIVE LEGAL STUDIES TODAY

Where the comparison is of 'different' and 'context', the comparison must extend beyond functionally equivalent rules, and other approaches are required. For

10 Zweigert and Kötz (n 8).

11 Jaakko Husa, 'Farewell to Functionalism or Methodological Tolerance?' (2003) 67 *RabelsZ* 419.

instance, it is generally accepted that the functional-institutional approach may not solve the issue of comparability as between a Western legal system and a religious system or a developing legal system. Moreover, if there is a problem in one legal system that has no counterpart in another, the functional approach faces another dilemma. There are yet other fundamental criticisms of this approach: the limitation of subject areas that can be compared and the fact that many areas of law are beyond the scope of comparison since they are regarded as 'not lending themselves to comparison', being determined by specific histories, mores, ethical values, political ideologies, cultural differences, or religious beliefs. Another problem is that posed by 'one institution or rule with many functions'.

Our first move should be to change the name of our subject from comparative law to its rival, 'comparative legal studies', and take seriously the claims of sociologists and anthropologists pushing us to get involved with context, be it economic, social, cultural, or religious. The more our subject becomes involved with context, the closer it moves towards sociology of law, and therefore, the name 'comparative legal studies' becomes more appropriate.

When we deal with hybrids, especially those that are complex,[12] we realize that comparative lawyers who also want to undertake the function of the so-called regionalists must move ahead. They must use the new approaches that have been added to the methodologies of the comparative law of our day. Some of these so-called postmodern developments are deep-level comparative research, critical comparative research, sociolegal methodology, and global comparative law.

One way of achieving 'deep-level comparative law', itself a 'critical' approach, is by linking comparative law with legal philosophy and taking a more jurisprudential approach rather than a technical one, and by stressing that what is important is looking at the ideas underlying positive law. Thus, whether one is looking for differences or indeed similarities, one should 'go deeper'. Depth is the crucial point of departure.

In addition, law is seen as embedded in culture and a by-product of legal culture. We know that Patrick Glenn did not favour the term 'culture' but rather used 'tradition', which is non-formalistic, dynamic rather than static, and shows the value of time rather than place in understanding law.[13] He noted that those who practise sociology of law have put forward the notion of culture as a substitute for that of system. This, for him, appeared to be a particularly Western construction, which does not advance any idea of normativity.[14] Tradition links past and present, and hence points to both continuity and innovation.

[12] Esin Örücü, 'What Is a Mixed Legal System: Exclusion or Expansion?' in Örücü, *Mixed Legal Systems at New Frontiers* (n 6).

[13] See H Patrick Glenn, *Legal Traditions of the World: Sustainable Diversity in Law* (4th edn, OUP 2010) (hereafter Glenn, *LTW*).

[14] Ibid, 142.

Towards the end of the twentieth century, however, the law-as-culture view became a prominent feature of comparative law literature – even dividing the community of comparatists into two camps. The law-as-culture view assumes that the mutual influence of law and culture, understood broadly, shapes differences between legal systems. The extreme position even negates the usefulness of comparative law research. In any case, in order to carry out this kind of research, the comparatist must be embedded into the 'millieu and social setting' that shapes the lawmaker and the interpreter of the law. In this context, we can also refer to the connection between law, religion, and tradition. Depending on the society, a cultural and anthropological perspective might be required. This is definitely the case when one is dealing with complex hybrids and legal pluralisms, or in Werner Menski's words, 'pluri-legality'.[15]

The word 'culture' has at least two very broad meanings in this context, as it generally appears in works on comparative law: one looks at legal cultures as 'the natural objects of comparison', with elements ranging from 'facts about legal institutions' to 'various forms of behaviour' or 'more nebulous aspects of ideas, values, aspirations, and mentalities'. The second meaning is related to a research approach to dealing with legal culture, that is, a method and methodology. Yet culture has many other connotations. Culture cannot just be the object and the method of comparative law.[16] Ideas about culture exist on a number of levels. One level considers culture as a 'set of understandings and expectations in terms of which human beings orient their behaviour towards one another'.[17] This includes any acquired capabilities, such as knowledge, art, belief, morals, law, and custom. Thus, law is a subset, an aspect, of culture.

Furthermore, the more we are involved in studying hybridity in jurisdictions, the more we start regarding law as legal pluralism. Here the underlying assumptions are that the state is not the only actor that can make law and that the social order is typically based on a variety of sources of normativity. Although in the West theorists have traditionally assumed that all are governed by one law for all, and that one legal system is present in any one particular state, with laws that have universal relevance, in fact 'pluri-legal law' is marked by either exceptions that are made for specific groups of people (customarily the original inhabitants of specific national jurisdictions) or even a combination of general law and personal laws coexisting as part of the official law.[18] When this view is pursued, the mainstream comparatist's job

15 See Werner Menski, 'Legal Simulation: Law as a Navigational Tool for Decision-Making' (special lecture at Japan Coast Guard Academy, 2015) <http://harp.lib.hiroshima-u.ac.jp/jcga/metadata/12172>.

16 David Goldberg and Elspeth Attwooll, 'Legal Orders, Systemic Relationships and Cultural Characteristics: Towards Spectral Jurisprudence' in Esin Örücü, Elspeth Attwooll, and Sean Coyle (eds), *Studies in Legal Systems: Mixed and Mixing* (Kluwer International 1996).

17 Ibid, 321.

18 Menski says that 'in terms of numbers, this is the dominant pattern globally'. Menski (n 15).

becomes rather daunting, as a deeper knowledge of the societies under survey becomes more significant, but also more taxing.

All the above can be regarded as various approaches to 'deep-level comparative law' overlapping with 'critical comparative law'. The interest here is in the differences between legal systems, which are sometimes seen as being irreconcilable.[19]

In addition, a new field of study has been born, the so-called transnational law, indicating that law transcends national states. The growth of EU law, international law, and the law of international organizations, along with their transposition into and implementation under domestic law and the problems created therein, have widened the scope of comparative law towards new fields. These developments cover both the private and the public sphere. For instance, Mathias Siems suggests that 'integrated approaches are most likely to provide a [more] meaningful comparative picture'.[20] It can also be useful in order to more fully embrace the methods of other social sciences.[21]

Here we must remember, however, that whichever approach we have been using, the standard or the new, we always end up with the question, Why do we compare? Whether this question is asked in order to understand the similarities between different legal systems or the differences between similar legal systems, it is always there. Therefore, following the description of our findings, always must come the explanatory stage, which has always involved factors such as tradition, culture, economy, ideology, religion, and, if no other answer can be found, historical accidents. So in fact, we can say that nothing is entirely new but is merely put in different terminology today.

In fact, the most important question seems to have become: What is 'law'? Tamanaha writes:

> What is law? is a question that has beguiled and defied generations of theorists. . . . Despite a continuous conversation about the character and nature of law ever since [the ancient Greeks], theorists have not been able to agree on how to define or conceptualize law.[22]

The answer to this question is especially vital in approaching complex hybrids and legal pluralisms. The challenge is to the definition of law as a collection of rules made by rulers, in other words as just 'state law'. If law is plural, that is, if it is more than just state law, then the claim is that legal rules are about morality and ethics (natural law), about social norms and customs (always present wherever people live), and increasingly, the acceptance that international law and human rights (new natural law) must be considered as forms of law. Thus state law or 'official law' is

[19] See Pierre Legrand, *Fragments on Law-as-Culture* (Willink 1999). Mathias Siems sees this approach as doing more harm than good. See Mathias Siems, *Comparative Law* (CUP 2014) 114.

[20] Siems (n 19) 186.

[21] Ibid, 187.

[22] Brian Z Tamanaha, 'Law', *Oxford Encyclopedia of Legal History*, vol 4 (2009) 17.

not the only form of law. All the sources of law must coexist, and legal positivism must compete with forms of natural law and sociocultural norms. Lawyers of our day must wear 'plurality-sensitive lenses', which reveal law to be always dynamic.[23] Such an approach definitely brings with it challenges for mainstream comparatists.

III THE COMPLEXITIES FACING COMPARATIVE LEGAL STUDIES IN MIXED LEGAL SYSTEMS

Today, comparative legal studies does not necessarily acquire a new meaning, but new interest in old subjects is rekindled. For instance, there is definitely renewed interest in our old friend, legal transplants. Although their value is hotly debated, in practice, legal transplants, whether through the activities of the judiciary or the legislature, have gained momentum in our century.[24] Their place in legal development cannot be refuted and seems permanently established. The presence of mixed legal systems is further proof, if further proof is needed, of the constructive role legal transplants have played and continue to play, since one of the by-products of legal transplants is mixed legal systems. In the past three decades, new interest in mixed legal systems and collaborative research efforts with new projects have quadrupled.[25] That is why it is appropriate to call our era the era of the *hybriditygeist*.

When we conceived the idea of producing a volume titled *Studies in Legal Systems: Mixed and Mixing* back in 1996,[26] Patrick Glenn's contribution, 'Quebec: Mixité and Monism',[27] which eventually appeared as the first chapter of the volume, was pivotal. From then on, our paths crossed on many occasions related to this theme. In the past decade, this crossing of paths extended beyond Patrick to Jane Matthews-Glenn in a number of projects.[28] I would like here to reminisce on these collaborations and reiterate my indebtedness to both colleagues.

Recent research has shown that in contrast to ninety-eight so-called civil law mono-systems and forty-seven so-called common law mono-systems, there are ninety-five mixed legal systems, the ingredients of which are various combinations of different laws (civil, common, customary,[29] Islamic, Jewish, and so on). This is indicated by an analysis and classification of the 'world's legal systems' offered by the

[23] See Menski (n 15) 2–3, 13.

[24] See the contributions in Nicola Lupo and Lucia Scaffardi (eds), *Comparative Law in Legislative Drafting: The Increasing Importance of Dialogue Amongst Parliaments* (Eleven International 2014).

[25] See eg, various publications in the last decade: Vernon Valentine Palmer (ed), *Mixed Jurisdictions Worldwide: The Third Legal Family* (2nd edn, CUP 2012); Örücü, *Mixed Legal Systems at New Frontiers* (n 6); Sue Farran, Esin Örücü, and Séan Patrick Donlan (eds), *A Study of Mixed Legal Systems: Endangered, Entrenched or Blended* (Ashgate 2014); Palmer, Matter, and Koppel (n 7).

[26] Örücü, Attwooll, and Coyle (n 16).

[27] H Patrick Glenn, 'Quebec: Mixité and Monism' in Örücü, Attwooll, and Coyle (n 16).

[28] See Farran and others (n 5); Farran, Örücü, and Donlan (n 25).

[29] Siems further analyses customary law and points out that there are four types, following Ubink, van Rooij, and also Menski: (1) living customary law, (2) textbook customary law, (3) codified customary law, and (4) judicial customary law. See Siems (n 19) 86–87.

University of Ottawa.[30] For comparative lawyers, however, a comprehensive study of 'mixed legal systems' or hybrids is a complicated task and a challenge both conceptually and in its many contexts. Yet such studies can make significant contributions not only to comparative law studies, but to sociolegal studies as well.

Comparative law teaching, study, and research by domestic scholars in Asia and Africa flourished in the postcolonial period. Earlier, it was Western comparatists who undertook such research and teaching. On the whole, this is the case even today. Yet some of these Western comparatists are now looking into what used to be called regional studies as well as jurisdictions that were not covered by mainstream comparative law. This shift is reflected in the renewed interest in the study of mixed jurisdictions and other mixed legal systems as well as legal pluralisms.[31]

Though the future of comparative law, or better still, comparative legal studies, is firmly established, we are in the process of renewing its image by being involved in areas other than private law, in regions other than the Western world (previously covered by so-called regional or area studies), and in embracing a multidisciplinary approach that befits our globalizing age, where understanding the 'other' has become the *sine qua non* of understanding ourselves.

If it is indeed the case that there are ninety-five mixed legal systems in the world and the majority of these are not just combinations of civil law and common law alone, then the whole picture changes. Looking at legal norms of the underlays and the overlays will not be enough in order to understand the legal systems at work in these jurisdictions. For instance, in Southeast Asia, where complex hybrids abound, Islamic, Chinese, Hindu, indigenous customary law, and European legal norms all are present and play their roles, both as to language, tradition, and culture.[32] The term 'multi-jural' has been used to indicate the coexistence of a number of legal systems or subsystems within a broader normative legal order to which they adhere. This is as opposed to 'bi-jural' systems where two components exist, such as in Quebec or indeed the EU (ie the common law and civil law).[33]

Some of the new approaches, the so-called postmodern developments seen earlier, such as deep-level comparative research, critical comparative research, sociolegal methodology, and global comparative law, are more appropriate for the study of mixed legal systems, especially the ones that we can call 'complex' rather than 'simple', and legal pluralisms.

Sociolegal approaches to comparative legal studies, which use quantitative data, qualitative data, or a mixture of both, also replace the formal understanding of 'law' (traditional comparative law) with a sociolegal one and use the term 'legal culture', looking at how law and society are linked in a causal way. Here, we also come across

30 N Mariani and G Fuentes, *World Legal Systems* (Wilson & Lafleur 2000) 16–17.

31 See, for instance, the sources cited in n 25.

32 See Glenn, *LTW* (n 13).

33 See Siems (n 19) 89.

the 'mirror' theory (or theories),[34] which assumes that law reflects the society in question; in other words, that there is a symmetrical relationship between law and society because law is a product of a society's history as well as its present, rather than adhering to the view of law as evolving in an independent, dysfunctional way related to the initiative of outsiders, minority groups, or elites. The mirror theory becomes rather problematic, however, in view of major transplants that have formed the very legal systems of our hybrids

In light of all this, the final and pivotal question must be: Whose laws, whose culture, whose tradition, and whose language?

IV WHOSE LAWS, WHOSE CULTURE, WHOSE TRADITION, AND WHOSE LANGUAGE?

In considering this question, and in trying to answer it, we can start by casting a brief look at Turkey. After the collapse of the Ottoman Empire, legal evolution in the Turkish Republic was instigated by a strong desire to become Western and contemporary; still today, rapid law reforms are underway in order to fulfil the requirements of the European Union's *acquis communautaire*, in the hopes of joining the Union. Rather than being homegrown, law reform has taken place through a succession of imports from the civilian world and has required major translation work.

Turkey is not a mixed jurisdiction in the classical sense, nor does it have an overt mixed legal system, much less one that is a mix of civil law and common law. However, it is mixed in two other significant senses. In the first sense, it has a synthetic and eclectic legal system, legislatively reconstructed (initially between 1926 and 1930) by receiving, adapting, and mixing laws from Switzerland, Germany, Italy, and France, and melting them in the Turkish pot to form the overlay: the civilian legal system. In fact, the legal system of the Turkish Republic has the appearance of belonging to the civilian tradition *in toto*. In the second sense, the legal system is a mix of these diverse laws with the lives of a people, the majority of whom have values and demands that reflect a different socio-culture, one related to a past element of the legal system, that of the Ottoman Empire – all its laws erased by the Turkish Republic – and significantly different from the socio-cultures represented by the incoming laws. The Ottoman legal system was legally pluralistic, enveloped in Islamic law until 1839, and thereafter until its collapse, a legally pluralist mixed legal system with added ingredients borrowed from the French system. It is this unique composite that makes it possible to consider the

[34] On mirror theories, see William Ewald, 'Comparative Jurisprudence (II): The Logic of Legal Transplants' (1995) 43 *Am J Comp L* 489. The reflection is of 'different (non-legal!) values: geography, religion, the *Weltgeist*, market economics, power-relations, the interest of the dominant class, or whatever.' Ibid, 493.

Turkish legal system 'a covert mix', a novel hybrid, as it now tries to accommodate Islamic law under the guise of 'tradition'.[35]

Thus, this synthetic and eclectic 'modern layer' of the Turkish legal system is the ultimate and predominant one, reflecting the civilian and laic nature of the law and embodying the mixing layers of the system. In fact, one can talk of the 'mixed modern layer' or 'modern layers' rather than a single 'modern layer' of law. The interaction between the modern layers is of utmost importance for the functioning of the legal system, but so is the interaction between the modern layers and the underlying layers, such as the traditional and religious. Whatever the future developments and shape of the mixture, both the legal and sociocultural systems will remain in a relationship that is mixed. Let us note then that the laws today are thoroughly Turkish, ninety years after their reception. The legal culture is civilian with a hint of Islam now; the traditions that were originally Swiss, German, Italian, and French have merged and mixed with what was there to become Turkish. The language is Turkish, which is unrelated to the source European languages, not having Latin as its base.

In all mixed legal systems, be they simple or classical ones (that is, a combination of civil law and common law) or complex ones (with more than two ingredients), there are at least two different legal cultures and traditions in operation. These ingredients reflect different socio-cultures that impact the legal cultures, traditions, laws, and languages. Thus each outcome is unique as to its past, present, and future.

If laws are reflections of legal cultures and if legal cultures are part of the general culture, then in a jurisdiction where at least two cultures – but in many cases a large number more – coexist and intermingle, what type of connection can be envisaged between law and culture? Furthermore, when at least two languages – but in many cases a large number more – are functioning in a given jurisdiction, we would have to query the relationship between law and language. In complex mixed legal systems, the challenge is both sociocultural and legal-cultural. Can we in fact talk about law-as-culture in such cases? And if we can, then are we going to agree that mixedness is the culture itself? How do we analyse and understand this mixedness in cultures? How do we go about deconstructing and then reconstructing such mixities in terms of language, tradition, and culture?

There are deep and contentious questions that are generally asked by comparative law scholars which have special significance in a hybridity context. For instance, 'if law lives in and through language, what happens to it when it is transferred into another language?'[36] If the structure of a language influences, or

[35] See Esin Örücü, 'How Far Can Religion Be Accommodated in Laic Turkish Family Law?' in Jane Mair and Esin Örücü (eds), *The Place of Religion in Family Law: A Comparative Search* (CEFL/Intersentia 2011). See also Esin Örücü, 'Turkey's Synthetic Civilian Tradition in a "Covert" Mix with Islam as Tradition: A Novel Hybrid?' in Palmer, Matter, and Koppel (n 7).

[36] Bernhard Grossfeld, *The Strength and Weakness of Comparative Law* (Tony Weir tr, Clarendon 1990) 101.

even determines, the mode and content of thought, might it not be that any one language can only express certain thoughts, and that these thoughts differ from culture to culture and language to language? More importantly, how strong is the link between the law or a legal system and the language of its statutes? Maybe even more vital are the questions related to capturing a tradition, since traditions can be reinvented and reconstructed. Since tradition and time should be considered together, how do we capture the past? When we know that there can be bureaucratic reconstruction of traditions, how is a tradition to be protected or promoted? Such questions are often discussed by linguists, sociologists, and anthropologists, and rarely by legal comparatists.

Glenn saw 'mixed jurisdictions' as places of confluence of common laws, and 'ongoing interdependence', places where we see an unsuccessful 'process of exclusive appropriation of one of the common laws'.[37] However, he also pointed out that 'with the increase in importance in the world of overlapping laws',[38] their significance may decline, possibly because more and more legal systems will become mixed. Thus, common laws were, and will continue to be, contemporary means of 'reconciliation and equilibrium'.[39] Therefore, we can say that in any mixed legal system, whether simple or complex, different traditions and cultures living in reconciliation and equilibrium will make up the culture of the mixed legal system, and finally either become entrenched or create a blend.[40] Although Vernon Palmer says that 'a mixed jurisdiction is the legal expression of unfinished cultural aspirations',[41] it could also be claimed that, unless these are systems in transition and we are talking about ongoing mixes, a mixed legal system can very well be settled and blended, thus creating a new culture of 'mixedness'.

European Commissioner Jean Dondelinger noted that 'cultural diversity [in Europe] forms the basis of our common cultural identity'.[42] Thus, standardization and uniformity run counter to this identity. We may adopt this claim that European culture is diversity for our hybrids: hybridity is the basis of their common cultural identities. In a mixed legal system, an ongoing permeability between the masses of laws derived from a number of sources that make up the legal tradition, also creates a unique socio-culture. Here the values are not tied to one particular past culture but have formed a blend, that is, the hybrid legal and socio-culture.

The task of teasing out this type of culture, which is hyphenated or with divided identities, multidimensional, and a composite or hybrid, will fall not on the shoulders of comparatists alone but will require the help of anthropologists and

37 Glenn, *OCL* (n 1) 119.

38 Ibid.

39 Ibid, 143.

40 For an analysis of entrenchment and blending, see 'Introductory Overview' and 'Endnote to Mixed Legal Systems: Endangered, Entrenched, Blended or Muddled?' in Farran, Örücü, and Donlan (n 25).

41 Palmer (n 25) 31.

42 Council Notice (EC) 90/C 90/01 Written Questions with Answers [1990] OJ C90/4.

sociologists. In fact, many laws are not even based on geographical boundaries, such as the 'Gypsy law' of the Romani peoples or the laws of the Quaker communities, which can be regarded as a variant of hybridity. Are future comparatists then to become socio-comparatists or even anthropologist-comparatists in order to understand and analyse the increasing number of mixed legal systems and legal pluralisms? Or should we be supporting 'combined comparative legal studies' and always work with proper sociologists, anthropologists, or psychologists, as the case may demand?

Even in 'classic' simple mixed jurisdictions there exists a civil law and a common law element. According to the law-as-culture approach, these two elements represent two different cultures and mentalities and are normally presented as existing in two separate jurisdictions such as the English and French legal systems, presumably as mono-systems and presumably pure. Now, this in itself is questionable since it has been demonstrated by many researchers, and particularly by legal historians, that even these two legal systems are mixed to some extent. Be that as it may, when institutions from these two diverse legal cultures – or legal traditions to use Glenn's preferred vocabulary – coexist in a jurisdiction such as Quebec, what can we be trying to explain? Should we present the picture as one of conflict or competition between the two diverse cultures and languages, or as an amalgam, a blend of some sort? Are we talking of an English Quebec and a French Quebec, or, with the passage of time, has the Quebec legal system become just the mixed system of Quebec?[43] For Glenn, for instance, structured and unstructured *mixité* characterized Quebec throughout its history. To him, the Quebec experience indicated that 'law is tolerant of high levels of complexity', various types of *mixité* that exist are 'capable of co-existence and mutual reinforcement', and *mixité* may extend through time.[44] Ongoing *mixité* preserves the sources of the mix.[45] The element of time in tradition then becomes the signifying touchstone for the outcome.

Another example to be teased out is Jersey.[46] Essentially a francophone country, after 1945 it underwent a linguistic transition from French to English that had an impact on Jersey law, which is also reflected in 'the linguistic balance amongst islanders'.[47] In such a situation, is the best way forward to bolster the 'mixedness' and give it stability and permanent status, as was done through the establishment of a Jersey legal education system started by the Institute of Law? How close are people to their laws?

What about jurisdictions such as the Island Republic of Vanuatu, where on many of its islands different languages are spoken? Although English, French, and Bislama

43 See Sophie Morin, 'Quebec: First Impressions Can Be Misleading' in Farran, Örücü, and Donlan (n 25) 165–82. See also Glenn, 'Quebec: Mixité and Monism' (n 27).

44 Glenn, 'Quebec: Mixité and Monism' (n 27) 16.

45 Ibid.

46 See Philip Bailhache, 'Jersey: Avoiding the Fate of the Dodo' in Farran, Örücü, and Donlan (n 25).

47 Ibid, 112.

(the national language that is a form of pidgin Franglais) are the official languages, there are more than 100 indigenous languages in these islands, and most residents speak at least 3 languages.[48] What can be the connecting factor there between culture, tradition, law, and language? Sue Farran suggests that a new mix may emerge, now taking into consideration customary laws (one aspect of *kastom*) in line with constitutional aspirations. She indicates that 'there are examples of pragmatic mixing taking place to address particular needs'.[49] The outcome of this mixing will illustrate once more the sociocultural challenges for comparative legal studies in mixed legal systems.

Can we say that there is an overarching but not necessarily a dominant culture of mixedness in every mixed legal system, maybe with its own languages, traditions, and cultures, preserving the sources of the mix but now blended into a novel entity? What about Turkey, where, as we saw, alien laws and cultures blended to create the Turkish legal system, with most inhabitants – even practicing lawyers – not even aware of the sources of the laws? Does this 'covert mix' demonstrate new inroads into the relationship between law, language, culture, and tradition, and justify once again the question: Whose laws, whose culture, whose tradition, whose language?

Think of the tasks facing comparative lawyers of our day looking at the increasing number of complex hybrids and deep legal pluralisms.[50] This may be 'irritating and messy', as Menski concludes, but it is 'an essential component' of comparative legal studies.[51] Comparative legal studies in mixed legal systems surely face sociocultural challenges that are tough but all the more exciting.

48 See Sue Farran, 'Pacific Punch: Tropical Flavors of Mixedness in the Island Republic of Vanuatu' in Palmer, Matter, and Koppel (n 7).

49 Ibid, 138.

50 Werner Menski talks of a 'plurality of pluralities' (POP), which is his nomenclature for deep legal pluralism. The challenge he points to is ensuring 'that local values and norms match the "official law"'. See Menski (n 15) 15.

51 Ibid, 21.

5

Breaking Barriers in Comparative Law

Michele Graziadei[*]

I PATRICK'S PATH

H Patrick Glenn's works have contributed to the renewal of comparative law studies in several ways. A major, lasting contribution has been the revitalization of the notion of 'tradition'. This is the cornerstone of his *Legal Traditions of the World*, the textbook that grew out of his courses at McGill University to become a standard reference for comparative law teaching around the world.[1] The intuition that the notion of 'tradition' – in the plural – could become the intellectual frame to compare a variety of laws under a shared, common roof has been fruitful and productive beyond expectation.

A fitting example is the use of the notion of tradition by the Treaty on the European Union. The Treaty speaks of 'tradition' with respect to fundamental rights 'as guaranteed by the European Convention for the Protection of Human Rights and Fundamental Freedoms and as they result from the constitutional traditions common to the Member States' recognizing that they shall therefore constitute general principles of EU law.[2] The Preamble of the EU's Charter of Fundamental Rights and Article 52(4) of the same document also reference that key notion to the same effect.[3] The European Court of Justice has relied on the notion of tradition to adjudicate over a hundred high-profile cases.[4] Still, the potential of the notion is

* I wish to thank Amy Cohen for her comments on the draft of this chapter. The usual disclaimer applies.

1 The fourth edition of the book was translated into Italian: see H Patrick Glenn, *Tradizioni giuridiche nel mondo: La sostenibilità della differenza* (Sergio Ferlito tr, Il Mulino 2011). For the relevance of Glenn's scholarship for legal historians, see Thomas Duve, 'Legal Traditions: A Dialogue between Comparative Law and Comparative Legal History' (2018) 6 *Comp Leg Hist* 15.

2 Consolidated Version of the Treaty on the Functioning of the European Union [2012] OJ C326/47, art 6(3).

3 Charter of Fundamental Rights of the European Union [2007] OJ C303/01. See Sabino Cassese, 'The "Constitutional Traditions Common to the Member States" of the European Union' [2017] *Rivista Trimestrale di Diritto Pubblico* 939.

4 Michele Graziadei and Riccardo de Caria, 'The "Constitutional Traditions Common to the Member States" in the Case Law of the Court of Justice of the European Union: Judicial Dialogue at Its Finest' [2017] *Rivista Trimestrale di Diritto Pubblico* 949. After the publication of this article, the ECJ

not exhausted. In 2018, the European Law Institute thus launched a collective project: 'To identify the source of Common Constitutional Traditions in Europe; their content; their relationship with national identity; whether they are an autonomous source of European law and the way in which they emerge as common to Member States and are expressed as such.'[5] Inevitably, this project will contribute to further highlighting the operative dimensions of the concept, showing why it is linked to a pluralistic approach to the development of law, and to the evolution of the law in the European Union.[6]

This is just one example, among many, of Patrick Glenn's ability to cast light on the direction of legal change, and to draw attention to the need to be prepared for it.[7] *Legal Traditions of the World* is the result of a sustained reflection on comparative law, focused on the current epistemological conditions of this academic subject. The ideas that lie at the root of that work were not widely shared in academic circles when they were first expressed. Patrick had to break down more than a few intellectual barriers to present comparative law neither as a complement nor as a supplement, to positivism, but as an alternative integrative enterprise, unfolding at the world level, and yet deeply interested in local knowledge. In this, he was all but a traditionalist, and this is also why, as Neil Walker rightly notes in his contribution to this collection, for Patrick, comparative law was always a subject in part defined against itself. Patrick coherently illustrated this vision over the years, and his wonderfully rich, thought provoking, and inspiring books on the cosmopolitan state[8] and on the common laws[9] of the world are powerful statements of it, along with the book chapters and scholarly articles in which he presented that vision.[10]

referenced the notion once more in the all important Case C-42/17, *Criminal Proceedings Against MAS and MB* (ECJ 5 December 2017) (*Taricco II*), para 53.

5 Sabino Cassese, Mario Comba, and Jeffrey Jowell, 'Freedom of Expression as a Common Constitutional Tradition in Europe', 2018, (*European Law Institute*) <www.europeanlawinstitute.eu/projects-publications/current-projects-feasibility-studies-and-other-activities/current-projects/cct-in-europe>.

6 In this context, the dynamic nature of 'tradition' vindicates Glenn's reconstruction of that notion. Indeed, as David Nelken makes clear in Part I of his chapter, for Glenn, '. . . tradition is more an engine of change than a guarantee of permanence . . . .' David Nelken, Chapter 8 in this volume. In the EU context, reference to 'constitutional traditions common to the Member States' plays a conciliatory role that is fully in line with Glenn's elaboration of the notion of tradition. Martin Krygier's chapter in this book shows, however, why thinking of law in terms of traditions will not always be conducive to the mutual accommodations among legal and social orders that Glenn intended to favour. See Martin Krygier, Chapter 6 in this volume.

7 H Patrick Glenn, 'Quel droit comparé?' (2013) 43 *RDUS* 23.

8 H Patrick Glenn, *The Cosmopolitan State* (OUP 2013) (hereafter Glenn, *TCS*).

9 H Patrick Glenn, *On Common Laws* (OUP 2005).

10 I am thinking in particular of H Patrick Glenn, 'Choice of Logic and Choice of Laws' in H Patrick Glenn and Lionel D Smith (eds), *Law and the New Logics* (CUP 2017); H Patrick Glenn, 'A Transnational Concept of Law' in Mark Tushnet and Peter Cane (eds), *The Oxford Handbook of Legal Studies* (OUP 2005); H Patrick Glenn, 'Are Legal Traditions Incommensurable?' (2001) 49 *Am J Comp L* 491; H Patrick Glenn, 'The Capture, Reconstruction and Marginalization of Custom' (1997) 45 *Am J Comp L* 613.

Patrick soon recognized that an unprecedented level of pluralism and cosmopolitanism was to shape the law in the twenty-first century. From the protection of the environment, to the management of health risks, from the regulation of labour conditions, to access to credit and payment systems, nearly all spheres of social and economic life are now affected by the tendency to inscribe the local dimensions of communities and individuals in the wider legal landscape, existing beyond and across state borders. Other factors as well work in the same direction, such as the direct or indirect influence of religious laws on individuals and their social life. The law of the state is thus interdependent with competing sources of authority. This dynamic is occurring on such a large scale because, contrary to what Kant and other thinkers suggested later on in the nineteenth century, no world government is established to rule the world in our time (and the demand for it has beaten a full retreat). The recent wave of nationalism that is reverberating around the world confirms this diagnosis. Highly contradictory and fragmented sets of regimes thus prevail beyond the state, as the effect of an integration process in which politics is not first in line.[11] It is mostly powerful socio-economic players, along with the availability of rapidly evolving technologies, that have driven globalization and have determined its concrete content. Politics and the state have adapted to this evolution, which has been supported by the growing weight of international and supranational institutions, and more widely by the rise of new global actors. The consequence is that the concrete form of globalization of law that we have is mostly a spill-over effect of particular developments occurring in various directions, and across many fields, in response to special interests and particular problems. This movement was matched at the constitutional and international level with increased convergence around certain values that are now more largely shared around the world.[12] The quest for justice, however, is far from being exhausted by the reference to these values, and is still precarious and uncertain in a world in which the distribution of wealth remains disproportionate both across countries and within them. The issue of justice on a world scale is thus emerging as a central subject for a number of academic disciplines, including political philosophy,[13] economics,[14] and international law.[15]

Within this landscape, two opposite representations of the law, arising in different arenas – from the field of international relationships and transnational commerce, to the more mundane areas of family law, property law, contracts and torts, administrative

[11] Gunther Teubner (ed), *Global Law without a State* (Dartmouth 1997) 3–28.

[12] See, eg, Dennis Davis, Alan Richter, and Cheryl Saunders (eds), *An Inquiry into the Existence of Global Values Through the Lens of Comparative Constitutional Law* (Bloomsbury 2015). For further considerations on this point, see John Bell, Chapter 3 in this volume.

[13] Chris Armstrong, *Global Distributive Justice: An Introduction* (CUP 2012).

[14] Dani Roderick, *The Globalization Paradox: Democracy and the Future of the World Economy* (WW Norton 2012).

[15] Frank Garcia, *Global Justice and International Economic Law: Three Takes* (CUP 2013); John Linarelli, Margot E Salomon, and Muthucumaraswamy Sornarajah, *The Misery of International Law: Confrontations with Injustice in the Global Economy* (OUP 2018).

law, criminal law, and so on – have come to dominate thinking about the law in the contemporary age, namely legal monism and legal pluralism. The great merit of Patrick's work was to show how both have been transformed by the impact of the transnational and cosmopolitan dimensions of the law. Patrick knew that in many jurisdictions legal monism remains, for most lawyers, *the* framework to think about the law. Legal monism is still, to many, the orthodoxy, but for legions of lawyers in many jurisdictions, legal pluralism is now the most promising intellectual frame and the way to meet the challenge posed by the multiplicity of competing legal orders, coexisting at the same time, over the same territory. Furthermore, legal pluralism is often considered the best option to understand the dilemmas of individual action under the law, when the law makes contradictory demands. Nonetheless, Glenn also knew that these two frameworks of analysis do not exhaust the legal imagination, nor capture all that is possible and that is real. In the following pages, I thus intend to follow his steps, and pay tribute to his scholarship by highlighting the role that comparative law, legal linguistics, and legal anthropology play in shaping new thinking about the law in our age. Should the reader detect familiar features in what is presented later, this is because Glenn's seminal ideas have become a common reference point for a very wide audience around the world, well beyond the lecturing halls of McGill University.

In the following pages, I will first turn to the two alternative poles of contemporary jurisprudence, namely legal monism and legal pluralism, to offer my take on them. I will then consider what contributions comparative law, studies of law and language, and studies of law and anthropology can jointly make to cast light on the evolution of the law in the present age, which is markedly more pluralistic and cosmopolitan than many would have ever predicted, or would have ever wished.

II LEGAL MONISM OR THE LAW OF THE STATE

Legal monism is an analytical framework that is based on the recognition of the notion of sovereign power, and of a sovereign state, from which all law emanates. We know the predicament: for each territory, there is a sovereign state and, in that territory, a population governed by the organs of the state through the law, for whom the state is responsible. The applicable law is the expression of the will of the state, as enforced by its agents.

With the advent of democracies, the will of the sovereign was turned into the will of the people, and the idea of democratic self-government was then upheld on the basis of democratic constitutions. The assumptions upholding this framework remained the same, however, and legal monism was not abandoned, although the transition to democratic governments posed several serious and, to an extent, unresolved challenges to it.

The structure of the state is not the same everywhere. A federal state would have multiple levels of government, and lawyers working in a federal jurisdiction are surely less prone to ignoring the possibility of multiple norms emanating from various centres of power. In the federal context, no general will of the people is to be implemented, as no centralized and homogeneous polity exists.[16] Nonetheless, legal monism often remains the principal tool of the trade, insofar as the law as an emanation of the state is still considered to be a generally accepted, legitimate means of government.

The law of the state is applicable to the generality of citizens, on the basis of the political bonds constituting citizenship. In this sense, it is of universal application and neutral as a means of government, given the formal equality of all citizens before the law. Often, the legitimacy of the law of the state was at first secured by the assumption of divine sanction of political power, then by its democratic legitimation under more inclusive democratic constitutions. The legitimacy of the law of the state also depended on the notion that state boundaries mark the limits of state power. This shaped the dynamic of international law, which was traditionally conceived as the law concerning the relations between states, each state being sovereign in its own territory.

The virtue of this great framework was its ideal simplicity. Apparently, the implication of this model was that the unity of the state implied the unity, rather than the multiplicity, of the law. Here I must stop to notice a first paradoxical fact, which Glenn duly emphasized in *The Cosmopolitan State*.[17] This ideal was never fully achieved in the old days of absolutistic rulers and legal regimes. The law of France, for example, was never completely unified under the King of France. During the *ancien régime*, customs of various kinds existed outside the domain of state law and thus posed a challenge to its effectiveness. State law did not claim to govern the life of French subjects in every respect. Apart from customs, religious laws and religious courts had a strong hold on the life of individuals and communities.[18] One has to wait for the collapse of the *ancien régime*, and the instauration of the Napoleonic rule, to actually have the monopoly of state law established over every other kind of law in every domain of social life, and even then custom (and canon law) did not completely disappear.[19]

Legal monism did not rule out the possibility of the evolution of a universal law for the entire world. Rather, it assumed that the development of such laws would have required the creation of a single sovereign and a single legal community constituted at the world level. Short of a world government, legal monism allowed for a law governing the relationship among the states, but could not conceive secular laws applicable across the entire world, which were not sanctioned by state authorities or resulting from state practices.

16 For penetrating reflections on this point, see H Patrick Glenn, 'Conflicting Laws in a Common Market? The NAFTA Experiment' (2001) 76 *Chi-Kent Rev* 1789.

17 Glenn, *TCS* (n 8) 49–50.

18 A case has been made for the productive effects of this duality: see Harold J Berman, *Law and Revolution* (Harvard University Press 1983); Paolo Prodi, *Una storia della giustizia* (Il Mulino 2000).

19 Cf H Patrick Glenn, 'The Capture, Reconstruction and Marginalization of "Custom"' (1997) 45 *Am J Comp L* 613.

III FACTORS UNDERMINING LEGAL MONISM

Over time, several factors undermined legal monism as a working hypothesis. The list of these factors is long.[20] Some of them have been more prominent than others. With respect to the European context, the rise of democratic governments and the development of transnational economic relationships probably have had a decisive impact. Beyond Europe and the Western world, legal monism has been defeated – if it ever ruled – by a more complex set of circumstances. They include the sheer complexity of the law on the ground and a persistent gap between the authority of the state and its laws on one side, and those followed by communities and individuals on the other side. In colonial times, the fault line also reflected the existence of unequal legal regimes established by the metropolitan state and its organs towards individuals and groups in the colonies.

The first set of factors I mentioned with respect to the European scenario, that is, the rise of democracy and the development of transnational economic relationships, show the working of forces pulling all in the same direction. These forces go together with the recognition of an unprecedented level of personal autonomy.[21] Democracy brings with it a new kind of pluralism, because democracy thrives thanks to the political and the legal recognition of a plurality of values and opinions.[22] Democratic constitutions accommodate a plurality of values, which are often in conflict. They preserve the possibility of finding an equilibrium among them, without suppressing one or the other. A well-known instance of this dynamic is the balancing exercises that are characteristic of all areas of the law under contemporary democratic governments. Indeed, the strength of contemporary democracies comes from the competence they have in handling such conflicts by upholding a plurality of values despite the tensions existing among them. Democracies declare and defend the equality of citizens before the law, but they also allow for individual diversity and personal and collective autonomy. A vibrant democracy must therefore be able to accommodate diversity under its constitution. This leads to a new kind of 'open' legal monism, which is inclusive rather than exclusive, and pluralistic in terms of citizens' participation in democratic life and life trajectories.[23] As

[20] For a brilliant, in-depth analysis of some of them, see Gunnar Folke Schuppert, Chapter 14 in this volume.

[21] The early diagnosis of this movement is linked to the name of HS Maine: see Henry Sumner Maine, *Ancient Law* (London 1861) 170 ('from status to contract'). On its present value, see Katharina S Schmidt, 'Henry Maine's "Modern Law": From Status to Contract and Back Again?' (2017) 65 *Am J Comp L* 147. For a revealing critical analysis of the contradictions in Maine's thought, see Veronica Corcodel, 'The Governance Implications of Comparative Legal Thinking: On Henry Maine's Jurisprudence and Liberal Imperialism' in Horatia Muir Watt and Diego P Fernández Arroyo (eds), *Private International Law and Global Governance* (OUP 2014).

[22] Harold Laski, a long-time correspondent of Oliver W Holmes Jr and other legal realists, was one of the most influential political thinkers who defended a pluralistic view of society. Since his time, political pluralism has branched off in many directions.

[23] Cf Marie-Claire Foblets, Michele Graziadei, and Alison Dundes Renteln (eds), *Personal Autonomy in Plural Societies: A Principle and Its Paradoxes* (Routledge 2018); Kyriaki Topidi (ed), *Normative Pluralism and Human Rights* (Routledge 2018).

such, it allows for reasonable accommodations, as well as principled compromise over ethical dilemmas, such as those relating to abortion or end-of-life decisions. Instances of pluralism within the framework of state law concern labour conflicts, citizen participation in administrative decisions about, for example, environmental governance, the regulation of matters relating to the freedom of religion, and so on. The framework of state law in modern times is needed to guarantee the possibility of such pluralism by establishing the equality of all citizens before the law. The rise of democratic governments in areas of the world where large parts of the population were excluded from government and did not enjoy full citizenship, or even full legal recognition as subjects of rights, eventually involved a turn towards a more inclusive and pluralistic approach to citizenship and democracy. The recent constitutional changes of countries like, Colombia, Peru, and Ecuador (which introduced the recognition of indigenous rights), for example, are telling in this respect. To be sure, at first democracy was not for all and everybody. Democracy in the United States did not mean equal rights for all for the greatest part of the history of the Union. The end of racial segregation and the emergence of the civil rights movement is still within memory for many US citizens. Canada's appalling assimilationist policies towards indigenous peoples were abandoned only gradually beginning in the 1970s. Significant gestures towards truth and reconciliation for past abuses are much more recent. Closer to home, in Europe, constitutions banning discrimination based on a variety of grounds became common only after the end of the Second World War. The job is clearly not finished if we consider gender-related issues.[24]

International regimes securing the respect of individual rights beyond the national sphere have a part in this story. National courts are often unwilling to secure justice in the presence of violations that are not perceived as such by national authorities, or which are perpetrated by actors protected by the state. This explains why, when the promotion of universally recognized values is in danger, the international community can consider intervention to support or – in extreme cases, such as those concerning the prosecution of war crimes – replace domestic judges, particularly in securing justice. This essentially means that even constitutional courts today may not be the ultimate arbiters of a dispute in which such values are involved. Indeed, constitutional courts and other supreme courts in Europe have gradually learned to defer to the jurisprudence of the European Court of Human Rights. Within the ambit of the European Union, constitutional courts have also begun to refer questions for a preliminary ruling to the European Court of Justice. The recognition of these obligations is inevitably a factor of crisis for any view of the law that considers state law as the only source of legal authority.[25] Unsurprisingly, political leaders tend to deny this reality in the name of national sovereignty, as happened when the European Court of Human Rights delivered important rulings

[24] Ruth Rubio-Marín, 'Women in Europe and in the World: The State of the Union 2016' (2016) 14 *ICON* 545.

[25] Sabino Cassese, 'The Globalization of Law' (2005) 37 *NYU J Int'l Law & Pol* 973.

in controversial cases, such as those concerning, for example, the voting rights of prisoners in the United Kingdom.[26]

As mentioned earlier, the second great force at work to undermine legal monism is the development of transnational economic relationships. The decision to end those beggar-thy-neighbour economic policies that were among the causes of the Second World War was a decisive step in this direction. The establishment of these relationships owes a great deal to the intrinsic means that private law has to develop cross-border interaction.[27] Although the state, through its organs, enforces private law as well as public law, private law has historically enjoyed a degree of autonomy from the state, being the expression of personal and group autonomy, namely of an independent capacity for self-organization. Indeed, human societies existed for millennia without resorting to state organization. Only under totalitarian dictatorships, in a war economy, or under similar regimes, does the state tend to absorb and suppress private law, as it did, for example, in the Soviet Union. As history shows, such regimes are exceptional, precisely because they suppress a capacity for autonomy that is inherent in individuals and communities. Apart from extreme cases represented by totalitarian regimes, private law arrangements are binding beyond the state, except when they are contrary to the local legal order, typically represented by *ordre public* rules. Drawing attention to this self-sustaining capacity of private law does not imply that private law is politically neutral or value free. Many private law rules reflect specific political arrangements, or certain sets of values, that are often common to public laws. Nonetheless, even when it pursues specific political goals or values, private law relies on mechanisms of decentralized decision-making that distinguish it from public law, a feature that is still evident beyond the decline of the idealised, classical versions of that distinction.[28]

The full implications of the establishment of networks of international economic relations for the state and its monopoly of legislative power were already clear to eighteenth-century thinkers, who reflected on the rise of international currency markets. They are set out with great clarity by Montesquieu in his *Spirit of the Laws*, a work that is a milestone in the history of comparative law studies and political science.[29] In that masterpiece, Montesquieu noticed that bills of exchange secured, for the first time in history, the possibility of transferring money from one

26 The leading case is *Hirst v UK (No. 2)* ECHR 2005-IX 681. It is significant that the UK judiciary distanced itself from the reaction of the government in this matter.

27 Daniel Caruso makes the point that '[i]n this context, private law is a central subject in globalization discourse, and contributes in many ways to the decline of the state'. Daniela Caruso, 'Private Law and State-Making in the Age of Globalization' (2006) 38 *NYU J Int'l Law & Pol* 1, 3.

28 For an instructive analysis, see Duncan Kennedy, 'The Stages of the Decline of the Public/Private Distinction' (1982) 130 *U Pa L Rev* 1349 (tracing the public/private distinction from its heyday to its collapse); for a thorough treatment, see Ralf Michaels and Nils Jansen, 'Private Law Beyond the State? Europeanization, Globalization, Privatization' in Nils Jansen and Ralf Michaels (eds), *Beyond the State: Rethinking Private Law* (Mohr Siebeck 2008).

29 Montesquieu, *De l'esprit des lois* (Geneva 1748). On what follows in the text, see in particular Albert O Hirschman, *The Passions and the Interests: Political Arguments for Capitalism before its Triumph* (2nd edn, Princeton University Press 1997) 70ff.

place to another quickly and cheaply, and that money exchanges introduced the possibility of buying and selling various currencies, and thus imposed new limits on the actions of rulers. The power of commerce domesticated rulers, so that under those new circumstances – according to Montesquieu – only the goodness of the government could confer prosperity. The violent exercise of state authority leads to the fall of the ruler, rather than to its success, as the local currency falls vertically on international markets. Montesquieu knew that the issuing of money is a manifestation of sovereignty, but he was also able to highlight the essential point: the value of a state's currency is in the hands of international markets. They operate beyond the powers of a single state, and unilateral action by a single state cannot govern them.

Transnational trade involves the integration of markets. There are many ways to obtain market integration. Some of them, once more, are conducive to a greater pluralism than a national legal system, in principle, would allow for. Market integration in Europe was carried out through harmonization measures and by regimes of mutual recognition in the provision of goods and services. Legal harmonization involves a hierarchical transfer of sovereignty between the member states and the EU, but mutual recognition involves a horizontal transfer of sovereignty, insofar as the rules of one country are given effect in another country: as long as goods or services are legally marketed in a member state, they can also be marketed in all other member states. As one commentator observed, under this regime, '[m]ember states can no longer guarantee a certain level of regulation of products marketed to their nationals as these regulations are being determined by other countries. The previous unity of territory, legitimation and the setting of rules is broken up'.[30] Transnational economic transactions, by requiring a certain degree of market integration, bring new problems. Legal monism cannot be the frame of reference to understand, analyse, or control those problems.

IV LEGAL PLURALISM: LAW BEYOND THE STATE

As a frame of reference to understand the law, pluralism has a remarkable history. This history shows that 'pluralism' must be defined in the plural, rather than in the singular: legal pluralism represents a group of conceptions that share certain common features, but differ in other respects.[31] Furthermore, other catchwords also convey ideas closely related to those currently put under the label 'legal pluralism'. For example, Masaji Chiba, a leading figure among scholars working on legal pluralism, rightly observed that the notion of legal culture evokes the multiplicity of sites where the law is produced, just like the notion of legal pluralism does.[32]

30 Susanne K Schmidt (ed), *Mutual Recognition as a New Mode of Governance* (Routledge 2008) 6.

31 Emma Patrignani, 'Legal Pluralism as a Theoretical Programme' (2016) 6 *Oñati Socio-Leg Series* 707.

32 Masaji Chiba, 'Other Phases of Legal Pluralism in the Contemporary World' (1998) 11 *Ratio Juris* 228.

In the European context, legal pluralism as a theoretical framework for exploring the interplay of state and non-state legal orders is at least a century old. The roots of the idea go back to the notion of social law and living law, linked to the autonomous practice of social groups and their interactions with state officials. Eugen Ehrlich, an opponent of both legal positivism and legal monism as represented by Hans Kelsen, was the eminent advocate of this conception of the law.[33] His valuable work never fully penetrated mainstream legal thinking in Europe, but his intellectual legacy was an important one for all those who rejected legocentric statism as an ideology. Recently, his work inspired Gunther Teubner's reflections on the structure of global law.[34] As mentioned earlier, with the rise of contemporary democracies, the protection of a plurality of beliefs, values, and modes of life, and the recognition of individual and collective autonomy as the foundation of democratic life vindicated a pluralist approach to democratic constitutionalism. Whenever this turn happened, this conception gained ground, becoming the norm as part of the development of democratic governments after the fall of dictatorial regimes.[35]

A second wave of interest in legal pluralism originates in the context of colonial and postcolonial regimes. In the colonies, a plurality of legal orders was in place. Those regimes were not operating on equal footing, as the colonizers refused to accept and live by local customs or local systems of law and justice, opting instead for the application of the legal regimes they brought to the colony. These regimes did not necessarily reflect the values and the structure of the system of government prevailing on the metropolitan territory. For example, colonial rulers ignored the division of powers, even when the metropolitan constitution was based on it. Furthermore, the local laws did not usually provide for institutions that governed certain types of transactions and relationships that were typical of a modern, industrialized economy, based on the division of labour (eg, commercial transactions, labour law). With independence, the foundations of the local power systems changed, and yet the newly independent states, whether they opted for democracy or not, often did not develop 'single, vertically integrated sovereignties sustained by a highly centralized state'.[36] A single law for the entire territory was very often beyond question. Legal pluralism was thus the condition of entire continents, either by choice or necessity.[37]

Probing deeper into this matter, it turns out that pluralistic legal arrangements are neither irregular occurrences in the history of European law nor are they to be found only in countries that once were subject to colonization. When the question is

[33] For a presentation and a discussion of some of the key notions and ideas presented in his work, see Marc Hertogh (ed), *Living Law: Reconsidering Eugen Ehrlich* (Hart 2008).

[34] Teubner (n 11).

[35] See the discussion in Nick W Barber, *The Constitutional State* (OUP 2010) 145ff.

[36] Jean Comaroff and John L Comaroff (eds), *Law and Disorder in the Postcolony* (University of Chicago Press 2006) 35.

[37] Brian Z Tamanaha, Caroline Sage, and Michael Woolcock (eds), *Legal Pluralism and Development: Scholars and Practitioners in Dialogue* (CUP 2012).

examined on an international scale, legal pluralism is to be recognized as the predominant way of living under the law, rather than the minor or marginal exception.[38]

Pluralism is not simply the outcome of the simultaneous interaction of different bodies of law or of norms. As the law changes over time, it simultaneously exhibits elements of the old and new order, operating in the same context. This part of the story is well known to legal historians. From monarchy to republic, from fascism to democracy, from socialism to capitalism, at every turn in history, legal historians detect the permanence of certain elements of the old in the new institutions, and in the new legal discourse. Overlapping normative regimes over time are yet another triumph of pluralism as an essential feature of the law.

Lastly, legal pluralism can be approached from the perspective of the subject, as Jacques Vanderlinden did when he abandoned his former rule-oriented approach to redefine legal pluralism in the following terms:

> [F]rom the standpoint of the individual . . . it is the condition of the person who, in his daily life, is confronted in his behavior with various, possibly conflicting, regulatory orders, be they legal or non-legal, emanating from the various social networks of which he is, voluntarily or not, a member.[39]

By adopting the perspective of the subject, this conception highlights the role of agency over structure in the law. The law can indeed be one of many tools available to advance individual purposes and ends, rather than the formal expression of an overarching social order. From here it is but a short step to think that state law does not play at all the dominant role that legal monists assign to it. Some enthusiastic adopters of pluralism seem to think that state law is almost a sort of dangerous collective (and malfunctioning) illusion.[40] Although the failures of state law are numerous, and the disasters brought about by certain experiments with modernization are immense,[41] what is done in the name of the state is not at all that illusory, preposterous, or ineffective.

The crucial point lies in a different consideration: the sanctity, legitimacy, morality, and effectiveness of state law is no longer self-evident, nor beyond discussion (if it ever was). Its goals and means are to be justified, its efficacy empirically tested, rather than assumed. The law emanating from the state intersects different notions of justice, morality, and social order in different social contexts, and may be called into question by a variety of forces. If those notions and those forces are sustainable over the long term, they may pave the way to a regime change. What was

38 This is also true with respect to religious systems of law, as shown in Ahmed Fekry Ibrahim, Chapter 9 in this volume.

39 Jacques Vanderlinden, 'Return to Legal Pluralism: Twenty Years Later' (1989) 8 *J Leg Plur* 149, 153–54.

40 Franz von Benda-Beckmann, 'Who's Afraid of Legal Pluralism?' (2002) 34 *J Leg Plur* 37 (providing a careful statement of the pluralist position in this respect too).

41 James C Scott, *Seeing Like a State: How Certain Schemes to Improve the Human Condition Have Failed* (Yale University Press 1999).

staunchly opposed by the state yesterday may become today's new code. Those who unthinkingly resisted change all along the way, turn out to be the losers in the game, losing the moral high ground.

V COMPARATIVE LAW IN THE AGE OF GLOBALIZATION

It is now time to turn to the three disciplines mentioned earlier to examine how they bring about a better, more realistic understanding of the contemporary legal landscape. The first pillar of a renewed approach to law still involves comparative law, a discipline that has been reinventing itself in recent decades. Why does comparative law remain an essential tool in carrying out serious legal analysis in our time?

In our epoch, a world government is not imminent, nor does there seem to be much appetite for it. Transnational and international legal regimes are the response to problems, concerns, and challenges spanning state borders. Climate change, large-scale environmental pollution, cross-border economic transactions, disease outbreaks, and the regulation of the internet, among others, are issues that require regulation at the world level. The institutions and norms that are in place around the world to tackle these problems constitute the present structure of the global legal order. But the order we have (to the extent we have it) is sector specific, and is fragmented rather than general as well as territorially limited. No government runs it. This is why we speak of *governance*, and not of *government* when these themes are addressed.[42] The study of this new world order is the study of the myriad of legal regimes that substantiate it, many of which are based on a dynamic of transplantation, or rather, of imitation and adaptation of specific legal institutions, as well as of original innovations, policies, and none of which is exclusively the product of a single ruling power.

A huge amount of comparative law literature is currently dedicated to analysing this dynamic and to the resulting tapestry of norms. I think this explains something about the field itself, which is characterized both by international tendencies to integrate different legal regimes and by a high level of fragmentation and regime collisions, which explains why 'pluralism' is a label that has been applied in this context too.[43] The task of studying this multiplicity of regimes is by and large a principal task for the community of comparative lawyers and their allies. If the comparative law community is not up to the challenge, others will step in to do the job. Consider that policymakers are already making wide use of comparisons that include elements of the law as well. Several international institutions and entities

[42] Jacob Torfing and Eva Sørensen, 'The European Debate on Governance by Networks: Towards a New Paradigm?' (2014) 33 *Policy & Society* 329.

[43] On this, see Paul Schiff Berman, 'Global Legal Pluralism' (2007) 80 *S Cal L Rev* 1155; Nico Krisch, *Beyond Constitutionalism: The Pluralist Structure of Postnational Law* (OUP 2010); Peer Zumbansen, 'Transnational Legal Pluralism' (2010) 1 *TLT* 141; Paul Schiff Berman, *Global Legal Pluralism: A Jurisprudence of Law Beyond Borders* (CUP 2012).

have been at work to produce indicators and rankings with the intention of representing how legal systems of the world perform in various sectors. These indicators and rankings are both sources of knowledge about societies and technologies of governance, as they are also used by market actors, NGOs, states, national administrations, and international organizations. Many of them draw explicitly upon the comparative law literature available on legal change, legal institutions, and law and development. It would be surprising if comparative lawyers were to miss the uptake of their discipline in understanding how the law is shaped at the world level.[44] Finding appropriate means to discuss the choices that are made around the world with respect to legal change and reform is a mission of the comparative law community in today's globalized world. Comparative law is deeply involved and interested in developing an informed critical debate about legal change at the world level, its effectiveness in pursuing democracy, social inclusion, justice and fairness, and the respect of legality across state boundaries.

VI LEGAL LINGUISTICS, TRANSLATION, AND COGNITION

Legal pluralists are often confronted with the argument that nobody today really believes anymore in the picture of legal monism and state law portrayed earlier.[45] In the twentieth century, the jurisprudential attack on mechanical jurisprudence opened up the Pandora's box of the law's indeterminacy. Under this condition, the plurality of interpretations that compete to respond to that indeterminacy seem to further strengthen the pluralist position. This theoretical move – the interpretivist turn – is not as iconoclast as it may seem, however.[46] The common wisdom shared by legions of lawyers is still that words frame the law and control its content.[47] Accordingly, the tendency is to assume that only in specific and somewhat exceptional cases is the link between language and law unstable, thus requiring a more prolonged and deeper analysis of the language employed by texts or proffered orally that should express the law. The fact that similar cases are regular occurrences all year long in the courts of every country has not been enough to shake this faith in the power of words.

44 For a view from the trenches, see David Trubek, 'Scan Globally, Reinvent Locally: Can We Overcome the Barriers to Using the Horizontal Learning Method?' [2014] *Nagoya U JL & Pol* 11. In a critical vein, see Kevin Davis and others (eds), *Governance by Indicators: Global Power Through Quantification and Rankings* (reprint, OUP 2015).

45 See, eg, Ido Shahar, 'State, Society and the Relations between Them: Implications for the Study of Legal Pluralism' (2008) 9 *Theo Inq L* 417.

46 This is my reading of Duncan Kennedy, A *Critique of Legal Adjudication: Fin de siècle* (Harvard University Press 1998).

47 Against it, see Roderick A Macdonald, 'Custom Made – For a Non-Chirographic Critical Legal Pluralism' (2011) 26 *Can JL & Soc'y* 301 (highlighting the significance of implicit and inferential legal norms in the working of written law as well, so that regimes of written rules too are consistently made over by those whose conduct they are presumptively meant to govern).

Language is indeed a much more complex affair than many lawyers and accomplished legal scholars would suspect, or would like to think, or openly admit. This point comes out dramatically when communication must take place across different languages and with reference to different legal systems. Considering how legal change occurs today around the world, the crucial point is that any transition from the law expressed in one language to that expressed in another language raises communication and translation problems. Just as there is no global universal law, but rather a whole set of fragmented transnational legal regimes aspiring to universality, there is no universal language that carries uniform meaning around the world; there is, rather, a multiplicity of languages that do not necessarily overlap in terms of possibilities of expression. This is a challenge for the framers of norms that should have transnational or international effects, as well as for operators who must work across boundaries. To take a relatively simple case, think of a company that must enact a set of rules for property investments to be followed by its management, in order to govern in a uniform way its property acquisitions in the different regions of the world. Can it frame those rules without regard to the law of any of the jurisdictions where a property acquisition may eventually occur? In which language should those rules be expressed? Which terms should such a company code use to achieve its purposes? Think of an NGO that speaks the language of human rights in carrying out its mission. How can it achieve its mission, and how should it convey the message to the local community?[48]

A good question for today's world is therefore how can we do justice to this plurality, which remains a challenge, even when there is broad convergence and agreement about what is to be done?[49] In other words to what extent are we able to cope with this linguistic and conceptual diversity? Most legal pluralists have not gone far enough in exploring this issue. By contrast, legal pluralists from Quebec, like Nicholas Kasirer, Daniel Jutras, and Patrick Glenn, who have produced outstanding contributions on this point, show an acute awareness of the problem.[50] The pity is that such awareness is not so widely shared by the rest of

48 Peggy Levitt and Sally Merry, 'Vernacularization on the Ground: Local Uses of Global Women's Rights in Peru, China, India and the United States' (2009) 9 *Global Networks* 441; cf Lisbeth Zimmermann, *Global Norms with a Local Face: Rule-of-Law Promotion and Norm Translation* (CUP 2017).

49 With respect to the framing of uniform law, see the brilliant essay by Gyula Eörsi, 'Unifying the Law (A Play in One Act, with a Song)' (1977) 25 *Am J Comp L* 658. See also Gerhard Dannemann, 'In Search of System Neutrality: Methodological Issues in the Drafting of European Contract Law Rules' in Maurice Adams and Jacco Bomhoff (eds), *Practice and Theory in Comparative Law* (CUP 2012).

50 Nicholas Kasirer, 'Le *real estate* existe-t-il en droit civil? Un regard sur le lexique juridique de droit civil de langue anglaise' in Rodolfo Sacco and others (eds), *Les multiples langues du droit européen uniforme* (L'Harmattan Italia 1999); Daniel Jutras, 'Énoncer l'indicible: Le droit entre langues et traditions' (2000) 52 *RIDC* 781; H Patrick Glenn, 'Qu'est-ce que la common law en français?' (2003) 5 *RCLF* 97. Esin Örücü, in Chapter 4 of this volume, provides a profound reflection on how mixed legal system challenges mainstream comparative law; this is a point not to be missed in considering the dimension of the languages of the law.

the pluralistic tribe outside Canada. The lesson to take home is that comparative law can only achieve its objectives if it does not unwittingly attempt to force upon one system the language of another. Meeting the challenge involves finding adequate linguistic mediations among the languages that come into contact by working through translations, by building shared terminologies, etc. Learning more about how natural languages actually work, and what they achieve as expressive means in the various contexts, as well as mapping the similarities and differences among them, is a significant enrichment of the comparative enterprise.

The frontier of these studies is represented by translation and terminology studies, writing systems research, sociolinguistics, cognitive research on preverbal and non-verbal communicative behaviour and on their relation to verbal behaviour, and linguistic anthropology. So far, however, the comparative law community as a whole has just caught a glimpse of what it means to take up the challenge originated by the plurality of languages that normative communities have and use.[51] Attention to law and language research is constantly growing, but much remains to be done. In all the above-mentioned fields of research, an intellectual and scientific revolution has been going on over the years. Our understanding of how language works, how translations work and what they achieve, and what cognitive structures are involved in verbal and non-verbal communication has changed dramatically in the past few decades. The time is ripe to turn to these fields and benefit from research carried out in this direction, to close the knowledge gap, and open up the gates of comparative law to contributions that are of the highest theoretical and practical value. They will help to dissolve a good number of false problems plaguing some comparative law debates, such as those raised by the question of whether it is ever possible to convey exactly the same normative meaning across two different languages.[52]

VII COMPARATIVE LAW AND THE ANTHROPOLOGY OF LAW

In tapping into these resources, comparative law is not alone. It has a confederate in the neighbouring field of anthropology, and more specifically in the field of the anthropology of law. Although there are anthropologists who were first trained as lawyers, and lawyers who have turned to social anthropology in the later part of their

[51] This assessment is based on how the new generation of comparative law handbooks in English fares in this respect. See eg, Mathias Siems, *Comparative Law* (2nd edn, CUP 2018) 19–21, 130–31; Jaakko Husa, A *New Introduction to Comparative Law* (Bloomsbury 2015) 193ff; Günter Frankenberg, *Comparative Law as Critique* (Edward Elgar 2016), and on it, in a critical vein, see Pierre Legrand and Simone Glanert, 'Law, Comparatism, Epistemic Governance: There Is Critique and Critique' (2017) 18 *Germ LJ* 702. For an essential critical update, see Vivian Grosswald Curran, 'Comparative Law and Language' in Mathias Reimann and Reinhard Zimmermann (eds), *The Oxford Handbook of Comparative Law* (2nd edn, OUP 2019).

[52] For some clarity on this issue, see David Bellos, *Is There a Fish in Your Ear?* (Penguin Books 2011); David Bellos, 'Halting Walter' (2010) 1 *Camb Literary Rev* 207. Bellos denies validity to translation theories that aspire to translate the ineffable. I agree with his stance. Unfortunately, some translation theories advanced in the legal community as well aim precisely at that.

professional life, it remains true that the core tenets of these subjects have little in common. Anthropology does not share the same normative commitments, and the law goes about its business without incorporating many of the insights about its ways and shortfalls that anthropology has acquired.

In the sub-domains of comparative law and of the anthropology of law, the overlapping of spheres of research becomes apparent, however.[53] Comparative law does not have normative ambitions as such, but has instead a certain empirical orientation, which is shared with anthropology, and which is necessary to explore the various dimensions of 'otherness' and 'sameness'.[54] Anthropology, on the other hand, regularly meets many of the methodological problems with which comparative lawyers are familiar, and which are encapsulated in the classical and still very much open question: How to compare?

It is tempting to draw the dividing line between the two disciplines by holding that comparative law mostly covers the laws of jurisdictions that belong to the industrialized world. Its boundaries would then be set by the presence of the familiar institutions and tools of the legal professions, namely legislatures, courts, a public administration, legislative enactments, court decisions, administrative practices, academic commentaries on the law, and similar paraphernalia. On the other hand, legal anthropology would be called upon where learned jurists and lawyers are on unfamiliar ground, because the law is not presented as a distinct field of learning and practice, power is not exercised through state institutions and the corresponding bureaucracy, and there is no specialized legal vocabulary to discuss, for example, binding obligations, forms of ownership and possession, norms governing family life, and succession.

Nonetheless, in a changing world, the distinction based on this rough rule of thumb is a thing of the past, and if I were to cite a single book that has made the point, that book would be Glenn's *Legal Traditions of the World*. Anthropologists are thus now active in contexts where lawyers intervene in everyday practice. The anthropological study of, for example, the administration of justice, financial markets regulation, human rights regimes, international criminal procedures, constitution making, indigenous rights, and cultural heritage, has become 'nothing less than a critical anthropology of the present.'[55] This critique involves all kinds of law makers and legal operators that are on the scene, both at home and in less familiar places.

[53] Cf Fernanda Pirie, 'Comparison in the Anthropology and History of Law' (2014) 9 *J Comp L* 88; Fernanda Pirie, *The Anthropology of Law* (OUP 2013), and see as well with respect to the question of interdisciplinarity in the sociolegal field, Annelise Riles, 'Comparative Law and Socio-Legal Studies in Language' in Reimann and Zimmermann (n 51).

[54] Mauro Bussani, 'How to Do Comparative Law: Some Lessons to Be Learned', Chapter 1 in this volume, eloquently shows that Glenn's rejection of positivism as well as his comprehensive notion of normativity, go precisely in the direction of rendering this exploration salient for comparative law studies, as I also have argued earlier, under Part I.

[55] Mark Goodale and Sally Engle Merry, *Anthropology and Law: A Critical Introduction* (NYU Press 2017) 5.

Comparative lawyers, having abandoned the narrow notions of the law that marked the beginnings of their academic discipline – once called comparative *legislation* – are now taking up the challenge to work in contexts where the interaction between formal and informal law, official and alternative kinds of normativity, traditional and modern systems of laws, is ever present. For them, the matter often is how to render effective under state law as well, institutions that are rooted in the norms of the community. The last barrier to fall is, of course, that which leads us to take notice of the necessity of an anthropology of law with respect to the jurisdictions that are considered to be at the centre rather than at the periphery of the Western world.

Legal anthropology and comparative law should therefore join forces. If we think, for example, of how property is regulated, there is a need for a lawyer to understand how property is recovered by bringing legal proceedings, but there is a need for an anthropologist to understand how it is exchanged and shared by informal arrangements that may trump formal arrangements, and how a certain ideology of property is produced and upheld by social and institutional practice. Similar examples could be given with respect to business practices, such as the taking of financial collateral to secure debts.[56] Family life, the regulation of adoption and reproductive technologies, the functioning of administrative law, the regulation of religious practices, and so on are fertile grounds for collaboration. The dialogue across disciplines in similar cases helps us understand the complexity of social and institutional interactions: it is a necessity, not a luxury.

CONCLUSIONS

My conclusions are brief. The path towards a richer understanding of the world of social relationships through the study of law has been marked by an attempt to build explanatory models of the law such as those I have examined. These models all have a tendency to take on a life of their own. Inevitably, actors rely on their perceptions of their social environment to structure their discourses and practices. Quite often these perceptions soon turn out to align with a preferred ideology. In the contemporary age, movements towards more integrated laws across the globe have not followed the path once indicated by those philosophers, political scientists, and jurists who first imagined a world government. What we have at the transnational level are mostly sectorial integrations of specific subsystems. This is brought about by fragmented law, spun out of networks of actors who often claim only technical competence and legitimation. Global law thus results from interactions between a variety of local regimes that have been transformed and integrated by forces pulling for the establishment of transnational regimes, which are often still in the making.

56 Annelise Riles, *Collateral Knowledge: Legal Reasoning in the Global Financial Markets* (University of Chicago Press 2011).

Within this framework, comparative law has a place of honour as a means to understand how this complex set of systems evolves. This central place can be maintained if comparative law remains open to change and engages with the theories, methods, and results that have produced substantial advances in a few neighbouring areas. This approach corresponds to a tradition of studies that Patrick Glenn cultivated admirably, in the spirit of true scholarship.

PART II

The Concept of Tradition

Potential and Challenges

6

Too Much Information

Martin Krygier[*]

INTRODUCTION

Imagine some bewildered heir of Rip Van Winkle and Monsieur Jourdain who wakes from a long slumber to discover he had 'been speaking prose for [almost] forty years without knowing it'.[1] That is roughly how, while preparing this chapter, I have come to feel. I spent much of the 1980s arguing that legal theory suffered from inattention to the profound *traditionality* of law.[2] About the end of that decade, however, with a manuscript of 'Law as Tradition' almost complete but unloved by the only publisher to whom I showed it, and also by me by then, I 'abandoned the manuscript to the gnawing criticism of the mice'.[3] Until very recently I had not looked at it again. When invited to contribute to this collection, it took me some time to find the text, of which I had one tattered paper copy. My electronic version, recorded on a long-discarded element of digital tradition (MS-DOS for the old and nostalgic), corrupted by age, and sullen from rejection, was reluctant to open its bran tub of information to me.

I then started to read Patrick Glenn's writings on legal traditions, which had been published (all five editions, et al!) while I slept. I discovered an erudite,

* I am grateful for discussions with Arthur Glass and Julie Hamblin.

1 Molière, *Le Bourgeois gentilhomme* (1670) act II, scene 4 (my substitution). The original was 'over forty years'.

2 See eg, Martin Krygier, 'Law as Tradition' (1986) 5 *Law & Phil* 237; Martin Krygier, 'The Traditionality of Statutes' (1988) 1 *Ratio Juris* 20; Martin Krygier, 'Tradition', *Dictionnaire encyclopédique de théorie et de sociologie du droit* (1st edn, 1988) 423; Martin Krygier, 'Thinking Like a Lawyer' in Wojciech Sadurski (ed), *Ethical Dimensions of Legal Theory* (Rodopi 1991); Martin Krygier and Adam Czarnota, 'Revolutions and the Continuity of European Law' in Zenon Bańkowski (ed), *Revolutions in Law and Legal Thought* (Aberdeen University Press 1991); Martin Krygier, 'Legal Traditions and Their Virtue' in Grażyna Skąpska and Krzysztof Pałecki (eds), *Prawo w Zmieniającym Się Społeczeństwie [Law in a Changing Society]* (Adam Marszałek 1992); Martin Krygier and Adam Czarnota, 'From State to Legal Traditions? Prospects for the Law after Communism' in Janina Frentzel-Zagórska (ed), *A One-Party State to Democracy: Transition in Eastern Europe* (Rodopi 1993). I revisit some of these themes in a somewhat more distanced fashion in Martin Krygier, 'Institutional Optimism, Cultural Pessimism and the Rule of Law' in Martin Krygier and Adam Czarnota (eds), *The Rule of Law after Communism* (Dartmouth 1999).

3 Karl Marx, 'A Contribution to the Critique of Political Economy' in Karl Marx and Frederick Engels, *Selected Writings* (first published 1859, Foreign Languages Publishing House 1951) 330.

engaging, and stylish speaker of the prose I had struggled with all that time ago, full of apt appreciation for the indispensable, ineradicable, normative presence of the past in law, hostile to (con-)temporally (and otherwise) parochial 'time-slice' characterizations of 'legal *systems*' and such, as though they all might have started yesterday or that it wouldn't matter if they hadn't. Hostile also to post-Western Enlightenment slightings of the traditional sources of form and content in societies and legal orders, modern as much as those relegated to benighted, custom-dominated, 'pre-legal', 'traditional' pasts (or presents in 'less developed', usually southern, climes). On commonly received views, Glenn sharply noted:

> 'Traditional' societies are . . . ones that are not dynamic or self-critical or rational, and we see everywhere in Western society, and Western academic discussion, the dichotomy between tradition and modernity. It is as though the modern Western world sprang somehow from nowhere and did not itself develop over thousands of years.[4]

Like Glenn, I believe that all of this is false, and it matters. Moreover, not only was Glenn's prose congenially familiar, and the argument retrospectively reassuring, but it was buttressed by a depth of legal scholarship I could only have dreamt about (had I, contrary to fact, still been dreaming about tradition).

Others who match Glenn's learning in one or other of the traditions he discusses, since they are unlikely to match it in several still less all, might speak of those.[5] My aim is more modest. I will return to where I started, to the foundational concept he deploys. Reading him has rekindled some of my early attachment to tradition; it is certainly worth waking up for. However, I cannot sustain the evangelical passion Glenn displays. Perhaps I never had it. I will try to explain both that shared attachment and the less-shared passion below. I start with the former in Section I and move on to the latter in subsequent sections.

I PASTNESS

The central characteristic of all traditions – the authoritative (Glenn would prefer 'normative'; in general I won't argue, though at times – in relation to traditions in which authority is explicitly, institutionally, mandated – I will insist on authoritative) presence of transmitted pasts – is so manifest in law that it is hard to understand how little attention has been devoted to it. Certainly as a conceptual matter, it has not been much emphasized, even if as a matter of fact we notice it, and have to deal with it, every day. Glenn himself confesses that he only came to appreciate its

[4] H Patrick Glenn, 'A Concept of Legal Tradition' (2008) 34 *QLJ* 427, 429.

[5] As they have, and not always sympathetically. See eg, Nicholas HD Foster (ed), 'A Fresh Start for Comparative Legal Studies? A Collective Review of Patrick Glenn's *Legal Traditions of the World*, 2nd Edition' (2006) 1 *J Comp L* 100.

significance inductively;[6] it grew on him from what he found as he came to read into different legal traditions. Having learnt it, he became dissatisfied with the standard taxonomic characterizations of law into systems, cultures, families, and nation states. Equally and for the same reasons, he came to reject the standard Western default models – the geographically anchored, law-monopolizing sovereign states of post-Westphalian European provenance, limited as they have been both in space and time – that fed these characterizations, and with them analytical legal philosophy's universalist overreachings.[7]

The reasons for Glenn's dissatisfaction with the conventional conceptual apparatus are several, some of them familiar, some quite novel and distinctive of his quasi-evangelical embrace of tradition. I find the former more persuasive than the latter, but only tentatively so, since both are intriguing and too rarely voiced, and Glenn's passion is infectious.

A fundamental and familiar objection to such temporally tone-deaf characterizations of legal orders, is endorsed by pretty well everyone who thinks traditions matter. It starts from the fact that elements of the past, or what is taken to be the past, are normatively significant in the present of so much that goes to shape the lives, mores, and laws of a society and, if one can talk sensibly of this, the character of the society as a whole.

Of course, as Glenn stresses, much of the past is no part of the present: unknown, lost, forgotten. A lot, too, though remembered or recorded as having occurred, has no current salience in the thoughts and practices of later generations; we know that this or that happened, but who cares? And who would care if the opposite had happened? And, though he says less about this than I think he should, there are also pasts that are objects of sustained attention by successor generations, often passionate and absorbed attention, that are treated purely as dead rather than alive, even if interesting nonetheless. Russian medievalists who study thirteenth-century England, say, or for that matter many English historians of the same period, might think of little else, but the historian's past is not the same as the traditionalist's present. Even if that disaffected historian and eponymous hero of Kingsley Amis' *Lucky Jim*, had evinced more interest in his 'strangely neglected topic', 'the Economic Effect of Developments in Shipbuilding Techniques, 1450–1485', and devoted his life to exploring it, this would not likely make those techniques part of

6 M Hildebrandt, 'The Precision of Vagueness, Interview with H. Patrick Glenn' (2006) 3 *Neth J Legal Phil* 346, 355:

> In my own personal experience I did not come to the concept of tradition until well in the process of thinking about the relations of different legal traditions, so in that sense it springs inductively or spontaneously from the examination at the same time of multiple traditions, as opposed to being in my own case any kind of a priori classification that was applied to all of them.

7 See Catherine Valcke's discussion of this issue, Chapter 7 in this volume.

any current tradition that was normative for him. Indeed, current generations might pore attentively over records of old doings, only to be struck by the extent to which 'the past is a foreign country. They do things differently there.'[8] Others, participants in traditions that incorporate such pasts into their lived present, might respond quite otherwise. Historians of the first sort might, indeed often do,[9] rebuke traditionalists of the second sort for not understanding the otherness of the pasts they claim to be continuing but are really, to use Glenn's term, 'massaging'.[10]

For the past in traditions is different from the simply historical past. It sticks around. That is to say, it is still around and it is sticky – normatively part of the present. What was or was done, or is believed to have been or been done, is normatively connected with what we are and do: '[T]his is what we have always done, and therefore should do', or just 'this is the way we do things here', whether with or without any conscious reflection on the pastness of the normative present. Often the pastness of traditions is unrecognized, but merely performed: we don't know why we here do or think as we do, until we find that they then did or thought in related ways, while they there – contemporary inheritors of different traditions – do not. Of such diachronic relationships, it is truer to say, 'the past is never dead. It's not even past.'[11]

Traditions in this sense are everywhere, and Glenn joins major contemplators of them, such as Edward Shils (and, for that matter, Edmund Burke) in lamenting how frequently these fundamental, unavoidable features of our ways of life are ignored or played down or relegated to 'pre-modern' or 'pre-legal' yore. Modern traditions differ from earlier ones in many ways of course. Today it is common to praisefully invoke originality or revolution in a novel way, the former not as returning to origins, but to be an origin; the latter not cyclical repetition, but the start of something quite new. That modernity came to embrace the new in such words and ways is a significant and distinctive aspect of modern traditions, but we have been doing it for some time now, and the traditions of modernity, borne as they have been over generations, are scarcely evidence that modernity has freed itself of tradition. It has rejected some and picked up others. Modern traditions have their normatively present pasts as well. In modern, just as in 'traditional', societies, as Shils puts it, '[e]very human action and belief has a career behind it'.[12]

When this is pointed out, it is rare that people object strenuously, but it is also rare that the pervasive normative presence of the past is regarded as a matter of conceptual salience. Returning to Shils:

[8] LP Hartley, *The Go-Between* (Hamish Hamilton 1953), *quoted in* David Lowenthal, *The Past Is a Foreign Country* (CUP 1985) xvi.

[9] See eg, Conal Condren, 'The History of Political Thought as Secular Genealogy: The Case of Liberty in Nearly Modern England' (2017) 27 *Intell Hist Rev* 115.

[10] See H Patrick Glenn, *Legal Traditions of the World: Sustainable Diversity in Law* (5th edn, OUP 2014) 16, 21 (hereafter Glenn, *LTW*).

[11] William Faulkner, *Requiem for a Nun* (Penguin Books 1960) 81.

[12] Edward Shils, *Tradition* (University of Chicago Press 1981) 43.

> Tradition is a dimension of social structure which is lost or hidden by the atemporal conceptions which now prevail in the social sciences.
>
> Social scientists avoid the confrontation with tradition and with their omission of it from explanatory schemes by having recourse to 'historical factors'. In this way they treat tradition as a residual category, as an intellectual disturbance which is to be brushed away.[13]

That traditions are pervasively important in our lives, then, is a general truth. So much of what matters in social arrangements and practices is comprised of beliefs, practices, and what Wittgenstein called 'forms of life', all of which are, or are believed to be – and are even if not known to be – transmitted from the past and retain authoritative significance in people's current beliefs, practices, and so on. Apart from explicit reference, traditional inheritances have pervasive consequences even where those consequences are not felt and reference is not made to them. They are the unreflected-upon context and medium of reflection, imagination, and action. And, for reasons I have discussed elsewhere,[14] we wouldn't, couldn't, have it any other way. There are many ways of responding to what traditions demand of us, and it is important to realize, more than Glenn likes to emphasize, how noxious it is possible for traditions to be, but there is a fundamental truth of which Karl Popper reminds us: 'If we start afresh, then, when we die we shall be about as far as Adam and Eve were when they died (or, if you prefer, as far as Neanderthal man).'[15]

It should already be clear that traditions are complicated and various phenomena, and any serious analysis of them would need to quickly move beyond generalities to tease out that complexity and variety. Some are simple matters of single behaviours transmitted over time; others are complex, such as the common law tradition.[16] Within complex traditions there are, paralleling Hart's primary and secondary rules, first order (what we do) and varying levels of higher order (what we do and/or think about what we do, and what we do or think about what we do or think, etc.) traditions.[17] Complex traditions, as Glenn emphasizes, contain many subtraditions that sometimes converge, sometimes compete, and that the larger traditions need to deal with. Long before sociolegal scholars began to notice 'legal pluralism', anthropologists had distinguished between the 'great' traditions of the learned and the 'little' traditions of the flock in complex societies,[18] and it doesn't

13 Ibid, 7–8.

14 Krygier, 'Law as Tradition' (n 2) 257–62.

15 Karl R Popper, 'Towards a Rational Theory of Tradition' in Karl R Popper (ed), *Conjectures and Refutations* (Routledge & Kegan Paul 1969) 129.

16 See David M Armstrong, 'The Nature of Tradition' in David M Armstrong (ed), *The Nature of Mind and Other Essays* (University of Queensland Press 1980) 89–90.

17 Popper (n 15) 127.

18 See Robert Redfield, 'Peasant Society and Culture' in Robert Redfield (ed), *The Little Community and Peasant Society and Culture* (University of Chicago Press 1973).

take much thought to realize how oversimplified this dichotomy is,[19] in law as much as in religion, or how varied lines of connection and direction might be. Again, one thing that distinguishes modern traditions from older ones is the degree of differentiation in modernity between one and another; religious, moral, legal, scientific, philosophical, and so on. This, as Max Weber insisted, is unprecedented. All these complications and others are important for a satisfactory appreciation of tradition. I will not pursue them in depth here, though, but will return to law.

Some traditions are more reflexive, more deliberately sustained, more institutionalized and *tended* in character (though not necessarily of greater social significance as a result; lawyers often mistake what they do for what is important). They are meant to endure and they do endure, with their pasts more explicitly treated as normative (some, notwithstanding Glenn's objections, literally authoritative) features of the present than others. Thus, the former commonly have authorized (and often authoritative) agents of interpretation, transmission, and implementation that are developed to sustain them; the latter leave things more to chance. Institutionalized religions are an example of the former, and so are legal orders.[20] As in all institutionalized traditions, many of the key practices, procedures, and institutions of the law are devoted to ensuring the preservation and transmission of normatively salient past texts, institutions, conventions, and so on. As in all ongoing traditions, what is inherited and transmitted is also transformed by those participants who receive it. In becoming participants, they too are transformed.

Law is sustained as and by complex, enduring, explicitly authoritative and institutionalized tradition. It contains many parts in complex interrelationship. It commonly has lasted a long time. Legal orders devote much of their structure, practice, and institutional arrangements to conveying authoritative elements of the legal past to the legal present, recording them, curating them, interpreting them, winnowing them, weeding some out and nurturing, not to say anointing, the claims of others, 'applying' the latter, attending to how they are to be passed on, and passing them on, where the process in turn continues. It includes and depends upon authoritative texts, writers, readers, and interpreters. These works and workers are screened, validated, tended, recorded, controlled, and connected by the incumbents, practices, and procedures of authoritative institutions.

As is well known, the common law makes a bit of a fetish of citing judicial 'authorities'. However, it is not alone among legal orders in requiring their present custodians to give deferential consideration to particular writers and writings (and not others) and specific *categories* of writers and writings (and not others). Among those writings that cannot be avoided are many that one might never have reason

19 SJ Tambiah, *Buddhism and the Spirit Cults in North-East Thailand* (CUP 1970) 368 (Indian Hinduism has 'a complexity which prohibits a simple reduction to these two levels').

20 I use the term 'order' here in the (perhaps vain) hope of finding a neutral placeholder which would not attract Glenn's ire. If I fail in that aim (after all, how ordered is a legal order, and by what or whom?), please just substitute 'X'.

even to look at if all one was after was the good, the true, or the beautiful. As Joseph Vining has observed of even the relatively freewheeling common law tradition of the United States:

> Whether brief or fulsome in the statement of their conclusions, lawyers dwell upon what has been said. In this they are like Isaiah Berlin writing on Tolstoy, Marx, or Vico, only the men whose words lawyers turn over in their heads are not Tolstoy, Marx, or Vico. They may be excellent men, but they are rarely so excellent as obviously to warrant such attention.[21]

It is unlikely one would 'dwell' on exactly the same folk if one's choice was uninformed or unconstrained by tradition, free to roam the planet as one pleased.

In almost every legal system, the maintenance of a normatively present past is attended to with a diligence matched only in institutionalized religions. What these present-pasts are made up of – statutes, interpretations, court judgments, the opinions of scholars, sacred texts – differs greatly among legal orders. Overarchingly, particular forms of what Clifford Geertz calls 'legal sensibility' also endure within traditions and differ, sometimes dramatically, between them.[22] The pervasiveness of such pasts, both real and imagined, their architectonic significance in the present of law, can scarcely be exaggerated.

This is true of law, as it is of all complex and enduring traditions. As a result of such practices, there are deep continuities. But such continuities do not long depend upon sameness. The present of any such tradition is profoundly influenced – much of it constituted – by what comes down to it from the past, but little that is important (perhaps liturgical rituals) remains without change. For characteristic of such traditions is a dialectical interplay between inherited layers which pervade and – often unrecognized – mould the present, and the constant renewals and reshapings of these inheritances, in which authorized interpreters and guardians of the tradition and lay participants indulge, and must indulge. Words change, meanings change, the world changes, we change; so does law. Continuously. The resulting traditions are more tangled, even mysterious, than pristine repetition or groundless, boundless, invention might appear to be. They are also more common and significant in social life. And law is an important one of them.

Glenn of course knows all this and more; so do many lawyers. However, far more than most who write on law, Glenn characterizes these central aspects of these easily observed features of legal orders in terms of tradition. It is his master concept. Talk of legal 'systems' conveys none of this, and this is one of Glenn's objections to such language: 'The diachronic nature of tradition would allow better understanding than the synchronic nature of momentary legal systems.'[23] Nor does 'legal culture'

[21] Joseph Vining, *The Authoritative and the Authoritarian* (Chicago University Press 1986) 154.

[22] Clifford Geertz, *Local Knowledge* (Basic Books 1983) 175.

[23] H Patrick Glenn, 'Doin' the Transsystemic: Legal Systems and Legal Traditions' (2005) 50 *McGill LJ* 863, 875.

draw attention to the normative presence of the *past*. We know things happened yesterday in systems, cultures, families, and that it often matters today, but the normatively present pastness of those key facts in the life of legal orders has no conceptual weight in or bearing on the 'static', 'momentary' kinds of concepts we typically deploy to characterize legal orders.

Moreover, Glenn insists not only that 'tradition' draws attention to something uncaptured in our standard-issue concepts, but that it exposes what is fundamental, underlying, in all legal, and he would add social and cultural, orders. It is myopic to start (and typically to finish) with what happens now, in this particular 'system' or 'culture' or indeed 'state' and tie all law to it. This slights the 'law which is more deeply rooted or profound than the law of legal systems, that which underlies and pervades all of them. . . . [T]he idea of legal tradition as the necessary foundation of legal systems and as the necessary means of teaching across, through, and beyond them.'[24] And of course, given the diachronic nature of traditions, to speak of them is not merely to turn to the past, but at the same time, to its interrelations with the present and then in turn to the relations between past, present, and future as well. In one of his most apt and frequently repeated metaphors, Glenn observes:

> Tradition is thus necessarily diachronic in character. It is very different from the idea of a 'momentary' legal system, the law that would be in force at a given time. Understanding tradition would be like looking at a film; understanding a momentary legal system would be like looking at a single frame of a film.[25]

Only the first frame of a film comes, as it were, from nowhere. The rest of the film precedes it or (apart from the end frame) follows it. What precedes moulds and informs what happens in it. So too does preparation for what is expected to come next, for what goes on afterwards must flow (or be thought to flow) from what went before. Ronald Dworkin's conceit, the chain novel, is apt here,[26] though he does not, I believe, pursue his insights far enough, into the extent to which earlier chapters might constitute, rather than simply inform, later readers and writers.[27]

This is not only a generic criticism of the use of time-poor concepts for time-rich practices; it is a particular one for several of the concepts involved – national legal systems, state-based law, legal culture – because not every legal tradition has them or can be made sense of in terms of them. They are specific products of relatively recent traditions. Several legal traditions do not have the idea that their law forms a 'system', do not consider that it must emanate from a territorially based state, do not have the concept of culture, which is of relatively recent vintage and coined, so Glenn insists, to distinguish 'us' from 'them'. These concepts belong to specific, recent, Western folk traditions; they should not be thought of as default analytical concepts apt for

24 Ibid, 867.
25 Ibid, 873.
26 See Ronald Dworkin, *Law's Empire* (Fontana 1986) esp ch 7.
27 See Krygier, 'Thinking Like a Lawyer' (n 2) esp 80–87.

universal application. To an extent, they reflect and capture the way we live and think now, but they are inadequate for comparative purposes and mute about the fundamental nature and contribution of tradition, which in our case, as in all cases, precedes the shape (state/national/systematic) that it has now been bent into[28] and might soon be bent out of.[29] The mistake is not to take account of the fundamental precedence and presence of tradition, and to mistake particular modern instances and products of legal traditions as self-standing in their current forms, and apt – even if only at a general taxonomic level – to frame the ways we approach all others.

II REIFICATION AND CONFLICT

Ignoring the normative presence of the past is obviously going to vex any partisan of tradition; having normatively present pasts is, after all, what traditions do, and it is significant that they do it. However, Glenn's criticisms of the concepts conventionally applied to law go much further than this. They reveal specific and distinctive aspects of his attachment to tradition and what animates an uncommon passion in relation to these issues.

One thing he believes the usual suspects do and tradition does not is *reify* legal orders: 'The most obvious form of social reification is found in the contemporary state or national legal system.'[30] And if lawyers reify systems and states, social scientists – better behaved in those domains than lawyers[31] – nevertheless do similarly with the black box, 'culture', which is always there as an all-purpose, presently available receptacle, into which any phenomena that don't fit neatly elsewhere, can be hoovered up.[32] In fact, there seems to be reification pretty well anywhere you look, at least in comparative law: '[M]any of the same criticisms which are made of the concept of culture may be made of similar constructions such as style, mentality and civilisation, to the extent that all lend themselves to the reification and categorisation of human groups, in an essentialising manner.'[33]

The problem here is not merely analytic, Glenn insists. It has real-world consequences. If laws are conceived as necessarily part of one 'system' or the other, their

[28] See H Patrick Glenn, 'Tradition in Religion and Law' (2009) 25 *JL & Relig* 503, 514–15 ('Only after the emergence of the state has the belief become widespread that the state is the exclusive source of law and that there was no law, properly so-called, prior to the state. In the early days of the emergence of the State, "no one doubted" that there was a normative, legal, foundation for the state, rooted in the legal traditions that led to the state, everywhere in Europe.'). And see Mauro Bussani, Chapter 1 in this volume, pts I and II.

[29] See Glenn, *LTW* (n 10) 53; See also H Patrick Glenn, 'The State as Legal Tradition' (2013) 2 *CJICL* 704.

[30] H Patrick Glenn, 'Com-paring' in Esin Örücü and David Nelken (eds), *Comparative Law: A Handbook* (Hart 2007) 97.

[31] Ibid.

[32] 'Everyone talks about culture these days, though no-one knows what it really is.' Ibid.

[33] H Patrick Glenn, 'Legal Cultures and Legal Traditions' in Mark Van Hoecke (ed), *Epistemology and Methodology of Comparative Law* (Hart 2004) 19.

participants sharing a particular and distinctive 'legal culture' as members, for example, of a particular *res*, so laws that are outwith that system or culture or state or family, must be part of another such entity and will potentially conflict:

> The reification process has thus manifested itself in terms of systems, cultures, civilisations, and further even in terms of 'mentalités'. These have all been boundary-tracing endeavours which both homogenise (within) and differentiate (without), in a way incompatible with com-paring ['bringing together with a peer, with that which is prima facie equal'[34]] and convivencia.[35]

Glenn believes that conflict is written into our normal ways of talking of legal orders:

> There cannot, therefore, be two legal systems operating in the same space, and so we have an entire legal discipline known as the conflict of laws that deals with cases that are somehow connected with two or more legal systems.
>
> . . . .
>
> If human groupings are thought of in reified, objectified or essentialized form, there will be conflict. The two objects cannot occupy the same space harmoniously. One must prevail over the other.[36]

Glenn argues that the concept of tradition, in its very nature, neither reifies nor separates, and this is clearly a central part of its charm for him. Why is this so? It can't be simply the presence of the past. One can at least imagine age-old traditions of conceiving that laws all come in systems or families or are always the spawn of states, shared in contemporary heads as a result of a shared 'legal culture', conceived so in the long distant past, and faithfully transmitted over generations that in turn faithfully so conceive of law and instruct their successors so to continue. Here we would have the normative presence of the past, but of a 'reified' past.

Glenn would not deny that a specific tradition could in fact take this shape – after all ours do – but he believes that the concept of tradition itself is not intrinsically apt for such reification, such totalizing closure. These are 'corruptions' of tradition, not implications, though they are a constant temptation and very frequently occur.[37] His reasons for thinking this seem to me to follow from a quite idiosyncratic and contestable conception of what traditions 'truly' involve, absent contingency or corruption which, he nevertheless allows, is far from rare. A lot of the 'conciliatory' hopefulness that seems, from reading him, central to (and attractive in) his own nature might be on more shifting ground, without this somewhat 'pollyannish'[38] conception of the concept of tradition as its foundation.

34 Glenn, 'Com-paring' (n 30) 92.

35 Ibid, 98.

36 Glenn, 'Concept of Legal Tradition' (n 4) 441–42.

37 See Glenn, *LTW* (n 10) 50–51.

38 Martin Shapiro, 'A Fresh Start for Comparative Legal Studies?' in Foster (n 5) 151. On the possible personal sources of Glenn's 'optimism', see Mauro Bussani, Chapter 1, pt VII in this volume.

III THE BRAN-TUB OF INFORMATION

Often the words we use are at the same time commonplace and weightless; we are comfortable using them and they loosely, often usefully, direct the flow of verbal traffic one way or another along paths we and others can understand, but they commit us to little. We know their referents when we see them and we don't bother about the details or about distinctions. Sometimes, when taken up by a stringent thinker, however, the same words get content and boundaries; at their deepest, they come both to embody a theory, or at least a considered view, and contribute in specific, even un-substitutable, ways to larger theorizing. 'Class' was such a word, made over into a central concept of social theory by Karl Marx; 'bureaucracy' another which Marx simply *used* fairly unreflectively but, after Weber explored it, carried a large part of the weight of his theory of modernity.[39] 'Rules' before and after Hart, 'principles' before and after Dworkin, are other such terms that have become sophisticated and distinctively elaborated elements in a theory.

'Tradition' comes to occupy a similar place in Glenn's contributions to comparative law. Notwithstanding his suspicion of other sorts of borders, he insists that those of tradition properly so-called, be closely delineated. Not just his analysis, but his view of it as opening legal orders up to greater mutual recognition, tolerance, conciliatory living together, depend upon this remapping. Redraw the borders and some of his claims become less obvious than they seem to him.

According to Shils, tradition is 'anything which is transmitted or handed down from the past to the present'.[40] Glenn disagrees. Though he allows that the *content* of traditions can vary hugely, Glenn sets a lot of store by a quite specific narrowing of what counts as a tradition: it is past *information*. True, that information can tell us pretty well anything; no specific content follows from the fact that it is traditional. Particular content is generated by particular traditions. But, while the uninformed might extend the term 'tradition' – for example, to practices, institutions, ways of life, to ways of transmitting any of the aforementioned and ways of responding to what has been transmitted – for Glenn it only applies to information.

It is not obvious why this has to be so;[41] lots of things can be handed down, and it is a potentially distorting stretch to call whatever comes down the pipe 'information'. However, it becomes clear why defining tradition as information comes to matter so

39 See Eugene Kamenka and Martin Krygier (eds), *Bureaucracy: The Career of a Concept* (Edward Arnold 1979) esp chs 2–4.

40 Shils (n 12) 12.

41 See William Twining, 'Glenn on Tradition: An Overview' in Foster (n 5) 113; John Bell, 'Civil Law Tradition' in Foster (n 5) 135 (on the definition of a legal tradition as a network of information: 'I would see this as a rather limited definition of law. For me, the law has a number of facets, which one can summarise with the mnemonics "CHIP" and "PIN": Concepts, Heuristics, Ideas, Power, Processes, Institutions and Norms.').

to Glenn. For information, on his account, resists reification, boundaries, separations. Anyone who finds out about it can learn from it, be influenced, or be challenged, by it. And thus:

> The conclusion that tradition is best seen as information is important for the resulting permeability of social structures. Information flows more freely than water and any process of reification or rigid separation of structures is impossible over time. Closure may be attempted but is rarely successful; put differently, there is no regress stopper in the face of informational challenge, whether internal or external.[42]

Similarly, Glenn once entertains, without much conviction but for the sake of argument, the possibility that the concept of tradition could go the reifying way of culture et al, but his heart is not really in it. Tradition 'has yet to undergo the same kind of reification and conflictualization as has occurred with the concept of culture. This may be because tradition is best conceived as simple information, lasting over time, which lacks the material dimension of social life present in the concept of culture.'[43] None of this really makes sense if we allow that institutions, say, or rituals might be thought of as traditional. But why not?

Glenn insists, however, that unlike the closed, walled-off qualifiers attached to law:

> If law conceived as system yields facts, silence and conflict, law conceived as tradition (as normative information) must yield normative claims, discussion and dialogue, as well as the possibility of reconciliation. Legal traditions thus speak to one another, and all the great legal traditions of the world say a great deal about their relations with one another.[44]

And how appealingly open and promiscuous those relations can be:

> [A]s normative information, tradition simply goes with the flow. There are no inherent boundaries to tradition, as is the case with systems, though particular traditions such as that of the nation state may construct boundaries for themselves. Traditions function according to multivalent forms of logic and tolerate diversity . . . . [T]hey have large and roomy middle grounds . . . . Traditions thus do not conflict and compete for space (though nothing prevents people from doing so), but rather influence, through a process of com-paring. . . . Traditions thus allow for convivencia.[45]

Indeed, it is not enough to say traditions are of their nature (when not subject to corruption) 'tolerant'; they are *beyond* tolerance, at least internally:

[42] Glenn, 'State as Legal Tradition' (n 29) 707.
[43] Ibid.
[44] Glenn, 'Concept of Legal Tradition' (n 4) 442.
[45] Glenn, 'Com-paring' (n 30) 105–06.

> [T]oleration doesn't seem to be the right word, or right concept, in describing the complexity of major legal traditions. They are complex, not because they are tolerant, but because they build real bridges. . . . The better notion seems to be one of interdependence, or of non-separation, and this emerges as the most basic idea in the existence of major, complex, legal traditions. It is the fundamental underlying characteristic of multivalence.[46]

It is hard for a sensitive new-age guy not to fancy tradition, as Glenn extolls it. Forget Marx's 'tradition of all the dead generations [that] weighs like a nightmare on the brain of the living';[47] Glenn's legal tradition is simply 'non-genetic information which influences but does not control legal practice. It is tolerant of argument, and argument has always been a useful antidote to reification and homogenisation, while allowing peaceful resolution of disputes.'[48] All those nation state, legal-systemic (and cultural) border guards don't have a chance: 'Tradition . . . comes with no clear markers, and it is difficult to identify traditions as autonomous or separate or pure. Traditions have fuzzy edges; they can only be identified in relation to other traditions; they contain within themselves elements of opposition . . .';[49] 'tradition conceived as information has no borders';[50] 'the flow of information is ultimately uncontrollable; closure is never complete.'[51]

So one image has all this information flowing like water, no one able to staunch the tide. Another, and a favourite of Glenn's, is of tradition as a 'bran-tub of information'. I had to google 'bran-tub' – 'noun (in Britain)' – but I understand it's like a bash-free piñata, 'a tub containing bran [I had got that far] in which small wrapped gifts are hidden, used at parties, fairs, etc'.[52] I imagine you can find all sorts of things there. Hard to know what you will get; and once the 'information' is in there, hard for those who would like to control what you take out, as well:

> One of the main criticisms of the use of tradition is that is a vague concept. There is of course a vagueness to it, because it simply points to the mass of normative information, which exists in the world. That is why the use of the bran tub is an accurate metaphor – everything goes into the bran tub, and there is no formal process of filtering or excluding what is in the bran tub. The particularisation of what's in the bran tub is not the function of tradition in general but of particular traditions, which define what is in the bran tub.[53]

I guess, from the point of view of a dipper into the tub it is pretty random what might be found inside, and so it seems: 'It necessarily contains varying and even [here the

46 Glenn, *LTW* (n 10) 373.
47 Karl Marx, 'The Eighteenth Brumaire of Louis Bonaparte' in Marx and Engels (n 3) vol 1, 255.
48 Glenn, 'Legal Cultures and Legal Traditions' (n 33) 20.
49 Ibid, 19.
50 Glenn, 'Doin' the Transsystemic' (n 23) 897.
51 Glenn, 'State as Legal Tradition' (n 29) 714.
52 'Bran-tub', *Collins English Dictionary* <https://bit.ly/2SbFHPk>.
53 Hildebrandt (n 6) 354.

metaphor starts to strain] conflicting views.'[54] And not only is conflict common in the bran-tub, but change comes out of it:

> Once tradition is seen as transmitted information, an ongoing bran-tub churned by new generations, with no inherent élites or hierarchy, the linking of tradition with stability becomes less obvious and less defensible. Tradition becomes rather a resource from which reasons for change may be derived, a legitimating agency for ideas which, by themselves, would have no social resonance. The past is mobilized to invent a future.[55]

So the bran-tub of tradition can deal with conflict. It is also a constant source of change, as it mixes with other bran-tubs (again the metaphor doesn't take us all the way):

> Since tradition is best defined as information . . . the (slightest) contact with another tradition implies a variation in the information base of the initial tradition. Its overall identity is no longer what it was, in the sense that the totality of information available to it has expanded. The bran-tub is larger. Given any form of contact between traditions, the overall identity of each becomes non-exclusive; each contains elements of the other, which may find support in the various tendencies in the receiving tradition. In today's world there are therefore no pure identities of tradition.[56]

It is a beguiling vision: open; proliferating choice, variation, and accommodation, available to all. You just have to stick your hand in and out comes a prize.

IV WITHIN THE BRAN-TUB; THE BRAN-TUB WITHIN

Though I have never seen it happen, I imagine that those who choose from a bran-tub do not sit in it. Most likely, they stand on the ground outside, and pick and choose among its random offerings. They are also, I guess, as free to reject them or throw them away as they are to choose them. But 'large and major' traditions of the sort with which Glenn is concerned[57] only offer themselves up this way to outsiders (unless, as happens with certain secret Aboriginal traditions in my own country, outsiders are simply not allowed in) who are not *within* the tradition and might have no clue what it has to tell initiates, still less what it might make them do, might indeed *make* them. In significant ways, however, strong traditions *constitute* the thoughts and practices of initiates, often to an extent hard for them even to guess at, and hard for outsiders to understand.

Traditions in this way constitute their members, not completely, not inescapably, always varyingly, mixed with other natural and social influences, but also often

54 H Patrick Glenn, 'Legal Traditions and *Legal Traditions*' (2007) 2 *J Comp L* 69, 72.

55 Glenn, *LTW* (n 10) 24.

56 Ibid, 34.

57 Ibid, 367.

deeply. As Clifford Geertz has memorably insisted, even common sense, that bedrock set of assumptions upon which most of us believe we act, and many assume needs no interrogation, indeed could not be interrogated, is (forgive the expression) a 'cultural system . . . not a fortunate faculty, like perfect pitch; it is a special frame of mind, like piety or legalism. And like piety or legalism (or ethics or cosmology), it both differs from one place to the next and takes, nevertheless, a characteristic form.'[58] And Geertz's pursuit of 'local knowledge' takes us well beyond common sense. Accompanying him on his attempt to render how several different legal traditions deal with what we call the distinction between fact and law, a reader quickly comes to see we are not just being introduced to different sources of information, or sources of different information, some familiar, some exotic, others sinister, others quaint. Rather, we get to feel the force of, as he defines legal sensibility, 'distinctive manner[s] of imagining the real'.[59] People brought up within powerful traditions do not choose with the ease with which one might choose from a bran-tub or between, say, discrete provisions of law, that might differ between legal systems. Legal sensibility is not a simple piece of information in the way that, say, differing provisions to deal with theft might conceivably be.[60] It is deeper, and commonly among initiates more inward, than that. It is internalized, in a way that bears analogy with Heinrich Popitz's notion of 'internal' (internalized) power, which unlike threats and promises, 'works even in a dark hole'.[61]

As Geertz puts it:

> Law may not be a brooding omnipresence in the sky, as Holmes insisted rather too vehemently, but it is not, as the down-home rhetoric of legal realism would have it, a collection of ingenious devices to avoid disputes, advance interests, and adjust trouble-cases either. An *Anschauung* in the marketplace. And: other marketplaces, other *Anschauungen*.[62]

I do not want to 'reify' the constitutive significance of traditions, still less make a claim for 'incommensurability' between traditions;[63] it's hard enough to disagree with Glenn even about simple things. However, I think he makes his case easier for himself by the conceptual minimalism of his concept of tradition. Partly that is because his bran-tub metaphor, like his account of tradition as information, has nothing to say of the deep ways in which, as participants in traditions, we don't simply choose between the bits of information they have to offer us, but in a real

58 Geertz (n 22) 11, fn 21.

59 Ibid, 173.

60 Those differences themselves may be far from simple, of course, depending on the meaning that theft has in a particular tradition.

61 Heinrich Popitz, *Phenomena of Power: Authority, Domination, and Violence* (Gianfranco Poggi tr, Columbia University Press 2017) 14.

62 Geertz (n 22) 175.

63 See Glenn, *LTW* (n 10) 46; H Patrick Glenn, 'Are Legal Traditions Incommensurable?' (2001) 49 *Am J Comp L* 133.

sense we 'belong to elements of tradition that reach us'.[64] Such belonging, particularly as Glenn emphasizes in times of global overlapping, is not total and rarely hermetic, but it is not just 'simple information'. In often profound ways it is always normative as, Glenn indeed often stressed: traditions always are.

V NORMATIVITY

It is common for complex phenomena and the concepts used to describe them to be 'abridged' and discussed as though some one element constituted their essence or, at least, was more important than any other. This has often happened in discussions of tradition, as was pointed out by the late (and great) Polish historian of social thought, Jerzy Szacki, in a major (though outside Poland unnoticed) contribution to understanding the phenomenon and the concept.[65]

Szacki distinguishes between three different 'ways of approaching the problem of links between present and past',[66] one or other of which he found dominated particular discussions of tradition in the literature of social science. One view focusses on the *process* of handing-on in traditions, the activities of transmission from one generation to another, and on the differing means by which such transmission can be accomplished. We speak of ideas, beliefs, myths, legends, rituals, practices, being passed down *by* tradition. This conception concentrates on the many and various ways transmission is accomplished. The post-Tridentine Roman Church emphasized this conception, when it spoke of 'active tradition' or *actus tradendi*.[67]

A second conception conceives of traditions as historical deposits, inheritances passed down from the past. The concern here is with *what* has been really or purportedly transmitted and received. The early Church generally spoke of 'tradition' in this sense: 'passive tradition', *traditum tradendum*. Early Church fathers thought of tradition, in the words of Saint Gregory of Nyssa, as 'the truth which has come down to us by succession from the apostles, as an inheritance'.[68] Burke, similarly, lauded the English recognition of their 'entailed inheritance derived to us from our forefathers, and to be transmitted to our posterity'.[69] And in a more analytical mode, Gadamer insists on the pervasive significance of tradition as effective history' – in the face of which

[64] H-G Gadamer, *Truth and Method* (Crossroad 1982) 420.

[65] Jerzy Szacki, *Tradycja: Przegląd problematyki [Tradition: A Review of the Problematic]* (Państwowe Wydawnictwo Naukowe 1971). Edward Shils knew Szacki, and told me he knew of his book, but he had never read it. The book is untranslated and out of print, but see Jerzy Szacki, 'Three Concepts of Tradition' (1969) 2 *Polish Sociolog Bull* 17.

[66] Szacki, *Tradycja* (n 65) 97.

[67] Cf David H Kelsey, *The Uses of Scripture in Recent Theology* (Fortress Press 1975) 95.

[68] Gregory of Nyssa, *Contra Eunomium* c 4 (PG 45, 653), *quoted in* Yves M-J Congar, *Tradition and Traditions: The Biblical, Historical, and Theological Evidence for Catholic Teaching on Tradition* (Michael Naseby and Thomas Rainborough trs, Basilica Press 1966) 42.

[69] Edmund Burke, *Reflections on the Revolution in France* (first published 1790, Penguin 1969) 119.

> [in] fact history does not belong to us, but we belong to it. . . . The self-awareness of the individual is only a flickering in the closed circuits of historical life. That is why the prejudices of the individual, far more than his judgments, constitute the historical reality of his being.[70]

This version puts such inherited tradition at the centre of all understanding.

The same conception is equally available to those who oppose tradition. Thus, though Marx's views on the significance of the past-in-the-present are complex – far more complex than those of any *tabula rasa* revolutionaries – he did as we saw manifest impatience with 'the tradition of all the dead generations [that] weighs like a nightmare on the brain of the living'.[71] Similarly, in its 'traditional' American translation by Charles Hope Kerr, the *Internationale* boasts that 'no more tradition's ties shall bind us'.

The third conception of tradition, which Szacki calls 'subjective' (but which in any enduring tradition is altogether inter-subjective, over generations among multitudes of subjects), has to do with 'that specific kind of value, whose defence (or criticism) involves calling on its descent from the past'.[72] In this third sense, tradition is a particular posture in relation to what are, or are thought to be, transmitted inheritances: one of deference, acknowledgement of their authority. Weber's traditional legitimacy, invoking 'the authority of the eternal yesterday'[73] was traditional in this sense, and would still have been even if yesterday had been altogether different from what we imagined. The legal scholar Max Radin was quite explicit in choosing to tie 'tradition' to such evaluative commitment to the past, rather than merely to the past or its survivals themselves:

> Strictly and properly speaking . . . a tradition is not a mere observed fact like an existing custom, nor a story that exhausts its significance in being told; it is an idea which expresses a value judgment. A certain way of acting is regarded as right; a certain order or arrangement is held desirable. The maintenance of the tradition is the assertion of this judgment.[74]

Following Radin, the Polish literary critic Roman Zimand, rather than equating 'tradition' with inheritance, focused on a particular sort of present selection from what is, or is said to be inherited: '[T]radition is a particular restricted kind of human activity. . . . [I]ts active source is he who actively resists or submits, and not he who transmits. The latter indeed is completely unnecessary.'[75] Szacki also recommends

70 Gadamer (n 64) 245.

71 Marx, 'Eighteenth Brumaire of Louis Bonaparte' (n 47) 224.

72 Szacki, *Tradycja* (n 65) 155.

73 Max Weber, 'Politics as a Vocation' in Hans Gerth and C Wright Mills (eds), *From Max Weber: Essays in Sociology* (Routledge & Kegan Paul 1970) 78.

74 Max Radin, 'Tradition', *Encyclopaedia of the Social Sciences*, vol 15 (1st edn, 1934) 63.

75 Roman Zimand, 'Problem tradycji' in M Janion and A Porunowa (eds), *Proces historiczny w literaturze i sztuce [The Historical Process in Literature and Art]* (Proceedings of a Conference May 1965, Warsaw 1967) 369.

thus narrowing the meaning of 'tradition'. A similar, though presumably independent, view is that of the French anthropologist Jean Pouillon. Tradition, he argues, both in 'traditional' and modern societies

> is a 'retro-projection': we choose what we say we are determined by, we present ourselves as the heirs of those we have made our predecessors.
>
> Consequently, to define a tradition we must go from the present to the past and not vice versa and understand it not as a *vis a tergo* to whose effects we submit, but a point of view from which we look at the past.[76]

Usually, conservatives who value transmitted, 'objective' traditions will seek to foster favourable 'traditional' commitment to them. Burke, for example, did not merely remark that English liberties were inherited; he praised them for that. Radicals are usually well aware of the existence and power of inherited or believed-to-be inherited patterns of thought and action, at least amongst others than themselves. Much of their activity is devoted to encouraging negative traditionality in this third sense; that's what radical traditions do (except about canonical forebears in their own traditions).

Often people writing about tradition will have one such conception of tradition in mind, or some undifferentiated combination of them all, without recognizing or acknowledging either their differences or their necessary interplays. Often some composite of all three conceptions will be intended, or a writer will slide unannounced from one to another. What in particular is meant, for example, by saying that modernity erases tradition? Are the transmission belts snapping? Is nothing getting through? Is no one interested? Frequently it is not obvious which, or which combination, of these is meant. Yet these three centres of attention are not the same, nor will an investigation in terms of one of them necessarily tell us much about the others, for one is dealing in each case with different issues. Indeed Szacki emphasizes these differences by giving each conception a separate name: the first conception he calls *social transmission*, the second 'objective' conception, *inheritance*, with *tradition* being reserved for the third 'subjective' conception alone.

I do not support the last two labels, since 'objective' tradition was often very different from what it is now imagined to be,[77] but a retrospective or often 'massaged'[78] representation, with little resemblance to whatever was taken up and made over by the tradition. Conversely, 'subjective' responses are rarely as individual as we might imagine. Even if the 'objective' item in the tradition was not in fact as it has come to be understood and transmitted in the tradition, attitudes of traditional deference often have a long and widespread provenance that imposes itself on (unwitting?) subjects.

76 Jean Pouillon, 'Traditions in French Anthropology' (1971) 38 *Soc Res* 78.

77 See Eric Hobsbawm and Terence Ranger (eds), *The Invention of Tradition* (CUP 1983).

78 Glenn, *LTW* (n 10) 21.

However Szacki is surely right to insist that these three conceptions of tradition focus on very different aspects of the phenomena involved:

> [T]he problem of inheritance is a problem of the *conditions* we find when we come to carry on our affairs; the problem of transmission is one of the *means* with the aid of which those conditions were and are formed; the problem of tradition is one of the *goals* with which we arrange our affairs, the hierarchies of values which we impose on the world we find.[79]

Glenn is well aware of all three of these aspects. Every *healthy*, *living* tradition (since many suffer poor health, and many die) depends on the 'capture' of deposits of the past (most of which, uncaptured, disappear without a trace) and then continuous transmission 'by way of a continual reflexive process, through looping or feedback';[80] its life depends not merely on something that was deposited then, or something we believe now but rather, as we have seen, it has a 'diachronic nature'[81] that 'can only be understood, like a film, as part of a larger story'.[82] And while the 'pastness' of the tradition is key, it is not enough. It is *normative* in the present of those who participate in the tradition. So that requires someone to require and someone to manifest Szacki's somewhat misdescribed 'subjective' aspect.

This is a crucial point. Though Glenn speaks of legal tradition as 'simple information', and that serves his purposes of stressing its essentially protean, amenable, uncontrollable character, it is clear that he understands that traditions, particularly 'large and major' traditions of the sort he explores, are and have to be complex and complicated from the start. Something *always* has to be added to 'simple information' to make it normative. After all, as he insists, most past information goes nowhere, is taken into no tradition, just forgotten or ignored. That is simple information, and it has a short life. Elsewhere and frequently he says, more precisely, that tradition is, and must be, not just simple but '*normative* information', but he does not examine the implications of the adjective, even though he stresses its importance and it is precisely what transforms information into tradition. Thus:

> Western theory of tradition teaches that all tradition is normative, that is, that it provides a model, drawn from the past, as to how one should act. Legal traditions, of all traditions, should not depart from this general phenomenon, since law is perhaps the most normative of human endeavours. . . . [I]n spite of some confusing signals, normativity is a constant feature of these legal traditions.[83]

But while Glenn notes the significance of the several elements that conspire in transmission of traditions, there are two distinctive aspects to his treatment of them.

79 Szacki, *Tradycja* (n 65) 152.
80 Glenn, 'Doin' the Transsystemic' (n 23) 874.
81 Ibid, 875.
82 Ibid, 893.
83 Ibid, 366.

First, recall that for Glenn tradition is only information, not its transmission or reception. So only one of Szacki's three types – inheritances – would constitute the tradition properly so called. Glenn explicitly distinguishes between that which has come down, on the one hand, and both the processes by which that happens, as well as the responses of those influenced by such inheritances. This turns out to be an important distinction for Glenn. Thus, '[i]n law . . . it has been said that tradition, and law itself, is "something which has come down to us from the past."'[84] The other elements work on the tradition but they are not the tradition itself. For Glenn, they are vital to the *life* of traditions; but they are not *parts* of the traditions themselves:

> If tradition is seen as information, it must be the object of transmission or *tradition* if it is to continue to function as an operative or living tradition. Tradition would be thus distinct from the process of its own transmission and maintenance. It would be then for us to decide what to do in particular situations, faced with the teaching of tradition and its availability to us, through transmission.[85]

Similarly,

> it should be recalled that a tradition is information, and information itself (as distinct from how it is used) is not dominating. It may give advice, but we always have to decide what to do. We always have to decide exactly how the advice applies to our particular problem. Tradition is persuasive authority; in itself it lacks authoritativeness.[86]

So you have the tradition proper, the transmission process that brings it to us members, and then there are we, free to pick and choose (blindly; that presumably is the point of the bran) from the bran-tub.

But the information that is the tradition can never be as essentially innocent as Glenn imagines, even less can it be *random*, for the very reason he insists upon: traditions are *normative* for those who participate in them. 'Tradition is unquestionably normative. It tells us how we should act. Its normativity derives from the collective judgment, exercised over time, that the content of the tradition is of value and should be of contemporary application.'[87] Normativity is part of the deal, but the information cannot provide it on its own, and it is never left to provide it on its own. Generations of 'normativizers' have worked on it to constrain wiggle room. They can never succeed in eliminating it entirely, but a lot of them work hard at it. By contrast, historians are deluged with information, much of it normative for

84 Ibid, 872.

85 Ibid, 873.

86 Glenn, *LTW* (n 10) 49. See also Glenn, 'Concept of Legal Tradition' (n 4) 431 ('The common law tradition is thus composed of the information base of the common law, over space and time, and while there may be different reactions to it, these are reactions *to* the tradition and not the tradition itself. So we reach a contemporary conclusion, for lawyers in an information age, that tradition is information, as opposed to its transmission or reaction to it. The study of tradition is therefore the study of the content and flow of large bodies of normative information over time and over space.').

87 Glenn, 'Legal Traditions and *Legal Traditions*' (n 54) 73.

others, but their vocation as currently understood excludes it from normativity for them in the exercise of their vocation. That is part of their tradition.

Typically, members of legal traditions are right to believe, and have a legal duty to believe, that a presently valid law was written for them, though not for them alone, to interpret and apply to now contemporary affairs, for it is part of the contemporary 'momentary legal system' which they are charged to uphold. Conversely, a law no longer valid is no longer applicable, though it might once have been significant and might be interpretable. Historians have no similar duty; no duty – rarely any right – to infer from survivals from the past that they are meant for them: 'This Minoan pot was made to cook a dinner or to carry water from the well, not in order to inform Sir Arthur Evans about a Minoan civilization which has not itself survived.'[88] And the difference is not merely between law and pots. Historians, constrained though they are by their 'horizons' seek to infer from survivals things about a past, even a legal past, which cannot be assumed to have them or their present situation in mind or to have any application to either. To insist that it does is to treat the historical evidence anachronistically. Interpretation of a law by jurists within its tradition must assume that presently valid past law has them potentially in mind, is intended to (normatively, often indeed authoritatively) affect the present in which they live. This is, of course, not a distinction between the subjective motivations of lawmakers and potters. It is a regulative norm of the authoritative tradition of law that its authorized guardians treat presently valid relevant law, the momentary legal system, as intended to have – and able to have – present consequences; as a contributor to the contemporary world. Such an assumption is not common among archaeologists about their discoveries, and not much more so among historians, even legal historians. The major reason for this is that traditions are normative for their participants in a way that they rarely are for outsiders.

Let us return to a second distinctive aspect of Glenn's account, the bran-tub. This comes to serve Glenn's analytical purposes less well than his programmatic ones. There's not much normativity in a bran-tub, at least as I understand it, neither for those who fill it nor those who empty it. Whoever loads up the bran-tub, I imagine, has little – or anyway low-grade – concern with what goes into it. Perhaps price, toxicity, size, and a few other things matter, but probably there's not much worry about what the items in the tub turn out to be, still less what information they convey. Traditions, again particularly institutionalized, large, and major ones, are different. They are managed by people concerned that some things be in, some out; some normative, others just simple information; some information, others just noise. And if I am a judge in a legal tradition, or a citizen in search of a result, I hope the law is not random. I want to be able to know it when I need to and, where things work as they should, many legal practices are designed to make that possible. Of course it's

[88] Michael Oakeshott, 'Present, Future and Past' in Michael Oakeshott (ed), *On History and Other Essays* (Blackwell 1983) 31.

not a simple matter, but if it's a lucky dip, then we're in bad shape legally. And when it is not as I believe it should be (for reasons traditions say a lot about), I or someone is likely to be involved in trying to 'massage' (Glenn's term) the material to have it interpreted one way or another, implemented one way or another, taken more or less seriously as a normative element in their lifeworld. All these responses are affected by the normativity that the purveyors over generations try to build into the 'information', and the extent to which receivers treat it as deserving of such normative weight. If all this sort of work is not happening to the 'information' in a tradition, you might still have the information lying somewhere, neglected (like my manuscript on tradition, come to think of it; jam-packed with information, but who knew?) or not, but you don't have a tradition; just information. In other words, while one can say of a person that s/he is human but needs air to breathe, without the air being part of her humanity, simple information is not part of a tradition, until the whole process of transmission and reception is under way. We're a long way from lucky dips into a bran-tub.

Simple information is just what it says (or is interpreted to say). Normative information is different. It gains its normativity *not* from its content in the first instance, but from responses to it, by those who capture it, those who sustain it, those who transmit it, those who receive it. Indeed, it is arguable that the normativity of the tradition never merely happens to traditional information, it preselects it. Thus:

> How has any . . . writing ever come to be regarded as holy? Obviously, not because it has been self-authenticating. . . . [T]he status of Holy Book has first to be established by some recognized spiritual authority within the community concerned. . . . [T]he authority that endorses the sacred character of the Book must clearly be the recognized embodiment or the Holy Tradition within the community concerned. Thus we reach the significant conclusion that the Holy Tradition precedes the Holy Book. . . . In studying any specific example of a Holy Book, we find that we must give prior consideration to the Holy Tradition, on which that Book is founded.[89]

Information does not produce the ways in which it is treated within specific traditions. On its own it is impotent. What it is understood to be, and the ways it is understood, by relevant interpreters depends on its being embedded as that-to-be-interpreted-in-certain-ways within traditions shared by members of the traditions' authorized interpretive communities.

If the information is *converted* into part of a tradition by being promoted and accepted as normative, then but only then will it become active in the present of the tradition. And if that occurs, its bearers and transmitters will have attachments to it, and to their preferred versions of it. These will often seek to exclude others and other

[89] SGF Brandon, 'The Holy Book, the Holy Tradition and the Holy Iko: A Phenomenological Survey' in FF Bruce and EG Rupp (eds), *Holy Book and Holy Tradition* (Manchester University Press 1968) 3.

interpretations, for a host of reasons, to do with piety, power, cupidity, temperament, honest belief in sacred truths, even simple difference.[90] Difference of location is often enough for people to confirm the 'rueful European saying' about nations that Karl Deutsch reports: '[A] group of people united by a mistaken view about the past and a hatred of their neighbours.'[91] What is necessarily less natural, more a 'corruption' of tradition, about any of this? These are just among the ways that normativity is manifested by people to whom traditions matter. We might prefer that they think and behave differently, and there are often strong moral reasons to prefer that too, but there is nothing in the normative presence of the past that tells us which way they will go, nothing that traditions in their nature do better than cultures or families, for example.

VI CORRUPTION

There is a revealing passage, that deserves to be quoted at length, in which Glenn responds to Martin Shapiro's suggestion that his view of tradition is 'pollyannish'. Glenn is stung by the suggestion, and responds:

> One of the innovations (I think) of *Legal Traditions* is to incorporate into the discussion of every tradition the problem of corruption. . . . Most law books do not even mention corruption, in spite of its widespread character in the world and its social importance. The general idea of tradition and normative information, however, appears to me to inevitably call for acknowledgment of the possibilities of corruption, and the existence of a gap between the formal teaching and (even criminal) deviation from it. Again, tradition allows much room for study of empirical phenomena. How much attention is given to the problem of corruption in philosophical discussions of legal systems? I have never encountered it. So, it does not appear appropriate to equate discussion of tradition with unbridled optimism. There are also acknowledged traditions of both crime and war.[92]

The problem with this defence is the default assumption, expressed in his acknowledgements that many traditions might come to disappoint Pollyanna only through 'corruption', 'gap[s]', '(even criminal) deviation' or the like. But what if there is no gap, no deviation, just crime and war? I don't believe I have pointed to any fact that Glenn does not know, indeed know better than I do. He does indeed often stress that traditions are prone to 'corruptions' of various sorts: social, intellectual, institutional. In ways that remind me of those defenders of

90 For striking illustration of, and commentary on, the complexity of such typical inter- and intra-traditional dynamics, tensions, divergencies, and rivalries, see David Nelken, Chapter 8 in this volume.

91 Karl W Deutsch, *Nationalism and Its Alternatives* (Alfred A Knopf 1969) 3.

92 Glenn, 'Legal Traditions and *Legal Traditions*' (n 54) 74.

ur-Marxism against its 'betrayals'[93] by 'really existing socialism', he emphasizes the myriad ways in which actual, really existing, traditions can be intolerant, closed, hostile to others. The problem, it appears to me, is that he wants to treat all these as *necessarily* corruptions, saving the essence of tradition for something altogether nicer. He seeks a conceptual basis to ground the 'better angels' of traditions in their inherent nature, rather than in the contingent, variable, and often distressing, workings of traditions in the world. But some traditions might have no better angels.

Tradition is never 'simple' information. Being normative, it is always 'information plus' and the 'plus' does a lot of work. That being the case, the beguiling images of free-flowing rivers or randomly assembled and chosen bits of information thrown into a tub, which might make plausible Glenn's contrasts between inherently borderless traditions and hermetically sealed systems and cultures, are overdone. They cannot support the normative load tradition places on them.

One could also come at the point from the other side. Systems theorists have long explored 'open systems', and many people have insisted, in terms that overlap with Glenn on tradition, that cultures typically mix, should not be 'essentialized', all the more today, and so on. Others, committed to those concepts, might argue for them in such ways. As a card-holding traditionalist, I won't go there. I am in Glenn's debt for reawakening my early affections, and I share his hostility to the 'can-do' arrogance of those who pay traditions no heed. We're stuck with them, we should understand that, and also recognize how much we depend upon them, indeed could not do without them. Nevertheless, he sees more to like in traditions than even I, their old friend, feel confident to find.

CONCLUSIONS

When European communism collapsed just as I (partly for that reason) abandoned my project on tradition, I was full of hope, like many, that authoritarian governments, ethnic and religious hatreds, and attitudes mixed of evasion and antagonism to law, manifest in the region over long periods, might be relegated to the (normatively non-present) past.[94] I have often been disappointed since.[95] One reason, to adapt to law the observation of two well-informed observers of post-communist societies after almost thirty years of optimistic experimentation, might be that

93 See Leon Trotsky, *The Revolution Betrayed* (Plough Press 1973).

94 See Krygier, 'Institutional Optimism' (n 2).

95 Martin Krygier, 'The Rule of Law after the Short Twentieth Century: Launching a Global Career' in Richard Nobles and David Schiff (eds), *Law, Society and Community: Essays in Honour of Roger Cotterrell* (Ashgate 2014); Martin Krygier, 'Why Rule of Law Promotion Is Too Important to Be Left to Lawyers' in Raimond Gaita and Gerry Simpson (eds), *Who's Afraid of International Law?* (Monash University Press 2017).

> [t]oday's political cleavages, political discourses, patterns of partisan affiliation, institutional choice, and the quality of democracy itself all appear to correlate to a remarkable degree with patterns from the 'deep past'. To date, social scientists, however, have not sufficiently reflected on what might explain this finding and how to study the impact of the general phenomenon of the long-run in the region.[96]

These legacies of the 'deep past' are not just differences in information. Information is cheap. However, often responses to it have socio-psychological roots at which we are only beginning to guess; often they are fed by strong traditions, many of them not at all nice.

Again, I have tried to follow the fate of 'rule of law promotion' programmes which have become a multibillion-dollar international industry over the last thirty years.[97] These too have rarely been blessed with much success. But they come with much enthusiasm, intelligence, money, and *so much information*, again and again only to hit brick walls they don't even see. It would be nice to think that enough mixing of essentially open, conciliatory, and so on, traditions would erode these walls. But why think that?[98]

The sorts of repetitive patterns and predicaments that seem to recur in post-communist societies, and probably everywhere, often reflect deep traditions of attitudes to law and the state, and to how law and the state should or shouldn't mess with people's lives, to what law does and should do, to what is relevant and who should be involved, and to many other relevant matters. These are the *Anschauungen* of which Geertz writes – they are often highly normative, and they seem to greet a lot of introduced legal information with scant respect.

We should acknowledge that law is typically founded on and in traditions, simply because these are facts, and important ones. I fear, however that such acknowledgement will do little to advance the mutual accommodations among legal and social orders that Glenn admirably favours. Nor does it necessarily block them. They still have to be promoted on independent grounds, not because to act conflictually or exclusively or arrogantly in relation to other legal traditions is in some way to betray

96 Grzegorz Ekiert and Daniel Ziblatt, 'Democracy in Central and Eastern Europe One Hundred Years On' (2013) 27 *E Eur Pol & Soc* 90.

97 See eg, Martin Krygier, 'The Rule of Law: Pasts, Presents, and Two Possible Futures' (2016) 12 *Ann Rev L & Soc Sci* 199; Krygier, 'Why Rule of Law Promotion Is Too Important' (n 95).

98 Cf WE Butler, 'Russia, *Legal Traditions of the World*, and Legal Change' in Foster (n 5) 142, 145. Butler quotes a passage from Glenn that includes: '[For] a western lawyer with no previous experience of Soviet or socialist law, there are no major conceptual problems in understanding it . . . . To reverse a communist legal order you simply reverse the process.' Butler's comment is painfully apt:

> Glenn is not the only comparatist to accept this falsehood. There is a certain amount of Bolshevism in the assumptions he sets out, for there is ample evidence that the early Soviet leadership massively underestimated how to go about introducing legal change on the scale and in the directions essential to achieve their objectives. Policymakers in major Western capitals did the same in the early 1990s and, on that basis, structured law reform projects and retained lawyers to assist. Some of the most misdirected and inept law reform assistance ever rendered was the result.

(or corrupt), or for that matter to honour, the very nature of legal tradition itself. Nothing in the essence of traditions tells you how they will behave. It is as available in their nature to be hostile to other traditions, or to sects and heretics within, as it is to be tolerant of them.[99] As Glenn himself notes, '[t]oleration is not easy, which may be why there is a tradition of intolerance'.[100] Quite; even the most skilled massaging of the concept of tradition is unlikely to end that any time soon.

99 See David Nelken, Chapter 8 in this volume.
100 Glenn, *LTW* (n 10) 51.

7

Legal Systems as Legal Traditions

Catherine Valcke[*]

INTRODUCTION

Whereas comparative law scholarship has traditionally focused on Westphalian legal systems, Patrick Glenn famously argued that the legal tradition offers a superior analytic focus point. His seminal *Legal Traditions of the World*[1] stands out from the 'legal family' (or *grands systèmes*) literature precisely in that it insightfully orders world law around seven dominant legal traditions, each one foreshadowing the various national legal systems commonly associated with it.[2]

The legal system is 'structurellement déficient, comme institution, comme manière de penser le droit',[3] Glenn explains, as it evokes physicality, staticity, territoriality, whereas law is fundamentally epistemic, normative, historical, thus ill defined and dynamic.[4] The notion of legal tradition, in contrast, would aptly convey law's fundamental intellectual nature, as the perpetuation of any tradition crucially calls on the intellectual skills, critical judgement, and concerted deliberate actions of its participants. In Glenn's words, tradition is best thought of 'as

* I would like to thank Jorge Fabra and the participants to the 2016 International Conference on the Philosophical Foundations of Global Law, in Cartagena, Colombia, as well as my colleagues at the University of Toronto Law Faculty Workshop, for their comments on the earlier drafts of this chapter presented at these gatherings. All remaining errors are mine.

1 H Patrick Glenn, *Legal Traditions of the World: Sustainable Diversity in Law* (2nd edn, OUP 2004) (hereafter Glenn, *LTW*). See also H Patrick Glenn, 'Comparative Legal Families and Comparative Legal Traditions' in Mathias Reimann and Reinhard Zimmermann (eds), *The Oxford Handbook of Comparative Law* (OUP 2006) 421.

2 See generally the symposium issue of the *Journal of Comparative Law* devoted to Glenn's treatise: Nicholas HD Foster (ed), 'A Fresh Start for Comparative Legal Studies? A Collective Review of Patrick Glenn's *Legal Traditions of the World*, 2nd Edition' (2006) 1 *J Comp L* 100.

3 H Patrick Glenn, 'La tradition juridique nationale' (2003) 55 *RIDC* 263, 265 ('structurally deficient, as an institution, as a manner of thinking about the law') (translated by author).

4 Glenn, *LTW* (n 1) 22–25, 37–41, 49–53 ('The identity of cultural or epistemic communities needs to dissociate from geo-political divisions of the globe.'). James Gordley likewise claims that the 'legal systems' we know of in fact lack the internal coherence and heterogeneity required for qualifying as 'systems' proper. James Gordley, 'Comparative Law and Legal History' in Reimann and Zimmermann (n 1) 761.

normative information'[5] that 'derives from the collective judgment, exercised over time, that the content of the tradition is of value and should be of contemporary application'.[6] As such, 'the concept of tradition allows us to perceive . . . three distinct phenomena – the tradition itself, the process of its transmission, and contemporary reaction to it'.[7] In sum, as legal traditions evolve from an accumulation of intellectual connections drawn between past, present, and future legal facts,[8] the tradition paradigm seems particularly apposite for underscoring the intellectual character of law and legal practice.

Glenn also favours the tradition paradigm on normative grounds. Whereas the system paradigm reflects and validates a legal structure inherited from colonial hegemony, the tradition paradigm denotes collective acceptance rather than domination.[9] That is, the tradition paradigm rejects any external definition of legal systems professedly imposed on emerging legal communities by colonial powers in favour of an internal definition, in particular, the legal communities' very own *self*-definition as such. Under the tradition paradigm, then, will qualify as a distinct legal order any epistemic community considered such on the inside by its participants acting collectively.[10]

Glenn is not alone in insisting on law's epistemic dimension and the consequent internal definition process of legal systems. Globalization and legal pluralism scholars, in particular, have repeatedly called on comparative lawyers to overcome the state paradigm and broaden their sights to account for informal sources of legal normativity.[11] There in fact appears to be wide consensus that, in the current global context of transnational lawmaking and conflict resolution, the state paradigm is obsolete, and comparative law must let go of it lest it too fall into

5 Glenn, *LTW* (n 1) 71.

6 Ibid, 73. Neil Walker likewise describes 'tradition' as 'selective specification in accordance with a recognised transmission procedure or formula which consciously ensures continuity between past and present'. Neil Walker, *Intimations of Global Law* (CUP 2014) 152. Glenn rejects as too imprecise Martin Shapiro's reduction of tradition to 'what people of a given society think and say about their law over time'. Glenn, *LTW* (n 1) 72.

7 Glenn, *LTW* (n 1) 72–73.

8 Walker refers to this as 'intimation': 'Intimation . . . is as much about what is implicit in the world as it stands and as it unfolds, as it is about our explicit pronouncements on the world to come . . . as much about anticipation as veneration.' Walker (n 6) 157–58.

9 Glenn, *LTW* (n 1) 31–41; H Patrick Glenn, 'The Nationalist Heritage' in Pierre Legrand and Roderick Munday (eds), *Comparative Legal Studies: Traditions and Transitions* (CUP 2003).

10 'Legal theorists (or legal comparatists), therefore, need not formulate a definition of a legal tradition because the (various) definitions are out there. One must simply work with them.' H Patrick Glenn, 'Legal Traditions and *Legal Traditions*' (2007) 2 *J Comp L* 69, 71.

11 Eg, Paul Schiff Berman, *Global Legal Pluralism: Jurisprudence Beyond Borders* (CUP 2012); Roger Cotterrell, *The Politics of Jurisprudence* (University of Pennsylvania Press 1989); Brian Z Tamanaha, A *General Jurisprudence of Law and Society* (OUP 2001); Boaventura de Sousa Santos, *Towards a New Legal Common Sense: Law, Globalization and Emancipation* (Butterworths 2002); Ralf Michaels, 'Global Legal Pluralism' (2009) 5 *Ann Rev L Soc Sci* 243; William Twining, 'Normative and Legal Pluralism: A Global Perspective' (2010) 20 *Duke J Comp & Int'l L* 473; Sean Patrick Donlan and Lukas Heckendorn Urscheler (eds), *Concepts of Law: Comparative, Jurisprudential, and Social Science Perspectives* (Ashgate 2014).

obsolescence.[12] It thus seems as if we are faced with an intractable dilemma: conventional comparative law scholarship and its static (for territorially bound) state legal systems, or else progressive global legal pluralism and its fluid (for intellectually self-determined) legal traditions.

I here propose to try to diffuse that apparent opposition by offering an account of the legal system as (intellectually self-determined) tradition that is nonetheless consistent with the Westphalian conception. As aptly formulated by Horatia Muir Watt, the question addressed here boils down to the following:

> [W]hether, despite globalizing trends towards transnational normativity and convergence through increased proximity, there are still distinct legal traditions, linked to stable communities (whether territorial or otherwise, connected or not to nation states), which are worth comparing . . . .[13]

My hope is to show that it is indeed possible to conceptualize legal systems in a way that validates conventional comparative law scholarship without, for that matter, evacuating their fundamental epistemic dimension.

In particular, I contend that an internal investigation of the kind advocated by Glenn (and others) yields an overall picture of legal systems as very much shaped like bee swarms. The relevant characteristic of bee swarms for present purposes is that they project elusive, fuzzy edges around a comparatively well-defined centre of gravity, namely, their queen bees. I here argue that legal systems, as internally delineated epistemic communities, likewise boast a well-defined institutional grounding (Part I) encircled by fluid edges (Part II).

I A WELL-DEFINED (MATERIAL) CENTRE OF GRAVITY

Under the description emerging from the literature, epistemic communities in and outside law are shown as revolving around 'actual practices in the field'.[14] Peter Haas's notorious analysis refers to community members interpreting their 'social *actions*' and 'common *practices*'.[15] Others evoke 'concrete patterns of social

[12] Ugo Mattei, *Comparative Law and Economics* (University of Michigan Press 1997) 74; Werner Menski, *Comparative Law in a Global Context: The Legal Systems of Asia and Africa* (CUP 2006); Mads Andenas and Duncan Fairgrieve, 'Intent on Making Mischief: Seven Ways of Using Comparative Law' in Pier Giuseppe Monateri (ed), *Methods of Comparative Law* (Edward Elgar 2012) 26; Horatia Muir Watt, 'Globalization and Comparative Law' in Reimann and Zimmermann (n 1) 580–83; Ralf Michaels, 'Globalization and Law: Law Beyond the State' in Reza Bankaar and Max Travers (eds), *Law and Social Theory* (2nd edn, Hart 2013) 303; Wolf Heydebrand, 'From Globalisation of Law to Law Under Globalisation' in David Nelken and Johannes Feest (eds), *Adapting Legal Cultures* (Hart 2001); Lawrence Rosen, 'Beyond Compare' in Legrand and Munday (n 9) 510. See also William Twining, *General Jurisprudence* (CUP 2009) ch 12.

[13] Muir Watt (n 12) 586.

[14] Baudouin Dupret, 'Legal Pluralism, Plurality of Laws, and Legal Practices: Theories, Critiques, and Praxiological Re-Specification' (2007) 1 *Eur J Leg Stud* 1.

[15] Peter M Haas, 'Introduction: Epistemic Communities and International Policy Coordination' (1992) 46 *Int'l Org* 1, 3, fn 4.

ordering'[16] or 'what people actually do'.[17] Yet others point to sets of 'common documents',[18] 'texts',[19] 'checklist[s] of facts [and] techniques',[20] all of which connote concrete things and actions, situated in time and space. Of course, the community draws its soul from the *meaning* attached to those things and actions; it is the similar way in which the community members go about interpreting them that ultimately ties the community together. But as Max Weber outlined, before there can be 'meaning', there must be 'meaningful acts'[21] – any interpretation is interpretation *of* 'something out there'.[22]

So what are, exactly, the 'meaningful acts' of law? Legal practice is commonly described as the combination of argumentation and implementation.[23] I would suggest that a better, more specific description would be to say that it is argumentation *geared at* implementation: argumentation as to what ought to be ultimately coded by the courts as legal or illegal, and enforced as such. That clearly describes the behaviour of litigating parties before a court, but it arguably also characterizes (though in lesser degrees of immediacy) the behaviour of all other legal actors. Legislation is typically drafted with a view to maximizing judicial enforcement: unconstitutional wording is generally avoided, as are texts so inconsistent with the system's other legal materials that they might end up being altogether ignored by the judges. Lawyers are hired to offer predictions as to how the courts will deal with their clients' predicaments. Contracting parties take care to draft contracts that they speculate will be enforced by the courts. Arbitrators and lower court judges aim to

16 Marc Galanter, 'Justice in Many Rooms: Courts, Private Ordering, and Indigenous Law' (1981) 19 *J Leg Plur* 1.

17 Brian Z Tamanaha, *Understanding Law in Micronesia: An Interpretive Approach to Transplanted Law* (Brill 1993). For a comparison of accounts of 'culture' as the mere transmission of ideas (eg, Glenn) and as including ideas and actual behaviour (eg, Bell, Kluckhohn), see Twining, *General Jurisprudence* (n 12) 119.

18 Annelise Riles, 'The Anti-Network: Global Private Law, Legal Knowledge, and the Legitimacy of the State' (2008) 56 *Am J Comp L* 605.

19 Julen Etxabe, 'The Legal Universe after Robert Cover' (2010) 4 *L&H* 115, 118–19 ('common authoritative texts').

20 Duncan Kennedy, 'Toward an Historical Understanding of Legal Consciousness: The Case of Classical Legal Thought in America, 1850–1940' in Steven Spitzer (ed), *Research in Law and Sociology* (Jay Press 1980) 6 ('something more influential than a checklist of facts, techniques, and opinions').

21 Max Weber, *Economy and Society*, vol 1 (Bedminster Press 1968) 4. Weber here follows Hegel's contention that ethical life requires concrete expression in a community, expression situated in public space: Charles Taylor, *Hegel and Modern Society* (CUP 1979) 84–95; Hannah Arendt, *The Human Condition* (University of Chicago Press 1958) ch 2. See also Clifford Geertz, *Local Knowledge* (3rd edn, Basic Books 2000) 31 ('[T]he object of cultural study is not to be found in an informant's unspoken subjectivity but is rather what is publicly available as symbols – the inscription in writing, the fixation of meaning.').

22 '[P]ractices are not self-identifying.' Luc Wintgens, 'Legisprudence and Comparative Law' in Mark van Hoecke (ed), *Epistemology and Methodology of Comparative Law* (Hart 2004) 309.

23 Eg, J Brunnée and Stephen Toope, 'Interactional Legal Theory, the International Rule of Law and Global Constitutionalism' in Anthony Lang and Antje Weiner (eds), *Global Constitutionalism* (CUP 2016) 5.

replicate what they speculate would be the higher courts' pronouncements on the issue(s) before them. Legal scholars likewise discuss and debate what they consider *should* be – or else *should* count as valid arguments towards – the courts' ultimate rulings on various questions. Even law students are constantly reminded to 'think like lawyers', and thus to adduce only 'valid legal arguments', that is, arguments that would be found persuasive by a court. All the various rules, arguments, source materials, and so on, that make up legal systems, it seems, are more or less directly aimed at the single question of what will or will not end up being implemented by the courts – what legal sociologist Niklas Luhmann has described as the legal/illegal binary 'coding' that takes place in all legal systems.[24] Thus, while what is in fact coded legal or illegal by the judges in the different systems varies,[25] that binary coding structure is constant.[26] We will see later that the arguments themselves of course can only be *relatively* 'good' or 'bad' (depending on how *likely* they are to lead to the particular legal/illegal coding sought). But for now the relevant point is that all legal arguments are ultimately directed at such binary coding.

If that is an accurate description of legal practice everywhere, it arguably makes sense to count as 'meaningful acts' in any given legal community all and only those operations ultimately directed at the community's particular legal/illegal coding. Indeed, the only arguments that really *matter* are those aired in front of the community's judges. For judges are uniquely empowered to trigger implementation, to turn 'mere' arguments into concrete measures directly affecting people's lives. Unlike other legal actors, judges in all legal systems indeed are bound (explicitly or implicitly) by 'the prohibition of denial of justice',[27] the requirement to 'decide all cases brought to them by themselves',[28] even those where there seems to be no good reason to favour one or the other of the 'legal' or 'illegal' coding options.[29] Moreover,

24 Niklas Luhmann, *Law as a Social System* (Klaus A Ziegert tr, Fatima Kastner and others eds, OUP 2009) 84–85.

25 See Etxabe (n 19) 124 ('[P]ractical decisions of validity are reached on a case by case basis and according to rhetorically tailored criteria of relevance that are contingent (because they depend on temporal and spatial considerations), heterogenous (because they are not enclosed on any list of permissible sources), and evaluative (because they depend on judgements).'). However, for Etxabe, such contingence confirms, contrary to the present argument, that legal systems cannot be described as 'systems' proper: ibid, 120, 124.

26 'The important point is that [all legal] communication defers to its regulation through coding.' Luhmann, *Law as a Social System* (n 24) 100. 'All systems code their environment .... But while the code is essential ... the content of these programmes is contingent.' Richard Nobles and David Schiff, 'Introduction' in Luhmann, *Law as a Social System* (n 24) 10.

27 Luhmann, *Law as a Social System* (n 24) 279.

28 Ibid.

29 As there is no third, 'neither legal nor illegal' option open to them, they 'inevitably, and regularly, have to decide the undecidable': 'Contracts and statutes can be drafted (or avoided) on the assumption that the legality of a particular matter cannot be known prior to the matter being decided. . . . But this avoidance is not open to the courts.' Nobles and Schiff (n 26) 32. See also ibid, 34 ('[A]rguments are operations of the legal system, but unlike decisions, they do not assign symbols of validity .... [T]his special role of the courts explains how it is that "errors" – decisions without reasons or applying inconsistent reasons – are nonetheless part of the system.').

only their decisions are final, thus amenable to imminent and irreversible implementation: the finality that individuals pine for in all legal communities[30] – having matters 'settled' once and for all – comes from the judges, and the judges alone. The arguments directed at them accordingly should be considered particularly weighty expressions of the community's collective commitments; precisely because such arguments carry the potential of real, imminent, and irreversible consequences for the parties involved, they likely reflect a degree of thoughtfulness unrivalled by inconsequential arguments, which in contrast are 'free', 'easy to make', thus likely less carefully thought through.[31] This is arguably confirmed by the notorious distinction drawn in common law systems between the ratio decidendi and obiter dicta of judicial decisions: ratios would be particularly significant precisely because they bear directly on the outcome of the case, and thus on what will materially affect the parties, whereas dicta would be less significant because they are by definition devoid of such imminent, material consequences.

However, it has been claimed that such strong emphasis on judges and adjudication, while perhaps warranted with respect to common law systems (as the example just given would confirm), is unrepresentative of most legal communities – in particular, of civil law systems.[32] I would resist such a claim on the basis that French and German legal scholars alike commonly echo their Anglo-Saxon counterparts[33] in describing their law as adjudication centred.[34] And while the ratio/dicta language indeed is peculiar to common law argumentation, the same

30 For an account of finality as inherent to justice and the rule of law, see Arthur Ripstein, 'The Rule of Law and Times' Arrow' in Lisa M Austin and Dennis Klimchuk (eds), *Private Law and the Rule of Law* (OUP 2015). Cf Leone Niglia, 'Pluralism in a New Key – Between Plurality and Normativity' in Leone Niglia (ed), *Pluralism and European Private Law* (Hart 2013) 254 (suggesting that finality matters *merely* for 'law as integrity' as purportedly distinct from law's normativity). Glenn links finality with legal hierarchy, which he views as normatively unattractive (Glenn, 'Legal Traditions and *Legal Traditions*' (n 10) 70), though elsewhere he recognizes the importance of finality at the level of individual rulings: H Patrick Glenn, 'Cosmopolitan Legal Orders' in Andrew Halpin and Volker Roeben (eds), *Theorising the Global Legal Order* (Hart 2009) 25.

31 I accordingly would object to describing 'legal systems' as mere 'sites of contestation' (eg, Hans Lindhal, 'A-Legality: Postnationalism and the Question of Legal Boundaries' (2010) 73 *MLR* 30, 44) on the same basis, namely, that only contestation conducted *in the shadow of implementation* 'matters' and hence ought to be seen as 'meaningful'.

32 Martijn W Hesselink, 'How Many Systems of Private Law Are There in Europe? On Plural Legal Sources, Multiple Identities and the Unity of Law' in Niglia, *Pluralism and European Private Law* (n 30) 209.

33 Most famously Justice Holmes, who described law as the 'bad man's prediction' of what the courts will do in any particular case: Oliver Wendell Holmes Jr, 'The Path of the Law' (1897) 10 *Harv L Rev* 457, and Ronald Dworkin, *Taking Rights Seriously* (Harvard University Press 1977).

34 Jean Carbonnier, 'Les hypothèses fondamentales de la sociologie juridique' in Jean Carbonnier (ed), *Flexible droit: Pour une sociologie du droit sans rigueur* (8th edn, LGDJ 1995) 21 ('. . . est juridique ce qui est propre à provoquer un jugement, ce qui est susceptible de procès, justiciable de cette activité très particulière d'un tiers personnage qu'on appelle arbitre ou juge.'); Beatrice Jaluzot, 'Cartographier les droits' in *Mélanges en l'honneur de Camille Jauffret-Spinosi* (Dalloz 2013) 689 ('. . . il s'agit de s'intéresser . . . au droit tel qu'il est dans la réalité et vérifié par l'expérience. Cette vérification est obtenue par la justiciabilité des règles observées, par leur aptitude à conduire à une

notion is arguably also present, though expressed differently, in civil law systems. While judicial decisions admittedly are considered less authoritative than written law, or perhaps even doctrinal writings, in civil law systems (at least in French and French-inspired ones, less so in German-inspired systems), that arguably is so only because their judicial decisions are much less explicit than the typical English case. The classic French judgment offers no more than the bare disposition of the case – what at common law is considered the judgemnt's 'conclusion' – leaving it to scholars to articulate the full reasoning. Considered on their own, French judgments accordingly offer very little juridical information. But the arguments afterwards expounded by scholars are very much those that *they attribute to their judges*. Another possible explanation for the apparent lesser importance of judicial decisions at French law might be that it is meant to signal a general preference for reason-based arguments of principles, directly derived from the Civil Code, over casuistic argumentation, proceeding instead from analogies across specific rulings. But here again, I would argue, the collective reflection is ultimately more about the kind of arguments likely to find judicial favour than about any measure of the downplaying of the judicial function.

Insofar as it can be accepted that all legal systems are (justifiably) ultimately centred on adjudication, it would seem that, though those indeed are discursive communities, self-defined in and through particular discourses, said discourses remain materially anchored in the specific institutions capable of implementing them on the community members. And insofar as implementation might require coercion, which in turn requires at least minimal territorial connection with the bodies and the assets of the individuals involved,[35] the systems themselves can arguably be described as necessarily ultimately so connected.[36]

décision judiciaire dotée d'une force contraignante étatique . . . .'). The same, moreover, has been said of Confucian jurisprudence (Norman P Ho, 'Confucian Jurisprudence, Dworkin, and Hard Cases' (2017) 10 *Wash U Jurisp Rev* 1) and contemporary Chinese law more generally (Mark Jia, 'Chinese Common Law? Guiding Cases and Judicial Reform' (2016) 129 *Harv L Rev* 2213).

35 '[T]he foundation of jurisdiction is physical power': *McDonald v Mabee* 243 US 90 (1917) 91 (Holmes J); '[A] state ought to assume jurisdiction only if it has a real and substantial link to the event': *R v Hape* [2007] 2 SCR 292, 328 (¶ 62). See also ibid 329 (¶ 65) (enforcement jurisdiction ultimately is strictly territorial); Jacco Bomhoff, 'The Constitution of the Conflict of Laws' in Horatia Muir Watt and Diego Fernandez Arroyo (eds), *Private International Law and Global Governance* (OUP 2014) 268 (scholarly consensus on the geographical limitations of enforcement powers); Sarah Song, 'The Significance of Territorial Presence and the Rights of Immigrants' in Sarah Fine and Leah Ypi (eds), *Migration in Political Theory: The Ethics of Movement and Membership* (OUP 2014); Kurt Siehr, 'Global Jurisdiction of Local Courts and Recognition of Their Judgments Abroad' in Peter Mankowski and Wolfgang Wurmnest (eds), *Festschrift für Ulrich Magnus zum 70. Geburtstag* (Sellier European Law 2014) 515 (state courts refusing enforcement of judgement entered on basis of 'transient jurisdiction' – individuals only temporarily present in state territory). The requisite degree of material connection may, however, vary across legal systems. Eg, continental inquisitorial procedure arguably presupposes a lesser such degree than Anglo-Saxon adversarial procedure.

36 Whether such minimal territorial connection necessarily entails that only (territory controlling) nation states can qualify as legal systems proper, however, remains an open question. See sources cited below in note 71, and the accompanying text.

II FLUID (INTELLECTUAL) EDGES

While legal systems, then, boast a relatively well-defined institutional, material centre of gravity, their edges, as indicated, are determined intellectually, which results in those edges being fluid, porous, elusive. Notably, that fluidity is both spatial and temporal; that is to say, the exact geography of legal systems, unlike that of their specific judicial institutions, is difficult to ascertain demographically (ie who counts as an actor of the system) and in terms of materials (ie what norms, rules, sources, etc., can be considered the system's own). That geographic indeterminacy moreover is compounded by historic indeterminacy: whatever individuals and materials can be earmarked as partaking of the system at any given time change constantly, and the precise moment at which those changes occur cannot be pinpointed with any degree of certainty. I will first look at the temporal indeterminacy of legal systems and thereafter turn to their spatial indeterminacy.

1 *Time*

There is little debate that legal systems are dynamic systems, whose reflexive quality results in their shape and content constantly changing over time.[37] As every legal operation involves looking backwards to prior legal operations while also projecting forward through speculations as to future such operations, and as every new operation in turn is included in the stockpile of operations that will inform future ones, the overall size of that stockpile is bound to increase. But its content is likewise modified at each turn, since every new operation involves (re)interpreting the existing stockpile, and interpretation, as we know, contributes to modifying, even ever so slightly, what is being interpreted. It is therefore the system's size and content alike that is bound to evolve through its self-regeneration process: the legal actors 'not only have to rebuild the ship as it sails, but they have to do so in a shifting sea whose nautical charts are subject to continuous adjustment'.[38]

The precise whereabouts of that process remain somewhat obscure, however. In particular, the thorny question of how the system emerges in the first place calls for

37 Michel van de Kerchove and Francois Ost, *The Legal System between Order and Disorder* (Claredon Press 1994); Hesselink (n 32) 209; Heydebrand (n 12) 117ff; Rosen (n 12) 502ff; Ugo Mattei, 'Three Patterns of Law: Taxonomy and Change in the World's Legal System' (1997) 45 *Am J Comp L* 5.

38 Walker (n 6) 162. See also ibid, 149–50: '[I]t is on account of that doubly "intimated" object – actively projected and obliquely sourced . . . that . . . law retains a fluid and contentious quality'; ibid, 151 (referring to '[law's] complex relationship to the legal past and to the legal future and so to legal "time" in general'). Likewise, see Nigel Simmonds, *Law as a Moral Idea* (OUP 2007) 162 ('never fully reducible to a great assemblage of enacted rules, but . . . always a system awaiting construction from those materials'); Sean Coyle, *From Positivism to Idealism: A Study of the Moral Dimensions of Legality* (Ashgate 2007) 16 ('constant revision and fragmentation [is] endemic to political ideals'); Luhmann, *Law as a Social System* (n 24) 91 ('Law is a historical machine in the sense that each autopoietic operation changes the system, changes the state of the machine, and creates changed conditions for further operations. . . . It is a machine that involves its own condition in each operation and so constructs a new machine with each operation.').

further reflection: if every new operation appeals to the existing stock of past operations, which themselves presumably appealed to pre-existing such operations, what did the very first operations appeal to? We are faced with a chicken and egg dilemma. For it now seems that, just like bee swarms which start in some elusive fashion but clearly self-magnify from the moment that they have in fact started, legal systems can really come into existence only from the moment that they . . . already exist.[39]

It is worth emphasizing at the outset that this dilemma indeed arises only under an internal definition of legal systems. Colonial history makes this clear: although the colonizing powers typically took it upon themselves to (externally) set a precise date at which their respective colonies would be considered created, those colonies did not *really* (internally) establish themselves as autonomous legal systems until they had already accumulated a minimum of local materials on which to draw for the purpose of adjudicating local disputes – as per the paradox discussed earlier.[40] Further compounding the problem was the fact that, as colonial legal materials naturally accumulated at different paces for different areas of law, it could be said that the colonial legal system came into existence at different times depending on the area of law in question. So if colonial legal systems were not born on the precise date externally set in colonial law, when did they, in fact, come into existence?

As it turns out, that dilemma is not quite as intractable as it first appears, at least not when it comes to law. (Fortunately, we can safely leave it to entomologists to deal with real bee swarms here.) Here again, Luhmann's sociological insights prove enlightening. On his account, the formation of legal systems proceeds in three stages.[41] First comes an accumulation of individual rulings: social life inevitably entails interpersonal conflicts, which need to be resolved one way or another.[42] The individuals charged with those resolutions at that point proceed on no other basis than their personal sense of right and wrong. They can rely on the Bible, Greek mythology, or whatever, even just their individual preferences. The sources determining conflict resolution at that early stage are infinite and infinitely varied: we are in a state of complete 'porosity',[43] 'permeability',[44] or as Luhmann calls it, 'informational openness'.[45]

39 Van de Kerchove and Ost (n 37) 147ff.

40 David Schorr, 'Questioning Harmonization: Legal Transplantation in the Colonial Context' (2009) 10 *Theo Inq L Forum* 49–53. On Canadian colonial history, see H Patrick Glenn, 'Persuasive Authority' (1987) 32 *McGill LJ* 261. On the US experience, see Rene David and Camille Jauffret-Spinosi, *Les grands systèmes de droit contemporains* (11th edn, Dalloz 2002) 301ff; Alan Watson, *Legal Transplants: An Approach to Comparative Law* (2nd edn, University of Georgia Press 1993) 65ff.

41 Luhmann, *Law as a Social System* (n 24) 230ff.

42 Nobles and Schiff (n 26) 25 ('long experience in arbitrating normative conflicts with the code legal/illegal').

43 William Twining, *Globalisation and Legal Theory* (CUP 2000) 85 ('the imprecision and porosity of the social contexts of most normative orders').

44 Etxabe (n 19) 124 ('law [as] an essentially porous entity, distinguishable from, and yet permeable by, its exterior'); Jaluzot (n 34) 691 ('relativité, mobilité et permeabilité de l'ordre juridique').

45 Luhmann describes self-regenerating, or 'autopoietic' systems as combining 'informational openness' with 'normative closure': while the legal process is initially open to a limitless diversity of factors and

Once a number of those rulings have taken place, however, the intellectual urge arises to 'attempt to order what is happening'.[46] The rulings are first recorded, in writing, or, in the case of oral legal traditions, through memory and narrative.[47] Patterns can then be detected in the justifications given for the various resolutions, some of which seem particularly consistent, robust, or somehow more legitimate, and hence worth retaining over the others. Only at this second stage, when a sufficient number of (actual) rulings have been gathered and it becomes possible to (intellectually) reflect back on them, can a form of 'legal consciousness' begin to emerge.[48] As the justification patterns initially retained recur in new conflict resolutions, their salience increases[49] to the point of gradually acquiring the status of 'norms',[50] which in turn allows community members to form 'normative expectations' as to future conflict resolutions.[51] The sum of those henceforth 'normative' rules, maxims, arguments, concepts, and so on, in time congeals into a body of 'legal materials' proper, soon to be attended with a particular technique ('legal

points of view, it will result in only a limited number of them actually becoming ('normatively relevant') law. Niklas Luhmann, *A Sociological Theory of Law* (Routledge & Keegan Paul 1985) 174–83; Luhmann, *Law as a Social System* (n 24) ch 2 ('The Operative Closure of the Legal System'). See also Gunther Teubner, *Law as an Autopoeitic System* (Blackwell 1993) esp ch 3; Hubert Rottleuthner, 'Les métaphores biologiques dans la pensée juridique' (1986) 31 *Arch Phil Droit* 215. As has been pointed out, Luhmann here is merely restating in abstract terms what many legal positivists, in particular Hart and Kelsen, have described in more concrete, legal terms: see Van de Kerchove and Ost (n 37) 5–6.

46 Nobles and Schiff (n 26) 27.

47 Luhmann, *Law as a Social System* (n 24) 234; ibid, 25 ('[We witness the] establishment of a level of secondary self-observation . . . writing recorded transactions that were worth recording.').

48 Nobles and Schiff (n 26) 51 ('a continued connection between consciousness and legal systems'); Etxabe (n 19) 118; John Gillespie, 'Developing a Framework for Understanding the Localisation of Global Scripts in East Asia' in Halpin and Roeben (n 30) 227 ('social institutions and regulatory practices are first created in the mind'); Kennedy (n 20) 15 (explaining how legal consciousness is experienced by legal actors: '[I]f your position about X puts a good deal of moral and intellectual pressure on you to take a particular position with respect to Y, then the two are part of [the same legal system]. If you experience no such pressure, they are not.').

49 'The differentiation process . . . can thus begin somewhere or other and somehow or other and reinforce the deviation that has arisen. One settlement among many comes to be preferred where the advantages of centralization are mutually reinforcing.' Niklas Luhmann, *Theory of Society*, vol 4 (Rhodes Barrett tr, Stanford University Press 2012) 3.

50 This distinction variously appears in the legal literature as that between 'what people actually do' and their 'felt sense of obligation' (Brian Z Tamanaha, 'The Folly of the Social Scientific Concept of Legal Pluralism' (1993) 20 *JL & Soc'y* 217, fn 71), 'actual behaviour' and 'beliefs or attitudes concerning its legitimacy, obligatoriness, and prescriptive power' (Twining, *General Jurisprudence* (n 12) 118), and 'existence empirique' and 'validité' (Jaluzot (n 34) 690).

51 'The function of law is to maintain normative expectations in the face of disappointment. Law's communications about what ought to occur must, if they are to continue as expectations, remain meaningful despite the inevitability that what ought to occur will not always occur.' Nobles and Schiff (n 26) 9 (paraphrasing Luhmann, *Law as a Social System* (n 24) 94). Also: 'The presence of expectations that captured and convicted thieves will be punished stabilizes expectations represented by the law of theft even if only a few criminals are punished relative to the amount of crime.' Nobles and Schiff (n 26) 15.

dogmatics'[52]) and concomitant body of expertise ('legal professionals'[53]). Only then does the initial 'informational openness' come to be accompanied with minimal 'normative closure', that is, the closure required for self-regenerating 'systems' to be recognizable as such.[54] As legal materials, legal dogmatics, and legal professionals slowly come together, so does a somewhat enclosed 'legal practice', distinct from other social practices.

Then comes the third and final stage of the formation process, on Luhmann's account: reflecting back on the practice itself. That is, it now becomes possible for, say, scholars to reflect on (and debate) not just the punctual outcomes of the conflict resolution process, but also the growing body of professional arguments that simultaneously supports and emerges from that resolution process, namely, the practice as such. We now have 'law' proper – law reflecting upon itself *as law* – as well as a 'legal system' proper – a system wherein individual conflicts are resolved by appeal to an objective law rather than the subjective opinions of unconnected individual arbitrators.[55]

There are three consecutive steps, then, respectively, staging judges, lawyers, and scholars. Moreover, while Luhmann himself does not say so explicitly, the *disappearance* of legal systems presumably proceeds similarly, through the same three steps in reverse. As particular materials, techniques, and voices somehow come to be ignored by the judges, they in turn move out of sight of the lawyers and scholars. They gradually exit adjudication, legal practice, and in time legal consciousness as a whole – and thus the system itself, which shrinks and eventually withers correspondingly.

To say of legal systems that they 'really come into existence only from the moment that they already exist' – or, in the reverse, that they 'really come out of existence only from the moment that they no longer exist' – is not quite as tautological as it might first appear. For the apparent circularity of such statements quickly subsides under Luhmann's account of law as inherently factual *and* intellectual. (What of real bee swarms, which do not boast the same duality?) Precisely because that account allows one to distinguish between what *is* in fact implemented as legal/illegal – the facts of law – and what *ought* to be so implemented – the norms of law – it can coherently be said of law on that account that it exists or does not exist (normatively) only from the moment that it already exists or no longer exists (factually). Or, in Luhmann's words, that 'autopoietic [self-regenerating] systems are always historical systems, which start from the state in which they have put themselves',[56] and that '[l]egal practice [as one such system]

52 Luhmann, *Law as a Social System* (n 24) 256.

53 Ibid, 298.

54 See above n 45.

55 'The long-term effect of all of this is a base of concepts, maxims, principles, and rules for decisions that forms the materials which are applied partly formally, partly critically, and which enable the judge to reject ad hoc and ad hominem arguments.' Luhmann, *Law as a Social System* (n 24) 249.

56 Ibid, 85.

always operates with a law that has historically always been there because it could not otherwise entertain the notion of distinguishing itself as legal practice.'[57]

The temporal indeterminacy of legal systems should be clear at this point. For, under the picture just laid out, there is no exact moment at which one can categorically affirm that a legal system, or any of its components, 'exists' or 'does not exist' – *normatively* speaking. Whereas the legal/illegal rulings that ground the system are categorical and punctual, the normative significance of these rulings, like that of the system's various other components – or of the entire system for that matter – is a question of interpretation, thus relative and never fixed once and for all, but rather gradually increased or decreased over time.[58]

Consider how the judicial reasoning process operates. In common law systems, the stockpile of accumulated legal operations consulted by the judges in any given case as we know is largely made up of judicial decisions, in particular, the parts of those decisions considered 'binding' (ratio), in contrast with their parts considered merely 'persuasive' (dicta). A similar distinction arguably is drawn in civil law systems between ('binding') legislative diktats and ('persuasive') diktats emerging from a *jurisprudence constante* (in France) or *ständige Rechtsprechung* (in Germany).[59] Yet analysts of the judicial process report that, despite such dichotomous labelling, no authority is, in fact, ever considered absolutely determinative (or not) by the judges in any legal system. Common law judges rather treat (purportedly binding) precedents as additional, more or less constraining reasons to favour one conclusion over the other, one important factor in that determination being the authoritative salience of the courts that issued them.[60] In other words, the weight of past decisions would be proportional to how 'loud' the decision-makers' voices are taken to be in the system at that particular time. In civil law systems, the legislative voice will likewise be considered 'louder' than the judicial voices at the source of any

57 Ibid, 91.

58 As obtains more generally under a 'coherence' rather than 'correspondence' standard of truth. See generally Andrei Marmor, 'Three Concepts of Objectivity' in Andrei Marmor (ed), *Law and Interpretation: Essays in Legal Philosophy* (Clarendon Press 1995); Matthew H Kramer, *Objectivity and the Rule of Law* (CUP 2007); Kent Greenwalt, *Law and Objectivity* (OUP 1992); Matti Ilmari Niemi, 'Objective Legal Reasoning – Objectivity without Objects' in Jaako Husa and Mark Van Hoecke (eds), *Objectivity in Law and Legal Reasoning* (Hart 2013) 69.

59 Alison Harvison Young, 'Stare Decisis – Quebec Court of Appeal – Authority v. Persuasiveness: *Lefebvre v. Commission des affaires sociales*' (1993) 72 *Can Bar Rev* 91, 98, 101. The same can be said of the Italian *dottrina giuridica* and the Spanish *doctrina juridica*. See generally Robert Alexy and Ralf Dreier, 'Precedent in the Federal Republic of Germany' in Neil MacCormick, Robert S Summers, and Arthur Goodhart (eds), *Interpreting Precedents: A Comparative Study* (Routledge 1997) 17, 50; Jean Carbonnier, 'Authorities in Civil Law: France' in Joseph Dainow (ed), *The Role of Judicial Decisions and Doctrine in Civil Law and in Mixed Jurisdictions* (Louisiana State University Press 1974) 91, 102; Michele Taruffo and Massimo La Torre, 'Precedent in Italy' in MacCormick, Summers, and Goodhart (n 59) 141, 180–81; Alfonso Ruiz Miguel and Francisco J La Porta, 'Precedent in Spain' in MacCormick, Summers, and Goodhart (n 59) 259, 272–73, 282–83.

60 Ronald Dworkin, *Law's Empire* (Harvard University Press 1986) 24ff; Stephen Perry, 'Judicial Obligation, Precedent and the Common Law' (1987) 7 *OJLS* 215, 239–45.

jurisprudence constante or *ständige Rechtsprechung* (though the difference is less marked with respect to the latter). In certain (easy) cases, of course, relevant authorities exist whose loudness seems well established and enduring. But where the stockpile of previous operations does not cover the case at hand, or is internally contradictory, the judge has no choice but to rely on less authoritative, perhaps even hitherto irrelevant, materials. As soon as that happens, however, those materials *ipso facto* become more authoritative – their normative salience increases – which in turn causes them to be reused in other cases (as per Luhmann's second stage of the formation process discussed earlier), to a point where they might eventually come to be treated as clearly entrenched and enduringly 'loud' materials. That arguably explains the rise to prominence of policy arguments in common law jurisdictions and the enviable status of doctrinal writings in civil law jurisdiction.[61]

The normative significance of each of the system's components, and the system's corresponding overall normative tightness, would accordingly be a matter of degree – and one that varies over time. That presumably is why legal systems are typically described as 'forming', 'emerging', 'developing', or else as 'declining', 'fading', 'deteriorating', rather than as categorically 'existing' or 'not existing'[62] – as is typically done with bee swarms. Unlike the centre of gravity of legal systems, then, their temporal boundaries are fluid: the size and content of those systems change constantly, and the exact moments at which those changes take place cannot be precisely identified.

2 *Space*

Luhmann's account of the formation of legal systems arguably likewise underscores these systems' spatial indeterminacy. He suggests that the three stages of these systems' formation confirm that they are not structured hierarchically (in a Kelsenian fashion) but rather circularly, in terms of 'centre' and 'periphery'.[63] However, he and I part company in the next step, when it comes to specifying the internal spatial organization of that circular structure (the system's 'internal differentiation'[64]).

Luhmann's account motions to an internal organization in terms of three concentric layers, corresponding to the three stages of the system's formation. The first layer is, as expected, made up of the judges – the system's very heart, its 'centre of gravity', as I described it. The second layer gathers the lawyers, who reflect on the

61 John C Reitz, 'How to Do Comparative Law' (1998) 46 *Am J Comp L* 617, 625, 629.

62 'If efficacy of law is a matter of degree, then we might have to concede that law's existence is likewise and thereby a matter of degree.' Gerald J Postema, 'Fidelity in Law's Commonwealth' in Lisa M Austin (ed), *Private Law and the Rule of Law* (OUP 2014) 24, fn 19.

63 Nobles and Schiff (n 26) 30 (referring to Luhmann, *Law as a Social System* (n 24) ch 7). Likewise: Gerard Timsit, 'L'ordre juridique comme métaphore' (2001) 33 *Droits* 8 ('un système d'appartenances ou d'inclusion des normes dans un ensemble non-hiérarchisé').

64 See above n 49.

judges' rulings with a view to extracting the rules and arguments that will inform future rulings – what Luhmann describes as 'second order' legal reasoning. Besides lawyers, that second layer includes all those who 'think like lawyers' and engage in 'second order' legal reasoning: the legislators, the contract drafters, even the judges themselves (in common law systems) when they overtly interpret previous cases rather than finally dispose of the one before them. The third layer comprises the scholars, as we saw, but also all those who 'think like scholars' – those who reflect on the materials produced through the second layer with a view to questioning and ultimately honing those materials' overall consistency and desirability. As the reflection of that last group of actors accordingly amounts to 'reflection on reflections', Luhmann dubs it 'third order' legal reasoning. Three concentric layers, then – much like the heart of an onion – represent the three forms of reasoning deployed at the three stages of formation.

I would resist this account of the internal organization of legal systems on the grounds that, while I do see the 'first order' reasoning deployed in the first layer (ruling on cases) as qualitatively different from the 'second' and 'third order' reasoning deployed in the next two layers (arguing over rulings), what Luhmann distinguishes as 'second' and 'third order' reasoning are in my view one and the same. That is to say that, while the scholars' 'third order' reflection is in a sense further removed from the judges' rulings than, say, the lawyers' 'second order' arguments before those very judges, it proceeds in exactly the same way. Insofar as any kind of legal interpretation necessarily involves passing judgment on the internal consistency and normative desirability of the materials interpreted, the task of extracting rules from past rulings would be 'normative' in exactly the same way as is that of overtly assessing these rulings' quality, however defined: in both cases, the debate ultimately centres on how judges *ought* to rule in any given case.[65]

Of course, there are different kinds of scholars. Some are more interested in reinventing the legal system along normative lines borrowed from neighbouring social systems (economics, literature, politics, etc.) than in honing the system's own normative apparatus. Theirs are the so-called 'external' critiques, in contrast to 'internal' ones, which instead seek to evaluate the system 'on its own terms'. Such external-critique scholars admittedly might be engaging in an intellectual exercise qualitatively different from that deployed by any of the actors just discussed. But as Luhmann himself seems to recognize, that might militate in favour of positioning them, not so much on a separate layer, as altogether outside the system[66] and seeing them as economists, literary critics, or political scientists more than 'legal scholars' proper. Accordingly, my

65 Of course, the judges' own reasoning could likewise be described as 'normative' insofar as they in principle should decide their cases by asking the very same question of how judges (here, themselves) objectively *ought to* decide the case at hand. But, crucially, we saw that they can in fact base their decisions on their own, personal values (as they do in the first stage of the formation process). Those decisions would nonetheless count as 'legal', whereas only the arguments based on the objective values of the system as a whole count as properly 'legal'.

66 Nobles and Schiff (n 26) 35.

point only applies to internal-critique scholars, insofar as their reasoning would indeed be qualitatively indistinguishable from that of any actor populating the purported second and third layers.[67] In sum, while I would retain (in fact insist on) the distinction drawn by Luhmann between the (first order) centre and the periphery of legal systems, I would resist his further (second and third order) distinction within the periphery.

That is not to say, however, that all legal actors and materials should be seen as equidistant from the centre, thus forming a single homogenous peripheral layer. Rather, their differences in normative salience warrants, I would argue, positioning them at correspondingly different distances from one another and the centre. At any given time, that is, the most salient actors and materials, those most likely to convince the judges – 'slam dunk' arguments, for example – can be pictured as sitting tightly together, very close to those judges. Conversely, the least salient actors and materials, those only remotely likely to convince the judges – highly 'creative' arguments – would sit further apart from one another and the judges. And in between would lie a flurry of unevenly distributed 'somewhat salient' actors and materials – arguments 'worth a shot'. Now, we saw that the actors' and materials' relative degrees of salience change over time, which would suggest that their relative distances from one another and the centre do as well. Indeed, when judges undertake to rely on hitherto ignored sources or materials, the resulting salience increase is reflected in those sources or materials moving correspondingly closer to the ones crowding the system centre. Conversely, as particular sources and materials become less frequently used in adjudication, their resulting reduction in salience is matched by a corresponding movement away from the centre.

If we now stand back to consider what that does to the spatial configuration of the system as a whole, we observe that any punctual movement of a system component towards or away from the centre, as it gains or loses salience, translates into a corresponding marginal variation in the system's overall coverage and density. The first judicial reference to hitherto ignored materials causes the system to stretch its boundary to reach towards and include the new materials, thus marginally increasing its overall coverage. But as those materials are being reused in subsequent cases, they make their way towards the centre, resulting in the system shrinking back and its density proportionally increasing. Conversely, materials moving away from the centre first cause an extension of the system's coverage, with a corresponding decrease in density. But if those materials move even further out, and come to exit the system altogether, the system's boundaries then pop back to a smaller overall coverage, yet without the proportional recovery in density as the system is now simply short of some of its initial components. That would entail that older, more mature legal systems,

67 Oddly, Luhmann seems to agree: '[T]he observation is itself an operation, and therefore everything applies to it that has been shown to apply to operations . . . . In this sense, self-reference always implies external reference, and vice versa.' Luhmann, *Law as a Social System* (n 24) 86.

whose composition has had the opportunity to stabilize over time, are knit more tightly, their breadth and density being, respectively, smaller and greater than those of younger, emerging systems – as is the case of long-standing, compared to newly emerging, bee swarms. In Luhmann's words, the 'normative closure' of mature systems is stronger, as those have had time to include and weave together high quantities of materials, and their informational openness is correspondingly weaker, since (and all else being equal) the strong normative closure eliminates the need to fish for new materials outside the system.

Thus, the fundamental normative character of legal systems, which makes it impossible to categorically affirm that those systems, or any of their elements, 'exist' or 'do not exist' at any particular *time*, also makes it impossible to ascribe exact *locations* to them or their elements at any given point in time. Certainly, there is no reason to assume that their locations can be determined territorially, by reference to the fixed territorial locations of the central adjudicative bodies that first produced them. All adjudicative bodies remain free to, and in fact commonly do, co-opt materials originating from other state territories. A Canadian judge referring to an English judicial decision for the first time, for example, would have the effect of extending the Canadian 'swarm' to include that decision without, for that matter, resulting in the Canadian and English swarms intersecting on the matter at hand, as the swarms' respective realms of authority would remain unchanged. (It would be an example of what Luhmann describes as 'structural coupling',[68] and what is sometimes dubbed 'legal pluralism' in the legal pluralism literature.[69]) Indeed, no comparative lawyer has ever suggested that foreign citations cause the host and foreign systems to intersect.[70]

In my view, then, the periphery of legal systems resembles that of bee swarms much more than that of onions. Whereas onions boast stable and well-defined concentric layers, legal systems are ill-shaped, elusively contoured, and unevenly dense at any particular time, and moreover, such shape, contours, and density change constantly.

CONCLUSION

Our internal investigation of the (self-)structuring process of legal systems allowed us to observe the emergence of an overall structure very much resembling, I argued, that of a bee swarm. In Part I, we saw that legal systems, like all epistemic communities, centre on a set of facts – their respective final courts' rulings – clearly identifiable in time and space. As such, those rulings are to their respective systems

68 Luhmann, *Law as a Social System* (n 24) ch 9.

69 Hesselink (n 32) 199.

70 Though they have suggested that such repeated citations justify grouping the Canadian and English systems within the same legal 'tradition' or 'family': Konrad Zweigert and Hein Kötz, *An Introduction to Comparative Law* (Clarendon Press 1987); David and Jauffret-Spinosi (n 40) 301ff.

what queen bees are to their respective swarms. We then saw in Part II that those centres of gravity are surrounded by argumentative practices whose edges in contrast are ill defined and constantly changing, again much like those of bee swarms. Building on Niklas Luhmann's account of the formation of legal systems, I argued that, as it is the normative salience of legal materials and arguments that determines the extent to which, and the time at which, they can be considered part of the system, their geographical and historical parameters indeed are bound to vary with that normative salience. From static and dynamic perspectives alike, then, legal systems very much resemble bee swarms, whose ever-fluctuating edges and opacity levels are determined by their elements' relative proximity to, and constant movement towards or away from, the queen bee.

The upshot of the bee swarm metaphor for comparative law is twofold. First, it arguably validates comparative lawyers traditionally focusing on state court rulings. Nothing said earlier admittedly precludes non-state communities that would be endowed with some kind of collective sanction-backed conflict-resolution process from qualifying, at least in principle, as autonomous swarms under the present account. Nonetheless, as state communities obviously so qualify, and may in fact stand as the prototypical swarm in the current Westphalian organization of world politics – the very same context in which comparative lawyers have themselves been operating to date – their ongoing focus on state legal systems seems entirely legitimate. Should the day come where adjudicative bodies other than national courts are endowed with real enforcement powers, that analytical framework indeed might need to be revisited.[71] But for now, there does not appear to be cause for worry.

[71] Kelsen famously denies that possibility as the political and legal realms, in his view, are inextricably interwoven, even at just a conceptual level. Hans Kelsen, *General Theory of Law and State* (Anders Wedberg tr, Russel & Russel 1961) 189; Hans Kelsen, *Introduction to the Problems of Legal Theory* (Clarendon Press 1992) 99 ('When the legal system has achieved a certain degree of centralization, it is characterised as a state.'). The primary aim of much of the global pluralist literature of course is to attempt to dissociate law from the political nation state. However, those who reviewed that literature seem to converge on the view that, first, it remains largely under-theorized, and second, none of it ultimately manages to steer clear of state law. See Stepan Wood, 'Transnational Governance Interactions: A Critical Review of the Legal Literature' (2015) Osgoode Legal Studies Research Paper Series Paper 109, 35–37 <https://papers.ssrn.com/sol3/papers.cfm?abstract_id=2644465>; Neil MacCormick, 'Juridical Pluralism and the Risk of Constitutional Conflict' in Neil MacCormick (ed), *Questioning Sovereignty* (OUP 1999) 102–05; Mattias Kumm, 'The Jurisprudence of Constitutional Conflict: Constitutional Supremacy in Europe before and after the Constitutional Treaty' (2005) 11 *Eur LJ* 262, 267, 306; Ralf Michaels, 'Globalization and Law' (n 12) 10, 14; Ralf Michaels, 'Territorial Jurisdiction after Territoriality' in Piet Jan Slot and Mielle Bulterman (eds), *Globalisaton and Jurisdiction* (Kluwer Law International 2004) 105; Oxana Golynker, 'European Union as a Single Working-Living Space: EU Law and New Forms of Intra-Community Migration' in Halpin and Roeben (n 30) 145; Nicole Roughan, *Authorities: Conflicts, Cooperation, and Transnational Legal Theory* (OUP 2013) 8; Alain Degenne and Michel Forse, *Introducing Social Networks* (2nd edn, Sage 1999); Mark Granovetter, 'Economic Action and Social Structure: The Problem of Embeddedness' (1985) 91 *Am J Soc* 481, 491; Pierre Larouche and Peter Cserne (eds), *National Legal Systems and Globalization: New Roles, Continued Relevance* (TMC Asser Press 2013); Jose E Alvarez, 'State Sovereignty Is Not Withering Away: A Few Lessons for the Future' in

At the same time, however, the bee swarm metaphor also clarifies that a focus on state courts does not entail that the corresponding swarms need be coextensive with their respective territorially bound nation states. State courts commonly co-opt norms and materials from one another, with the result that any given state swarm can be expected to boast some degree of norm or material hybridity. And while some national courts have recently expressed concern that such co-opting might ultimately erode the integrity of their respective national swarms,[72] the preceding analysis suggests that worry is unfounded: so long as those courts reserve to themselves the authority to determine what materials deserve to be co-opted in any given case, the integrity of their respective swarms is safe. As Luhmann, again, would put it, no amount of 'informational openness' threatens the system's integrity so long as that system remains properly 'normatively closed'.[73] As it turns out, comparative lawyers have long been attuned to, and in fact militated in favour of, such norm hybridity, as they have not typically confined their own investigations of any given state legal system to the norms and materials originally produced by that state's courts, but rather followed those courts wherever they have decided to go. If anything, moreover, comparative lawyers have actively advocated state courts becoming better informed as to what is being done elsewhere.[74]

On both counts, then, it appears that conventional comparative law scholarship has not gone too far astray, if at all.

Antonio Cassese (ed), *Realizing Utopia: The Future of International Law* (OUP 2012) 26, 27–37; Noah Feldman, 'Cosmopolitan Law?' (2007) 116 *Yale LJ* 1022, 1032; Jack Goldsmith, 'Liberal Democracy and Cosmopolitan Duty' (2003) 55 *Stan L Rev* 1667, 1673–75; George Bermann and Alan Scott Rau, 'Gateway-Schmateway: An Exchange between George Bermann and Alan Rau' (2016) 43 *Pepp L Rev* 469, 472; David Nelken, 'Signaling Conformity: Changing Norms in Japan and China' (2006) 27 *Mich J Int'l L* 933, 945.

72 For a taste of the vigorous debate surrounding the US Supreme Court's such concern, see Cass R Sunstein, *The Constitution of Many Minds* (Princeton University Press 2009); Raymond Legeais, 'L'utilisation du droit comparé par les tribunaux' (1994) 2 RIDC 339; Mark Tushnet, 'The Possibilities of Comparative Constitutional Law' (1999) 108 *Yale LJ* 1225, 1307; Martin Gelter and Mathias M Siems, 'Citations to Foreign Courts – Illegitimate and Superfluous, or Unavoidable? Evidence from Europe' (2014) 62 *Am J Comp L* 35; Ulrich Drobnig, 'The Use of Comparative Law by Courts' in Ulrich Drobnig and Sjef van Erp (eds), *The Use of Comparative Law by Courts* (Kluwer Law International 1999); Shirley S Abrahamson and Michael J Fischer, 'All the World's a Courtroom: Judging in the New Millennium' (1997) 26 *Hofstra L Rev* 273; Bruce Ackerman, 'The Rise of World Constitutionalism' (1997) 83 *Va L Rev* 771; Taavi Annus, 'Comparative Constitutional Reasoning: The Law and Strategy of Selecting Human Rights Arguments' (2004) 14 *Duke J Comp & Int'l L* 301, esp 309ff; Eric Posner and Cass R Sunstein, 'The Law of Other States' (2006) 59 *Stan L Rev* 131; Eric Posner and Cass R Sunstein, 'Response: On Learning from Others' (2007) 59 *Stan L Rev* 1309, 1313; Fredrick Schauer, 'Authority and Authorities' (2008) 94 *Va L Rev* 1931.

73 '[E]xternal reference is not an indication for us that the autonomy of a system is limited because the operation of referring remains an operation of the system . . . .' Luhmann, *Law as a Social System* (n 24) 106.

74 See n 72.

8

Learning from Patrick Glenn: Tradition, Change, and Innovation

*David Nelken**

Rab Judah said in the name of Rab, 'When Moses ascended on high he found the Holy One, blessed be He, engaged in affixing coronets to the letters. Said Moses, "Lord of the Universe, Who stays Thy hand?" He answered, "There will arise a man, at the end of many generations, Akiba b. Joseph by name, who will expound upon each tittle heaps and heaps of laws." "Lord of the Universe", said Moses; "permit me to see him." He replied, "Turn thee round." Moses went and sat down behind eight rows [and listened to the discourses upon the law]. Not being able to follow their arguments he was ill at ease, but when they came to a certain subject and the disciples said to the master "Whence do you know it?" and the latter replied "It is a law given unto Moses at Sinai" he was comforted.'

Babylonian Talmud, Tractate Menachot[1]

INTRODUCTION

I am grateful for this opportunity to contribute to a book honouring Patrick Glenn. Patrick was an exceptionally erudite, wide-ranging, and gentle scholar whom I enjoyed meeting at conferences and whose work is a great source of intellectual stimulation. I remember well, at the workshop where I first met Patrick,[2] the way he first shook hands in turn with every one of us, and once proceedings got started, was soon arguing with facility and good-humoured intensity about the difference between incommensurability and incomparability[3] and the significance of Maimonides' medieval codification of Talmudic law.

* I gratefully acknowledge help from Laurenz Ramsauer (LLB, Kings College 2016) who, as my research assistant, analysed Patrick Glenn's ideas of tradition in relation to those of other scholars. Thanks also to Maurice Adams, Albert Baumgarten, Peter Cserne, Helge Dedek, Mark van Hoecke, Jaako Husa, Martin Krygier, Amber Lynch, Ralf Michaels, Robert Reiner, Mathias Siems, and Peer Zumbansen for their comments on this chapter. None of the above should be assumed to agree with the claims it makes.

1 Babylonian Talmud, *Tractate Menachot* 29B <https://halakhah.com/pdf/kodoshim/Menachoth.pdf> (Soncino translation).

2 See, based on his contribution to this workshop, H Patrick Glenn, 'The Nationalist Heritage' in Pierre Legrand and Roderick Munday (eds), *Comparative Legal Studies: Traditions and Transitions* (CUP 2003).

3 See H Patrick Glenn, 'Are Legal Traditions Incommensurable?' (2001) 49 *Am J Comp L* 133; H Patrick Glenn, 'Com-paring' in Esin Örücü and David Nelken (eds), *Comparative Law: A Handbook* (Hart 2007).

In this chapter I shall first discuss Patrick's effort to reinvigorate the idea of tradition, probably his major theoretical input to comparative law scholarship. I then go on to put some of his ideas to the test by examining a controversial episode involving the renewal of tradition that is recorded in the Talmud, one of the less accessible of the seven legal traditions that Glenn reviews in his magnum opus, *Legal Traditions of the World*.[4] His textbook has not satisfied all of the specialists in the fields it covers.[5] But this is at least in part a result of its considerable ambition. As William Twining has pointed out, Glenn's thesis

> has implications for some issues of contemporary concern that have hardly featured in the orthodox texts: economic and cultural globalisation; 'the clash of civilisations'; corruption; fundamentalism; diffusion and convergence; nationalism and identity politics; universalism, relativism and incommensurability; multivalent logic; and even chaos theory.[6]

It is a book with a mission, and there is no question about its topicality. We are witnessing increasing efforts by groups to recreate historical connections with the past by appealing to the bonds and identities constituted by membership in supposedly long-standing, distinctive religious and national traditions. But this too may be seen as a reaction to the weakening of boundaries and perceived shrinking of space characteristic of globalization. The purpose of Glenn's survey, on the other hand, is to build a case for what he calls – in his subtitle – 'sustainable diversity in law'. 'A concept of legal tradition', he argues, 'appears necessary in a diversified world, since it provides the conceptual and conciliatory devices necessary for the peaceful coexistence of different ideas and peoples.'[7]

In what follows, I first pick out some of the relevant characteristics of what Glenn means by tradition, and I will then use a case study to test some of his ideas. As my title suggests, I am interested in the relationship between legal tradition and innovation or, more exactly, in the problem of how far the dynamics of tradition and change can be illuminated through a better understanding of how tradition is (re)produced. This involves understanding how tradition emerges, how appeals to tradition serve to justify decisions, and, perhaps most interestingly, in what ways the need to justify choices in terms of tradition exercises a constraint over the kind of decision that can be made. Within the sociology of law (where I have my primary academic allegiance), mainstream writers such as Lawrence Friedman have long argued that a social science approach is an important corrective to the stories that 'taught tradition' tells

4 H Patrick Glenn, *Legal Traditions of the World* (5th edn, OUP 2014) (hereafter Glenn, *LTW*).

5 See Nicholas HD Foster (ed), 'A Fresh Start for Comparative Legal Studies? A Collective Review of Patrick Glenn's Legal Traditions of the World, 2nd Edition' (2006) 1 *J Comp L* 100.

6 William Twining, 'Glenn on Tradition: An Overview' (2006) 1 *J Comp L* 107, 108.

7 H Patrick Glenn, 'A Concept of Legal Tradition' (2008) 34 *QLJ* 427, 445.

about its own history, especially when such narratives underplay the wider social forces that are the real movers of change.[8]

But, as will be seen, a positivistic type of social science enquiry into what explains tradition, or even what tradition explains, is not central to Glenn's project. We do find some thought experiments, as when Glenn tries to make sense of the growth of the English common law after the Norman invasion in terms of the rational choices that would have led to that form of law. And he tells us, for example, how legal traditions helped shape an idea of the state that is now on its way out.[9] But the issue that mainly concerns him is what comparative lawyers have to gain by exploring differences in law in terms of overlapping traditions rather than by adopting other frameworks. In what follows, I argue that there is much to learn – perhaps even for those who seek to 'explain' sociolegal change – from what Glenn has to say about the way traditions reproduce themselves, though there is need for yet further investigation of the way tradition combines change and stability.[10] On the other hand, I cast doubts on how far his proposal that adopting the term 'tradition', rather than say culture, will lead scholars to a more appreciative stance to other ways of learning from the past.

I GLENN ON TRADITION

Glenn's interest in tradition can be seen even in his earliest work tracing the survival of regional, subnational, or local approaches to law, whether it be the civilian profession of *avocats*, the circumstances in Alsace-Lorraine, or the situation in his home jurisdiction of Quebec.[11] And his fascination with hybrid jurisdictions continued. Here I am mainly concerned with those writings in which he treats tradition more as an ideological structure than as something linked to a geographical location. As compared with those social-scientific writings that still contrast the traditional and the modern, for him, modernity and even rationality also count as types of tradition.[12] The key to

8 Lawrence Friedman, *History of American Law* (3rd edn, Simon & Schuster 2005), sees tradition in terms of 'friction and inertia' (Ibid, 113). He argues that it can 'limp along' provided it does not block social developments (Ibid, 173). Generally, only that which is fit and functional survives. A well-known, if controversial, effort to link legal traditions to social outcomes can be found in the work of the so-called 'legal origins' school, whose adherents emphasize the differences between economic development in countries influenced by the common law and civil law. For a recent summary by the pioneers of this work, see Rafael La Porta and others, 'The Economic Consequences of Legal Origins' (2008) 46 *J Econ Lit* 285. Evidence that the line should rather be drawn between colonies shaped by the United Kingdom and Germany on the one hand, and France on the other, can be found in Thierry Kirat, 'Legal Tradition and Quality of Institutions: Is Colonization by French Law Countries Distinctive?' (2013) 11 *Revista Criterio Libre* 25 <http://econpapers.repec.org/article/col000370/010834.htm>.

9 H Patrick Glenn, 'The State as a Legal Tradition' (2013) 4 *CJICL* 704.

10 See Ahmed Fekry Ibrahim, Chapter 9 in this volume.

11 See eg, H Patrick Glenn, 'La civilisation de la common law' (1993) 45 *RIDC* 559; H Patrick Glenn, 'The Capture, Reconstruction and Marginalization of "Custom"' (1997) 45 *Am J Comp L* 613.

12 H Patrick Glenn, 'Tradition in Religion and Law' (2009) 25 *JL & Relig* 503, 512.

tradition for Glenn is the idea of 'information', '[t]hat which is brought from the past to the present, in a particular social context'.[13]

The information transmitted through tradition 'can include stories, concepts, beliefs, facts, symbols, values, political theories, heuristics and, if not actual institutions, at least ideas about institutional objectives, design and significance'.[14] What makes the information relevant to today is the binding messages it sends us: 'That which has been captured from the past is inherently normative; it provides present lessons as to how we should act.'[15] But the extent of this can vary. In Glenn's approach,

> Western tradition is normative, that is, it provides a model, drawn from the past, as to how one should act. Legal traditions should not depart from this general phenomenon, since law is perhaps the most normative of human endeavours. There are clear differences, however, amongst legal traditions in terms of the extent to which they claim to regulate human conduct. Chthonic law doesn't appear to regulate much, yet in proscribing all conduct incompatible with a recycling cosmos its normativity is unquestionable. Talmudic and Islamic law regulate most of life; they are normative in all directions.[16]

Most important, tradition does not speak for itself; it is called on selectively,[17] or, in his words, 'massaged'.[18] As Glenn puts it:

> The pool of information captured by the adherents of a particular tradition therefore cannot be entirely controlled by the tradition itself. . . . The variety of information captured will increase as the tradition increases in size, each generation capturing its own understanding of, and adherence to, the tradition. The reporting of current cases, in law, is an example of this large, reflexive, looping characteristic of a living tradition, an iterative process.[19]

Glenn's most controversial claims have to do with his benign view of how traditions maintain their hold. He sees traditions as open; whilst '[a] tradition typically has a stable core' it has 'no fixed boundaries'.[20] This follows from the complexity of mature traditions. As he puts it:

13 Glenn, *LTW* (n 4) 13.
14 Twining, 'Glenn on Tradition' (n 6) 113.
15 Glenn, *LTW* (n 4) 17.
16 Ibid, 366.
17 See also Martin Krygier, 'Law as Tradition' (1986) 5 *Law & Phil* 237, 254 ('The umbrella-concept tradition shelters many different types of phenomena with different characteristics. Any complex tradition, such as law itself is likely to be made up of different sorts of traditions: traditions of claims about the world; "second-order" traditions about such "first-order" traditions and how one should respond to them.').
18 The massage is the message?
19 Glenn, *LTW* (n 4) 15.
20 William Twining, *General Jurisprudence: Understanding Law from a Global Perspective* (CUP 2008) 80.

> All of these complex, major traditions thus achieve complexity because of their proven ability to hold together mutually inconsistent sub-traditions. They all involve a particular way of thinking, which has become explicit in some of them though remaining implicit in others. It is a way of thinking which has been described as multivalent, as opposed to bivalent, because sub-traditions are not either right or wrong but may be right in different, multiple (inconsistent) ways.[21]

Or, as Twining tells us, for Glenn:

> Major traditions are complex, constituted by traditions within traditions, which are often competing or conflicting with each other. They accordingly accommodate internal controversy and debate, provided that the core of ideas is stable or only changes slowly. If a tradition is undermined by doctrinaire lateral movements, such as fundamentalism or universalism, the tradition is corrupted and, in extreme cases, ceases to exist.[22]

But if it is intuitively plausible to think that the complexity of tradition makes necessary a tolerance of potentially conflicting ideas, it is less obvious that the same applies to the relation between traditions. For Glenn, however, the two forms of openness are connected.[23] 'Given any form of contact between traditions, the overall identity of each becomes non-exclusive.'[24] According to him:

> To recognize another tradition there are threshold requirements of knowledge and understanding. . . . Since tradition is best defined as information, however, the (slightest) contact with another tradition implies a variation in the information base of the initial tradition. Its overall identity is no longer what is was, in the sense that the totality of information available to it has expanded.[25]

But do we not also need to take account of the ways traditions seek to defend themselves from challenge? Glenn asks whether 'a tradition can take specific measures to protect its underlying or basic elements, whether it can specifically protect its identity' and admits that '[m]ost apparently do, and the means may range from a simple ethical obligation to remember . . . to instruments variously known as heresy, treason or sedition.'[26] But he asserts nonetheless that 'the authority of tradition is persuasive only'.[27] It allows for dialogue and 'normative engagement, as opposed to hierarchical dominance'.[28] On the other hand, whilst it is possible to

21 Glenn, *LTW* (n 4) 368.

22 Twining, 'Glenn on Tradition' (n 6) 110.

23 As Glenn put it in 2008, 'law conceived as tradition (as normative information) must yield normative claims, discussion and dialogue, as well as the possibility of reconciliation. Legal traditions thus speak to one another, and all the great legal traditions of the world say a great deal about their relations with one another.' Glenn, 'Concept of Legal Tradition' (n 7) 442.

24 Glenn, *LTW* (n 4) 34.

25 Ibid.

26 Ibid, 40–41.

27 Ibid, 42.

28 Glenn, 'Concept of Legal Tradition' (n 7) 443.

resist particular traditions, this does not undermine the force of tradition (or 'Tradition') as such.[29]

When it comes to law, Glenn is interested in understanding how it unfolds as it is developed.[30] He prefers the idea of tradition to the conception of law employed by legal positivists because it is more apt for dealing with cases of legal pluralism. But his strong advocacy of the term 'tradition' in the context of comparative law arises from its ability to disrupt the goal of classification that guides so much of such scholarship:

> In contrast to the taxonomic objective underlying the concept of legal families, that of legal traditions has no explicit taxonomic purpose. Indeed, it may well be impossible to categorize national legal systems according to legal traditions, since the concept of tradition is simply that of normative information and national systems may repose on different and varying amounts of (traditional) normative information.[31]

Glenn is especially critical of what he treats as the nearest competing concepts,[32] '(legal) system' and '(legal) culture'.[33] These, he says, 'are often driven by the

[29] Glenn, 'Tradition in Religion and Law' (n 12) 512:

> If resistance to tradition is futile, in this sense, then resistance to tradition cannot bring about an absence of tradition, but only a shift in allegiances, a movement from one tradition to another (including those traditions known as 'rationality' or 'modernity'), or the restraining or limiting of a particular tradition in favor of another.

[30] Compare the works of James Boyd White: eg, James B White, *Heracles Bow* (University of Wisconsin Press 1985). But Glenn pays less attention to the elements of rhetoric and communication that are the focus of his works.

[31] H Patrick Glenn, 'Comparative Legal Families and Comparative Legal Traditions' in Mathias Reimann and Reinhard Zimmermann (eds), *The Oxford Handbook of Comparative Law* (OUP 2006) 425. Jaakko Husa's comments are interesting here:

> The true quality (of Glenn's textbook) can be understood only if it is being compared to legal families and/or legal cultures approaches. (It is his way of trying to get out of all that (ie, conflicting systems, taxonomies, civil law + common law emphasis, West and the Rest etc.) . . . . But scholarly path-dependence has a role . . . . [I]t was not authored in 'a disciplinary free space'. . . . Also his background in private international law (ie, conflict of laws) has significance: I will always remember his way of explaining how he tried to follow the Indian Kuchipudi dance (hands going together peacefully; fingers overlapping each other) instead of private international law (fists banging against each other in aggression). But, and here is the thing, if you . . . compare it superficially with older macro-comparative classifications it appears rather similar. In fact, I made this question/point to him many times and he never liked it. He always explained that traditions only look similar to legal families but they are constructed differently. This is, I think, the genuine paradox of his legal traditions: it is built on different thinking and yet it kind of looks all the same.

Email from Jaakko Husa to author (29 March 2017).

[32] Potentially competing and overlapping terms of course range more widely and include 'law in action', 'legal discourse', 'legal ideology', 'legal consciousness', 'legal mentalities', 'legal styles', 'legal complex', 'legal epistemes', 'legal formants', 'path-dependency', 'regulatory styles', and even 'legal autopoiesis'. See David Nelken, 'Using Legal Culture: Prospects and Problems' in David Nelken (ed), *The Uses of Legal Culture* (Wildys, Simmonds, and Hill 2012).

[33] See also H Patrick Glenn, 'Doin' the Transsystemic: Legal Systems and Legal Traditions' (2005) 50 *McGill LJ* 863.

Western tendency to emphasise the internal unity of groups and systems and thus to stress separation and difference rather than permeability and continuities.'[34] Law conceived as a system yields facts, silence, and conflict, and wrongly suggests a self-contained unit. And he has a particular quarrel with the concept of culture because it lends itself to being used as an euphemism for race and to justify colonialism.[35] The term, he says, is 'largely a creation of the western enlightenment, though suffering from a remarkable level of ambiguity. In concentrating on current forms of human thought and activity, moreover, it appears antithetical to whatever normativity may be derived from the past.'[36]

By contrast, he sees the term 'tradition' as (supposedly) culture free: 'It does not appear to be the product of any particular civilization, yet appears present, explicitly or implicitly, as a formative influence in the law of all of them. . . .'[37] Moreover, it can be used for the purposes of making comparisons, because 'although different cultures may have different conceptual schemes, traditions are comparable because every tradition has to address four issues: the nature of the core that constitutes its identity; its underlying justification; its conception of change; and how the tradition relates to other traditions.'[38]

Glenn's ideas about tradition certainly have not gone without challenge.[39] Some commentators argue that his approach seeks to cover too much ground and too many disparate phenomena. For Andrew Halpin, for example, Glenn's readiness to embrace tradition as both setting the question and providing the answer is dangerously misconceived. His insistence that all conflict within and between traditions is resolved by tradition 'detracts from anything we might learn from empirically examining true points of conflict'.[40] Other scholars charge him with turning tradition into the history of ideas and giving too little attention to the role of attitudes, expectations, institutions, habits, and actual practices.[41] Martin Shapiro argues that the limited attention paid to the actual effects of traditions in practice means that his

34 Twining, *General Jurisprudence* (n 20) 80 (citing H Patrick Glenn, *Legal Traditions of the World* (2nd edn, OUP 2004) xxv).

35 In practice, the terms 'culture' and 'tradition' are often used in similar ways. See Jaakko Husa, 'Legal Culture vs. Legal Tradition – Different Epistemologies?' (2012) Maastricht European Law Institute Working Paper 2012/18 <https://papers.ssrn.com/sol3/papers.cfm?abstract_id=2179890>. For a recent overview of uses of the term 'legal culture', see David Nelken, 'Comparative Legal Research and Legal Culture: Facts, Approaches, and Values' (2016) 12 *Ann Rev L & Soc Sci* 45. See also Esin Örücü, Chapter 4 in this volume.

36 Glenn, *LTW* (n 4) xxv.

37 Ibid.

38 Twining, *General Jurisprudence* (n 20) 81–82.

39 See especially the contributions to the 2006 issue of the *Journal of Comparative Law* and Glenn's replies there, and in his interview with Hildebrandt: M Hildebrandt, 'The Precision of Vagueness, Interview with H Patrick Glenn' (2006) 3 *Neth J Legal Phil* 346.

40 Andrew Halpin, 'Glenn's *Legal Traditions of the World*: Some Broader Philosophical Issues' (2006) 1 *J Comp L* 116, 119.

41 See eg, John Bell, 'Chapter Five: Civil Law Tradition' (2006) *J Comp L* 130; James Q Whitman, 'A Simple Story' [2004] *Rechtsgeschichte/Legal Hist* 206.

account risks being overly idealistic, '[f]or in most societies, law talk is far more aspirational than law practice'.[42]

My special focus here, however, is on what follows from his approach to the relationship between tradition, change, and innovation. Glenn tells us that traditions can be living, submerged, frozen, or suspended, that they can be well established or still young, and that time will show us their staying power.[43] He argues further that it is the normativity of tradition that helps explain why rules endure and how they shape social life. On the one hand, tradition contributes to stability. He accepts that change relies on claims to coherence. In religious legal traditions, for example, it is the key to showing faithfulness to what Glenn, in his chapter on the Talmudic tradition, calls 'the Perfect Author'.[44] Similarly, for Edward Shils, a sociologist whose writings on this topic have been fundamental, 'traditionalism' may be the corruption of tradition, but '[t]he normativeness of tradition is the inertial force which holds society in a given form over time'.[45] For Martin Krygier, '[t]his traditionality of law is one more reason why "time-slice" explanations of doctrine which relate it purely to contemporary social, political and economic forces – which look relentlessly outside, as it were, rather than backwards – are likely to be misleading'.[46]

Nonetheless, for Glenn, tradition is more an engine of change than a guarantee of permanence. 'Once tradition is seen as transmitted information, an ongoing bran-tub churned by new generations, with no inherent élites or hierarchy, the linking of tradition with stability becomes less obvious and less defensible.'[47] Or as he puts it, in writing about religion and law, '[l]egal traditions thus have the capacity of change over time and may even be the single greatest source of what we know as change, as proponents of change look for, and cite, historical justification for the particular changes they are urging'.[48] Although he says only little[49] about work on the 'invention' of tradition,[50] he makes no suggestion that this approach is fundamentally inconsistent with his own.

To be useful in empirical research, Glenn's ideas about the connection between coherence and change need to be unpacked carefully. His analyses of social change tend to rely on a variety of not always consistent and sometimes mixed metaphors.[51]

42 Martin Shapiro, 'Common Law Traditions' (2006) 1 *J Comp L* 151. But Glenn explained that he deliberately preferred tradition over culture because he wanted to make it clear that practice does not always follow what tradition says. See Hildebrandt (n 39).

43 Glenn, 'Concept of Legal Tradition' (n 7) 435.

44 Glenn, *LTW* (n 4) 98ff.

45 Edward Shils, *Tradition* (Chicago University Press 1981) 25.

46 Krygier, 'Law as Tradition' (n 17) 242.

47 Glenn, *LTW* (n 4) 24.

48 Glenn, 'Tradition in Religion and Law' (n 12) 511.

49 Glenn, *LTW* (n 4) esp 5–6.

50 Eric Hobsbawm and Terence Ranger, *The Invention of Tradition* (CUP 1983).

51 Martin Krygier queries Glenn's favourite bran tub metaphor, asking whether we are in the bran tub or it is in us – email from M Krygier to author (8 April 2017). Peter Cserne doubts that '"normative information" is a satisfactory characterization of what tradition is' and suggests 'how can such

We are told, for example, that '[a] given tradition emerges as a loose conglomeration of data, organised around a basic theme or themes', and is variously described as a 'bundle', a 'tool box', a 'language', a 'playground', a 'seedbed', a 'rag-bag', or as a 'bran-tub'.[52] It is hard not to see a connection between his idea of the basic elements of tradition – (bites of) information – and current reliance on information technology. But in many religious traditions the key idea of tradition is more linked to a 'way' or 'path' (an interestingly forward-looking metaphor).

More, unless used with care, Glenn's approach can equally explain opposite outcomes. Where legal systems converge, law as tradition would have an explanation by referring to the openness and accommodative logic of all traditions. And, where legal systems conflict, law as tradition has an explanation by referring to the epistemic barrier that tradition provides by structuring our perceptions and attitudes.[53] How exactly is tradition supposed to shape social behaviour? Does it do this by limiting the reasons that social actors can use to justify their decisions, or does it exert its influence more because of what it helps keep as taken for granted? For Krygier, the normativity of the past is strongest when we are unaware of it.

> Dig into this diachronic quarry at any particular time to discover what the law is and the 'present' will be a revealing mixture of fossils, innovations of the long gone, provisional answers to different problems which stick because nothing better can be found or because participants in the tradition take this answer, once embedded, as satisfactory, or because they do not think of any alternative but think through this answer.[54]

But Glenn emphasizes more the ways tradition 'becomes rather a resource from which reasons for change may be derived, a legitimating agency for ideas which, by themselves, would have no social resonance. The past is mobilized to invent a - future . . . .'[55] For him:

> A tradition, in the form of received information, is thus a fragile thing. It bears within itself the seeds of diversity or, more radically, change. It also bears within itself the seeds of corruption, the various forms of human frailty which would convert it to an instrument of perverse and personal ends.[56]

normative information be "submerged, frozen suspended etc" is not easy to grasp' – email from P Cserne to author (28 April 2017). For a discussion of how (far) to take the metaphors, see David Nelken 'Legal Transplants and Beyond: Of Disciplines and Metaphors' in Andrew Harding and Esin Örücü (eds), *Comparative Law in the 21st Century*, vol 4 (Kluwer 2002) 19–34.

52 Glenn, *LTW* (n 4) 16.

53 Husa (n 35). Of course both explanations could be true under different circumstances.

54 Martin Krygier, 'Critical Legal Studies and Social Theory – A Response to Alan Hunt' (1987) 7 *OJLS* 26, 35.

55 Glenn, *LTW* (n 4) 24.

56 Ibid, 30. The idea of 'corruption' is asked to play too many roles in Glenn's account. He seems confident that we can distinguish the pure from the corrupt form of tradition, whereas the difficulty in making that distinction is the very point in question in many internal debates within traditions.

John Bell insists nonetheless that Glenn underplays the importance of coherence. For Bell, the information metaphor does not grasp the coherence requirement, however it is conceived. 'The law is not just a "bran tub" of information that can be reprocessed in the modern time. It has a coherence that is renegotiated over time.'[57] But what exactly is meant by coherence over time? And how does tradition achieve such 're-negotiation'? To throw further light on these questions, I now turn to a case study of the contestation of tradition (and the tradition of contestation) in Talmudic law, which is one of the traditions that Glenn includes in his textbook.

II TRADITION AND INNOVATION – A CASE STUDY OF THE PROZBUL

A famous episode of tradition and innovation reported in the Talmud concerns the institution of the Prozbul,[58] a rabbinical enactment (or takkana)[59], attributed to the Mishnaic[60] authority, Hillel the Elder, who lived at the end of the period of the second Temple. As I will show (and this in itself confirms Glenn's insights), even among adherents to the Jewish tradition there is no neutral and uncommitted way of describing what Hillel did. But the basic outline runs something like this.[61] 'The Torah mandates a Sabbatical year, or Shmita year, every seventh year. Among other things, the departure of the year cancels all debts and is one of the many laws in the Torah meant to protect the poor and disadvantaged, affording them a chance to escape from eternal debt.' However, though the Torah explicitly warned lenders not to stop lending even though they would lose their capital (Deuteronomy 15:9) this is what ended up happening in practice. Hence:

> The rabbis, under the suggestion of Hillel the Elder, created a loophole in Jewish law, in which a legal document would accompany the interest-free loans (charging interest to fellow Jews was forbidden in the Torah) issued by individuals that stated that the loans were to be transferred to the courts as the law of remission does not apply to loans within the public domain. This groundbreaking institution benefited

[57] Bell (n 41) 138.

[58] There are a variety of ways of spelling this transliterated word, which means 'before the court' and refers to a document drawn up in front of three judges. It is of course interesting for the purposes of this chapter that this term, as well as, eg, the term 'Sanhedrin' to name the higher courts, are loan words from Greek.

[59] There are over thirty examples of rabbinical decrees throughout the Talmud (including ones dealing with difficult issues involving personal status or the ransoming of captives). This is one of eighteen examples of Tikkun Olam. According to Ran Hirschl, *Comparative Matters: The Renaissance of Comparative Constitutional Law* (OUP 2014), such rabbinic enactments were intended to work for the 'repair of social and economic order' (Ibid, 100). See generally David Birnbaum and Martin S Cohen (eds), *Tikkun Olam: Judaism, Humanism and Transcendence* (New Paradigm Matrix 2015).

[60] The Mishna is the legal codification of biblical and post-biblical law, attributed to Rabbi Judah the Prince, which is debated and incorporated in published editions of the Talmud.

[61] See 'Prozbul' (*Wikipedia*) <https://en.wikipedia.org/wiki/Prozbul>. (This should not be confused with the *Jubilee* year, which is the year following seven cycles of Shmita).

both borrower and lender; because lenders knew their money was safe even following the Sabbatical year, they were likely to loan to the poor.[62]

The debates that surround this intervention centre on the authority of the rabbis in general, and, more specifically, of Hillel the Elder, to create a legal instrument/fiction that de facto apparently abrogates scriptural law. Some argue that the obligations that Hillel's decree set out to circumvent were ones only based on rabbinic authority at the time, because the Shmita laws, having to do with the homeland, only have biblical status when a majority of Jews live in Israel. Other matters raised by Jewish commentators of later generations have to do with whether Hillel intended his decree for his time (of emergency) and for his generation, or for all time,[63] and the possibility that all he was doing was making public – and acceptable – what had previously only existed as a theoretical possibility. Even today many practising Orthodox Jews make sure that where necessary, in their business affairs, they have a Prozbul drafted in the appropriate manner (though there are learned disagreements about when and where this is required, and what sort of court is needed).[64]

What is especially interesting for present purposes is the way the contested understanding of Hillel's decree has become a site of *meta*-debate about the scope and limits of innovation in Jewish tradition, as between the Orthodox, Conservative, and Reform groupings that have contested the tradition since the European Enlightenment.[65] Those in the Orthodox camp normally tend to choose a narrow interpretation of the scope of Hillel's innovation – and emphasize how it employed well-accepted techniques of Jewish law (the Halacha). Many of these argue that Hillel created the loophole only so as to reinforce a more serious law, that is, the biblical obligation to lend to the poor, so as to ensure that people did not stop lending to them. Hence, rather than prioritizing rabbinical discretion to undo biblical texts, he was using rabbinical power to reinforce biblical authority. By

62 Ibid. The proof text here (Deut. 15:3) speaks of an individual demanding repayment 'from his brother', which it is possible to read as excluding demands made by the courts. The power of the Jewish Court or Beth Din includes, under certain circumstances, the right to confiscate goods, and is much greater in civil than ritual matters.

63 'If he ruled only for his own generation but thereafter people continued the practice of their own volition, then any later *beth din* may alter or suspend his *takkana* as it sees fit.' 'Practical Implementation' (*Jewish Law Articles: Examining Halacha, Jewish Issues and Secular Law*) <www.jlaw.com/Articles/pruzbul3.html>.

64 Yisroel Reisman, *The Laws of Ribbis: The Laws of Interest and Their Application to Everyday Life and Business* (3rd edn, Mesorah 2004).

65 The terminology used to describe the contending groups can sometimes be misleading. The Reform (and Liberal) wings of Judaism stand, as the names suggest, for freedom to innovate with changing times. But the so-called conservative movement (also called, especially in Israel, the Mesorati, which in Hebrew means 'traditional') is considered by the (more) Orthodox to be insufficiently respectful of traditions. The Orthodox world itself is highly variegated (and includes the so-called Modern Orthodox). Most of those who see themselves as taking a stricter view of Jewish practice would not apply terms like Ultra-Orthodox to themselves; they prefer to call themselves, following a text in Isaiah, 'Charedim', 'those who are God-fearing'.

contrast, most Conservative[66] and, even more, Reform thinkers stress the way in which Hillel's enactment shows that biblical texts can, where necessary, be outflanked.[67] Some on the Orthodox side reply that these thinkers are choosing a reading of events that (only) serves to justify their preference for introducing illegitimate radical changes.[68]

But even amongst those who self-identify as Orthodox, a minority do take the introduction of the Prozbul to be a model for deliberate innovation, a way of enabling tradition to keep up with new challenges and changing times. Thus David Hartman, a leader of the so-called 'Modern Orthodox' camp, describes Hillel as a groundbreaking example of religious leadership that reflects the 'Mishnaic sensitivity and responsiveness' that makes space for the human condition and takes seriously its most pressing needs. He contrasts this with what he sees as the less courageous interpretation offered by the Talmud itself.[69] In his words, '[i]nstead of relying on halachic precedent, Hillel relied on his own moral conviction. He employed a system of creative reasoning – couched in halakhic language – to significantly circumscribe the biblical *shmita* law and arrive at an alternative outcome.'[70]

66 See eg, Neil Gillman, *Conservative Judaism: The New Century* (Behrman House 1993). Hillel 'used a legal fiction to circumvent a biblical law that because of changing economic conditions had come to subvert the broader social vision of the Torah' Ibid, 23.

67 These groups have a more evolutionary understanding of the development of tradition by rabbinic authorities in different social circumstances. Other examples they use include the Talmudic reinterpretation of the meaning of 'an eye for eye' to mean monetary damages, the imposing of requirements sufficient as to nullify the practical applicability of the rules regarding 'the rebellious son', or Rabbi Akivah's apparent willingness to abrogate de facto the death penalty by making it procedurally impossible to convict offenders at risk of such a penalty.

68 'Intermarriage – Question for Reform Jews' (*Google Groups*) <https://groups.google.com/forum/#!topic/soc.culture.jewish/JmKOCdRRHBU%5B126-150%5D>. What is interesting here is the adoption of the somewhat un-Jewish contrast between 'spirit' and 'letter':

> . . . Pruzbul was never a change in halacha. I don't see why pruzbul has become the slogan of reformers. In what way did Hillel change the halacha? In what way was halacha different after Hillel than before? All Hillel made was an administrative change to the procedures of courts, elevating an existing practise from the realm of 'dubious rort' to that of 'normal legal procedure'. The only change is in the 'spirit of the law', not in the letter.

69 Of course a common trope in arguments within a tradition is to seek to 'go back' to an earlier, more pure or authoritative, source.

70 David Hartman, *From Defender to Critic: The Search for a New Jewish Self* (Jewish Lights 2012) 233 (emphasis added). Another valuable contribution from within the Modern Orthodox camp comes from Meesh Hammer-Kossoy, 'Daring Decrees and Radical Responsibility: Why Rabbinic Tikkun Olam Is Not What You Think' in Birnbaum and Cohen (n 59). Interestingly, the author is herself an example of the recent and controversial innovation of female Orthodox rabbis. For other contemporary interpreters, Hillel should be seen as an early proponent of the 'law and economics' approach. Thus Ohrenstein and Gordon argue (admiringly) that Hillel 'combined rational thought with the power of observation. This empirical approach enabled him to suggest a practical solution by way of modifying the law.' See Roman Ohrenstein and Barry Gordon, *Economic Analysis in Talmudic Literature: Rabbinic Thought in the Light of Modern Economics* (3rd edn, Brill 2009) 11.

If disagreements *within* Jewish tradition go deep, there are also a variety of responses in the related traditions of Christianity and Islam. These touch on the theological question about whether it is permissible to lend with interest as well as evaluations of the empirical evidence of whether religions traditions that have tried to restrict lending for profit have succeeded in doing so, and, more generally, what effects they have actually had on economic development. A recent widely reviewed academic contribution argues that Islamic commercial law and tradition was responsible for holding back the development of capitalism in Muslim countries and hence contributed to the 'long divergence'.[71] Interestingly, critics of this thesis who identify strongly with the tradition argue that other political and economic variables should be given more importance than tradition. For them it was not so much Islamic law that constituted an obstacle as the political and economic interests that benefitted from the status quo and did not welcome potential modifications or workarounds.[72]

But views of other traditions do not always reflect the openness that Glenn would have wished for. Rather we find polemical apologetics and zero-sum arguments that urge us to choose between supposedly incompatible ideologies. For some traditionalist Christian commentators, for example, the Prozbul is only another example of the way Jews circumvent 'The Law' through subterfuge – so making the word of God to no effect and using the letter to kill the spirit.[73] For many Islamic writers the superiority of the religious rules of their faith is well shown by the architecture of Islamic finance, which maintains a prohibition on lending with interest, but has successfully introduced a variety of alternative methods of co-participation in the success of enterprises.[74]

A striking example of a critical approach to another tradition is that put forward by the scholar, Werner Sombart, in his book *The Jews and Modern Capitalism*.[75] He tells us:

71 Timur Kuran, *The Long Divergence: How Islamic Law Held Back the Middle East* (Princeton University Press 2010).

72 See eg, Abdul Azim Islahi, 'Book Review: *The Long Divergence: How Islamic Law Held Back the Middle East by Timur Kuran*' (2012) 25 *JKAU: Islamic Econ* 253, 256–57.

73 Harold F Roellig, *The More Excellent Way: 2000 Years of Jesus' New Way of Life* (Crucifer Press 2006) 50–51. But little is said about the centrality of banking to modern capitalism in the Christian West.

74 See eg, Jamaal al-Din Zarabozo, 'Islam – Interest and Its Role in Economy and Life' (*Islam Religion*, 2007) <www.islamreligion.com/articles/538/viewall/interest-and-its-role-in-economy-and-life>. See generally 'Islamic Banking and Finance: Studies' (*Wikipedia*) <https://en.wikipedia.org/wiki/Islamic_banking_and_finance#Studies>. But other voices in that tradition point out that only a small proportion of Islamic business is conducted in terms of the religious rules, and that capitalist-like activity proceeds just as successfully when they are in place: see eg, AK Muhammad, *What Is Wrong with Islamic Economics? Analysing the Present State and Future Agenda* (Edward Elgar 2013); Feyyaz Zeren and Mehmet Saraç, 'The Dependency of Islamic Bank Rates on Conventional Bank Interest Rates: Further Evidence from Turkey' (2015) 47 *Applied Econ* 669.

75 Werner Sombart, *The Jews and Modern Capitalism* (Mordecai Epstein tr, first published 1911, Batoche Books 2001).

> [W]hen we recall the period in which the Talmud came into being (200 BC to 500 AD) and compare what it contains in the field of economics with all the economic ideas and conceptions that the ancient and the mediaeval worlds have handed down to us, it seems nothing short of marvellous. Some of the Rabbis speak as though they had mastered Ricardo and Marx, or, to say the least, had been brokers on the Stock Exchange for several years, or counsel in many an important money-lending case.[76]

He adds, more specifically, that '[t]he Prosbul, too (by means of which it was possible to ensure the existence of a debt even over the year of release), is a sign of a highly organized system of lending'.[77]

But this (backhanded) compliment forms part of an altogether less sympathetic socio-historical account in which Hillel's Prozbul is seen less as a method to ensure that the poor continue to find people who will lend to them, and more as an anticipatory step in the chain that links Judaism to modern capitalism. Sombart's aim is to offer an alternative to Max Weber's thesis about the role of Protestantism in shaping capitalism.[78] Like Weber, he tries to get inside another tradition so as to explain its influence in history. But his characterization of Jewish tradition as a source of the capitalist ethic is cruder and more problematic than Weber's portrait of Protestantism (perhaps because Weber had more direct links with that tradition through his devout mother).[79]

While Sombart's work shows flashes of genius, its reasoning is too often badly flawed. He is on strongest grounds when writing about the (unintended?) economic effects of the prohibition on lending on interest being restricted to insiders, arguing that

> [i]f we have called the Jews the Fathers of Free Trade, and therefore the pioneers of capitalism, let us note here that they were prepared for this role by the free-trading spirit of the commercial and industrial law, which received an enormous impetus towards a policy of laissez-faire by its attitude towards strangers.[80]

But in seeking to explain historical developments as a direct outcome of Jewish tradition he essentializes 'the Jew' across all times and places, and applies his

76 Ibid, 219.

77 Ibid, 220.

78 Max Weber, *The Protestant Ethic and the Spirit of Capitalism* (first published 1905, OUP 2010).

79 At points, Sombart even draws on what could easily be seen as vulgar anti-Judaic tropes, as in the following passage:

> Now think of the position in which the pious Jew and the pious Christian respectively found themselves in the period in which money-lending first became a need in Europe, and which eventually gave birth to capitalism. The good Christian who had been addicted to usury was full of remorse as he lay a-dying, ready at the eleventh hour to cast from him the ill-gotten gains which scorched his soul. And the good Jew? The evening of his days he gazed upon his well-filled caskets and coffers, overflowing with sequins of which he had relieved the miserable Christians or Mohammedans. It was a sight which warmed his heart, for every penny was almost like a sacrifice which he had brought to his Heavenly Father.

Sombart (n 75) 170–71.

80 Ibid, 172.

theories indiscriminately to both the worldly and other worldly strains of Jewish piety.[81]

Sombart tells us:

> No consideration whatever is had for the personality of the sinner or his ethical state, just as a sum of money is separated from persons, just as it is capable of being added to another abstract sum of money. The ceaseless striving of the righteous after well-being in this and the next world must needs therefore take the form of a constant endeavour to increase his rewards. Now, as he is never able to tell whether at a particular state of his conscience he is worthy of God's goodness or whether in his 'account' the rewards or the punishments are more numerous, it must be his aim to add reward after reward to his account by constantly doing good deeds to the end of his days. The limited conception of all personal values thus finds no admission into the world of his religious ideas and its place is taken by the endlessness of a pure quantitative ideal.[82]

He continues:

> What in reality is the idea of making profit, what is economic rationalism, but the application to economic activities of the rules by which the Jewish religion shaped Jewish life? Before capitalism could develop the natural man had to be changed out of all recognition, and a rationalistically minded mechanism introduced in his stead. There had to be a transvaluation of all economic values. And what was the result? The homo capitalisticus, who is closely related to the homo Judeus, both belonging to the same species.[83]

Sombart passes over most of the Jewish laws and regulations that stress collective responsibility and seek to realize a scheme of divinely mandated social solidarity and fair dealing, injunctions that could, in other historical circumstances, have produced a social system far removed from modern capitalism.[84] The link between Jewish tradition and capitalism thus remains highly controversial. It has even been

[81] Eg, when dealing with the other-worldly strain in Judaism, Sombart tells us:

> How deeply the teleological view of things is embedded in the nature of the Jew may be seen in the case of those of them who, like the Chassidim, pay no attention to the needs of practical life because 'there is no purpose in them'. There is no purpose in making a living, and so they let their wives and children starve, and devote themselves to the study of their sacred books.

Ibid, 186. As Mendes-Flohr writes:

> Sombart is apparently implying, if these sequential statements are to be logically meaningful, that the teleological attitude induced by Judaism is a phenomenological set, whose object may be this or other worldly. In seeming disregard to this observation that Judaism may be indeed other-worldly, Sombart later insists that Judaism has consistently taught the Jews 'to look for their chief happiness in the possession of money'.

Paul R Mendes-Flohr, 'Werner Sombart's *The Jews and Modern Capitalism*: An Analysis of Its Ideological Premises' (1976) 21 *Leo Baeck Inst Yrbk* 87, 108.

[82] Sombart (n 75) 212.

[83] Ibid.

[84] The institutions of Shmita and the Jubilee both emphasize that land (the source of wealth in the economy) belonged to the Lord and operated to prevent the accumulation of resources. There are

asserted that the influence of tradition is felt more in its breach. Critics have pointed out that Sombart refused to recognize, as Weber did, that wherever these religious systems, including Judaism, were at their most powerful and authoritarian, commerce did not flourish. Jewish businessmen, like Calvinist ones, tended to operate most successfully when they had left their traditional religious environment and moved on to fresher pastures.[85]

CONCLUSIONS

In this chapter I have discussed some of Glenn's ideas about tradition and then summarized some of the debates surrounding a remarkable innovation recorded in the Talmud. My claim is that Glenn's insights can help us bring out some of the important lessons of this case study, but that it also helps us see why some of his points may need modification.

Most obviously, I have shown the high level of disagreement within the Jewish tradition as to the meaning and implications of Hillel's enactment of the Prozbul. We have also seen how this is linked to the wider claims about the proper scope of innovation that the interpreters are trying to justify. As Glenn puts it:

> The necessity of massaging the information of tradition thus extends through the entire range of attitudes towards it. It occurs amongst the most faithful of adherents to it, as they seek to perpetuate it; it occurs amongst the most vigorous of opponents to it, as they seek to overcome it; and it occurs between both groups. . . . In the theoretical discussion of tradition, this emerges in the conclusion that tradition never reaches definitive form, but is rather, in the present, a series of interactive statements of information.[86]

Glenn is also right to argue that, even if different traditions have their own ideas of how to bring about change, traditions can also be intelligible to others, especially, of course, those with common roots. As we have seen, there would certainly be at least some communality between the debates here and those that have taken place in religious legal traditions such as the Islamic tradition. By his own definition of traditions, Glenn is correct to say that they are necessarily 'open' if they are to embrace complexity and survive.

On the other hand, we should not minimize the extent to which traditions often thrive by distinguishing themselves internally and externally and, sociologically speaking, seem to need 'enemies'.[87] We might expect traditions to be more resistant to rival traditions. But in practice it may be particularly important to overcome

many stringent rules against direct competition and overcharging, great emphasis on the need to pay workers fairly and on time, and welfare provisions for the needy and for strangers. There are many Talmudic narratives whose point is to celebrate the piety of those Sages whose conduct in business matters went beyond the requirements of the law.

85 Mendes-Flohr (n 81).

86 Glenn, *LTW* (n 4) 20–21.

87 See Martin Krygier, Chapter 6 in this volume.

competing claims from bearers of the same tradition.[88] How traditions differentiate themselves internally and externally are in large part empirical questions that cannot be resolved a priori. Ran Hirschl, for example, argues that the Jewish tradition became more resistant to other traditions in those parts of the diaspora where there was more fear of assimilation than in others.[89]

Glenn's claim that tradition is as much concerned with change as with stability likewise finds ample confirmation. The Prozbul innovation well demonstrates how traditions need to show how they respect coherence even whilst producing change. Because it is presented as an exception to the normal way in which law is unfolded (more similar to what we now call legislative activity, or what Weber helpfully called law-making rather than law-finding), it directly and indirectly (by following defined procedures) reinforces the authority of the rest of the system. But, beyond the case of exceptional decrees, change over time through tradition is made possible by the need and possibility of interpreting texts and cultural practices in different ways under different circumstances. Hence tradition, like culture in general, can be seen as a resource as much as a constraint. Insofar as we are dealing with reasons for action, not external causes, what happens will depend on how people make use of these resources.

In the case of religious and legal traditions, there may be a special need to anchor the authority of those who make the past speak to us, as is highlighted in the Talmudic fable that forms the epigraph of this chapter. But this retrospective anchoring is normally confined to existing practices that need justification (as compared to the making of new enactments such as Hillel's Prozbul). In any case, such reference back cannot be overdone.[90] The text in the epigraph leads on to an account of Rabbi Akivah's martydom! Introducing whatever seems 'new' depends on the ability of interpreters to convince the relevant audience(s) that they embody the best efforts to continue the tradition.[91] In situations of anxiety and high contestability

88 See further Noam Zion, *'Elu v'Elu: Two Schools of Halakha Face off on Issues of Human Autonomy, Majority Rule and Divine Voice of Authority* (Shalom Hartman Institute 2008).

89 Hirschl (n 59).

90 The (relatively few) attributions of rulings back to Moses under the rubric of *Halakhah le-Moshe- Sinai* were more common in the Talmudic period than the Mishnaic one. See Christine Hayes, 'Halakhah le-Moshe-Sinai in Rabbinic Sources: A Methodological Case Study' in Shaye JD Cohen (ed), *The Synoptic Problem in Rabbinic Literature* (Providence Brown University 2000). More generally, Gunther Teubner, *Law as an Autopoietic System* (Blackwell 1993), cites the Talmudic story concerning the *Oven* of *Akhnai* (*Tractate* Bava Metzia 59a–b), which appears to argue that even the claims of what Glenn calls 'the Perfect Author' count less than those of the interpreters of tradition. In accordance with his (selective) commitment to Luhmanian theory, Teubner views this type of assertion of authority as paradoxical. But it is important also to recognize that this tradition (like others) generally manages to normalize the role of interpreters in ways that involve less drama than in that unusual story. See most recently Karl Heinz Ladeur, 'Report zu Ronen Reichman, Autorität, Tradition, Argumentation bei der Formierung des rabbinischen Rechtsdiskurse' ['Report on Ronen Reichman's Authority, Tradition, and Argumentation in the Formation of Rabbinical Legal Discourse'] [2016] *Ancilla Iuris (anci ch)* 111, (translated by Alison Lewis) who concludes that 'Jewish law is different' and 'there is a great deal that Western law can learn from this different law' (ibid, 120).

91 'The achievement of these scholars, who established a tradition rooted in the Torah and growing out of it, is a prime example of spontaneity in receptivity. They are leaders because they know themselves

it can be crucial to be able to claim (as with Hillel) to be 'safeguarding' the tradition by innovating through it.

But even the most successful effort at understanding how a given tradition understands itself is unlikely to tell us why and when it constitutes a block on wider social change or makes it possible. Was it what Glenn would call 'a core value' of Judaism (or Islam) to frustrate or to encourage capitalist development? Does that question even make sense? We know too little about the events that precipitated Hillel's decision or their social and economic consequences.[92] Whether or not lack of historical contextualization by traditional authorities is deliberate,[93] tradition usually has other priorities.[94] Even in the contemporary debate within the Jewish tradition, the question fought over is how much importance to give to the more technical one of how Hillel's actions were warranted and justified as opposed to speculation about *why* he chose to take them.

Glenn's emphasis on ideas and values in talking about tradition thus mirrors the way tradition talks about itself. Disagreements within tradition are focused on its meaning for today, not on a disinterested search for what larger forces shape its path. Anachronism seems to be the price we need to pay if fidelity to tradition is to be more than antiquarianism.[95] If from one point of view it is a weakness of traditional ways of

to be led.' See Gershom G Scholem, 'Tradition and Commentary as Religious Categories in Judaism' (1969) 3 *Stud in Comp Relig* 2.

92 Some commentators do think they know enough. For Michael Hudson,

> [t]he fact that Hillel could establish the prosbul waiver as part of Jewish religion showed how far Israel had moved with the same tide of privatization that was sweeping the rest of antiquity into a new Dark Age. (Still, the obedience paid to the Jubilee Year debt forgiveness was strong enough as late as thirteenth-century Spain to inspire Rabbi Maimonedes and Ibn Adret to insist that without the prosbul waiver, debts among Jews were to be forgiven.)

Michael Hudson, 'The Lost Tradition of Biblical Debt Cancellations' (1993) 39–40 <https://michael-hudson.com/wp-content/uploads/2010/03/HudsonLostTradition.pdf>. See also Michael Hudson, 'The Land Belongs to God' (2017) <http://michael-hudson.com/2017/01/the-land-belongs-to-god>.

93 But the earlier historical context may turn out to be relevant as situations change. Thus, in modern Israel, Shmita is again fundamentally linked to the land and only secondarily to the remission of debts. See <www.daat.ac.il/mishpat-ivri/skirot/326-2.htm>. Some authors seek to show the relevance of the Shmita rules for ecological challenges and environmental sustainability. David Krantz, 'Shmita Revolution: The Reclamation and Reinvention of the Sabbatical Year' (2016) 7 *Relig* 100.

94 As Scholem puts it, '[i]n considering the problem of tradition, we must distinguish between two questions. The first is historical: How did a tradition endowed with religious dignity come to be formed? The other question is: How was this tradition understood once it had been accepted as a religious phenomenon?' Scholem (n 91) 1.

95 A good example of the distance between contemporary robust American common sense and ancient tradition is found in this question posted by a rabbi on an Orthodox Jewish website:

> It seems to make no sense. Why does Hashem (ie, God) want loans to be cancelled at the end of the Shemitah year? There are no free lunches in life – why does the borrower receive a free pass and not have to repay his loan? . . . One who refuses to extend loans at that time seems not to be evil but rather acting in a financially prudent manner. . . .

Rabbi Haim Jachter, 'Making Sense of Shemitat Kesafim and Prozbol' (*Jewish Link*, 3 September 2015) <www.jlinkbc.com/index.php?option=com_content&id=9401%3Amaking-sense-of-shemitat-kesafim-and-prozbol&Itemid=585>.

telling their history that they tend to marginalize explanations that have little to do with the tradition itself that may also be a key to their strength in maintaining the loyalty of their followers.

At the same time, we should also be wary of drawing too sharp a line between external explanation and the self-understanding of tradition. If people argue that tradition constrains, then that itself may give it the potential to do that – for better or worse.[96] And, as we have seen in the case of Sombart's arguments, apparently 'external' investigations of tradition may also be as much concerned with its meaning for today as with explaining the past. As against Glenn's arguments in favour of the concept of tradition over rivals such as system and culture, Sombart's work shows that the concept of tradition, as much as culture, can be used by scholars in a way that is racist, essentialist, and over-determining.

96 Martin Krygier, 'Is There Constitutionalism after Communism? Institutional Optimism, Cultural Pessism and the Rule of Law' (1996/1997) 26 *Int'l J Socio* 17, pointed this out in the context of early doubts about the possibilities for legal change in the ex-communist world. He argues that there was a need to find a language that avoided institutional optimism, and ignored cultural differences and cultural pessimism about the possibility of changing or importing new institutions.

9

The Sunni Legal Tradition: An Overview of Pluralism, Formalism, and Reform

Ahmed Fekry Ibrahim[*]

INTRODUCTION

Describing Islam, Dale Eickelman opines that the main challenge facing students of Islam is describing how the religion's universal principles are reflected in specific social and historical contexts without representing Islam 'as a seamless essence on the one hand or as a plastic congeries of beliefs and practices on the other'.[1] Sunni Islamic law presents a similar challenge due to its pluralism. Western scholars writing in the first half of the twentieth century, such as Schacht and Coulson, argued that Islamic juristic discourse was rigidly fixed according to the doctrine that 'legal conformism' (*taqlid*) dominated juristic writings from around the tenth century. By the end of the twentieth century, the pendulum had swung in favour of assuming greater interpretive freedom (*ijtihad*), multiple Islams, and many Islamic legal systems that are almost beyond analysis due to their multifariousness.[2] What is Islamic law? How can we reconcile the tension between change and rigidity, unity and diversity? In order to answer these questions, I address three main themes that have a bearing on an eventual definition of the Sunni Islamic legal tradition: (1) legal pluralism, (2) legal determinacy, and (3) legal reform. As an introduction to these three themes, I offer a brief overview of the concept of *tradition*, which informs my analysis of Sunni Islamic law.

* I am grateful to Talal Asad for his helpful comments on a draft of this chapter. I am also indebted to Brinkley Messick for inviting me to present an early version of this chapter at the Sharīʿa Workshop of the Middle East Institute, Columbia University, in March 2017, as well as to Wael Hallaq, Marion Katz, Najam Haider, Omar Farahat, Aseel Nabeel Najib, and others in attendance for their comments and critiques, from which I benefitted greatly, but of course any faults that remain are my own. I would also like to thank the Social Sciences and Humanities Research Council (SSHRC) and Fonds de Recherche du Québec – Société et Culture (FRQSC) for their generous grants (2014–2017), which enabled me to conduct the research for this chapter.

1 Dale Eickelman, 'Changing Interpretation of Islamic Movements' in William R Roff (ed), *Islam and the Political Economy of Meaning: Comparative Studies of Muslim Discourse* (Croom Helm 1987) 18.

2 For a discussion of the notion of multiple Islams, see Abdul Hamid el-Zein, 'Beyond Ideology and Theology: The Search for the Anthropology of Islam' (1977) 6 *Ann Rev Anthropology* 227; Wael B Hallaq, 'Was the Gate of Ijtihād Closed?' (1984) 16 *Int'l J Mid E Stud* 3.

Before we discuss tradition, a word about the subject matter of Islamic law is in order. Islamic law (sharia) is different from other legal systems in that it includes ritual and ethical rules, such as etiquette, hygiene, and prayer.[3] Although the coercive power of the state is employed to ensure observance of many aspects of the law, the violation of some ritual and ethical rules does not carry any punitive measures, and therefore a primary concern of Islamic law is care of the self. Even the strictly punitive, legal aspects of Islamic law to be found, for instance, in criminal law carry eschatological consequences that are, for some Muslims, more serious than the worldly consequences. Put differently, the coercive power of Islamic law resides in both worldly, physical punishments and in the other-worldly. The job of the Muslim jurist is therefore to determine whether any given human act belongs to one of five categories: prohibited (*haram*), obligatory (*wajib*), recommended (*mandub*), discouraged (*makruh*), or neutral (*mubah*), with the last three falling outside the purview of the law in Euro-American legal traditions.

For many anthropologists, tradition refers to a set of practices and established folkways, including 'tacit knowledge', which cannot be described in words, but rather must be experienced. In philosophy, religion, and law, according to Mark Phillips and Gordon Schochet, tradition is identified with bodies of ideas consciously interpreted and transmitted over time. The essence of tradition in these conscious systems therefore resides in language. In this hermeneutic process, the present is in dialogue with the past tradition as established and policed by interpretive communities.[4] Tradition is in a constant state of invention and reinvention by those who inhabit it, and reform is a moment when they separate the essential elements from the contingent elements of tradition.[5] I contend that the malleability of memory and hermeneutics is an essential mechanism by which tradition is reconstituted and reimagined. This malleability is not a perversion, but rather is essential to the survival of tradition.

Martin Krygier outlines three elements that are essential to any tradition: (1) its past origins, whether real or imagined; (2) being passed down over intervening generations, rather than simply unearthed from a past discontinuous with the present; and (3) its possession of authority in the present. In a legal tradition, the past speaks with many voices, since the present consists of deposits made by many

[3] I use 'sharia' and 'Islamic law' in this chapter interchangeably. Wael Hallaq, however, makes a clear distinction between sharia and Islamic law. See Wael B Hallaq, 'Groundwork of the Moral Law: A New Look at the Qur'ān and the Genesis of Sharī'a' (2009) 16 *Islam L & Soc'y* 239.

[4] Mark Phillips and Gordon J Schochet, *Questions of Tradition* (University of Toronto Press 2004) ix–xv, 4–7, 18–22; EJ Hobsbawm and TO Ranger, *The Invention of Tradition* (CUP 2012) 1–14; Hans Georg Gadamer, *Truth and Method* (Joel Weinsheimer and Donald G Marshall trs, Continuum International 2004) 299–306; Edward Shils, *Tradition* (University of Chicago Press 1981) 23; Stanley Eugene Fish, *Is There a Text in this Class? The Authority of Interpretive Communities* (Harvard University Press 1980) 1–17, 303–56; Michael Polanyi, *The Tacit Dimension* (Doubleday 1966).

[5] Phillips and Schochet (n 4) 4–7; Hobsbawm and Ranger (n 4); Shils (n 4) 23.

generations with varying values and beliefs.[6] This past is arguably reconstituted and recast through a dialogic interaction between the various layers of tradition and the present, a form of *Wirkungsgeschichte* or effective history in Gadamerian terms, which regulates the hermeneutic engagements with the tradition's various historical deposits. This process of recasting and reconstitution inevitably leads to tensions and inconsistencies that are often smoothed over by jurists and other participants in the tradition, but can also create moments of crisis, leading to radical changes.[7] Yet these revolutions in law are both rare, as Krygier argues, and almost never total.[8] Conceptualizing law as a tradition tallies well with Alan Watson's concept of legal inertia,[9] or the law's resistance to change. However, despite their relative resistance to change through the authoritative interpreters' policing of the present, traditions sometime undergo significant transformations, and therefore the Enlightenment antinomy between tradition and change denotes a severe misunderstanding of the nature of tradition.[10]

One paradox is that systems of thought premised on the destruction of tradition often conform to the parameters of tradition in order to survive as intellectual and social phenomena.[11] Enlightenment rationalism is a case in point.[12] This paradox has an analogy in the purist tendency in Islamic law (known in the modern period as 'Salafism'). Its proponents opposed the accumulated interpretive tradition of jurists and fought against 'blind imitation' of the accumulated lore of jurisprudence. Does Salafism fall outside of the legal tradition of Sunni Islam in the same way Enlightenment rationalism is a tradition distinct from the earlier supposedly 'non-rational' tradition that it sought to dismantle? How do Salafism and reform fit into the Sunni legal tradition?

In order to offer a descriptive and analytical account of the Sunni legal tradition that captures both its unity and diversity, I suggest, in the remainder of this chapter, the following: (1) To understand the Sunni legal tradition, we must include the practices of judges in a given time and place in our analysis, rather than focus exclusively on the seemingly timeless discourse of 'author-jurists' who compile manuals of substantive law and function outside the courtroom.[13] Including the

6 Martin Krygier, 'Law as Tradition' (1986) 5 *Law & Phil* 237. In the Islamic context, some purist jurists often argue, *pace* Krygier's definition, for discontinuities between an authoritative tradition in the distant past and their point in the present.

7 On revolutions in scientific traditions, see Thomas S Kuhn, *The Structure of Scientific Revolutions* (University of Chicago Press 1970).

8 Krygier (n 6) 248.

9 Alan Watson, *Society and Legal Change* (Scottish Academic Press 1977) 1–11, 115–27.

10 Krygier (n 6) 251.

11 On tradition generally, see also Alasdair C MacIntyre, *Three Rival Versions of Moral Enquiry: Encyclopaedia, Genealogy, and Tradition* (University of Notre Dame Press 1990) 127–48; Alasdair C MacIntyre, *Whose Justice? Which Rationality?* (University of Notre Dame Press 1988); Alasdair C MacIntyre, *After Virtue: A Study in Moral Theory* (University of Notre Dame Press 1984).

12 Phillips and Schochet (n 4) 7; Shils (n 4) 23.

13 Hallaq uses the term 'author-jurist' to refer to authors of juristic discourse, the framers of the law. I use 'author-jurists' and 'jurists' interchangeably to mean those who articulated the law, in

localized, pluralistic practices of the law naturally leads to more divergence in legal norms than would be the case if we were to focus exclusively on the discourse of author-jurists. (2) Thus, the legal historian should study Sunni Islamic law as a series of localized iterations of a larger tradition situated in time and place. These iterations represent the local variations of the contingent (and often contradictory) elements of the tradition in dialogue with the intellectual accretions and practices of Muslim jurists and judges over centuries. (3) This approach promises to open up more avenues of legal reform grounded in a more authoritative period far removed from the negative baggage of modernity. I make these three contentions in my following discussions of legal pluralism, determinacy, and reform.

I LEGAL PLURALISM

There is no consensus on the meaning of legal pluralism, a concept coined in the 1970s as a reaction against the idea that the law is exclusively the prerogative of the state, known as 'legal centralism'. In its broadest sense, legal pluralism refers to the situation when more than one source of law is applied in a given social field.[14] According to Griffiths, there are two types of legal pluralism. Strong legal pluralism exists where there are multiple sources of law, developed by private social groups and uncontrolled by the state. Weak legal pluralism exists when the state designates legal rules for different sectors of the population, such as when the state permits tribunals for religious or ethnic minorities. In other words, the state's recognition of a system of law makes it part of the state's legal apparatus, and therefore some scholars do not consider this type to be 'real' legal pluralism.[15]

contradistinction to judges, who by the thirteenth century were required to follow the discourse of jurists in their court adjudication. This distinction is important because it was the legal manuals penned by jurists, rather than the precedent of judges, that constituted the normative doctrine of Islamic law. Unlike Hallaq, however, I include jurisconsults (muftis), who authored non-binding legal opinions, known as fatwas, in this category. See Wael B Hallaq, *Authority, Continuity, and Change in Islamic Law* (CUP 2001) 166–235.

14 John Griffiths, 'What Is Legal Pluralism?' (1986) 24 *J Legal Pluralism* 1; Brian Z Tamanaha, 'The Folly of the "Social Scientific" Concept of Legal Pluralism' (1993) 20 *JL & Soc'y* 192; Ido Shahar, 'Legal Pluralism', *The Oxford Encyclopedia of Islam and Law* (2017) <www.oxfordislamicstudies.com>; Brian Z Tamanaha, Caroline Mary Sage, and Michael JV Woolcock, *Legal Pluralism and Development: Scholars and Practitioners in Dialogue* (CUP 2012).

15 In a similar fashion albeit using different nomenclature, Gordon Woodman draws a distinction between 'state law pluralism', which refers to two bodies of norms applied to different sections of the population and accepted by the state, and 'deep legal pluralism', which refers to laws that are not sanctioned by the state. See Gordon R Woodman, 'Legal Pluralism and the Search for Justice' (1996) 40 *J Afr L* 156; Griffiths (n 14); Murielle Paradelle, 'Legal Pluralism and Public International Law: An Analysis Based on the International Convention on the Rights of the Child' in Baudouin Dupret, Maurits Berger, and Laila Al-Zwaini (eds), *Legal Pluralism in the Arab World* (Kluwer Law International 1999); Ido Shahar, 'Legal Pluralism and the Study of Shariʿa Courts' (2008) 15 *Islam L & Soc'y* 112; Gordon R Woodman, 'The Idea of Legal Pluralism' in Baudouin Dupret, Maurits Berger, and Laila Al-Zwaini (eds), *Legal Pluralism in the Arab World* (Brill 1999).

Ido Shahar argues for a reconceptualization of the strong/weak distinction based on the institutional functions of legal pluralism. In his view, strong legal pluralism exists when the subjects of the law can choose the forum of adjudication. Weak legal pluralism obtains when the state forecloses forum shopping by assigning tribunals to different categories of the population.[16] By contrast, Brian Tamanaha rejects the very notion of legal pluralism, calling into question the legal pluralists' insistence that the state does not have a monopoly on law, which in his estimation leads to the conclusion that all forms of social control are law. According to Tamanaha, without the state, the term 'law' loses its meaning as it becomes synonymous with 'normative order', which may include moral and political norms, customs, habits, and rules of etiquette. Instead, he proposes to use alternative terms such as 'normative pluralism' or 'rule system pluralism'.[17] Despite Tamanaha's critique, the term 'legal pluralism' has been widely used as a conceptual framework over the past forty years.[18]

I use legal pluralism in this chapter in a broad sense to refer to three main types: First, 'Sunni juristic pluralism' refers to the existence of multiple legal rules that are considered equally normative in the discourse of Muslim jurists. Second, 'sharia and state law pluralism' refers to the tension between the jurisdiction of sharia and that of state courts and laws, such as Mamluk complaint courts (*mazalim*) and Ottoman state law (*qanun*) in the premodern period. The distinction made by Muslim jurists between sharia and state law is rooted in the assumption that the latter derives its *direct* authority from the state, rather than from Muslim jurists. Sharia and state law were the two main components of the legal apparatus of premodern Muslim states. Third, 'sharia and customary law pluralism' refers to the tension between customary tribunals and laws, on the one hand, and sharia jurisdiction, on the other. The first two kinds of legal pluralism are state sponsored (representing weak legal pluralism in Griffiths' terminology), but the third type is often not sanctioned by the state (representing strong legal pluralism). In what follows, I provide a brief historical overview of these three types, placing more emphasis on Sunni juristic pluralism for two reasons. First, it is a type about which we know more than the third type, for instance, owing to juristic pluralism's validation by the state and incorporation into its legal apparatus. Second, it is a site where subjects of the law are best able to take advantage of legal pluralism to accommodate their evolving social and economic needs, and therefore juristic pluralism affords us a look at the functioning of the law at the point of contact between state and society.

During his life, Prophet Muhammad combined political and spiritual authority, acting as a statesman, a judge, and a prophet. After his death in 632, four of his Companions ruled the early Muslim state, making pragmatic decisions that sometimes departed from Muhammad's legacy, or, some may argue, paying more attention

16 Shahar, 'Legal Pluralism' (n 14) 118–26.

17 Tamanaha, 'Folly of the "Social Scientific" Concept' (n 14).

18 On legal pluralism and the relationship between jurists and the state in Islam, see Sherman A Jackson, 'Legal Pluralism between Islam and the Nation-State: Romantic Medievalism or Pragmatic Modernity?' (2006) 30 *Fordham Int'l LJ* 158.

to the spirit of the Qur'an and the memory of Muhammad rather than to the letter of revelation. After the death of Ali (d 661), the last of the four caliphs considered by Sunnis to be models of piety, Umayyad dynasty (661–750) administrators and judges relied on local practices to resolve the legal problems they encountered. In the fast-expanding new cities that the Arab conquerors established in the Near East, many pious jurists debated whether the legal and administrative practices of the Umayyads represented the values of the Qur'an and the legacy of the Prophet. This concern was reinforced by the view widely held in some scholarly (and popular) circles that the Umayyads were impious and unjust usurpers of power. These scholars sought to develop the law, largely independent of the state and its machinations. Great centres of Islamic legal scholarship emerged by the late seventh and early eighth centuries, including Kufa, Basra, Medina, and Damascus.[19] In the course of their legal systematization during this period, jurists introduced new elements of juristic disagreement through their divergent legal methodologies, further increasing Islamic law's discursive pluralism. Given the Qur'an's sparse treatment of legal issues, the scholars of the centres of the Islamic lands had to rely on non-qur'anic solutions. These included the practices of the early generations of Muslims, localized customary practices, analogical reasoning, and pragmatic reasoning.

The early sources of Islamic law, which go back to the late eighth and early ninth centuries, draw a picture of extreme doctrinal pluralism (my first type of legal pluralism) in different regions of the Abbasid Caliphate (750–1258), which stretched from central Asia to North Africa. Influential cities within this vast empire had different methodological and substantive legal views to the extent that this diversity caused concern in some quarters of the Abbasid government. Early Islamic legal sources often assume a level of geographical unity as they make references to the views of Kufans, Basrans, Meccans, Syrians, Medinese, or the Iraqis. Thus, the jurist Ibn Hanbal (d 855) was reported by his son to have said that if someone were to follow the people of Kufa on date wine, the people of Medina on music, and the people of Mecca on *mut'a* marriage, she would be a sinner.[20] These differences were the result of regional, pre-Islamic social, administrative, and judicial practices, the legacy of the peoples of the Near East who were ruled by the Byzantines and Sassanids for centuries before the Islamic conquests of the region started in the 630s, as well as individual hermeneutic approaches.[21]

19 Marshall GS Hodgson, *The Venture of Islam: Conscience and History in a World Civilization* (University of Chicago Press 1974) 217–30; Jonathan Porter Berkey, *The Formation of Islam: Religion and Society in the Near East, 600–1800* (CUP 2003) 76–101; Fred McGraw Donner, *Muhammad and the Believers: At the Origins of Islam* (Belknap Press 2010) 145–217; Hugh Kennedy, *Caliphate: The History of an Idea* (Basic Books 2016) 33–61.

20 Aḥmad Ibn Ḥanbal, *Masā'il Al-Imām Aḥmad Ibn Ḥanbal Riwāyatu Ibnihi 'Al- Allāh Ibn Aḥmad* (Zuhayr al-Shāwīsh ed, al-Maktab al-Islāmī 1981) 449; Abū Muḥammad al-Ḥasan b 'Alī b Khalaf al-Barbahārī, *Sharḥ Al-Sunna* ('Abd al-Raḥmān b Aḥmad al-Jumayzī ed, Dār al-Minhāj 2005) 116.

21 Joseph Schacht, *An Introduction to Islamic Law* (Clarendon Press 1964) 19–22; Noel James Coulson, *A History of Islamic Law* (Edinburgh University Press 1962) 27–28, 50–52; Joseph Schacht, *The Origins*

Although judges and administrators, associated as they were with the state as its representatives, played an important role in developing the law in the first century of Islam, by the middle of the eighth century it was author-jurists whose articulation of the law set the norms. Judicial precedent, therefore, had no legal weight unless it received a stamp of approval from jurists, a reality which increased Sunni juristic pluralism. The picture was further complicated by the fact that in addition to geographical differences, there were also juristic Sunni disagreements within each city or region. In other words, from the very formative period of Islamic law, there were intra-regional and interregional doctrinal differences. Intra-regional doctrinal differences resulted from hermeneutic considerations and the personal authority of certain jurists, whereas at least some of the interregional differences resulted from administrative, social, and legal structures and practices predating Islam.

This legal pluralism, where different legal doctrines were operative in different regions under Ummayad and Abbasid rule, was never centrally circumscribed due to the historical relationship between jurists and the state. In the early period of Islam, a tension existed between the state and jurists due to the trauma of the early Muslim civil wars in 656–661 and 680–692, which led to the accession to power of rulers who were considered illegitimate or at least impious by many scholars, as already mentioned. As early as the eighth and ninth centuries under the Abbasids (750–1258), there was hostility among many scholars to state intervention in matters of law and theology, as evidenced by the jurists' position on the Abbasids' desire to centralize Islamic law and remove legal pluralism during the reign of al-Mansur (r. 754–775), as well as the Qur'an Inquisition of 833–848.[22]

The prevalence of pragmatic juristic reasoning in lawmaking and its concomitant legal pluralism characteristic of this period led to the emergence of a group of jurists by the late eighth century who were staunchly opposed to 'human' rather than 'scriptural' (and therefore purely Islamic) reasoning. These legal purists called their opponents *ahl al-ra'y* ('partisans of personal reasoning') and advanced the thesis that the Prophet's sayings and teachings (*hadiths* or prophetic traditions) should replace non-scriptural forms of juristic reasoning. These purists – whose main opponents were the rationalist scholars of Kufa led by Abu Hanifa (d 767) – were known as *ahl al-hadith* ('partisans of prophetic traditions'); I will henceforth refer to them as 'traditionalists' or 'purists' interchangeably. The traditionalists sought to collect the Prophet's traditions, giving rise to the acute proliferation of prophetic traditions in the course of the eighth and ninth centuries, until the corpus of *hadith* was canonized in the second half of the ninth century.[23] Although these purists influenced the

of Muhammadan Jurisprudence (Clarendon Press 1967) 6–10; Patricia Crone, *Roman, Provincial, and Islamic Law: The Origins of the Islamic Patronate* (CUP 1987).

[22] Dimitri Gutas, *Greek Thought, Arabic Culture: The Graeco-Arabic Translation Movement in Baghdad and Early 'Abbāsid Society (2nd-4th/8th-10th Centuries)* (Routledge 1998) 75–83; Ahmed Fekry Ibrahim, *Pragmatism in Islamic Law: A Social and Intellectual History* (2nd edn, Syracuse University Press 2017) 35–36.

[23] Jonathan Brown, *Hadith: Muhammad's Legacy in the Medieval and Modern World* (Oneworld 2009).

direction of Sunni Islamic law, they did not completely do away with pragmatic juristic reasoning. A jurist from Medina by the name of al-Shafi'i (d 820) was credited by many historians for creating a synthesis between the rationalist and traditionalist positions, according to which the sources of Sunni Islamic law were the Qur'an, the *hadith* (prophetic traditions), analogical reasoning, and the consensus of the community. However, many traditionalists – notable among whom was Ahmad Ibn Hanbal (d 855), the champion of the Qur'an Inquisition – continued their attack on rational modes of reasoning and the four-source theory.[24]

At the end of the tenth century, when the dust had settled, five Sunni schools survived: the Hanafis, who were associated with the early rationalists; the Malikis, who were associated with a unique mix of rationalist and traditionalist thought;[25] the Shafi'is, who championed a synthesis between the traditionalist and rationalist theses; the Hanbalis or followers of Ibn Hanbal (d 855), the traditionalist who launched a sustained attack against the rationalists; and the Zahiris, followers of Dawud al-Zahiri (d 884), a literalist whose school died out by the eleventh century. The Hanafi school had to abandon elements of its early rationalist methodology and accept the dominance of the textual sources,[26] while the Shafi'is and some Hanbalis accepted limited forms of reasoning such as analogical reasoning, which were anathema to early traditionalists.

Al-Shafi'i's legal methodology does not *in theory* have space for pragmatic or utilitarian considerations in lawmaking, but this is misleading because pragmatic considerations made their way into the law through many doors. After the dominance of the purists' thesis regarding the centrality of prophetic traditions to law, the Prophet's legacy was remembered severally in many contradictory *hadiths*, lending legitimacy to pragmatic solutions that by the early ninth century needed a textual justification to pass muster. Pragmatic solutions were incorporated into the law when jurists sifted through a vast *hadith* literature to determine which one to accept or reject, sometimes based on what legal point they supported. Other forms of subjective pragmatic reasoning continued to be a means to derive or justify laws,

[24] Joseph Lowry argues against the common wisdom that al-Shafi'i created a synthesis between traditionalism and rationalism in the form of a four-source theory, contending that this supposed theory was a back-projection of later Shafi'i jurists onto the eponym's treatise on legal theory, *al-Risala*. Joseph E Lowry, 'Does Shāfi'ī Have a Theory of "Four Sources" of Law?' in Bernard G Weiss (ed), *Studies in Islamic Legal Theory* (Brill 2002) 23–50; Joseph E Lowry, *Early Islamic Legal Theory: The Risāla of Muḥammad Ibn Idrīs al-Shāfii'ī* (Brill 2007) 1–7, 23–51; Wael B Hallaq, *Sharī'a: Theory, Practice, Transformations* (CUP 2009) 55–60; Wael B Hallaq, 'Was al-Shāfi'ī the Master Architect of Islamic Jurisprudence?' (1993) 25 *Int'l J Mid E Stud* 587; Wael B Hallaq, A *History of Islamic Legal Theories: An Introduction to Sunnī Uṣūl Al-Fiqh* (CUP 1997) 21–35; Schacht, *Introduction to Islamic Law* (n 21) 37–68; Ahmed El Shamsy, *The Canonization of Islamic Law: A Social and Intellectual History* (CUP 2013) 17–90; Ahmed El Shamsy, 'Rethinking *Taqlīd* in the Early Shāfi'ī School' (2008) 128 *Am Oriental Soc'y J* 1; Christopher Melchert, *The Formation of the Sunnī Schools of Law, 9th–10th Centuries* C.E. (Brill 1997) 1–67.

[25] Yasin Dutton, *The Origins of Islamic Law: The Qur'an, the Muwaṭṭa' and Madinan 'Amal* (Curzon 1999).

[26] Melchert (n 24) 48–60.

especially in the Hanafi school, including the by now highly maligned subjective and pragmatic forms of reasoning such as 'juristic preference' (*istihsan*). Traditionalists often blamed these forms of subjective and pragmatic reasoning for Sunni Islam's doctrinal pluralism, which they strongly opposed.

Most of the doctrines of Islamic law had already been developed by the end of the eighth century when the rationalist–purist debate was ignited, yet little substantive law was changed as a consequence of the nascent legal theory. It was the jurists' memory of the Prophet's legacy as well as their sophisticated hermeneutic engagements that brought about consistency between the nascent legal theory and the existing regional legal doctrines predating it. Instead of launching a substantive legal revolution disrupting the administration of law, most jurists found ways to maintain the four-source theory (despite significant modifications over the course of the ninth to thirteenth centuries) without introducing radical changes to the legal doctrines predating it. The jurists' success in reconciling the pluralistic legal tradition of the first two centuries of Islam with the successful thesis of traditionalists was achieved by (1) opting for a less radical version of the traditionalist thesis represented by al-Shafiʿi's synthesis; (2) choosing a flexible hermeneutic that allowed different substantive rules to coexist;[27] and (3) devising a flexible system of *hadith* criticism,[28] which also allowed for considerable disagreements over the authenticity of prophetic reports. In other words, the memory of the Prophet was variously constructed, ensuring the continuity of the pluralistic Sunni legal tradition.

The Islamic tradition of the first two centuries of Islam was thus able to ward off traditionalism, which represented the first major threat to the Sunni legal tradition as it accumulated over the first two centuries of Islam, maintaining the rationalist (read: subjective, pragmatic) solutions of the early centres of Islamic legal scholarship as an essential part of the heritage of Sunni Islamic law. In a word, Islamic law from its very beginning was the result of the interaction between formalist textualism and pragmatism, leading to considerable 'Sunni juristic pluralism' within the discourse of jurists. This was the case both before and after the traditionalist onslaught. By the end of the ninth century, the majority of Sunni jurists continued to gravitate towards a legal theory that incorporated formalist and pragmatic solutions to legal problems.

On the margins of the Islamic legal tradition, there have always been jurists who opposed 'human reasoning', subjectivism, and their corollary, legal pluralism. They rejected the synthesis between rationalism and traditionalism and the very notion of traditionality inherent in the Sunni *madhhabs* (schools of law), thus basing their

27 David Vishanoff, *The Formation of Islamic Hermeneutics: How Sunni Legal Theorists Imagined a Revealed Law* (American Oriental Society 2011)

28 This system was often subjective. See Jonathan AC Brown, 'How We Know Early Hadith Critics Did *Matn* Criticism and Why It's So Hard to Find' (2008) 15 *Islam L & Soc'y* 143; Brown, *Hadith* (n 23) 1–172.

tradition on the dismantlement of tradition. Despite their claim to *ijtihad* in the sense of applying one's mental capacities directly to the textual sources (the Qur'an and *hadiths*) to derive the law, purists could not escape the prison-house of tradition[29]: the accumulated heritage of *hadith* criticism, qur'anic commentary, and the Arabic lexicon itself. This legal hermeneutic tradition had stabilized by the second half of the ninth century, making it hard for jurists following an *ijtihad* methodology to introduce considerable change to the legal legacy of the first two centuries. The purist and de-constructivist tradition to whom the very notion of 'school' (*madhhab*) was anathema formed a legal canon corresponding mostly to the Hanbali school with occasional variations by some mavericks like the Syrian polymath Ibn Taymiyya (d 1328). The framers of this canon could only claim to be in a constant state of deconstruction based on the fiction that they could somehow operate outside of tradition, its lexicon, *hadith* criticism, and qur'anic commentary, all of which were themselves produced by the tradition and productive of it.[30] Thus, the purists' 'tradition-less' tradition congealed with the other Sunni schools on many points of agreement, under the umbrella of consensus (*ijma*ʿ), itself a source of Sunni Islamic law. The fiction of constant reconstruction (or at least constant verification) largely remained just that,[31] a fiction.

Due to the events of early Islamic history, especially the Qur'an Inquisition, it was the interpretive communities' policing of meaning, rather than state intervention, that kept Sunni juristic pluralism at bay. The trauma of the Qur'an Inquisition in the collective Islamic imaginary and the failure of the Abbasid state to impose one theological doctrine in a manner similar to Byzantine interventions in Christological debates made it hard for future Islamic states to make claims to theological or legal orthodoxy. These events gave rise to a unique theory of the relationship between state and scholars in Sunni Islam, best articulated in a treatise written by an eleventh-century jurist from Baghdad. According to this theory, there was a division of labour between state and jurists (my second type of Islamic legal pluralism), whereby the latter made law, while the state enforced it; indeed, the state derived its legitimacy from the enforcement of the jurisprudence of jurists.[32] Despite the assumption that the state was only to make law in limited domains and so long as they did not contradict the jurisprudence of jurists, there were many periods of

29 Spinoza encountered a similar problematic as cited in Jonathan Brown, *Misquoting Muhammad: The Challenge and Choices of Interpreting the Prophet's Legacy* (Oneworld 2014) 204–06.

30 Ibn Hazm (d 1064) remarked that many jurists who claim to exercise *ijtihad* are in fact simply paying lip service to the deconstruction of tradition, since despite their hermeneutic claims, they do not in reality depart from the doctrines of their given schools. In other words, they find hermeneutic ways to maintain their doctrines all while claiming to be neutral interpreters of the scripture. Ahmed Fekry Ibrahim, 'Rethinking the *Taqlīd-Ijtihād* Dichotomy: A Conceptual-Historical Approach' (2016) 136 *Am Oriental Soc'y J* 285, 299.

31 On the purist reconstruction or verification of the authenticity of the legal tradition, see Ahmed Fekry Ibrahim, 'Rethinking the *Taqlīd-Ijtihād* Dichotomy' (n 30) 285–303.

32 ʿAlī b Muḥammad Māwardī, *The Ordinances of Government: A Translation of Al-Aḥkām Al-Sulṭāniyya Wa'l-Wilāyāt Al-Dīniyya* (Wafaa Hassan Wahba tr, Garnet 1996).

tension between the two bodies of law.[33] This theory justified the existing 'constitutional arrangement' between jurists and the state,[34] where encroachment of the state was kept at bay, ensuring that matters of lawmaking would remain the primary responsibility of jurists.

This unique politico-legal context gave rise to potentially unlimited legal pluralism and uncertainty. Since the legal system was not centralized by a government or a clergy, most jurists perceived potentially extreme legal pluralism as a threat to legal predictability and the efficient administration of justice. It fell to jurists to balance the requirements of justice and legal predictability by managing two competing legal modes of lawmaking – 'personal interpretive freedom' (*ijtihad*) and 'interpretive conformism' (*taqlid*) within the school unit. They gradually limited interpretive freedom over the course of the eleventh to thirteenth centuries by arguing for the dearth of legal skills.[35] Jurists also controlled legal pluralism in court practice by determining which view in a given school was the dominant position of that school, which was supposed to be applied by judges.[36] Despite the jurists' efforts to rein in doctrinal diversity through the limits they placed on *ijtihad*, Sunni Islamic law retained much of its pluralism in the four extant schools as well as in intra-school doctrine.

The third type of legal pluralism pertains to the competing jurisdictions of sharia on the one hand and customary tribunals and laws on the other. Like state law (*qanun*), customary law was assumed by Muslim jurists to complement rather than compete with sharia. Yet this was not always the case, as we will see in the discussion of legal formalism below. It is hard to know both the extent of the utilization, in the premodern period, of non-state customary laws by Muslims outside of the jurisdiction of the sharia judge (*qadi*) and the nature of tribunals that applied non-sharia (and non-state) customary law. However, it is safe to assume that many legal disputes were resolved out of court in private arbitration tribunals. This can be seen often in references to arbitration and reconciliation tribunals in the theories of premodern Muslim jurists and in the sharia court records of the premodern period.[37]

33 Kristin Stilt argues for a broader conception of sharia that includes not only the jurisprudence of jurists but also some of the actions of the state. On some of the areas of tension between sharia and state law, see Kristen Stilt, *Islamic Law in Action: Authority, Discretion, and Everyday Experiences in Mamluk Egypt* (OUP 2011).

34 On this 'constitutional arrangement' generally, see Noah Feldman, *The Fall and Rise of the Islamic State* (Princeton University Press 2008).

35 Ahmed Fekry Ibrahim, 'Rethinking the *Taqlīd* Hegemony: An Institutional, *Longue-Durée* Approach' (2016) 136 *Am Oriental Soc'y J* 801.

36 On the process of establishing the school's most preponderant position (*tarjih*) and on the requirement that judges follow it, see Hallaq, *Sharī'a* (n 24) 73–77; ibid.

37 On *sulh* (reconciliation) and *tahkim* (arbitration), see Aida Othman, '"And Amicable Settlement Is Best": *Sulh* and Dispute Resolution in Islamic Law' (2007) 21 *ALQ* 64; Hamad al-Humaidhi, 'Ṣulḥ: Arbitration in the Arab-Islamic World' (2015) 29 *ALQ* 92. On selection bias in the study of Ottoman court records with respect to cases that were resolved out of court, see Metin M Coşgel and Boğaç A Ergene, 'The Selection Bias in Court Records: Settlement and Trial in Eighteenth-Century Ottoman Kastamonu' (2014) 67 *Econ Hist Rev* 517.

The modern state (both colonial and postcolonial) sought to create legal unicity by removing many aspects of premodern Islamic legal pluralism. With respect to the first and second types of Sunni juristic pluralism, the nineteenth-century Egyptian state, for instance, unified Islamic law under the Hanafi school and slowly restricted Islamic law to the realm of family and succession law over the course of the nineteenth and twentieth centuries. In other words, one Sunni school become the representative of Islamic law, eliding much of our first type of pluralism. With respect to the second type, secular state law replaced many aspects of the legal system that used to be based on Islamic law in the premodern period. In the twentieth century, the Egyptian state combined rules from different bodies of Sunni law in state statutes, which coexisted within a unified legal system largely of European provenance.[38] The second and third types of legal pluralism, however, have continued to play a role in the modern period despite the centralization efforts of the modern state. For instance, Rudolph Peters shows the complementarity and tensions between sharia and statute law in Egypt in the second half of the nineteenth century, whereas Sarah Ben Nefissa examines customary arbitration in contemporary Egypt.[39]

II LEGAL DETERMINACY: TWO FORMALISMS

In his award-winning *Legal Traditions of the World*, the late Patrick Glenn reasoned, 'So while an islamic tradition is one in which the notion of stability is taken further than perhaps in any other, in its working it can no more guarantee stability, or precise and constant results, than can any other legal tradition.'[40] Glenn's comments raise the important question of determinacy and formalism in Islamic legal rules. The theory of formalism, whose proponents tout its ability to ensure stability and the rule of law, assumes that adjudication is the mechanical application of the law, understood as a body of pre-existing rules to be found in canonical legal materials, to known facts. According to the theory of formalism, the judge's *Weltanschauung* is irrelevant to the application of law or the establishment of the relevant facts. Legal decisions are therefore 'the product of a syllogism in which a rule of law supplies the major premise, the facts of the case supply the minor one, and the decision is the conclusion'.[41]

38 On Hanafization and partial unification through state statutes, see also Woodman, 'Idea of Legal Pluralism' (n 15) 18; Kenneth M Cuno, *Modernizing Marriage: Family, Ideology, and Law in Nineteenth and Early Twentieth Century Egypt* (Syracuse University Press 2015) 123–57; Ahmed Fekry Ibrahim, *Pragmatism in Islamic Law* (1st edn, Syracuse University Press 2015) 202–29.

39 Peters argues that sharia and statute law complemented each other and only rarely overlapped. See Rudolph Peters, 'An Administrator's Nightmare: Feuding Families in Nineteenth Century Bahariyya Oasis' in Dupret, Berger, and Al-Zwaini (n 15); Sarah Ben Nefissa, 'The *Haqq Al-'Arab*: Conflict Resolution and Distinctive Features of Legal Pluralism in Contemporary Egypt' in Dupret, Berger, and Al-Zwaini (n 15).

40 H Patrick Glenn, *Legal Traditions of the World: Sustainable Diversity in Law* (OUP 2000) 183.

41 Richard A Posner, *How Judges Think* (Harvard University Press 2008) 41. Schauer suggests that there is no consensus on what formalism really means. Frederick Schauer, 'Formalism' (1988) 97 *Yale LJ* 509.

In the context of Islamic law, there are two types of formalisms. The first type relates to the judge's 'mechanical' application of the rules of author-jurists in the courtroom based purely on the law and the facts of a case. With respect to this formalism, most premodern Muslim jurists assumed that courts applied juristic discourse in a formalist manner in the age of *taqlīd* (legal conformism), especially after the thirteenth century, although they accepted the judge's accommodation of social custom (*'urf*) so long as it did not contradict the discourse of author-jurists. However, scholars like Joseph Schacht, taking an anti-formalist position, have argued that Islamic criminal law, for instance, was so austere that it was rarely applied in practice, suggesting that the rigid rules of legal theory did not always predetermine legal outcomes.[42]

The second type of formalism pertains to the activities of author-jurists who 'discover' the law from the sources: the Qur'an, *hadith*, and consensus. Premodern Sunni jurists assumed that legal theory's function was to guide jurists to the divine law, despite the fact that Islamic legal theory accommodated pragmatic and utilitarian avenues of lawmaking through concepts such as *maslaha* and *istihsan*, as already noted. Vishanoff showed that the legal hermeneutic that dominated Islamic law was flexible enough to allow for many possible outcomes, despite the claim of legal theorists that their rules were the will of God. This discussion is similar to the debate over formalism among American legal theorists in that the interpretation of the Islamic scriptural sources to devise new legal rules can be analogized to an American judge's interpretation of precedent or the constitution.[43]

We should, however, go beyond the two formalisms: juristic discursive formalism, that is, the assumption that the law of jurists, found in legal manuals, is the law applied mechanically in the court; and hermeneutic formalism, that is, the assumption that Islamic legal theory was always creative of legal rules by following a clear methodology. Hermeneutic formalism has been potently challenged recently by Sherman Jackson, who argues that pragmatic and utilitarian concepts such as *istihsan* and *maslaha* were designed to reverse the negative effects of strict hermeneutic formalism. Those who challenge hermeneutic formalism have also concluded that Sunni legal theory did not really play the creative role assigned to it by legal theorists.[44] However, the first type of formalism (juristic discursive formalism) is only beginning to be challenged in a substantive way. Although there are excellent

42 Schacht, *Introduction to Islamic Law* (n 21) 75–85.

43 On formalism and pragmatism, see Daniel A Farber, 'The Inevitability of Practical Reason: Statutes, Formalism, and the Rule of Law' (1992) 45 *Vand L Rev* 533; Thomas F Cotter, 'Legal Pragmatism and the Law and Economics Movement' (1996) 84 *Geo LJ* 2071; Daniel A Farber, 'Legal Pragmatism and the Constitution' (1987–1988) 72 *Minn L Rev* 1331; BZ Tamanaha, 'Pragmatism in U.S. Legal Theory: Its Application to Normative Jurisprudence, Sociolegal Studies, and the Fact-Value Distinction' (1996) 41 *Am J Juris* 315; Evan Simpson, *Anti-Foundationalism and Practical Reasoning: Conversations Between Hermeneutics and Analysis* (Academic Print 1987); Ibrahim, *Pragmatism in Islamic Law* (n 22) xi–xiii.

44 Jackson also utilizes Stanley Fish's 'New Legal Formalism' to argue that theory validates, rather than produces, law. See Sherman Jackson, 'Fiction and Formalism: Toward a Functional Analysis of *Uṣūl*

studies that have dealt with court records in Ottoman Syria,[45] Ottoman Aintab,[46] Ottoman Aleppo,[47] and Ottoman Egypt,[48] to mention a few, the objectives of these authors were not to challenge the formalist hypothesis head-on. They explored other equally important legal and historical questions, especially relating to gender. Looking at Islamic law holistically as a tradition incorporating various participants both inside and outside the courtroom (such as judges, muftis, legal subjects, and scribes) requires us to consider both the pragmatic adjudication of Ottoman-Egyptian judges and their formalistic adherence to the rules of author-jurists in our assessment of the tradition. After all, the mix of formalism and pragmatism has indeed existed in Islamic law from its birth.

In order to transcend the two formalisms, we must consider the interplay between legal rules and court adjudication. Many American legal theorists would acknowledge that there are hard cases that warrant a higher level of indeterminacy, but with most easy cases there is greater determinacy. This explains why a well-known legal theorist like Judge Posner argues that American judges have historically used a mix of formalism and pragmatism in their decision-making.[49] Islamic law is no different. I have shown elsewhere that despite the formalism of Ottoman judges on many of the rules of child custody,[50] there were some issues over which judges exercised pragmatic adjudication, departing from formalist adjudication to ensure family stability.[51] Judges, muftis, and even the laity knew what the operative rules were. In fact, we know that each region had books of high repute containing the dominant legal doctrines that judges were required to follow in their adjudication and legal education. In order to answer the question 'What is premodern Islamic law?' in a *descriptive* mode (as opposed to a *prescriptive* mode, as discussed later in the section on legal reform), we must conduct a series of historical studies of court practices in different regions, as well as studies of the books of high repute to comprehend the formalism–pragmatism mix that Judge Posner refers to and which applies perfectly to Islamic law, especially in the premodern period.

Al-Fiqh' in Weiss (n 24); Mohammad Fadel, '"*Istiḥsān* Is Nine-Tenths of the Law": The Puzzling Relationship of *Uṣūl* to *Furūʿ* in the Mālikī *Madhhab*' in Weiss (n 24).

45 Judith E Tucker, *In the House of the Law: Gender and Islamic Law in Ottoman Syria and Palestine* (University of California Press 1998).

46 Leslie P Peirce, *Morality Tales Law and Gender in the Ottoman Court of Aintab* (University of California Press 2003).

47 Elyse Semerdjian, *'Off the Straight Path': Illicit Sex, Law, and Community in Ottoman Aleppo* (Syracuse University Press 2008).

48 Reem A Meshal, *Sharia and the Making of the Modern Egyptian: Islamic Law and Custom in the Courts of Ottoman Cairo* (American University in Cairo Press 2014).

49 Richard A Posner, *The Problems of Jurisprudence* (Harvard University Press 1990) 32.

50 Ahmed Fekry Ibrahim, 'The Best Interests of the Child in Premodern Islamic Juristic Discourse and Practice' (2015) 63 *Am J Comp L* 859.

51 Ahmed Fekry Ibrahim, *Child Custody in Islamic Law: The Best Interests of the Child in Theory and Practice* (CUP 2018).

In trying to understand the premodern Sunni legal tradition both inside and outside the court, we are faced with a problem with respect to periods for which there are no extant court records. Although legal historians are fortunate to have access to vast collections of Ottoman court rulings covering different provinces from the fifteenth to nineteenth centuries, other periods prior to the fifteenth century are less accessible. Save for limited Fatimid (909–1171) and Mamluk period (1250–1517) documents of legal value and some references in the biographical literature and chronicles to important court cases, as well as manuals of legal formularies, legal procedure, and scribal practices, there is very little information about court practice prior to the Ottoman period. It is therefore almost impossible to write a full history of the practice of Islamic law before the mid-fifteenth century or in non-Ottoman territories. By contrast, Ottoman legal historians have millions of court records at their disposal. In regions and periods in which court records are not available, we are forced to take a formalist approach out of necessity.

The Ottoman period is therefore superbly positioned to offer deep insights into the tradition of Sunni Islamic law. Treating the Sunni legal tradition as comprising both the jurisprudence of author-jurists and the adjudication of judges in dialogic interaction with society, the Islamic legal historian can best reconstruct this tradition by studying the books of high repute in a particular Ottoman province in order to gain an understanding of legal doctrine. Ottoman court records can then complement that picture with the pragmatic choices made in the courtroom on a narrow topic of substantive or procedural law.

Consider the following example: the premodern Ḥanafi school had two competing positions over the age at which a girl should be transferred from the custody of her mother to the custody of her father. One of these positions requires the transfer at physical maturity, which is either menstruation or a presumptive age of around fifteen years. This position was attributed to the eponym of the Ḥanafi school, Abu Hanifa (d 767). Another position, attributed to Abu Hanifa's famous disciple, Muhammad al-Shaybani (d 805), placed the age simply at nine. In order to know the dominant position within the juristic discourse of say, sixteenth-century Egypt, one should examine the books of high repute from that period. Coming up with a list of these books is no easy task. One must examine such diverse historical sources as probate inventories, which tell us what books scholars had in their libraries; citations of books in the court records themselves; and references to important books in the biographical dictionaries. No thorough list of such books exists in Islamic legal studies.[52] This juristic discursive knowledge can then be analysed against Ottoman

[52] There have been limited, albeit laudable, attempts to compile such lists. See eg, Guy Burak, *The Second Formation of Islamic Law: The Hanafi School in the Early Modern Ottoman Empire* (CUP 2015); Scott C Lucas, 'Justifying Gender Inequality in the Shāfiʿī School: Two Case Studies of Muslim Legal Reasoning' (2009) 129 *Am Oriental Soc'y J* 237; Ya 'akov Meron, 'The Development of Legal Thought in Hanafi Texts' (1969) 30 *Studia Islamica* 73; N Cottart, 'Mālikiyya', *Encyclopaedia of Islam* (2nd edn, 2012).

Egyptian court practice in the sixteenth century. While juxtaposing legal doctrine with the pragmatic practices of Ottoman judges has much descriptive value, it can also be a tool of reform in the modern period, to which we now turn.

III MODERN LEGAL REFORM

The very notion of Islamic legal *reform* implies that there is a fixed system of rules and methodologies that have ceased to serve our modern sensibilities, and therefore certain aspects of the tradition must be modified. Traditions, as we saw in the introduction, are subject to adjustments and changes, sometimes so radical that they cause a paradigm shift or a legal revolution. I have argued that the traditionalist hermeneutic revolutionaries in their multifarious varieties were largely contained and tamed by tradition.

Talal Asad's notion of 'discursive tradition', a concept that he uses to describe the living tradition of contemporary Islam, successfully resuscitated 'Islam' as an analytical category and helped conceptualize its internal contradictions.[53] Similarly, Asad mobilized the concept to explain that the contradictions within liberalism are due to it being 'an evolving discursive tradition'.[54] I contend that it is useful to extend this concept to Islamic law in order to think through one of Asad's claims, namely that traditions have essences that make them what they are, and therefore contradictions within the tradition can only affect its contingent rather than essential elements. If we agree with this claim, then how much reform can the contemporary Sunni legal tradition, viewed as a discursive tradition, sustain without losing its essence and becoming something else that is not 'Islamic'?

Before we address this question, we should think about the historical approaches to reform that have dominated Islamic legal modernity. One approach seeks to deal with the clearly contingent elements of the law by taking advantage of Sunni legal pluralism. Thus, early modernists such as Muhammad Abduh (d 1905) and Rashid Rida (d 1935) sought to offer solutions to legal problems through forum and doctrinal selection, a process which I have elsewhere termed 'pragmatic eclecticism'. This approach breaks down the boundaries between the four Sunni schools, allowing state legislators to create legal systems out of the entirety of Islamic juristic discourses. This approach, which is as old as the Islamic legal tradition, is not a by-product of modernity.[55]

53 Talal Asad, *The Idea of an Anthropology of Islam* (Center for Contemporary Arab Studies, Georgetown University 1986); Talal Asad, *Genealogies of Religion: Discipline and Reasons of Power in Christianity and Islam* (Johns Hopkins University Press 1993) 18; Ovamir Anjum, 'Islam as a Discursive Tradition: Talal Asad and His Interlocutors' (2007) 27 *Comp Stud S Asia, Africa & Mid E* 656.

54 Talal Asad, Judith Butler, and Saba Mahmood, *Is Critique Secular? Blasphemy, Injury, and Free Speech* (University of California Press 2009) 26.

55 Ibrahim, *Pragmatism in Islamic Law* (n 22).

The other approach, which also focuses on juristic discourse, is hermeneutic. It assumes that if legal pluralism does not provide an already extant legal opinion that can serve our modern sensibilities, we must turn to new interpretations of the textual sources of Islamic law. One famous example is Abduh's reinterpretation of the qur'anic verse that had historically been understood by jurists to sanction polygamy, arguing that the verse did not in fact allow polygamy. This hermeneutic approach is usually concerned with offering new ways of reading the same text or giving it a new context to construct a novel meaning. This approach does not challenge the premodern atomistic hermeneutic methodology in which a text is read verse by verse to construct a series of legal rules. Yet the atomistic methodology does not exclude intertextuality as an essential part of the hermeneutic process. It rather presumes that despite the impact that intertextuality bears on a specific verse, it is the latter that remains the final unit of analysis vis-à-vis a legal rule. Thus, the textual support for rules produced through the atomistic hermeneutic methodology is often simply given as a specific verse, and the rest is lexical and historical context.

Given the tremendous challenges that Islamic law faces today due to its encounter with modern discourses of human rights, some Muslim scholars have utilized a hermeneutic approach that they hoped would lead to a legal revolution, rather than limited changes based on pragmatic eclecticism or limited hermeneutic manoeuvres circumscribed by the accumulated contextual and lexical interpretive tools of the tradition. The holistic hermeneutic approach of twentieth- and twenty-first-century Islamic modernists and feminists such as Fazluar Rahman, Amina Wadud, Asma Barlas, and Jamal al-Banna is so radical that if successful it would upend the entire legal hermeneutic tradition of Islamic law. This hermeneutic Armageddon could lead to changing many of the doctrines of Islamic law beyond recognition. The very manner in which a Muslim reads the scriptural sources to understand the divine law would be completely annihilated.[56]

Might the traditional atomistic hermeneutic mode of reading scripture be part of the essence of the Islamic legal discursive tradition in Asadian terms? The only way we can answer this question is in hindsight, because the success or failure of a reinvention of tradition, a process which I consider to be essential to the survival of traditions, can only be judged by examining the reception of that reinvention by the tradition's participants. I therefore disagree with Hallaq's claim that the tradition of Islamic law is essentially incompatible with the tradition of the modern liberal state. On the basis of the success of some Islamic states both as theorized by their proponents and as actual entities existing in the modern period, the term 'Islamic

[56] Fazlur Rahman, *Islam and Modernity: Transformation of an Intellectual Tradition* (University of Chicago Press 1982) 2–25, 144; Asma Barlas, *'Believing Women' in Islam: Unreading Patriarchal Interpretations of the Qur'an* (University of Texas Press 2002); Jamāl Bannā, *Tathwīr Al-Qur'ān* (Dār al-Fikr al-Islāmī 2003); Ahmed Fekry Ibrahim, 'Jamāl Al-Bannā's New Jurisprudence and Post-Mubarak Egypt' (2015) 6 *Encounters* 219.

state' is not an oxymoron.[57] As for holistic hermeneutics, we will not know whether the atomistic hermeneutic method itself is part of the essence of Sunni Islamic law's discursive tradition or at least, not until we see whether the holistic discourse is able to gain momentum among participants in the tradition. Unlike the concept of an Islamic state, there is no actual Islamic legal system that boasts a holistic hermeneutic. What is clear so far is that the holistic approach, notwithstanding its importance and the creativity of its proponents, has not gained much support except among limited elite groups, mostly in Western academia.

We have thus far seen approaches to reform of the Islamic legal tradition that are based on grappling with the high discourse of jurisprudence. Since the premodern Muslim judge's decisions were not binding on future judges, Muslim jurists have understandably paid little attention to legal practice. Neither modern nor premodern Muslim jurists busied themselves with studying the jurisprudence of Muslim judges of the premodern period. After all, according to the formalist assumptions of premodern Muslim jurists, by the thirteenth-century judges were simply supposed to mechanically 'apply' the law without much intervention (of course, this was not the case in reality, as I have already noted[58]). Under the spell of this formalist sensibility, Muslim reformers therefore utterly ignored another avenue of reform, that is, the practice of Muslim courts for many centuries predating modernity.

In a manner similar to the late Shahab Ahmed's attempt to make sense of the non-commensurate doctrines and practices of Islam, or the contradictions within the religious tradition known as Islam, whether 'between doctrine and doctrine, doctrine and practice, or practice and practice', I contend that reformers should mine the legal tradition's practices for potential solutions to legal problems brought about by the encounter with modernity.[59] With respect to Islam, Shahab Ahmed reasoned, 'we are actually talking not so much about conceptualizing unity in the face of diversity, but rather about conceptualizing unity in the face of *outright contradiction*'.[60] He cited examples in which many Muslims valorized practices such as wine drinking and the production of figural representations, both of which were prohibited by jurists.[61] In the earlier section on legal determinacy, I have already argued for juxtaposing court practice with juristic discourse in a descriptive mode to gain an understanding of the historical tradition of Sunni Islamic law. What I am proposing in this section is to endow premodern Islamic judicial practices with legal normativity by using categories and arguments developed by premodern Muslim jurists whose discourse adapted the law to changing social and judicial practices.

57 Wael B Hallaq, *The Impossible State: Islam, Politics, and Modernity's Moral Predicament* (Columbia University Press 2013).

58 Ibrahim, 'Rethinking the *Taqlīd* Hegemony' (n 35).

59 Shahab Ahmed, *What Is Islam? The Importance of Being Islamic* (Princeton University Press 2015) 119.

60 Ibid, 72.

61 Ibid.

In premodern Sunni juristic discourse, two concepts were often used to justify judicial practice in tension or contradiction with the law, to wit, 'custom' (*'urf*) and 'practice' (*'amal*), which I have briefly discussed earlier in the context of legal pluralism. Custom, a subsidiary source of the law, was conceptualized by jurists as a broad *social* practice inhabiting the larger society and in full harmony with juristic discourse.[62] Although jurists were not supposed to use *'urf* as a source of law when it contradicted Islamic law *qua* juristic discourse or when it was not widely practised in society, there are many examples of premodern author-jurists incorporating such customs into the law.[63] Another concept invoked by Muslim jurists to justify judicial practices, especially in the Maliki school, is 'practice' (*'amal*).[64]

Although social and judicial customs sometimes overlap, judicial customs, which have an etymological connection to society in that judges are situated within their communities, often privilege one social vision over another. It is author-jurists who have the prerogative to inscribe into legal manuals customs – that is, judicial or social practices, embodied in the concepts of 'urf and 'amal – that they deem palatable to their sensibilities and exclude others that they consider anathema to their own values, which may or may not correspond to those of the larger society. In the Ottoman period, some jurists valorized controversial court practices, bringing about conformity with the law.[65] Once a certain premodern custom was incorporated into juristic discourse through a process of valorization and justification, the practice became part of the tradition of Islamic law.[66] At other times, for a host of reasons, some premodern customs were left to stand in tension or contradiction with the discourse of jurists.[67] In this sense, the juristic class was the final arbiter on what constituted acceptable customs. Once valorized and incorporated into Islamic legal texts, customs no longer constituted instances of legal pluralism in tension with sharia, but this tension persisted for customs that were not valorized by author-jurists.

62 For a broader definition of custom, which goes beyond the social, see Meshal (n 48) 41–69. On the history of custom, see Ayman Shabana, *Custom in Islamic Law and Legal Theory: The Development of the Concepts of 'urf and 'ādah in the Islamic Legal Tradition* (Palgrave Macmillan 2010); Gideon Libson, 'On the Development of Custom as a Source of Law in Islamic Law: Al-Rujū'u Ilā Al-'urfi Aḥadu Al-Qawā'idi Al-Khamsi Allatī Yatabannā 'alayhā Al-Fiqhu' (1997) 4 *Islam L & Soc'y* 131.

63 Ottoman jurists endowed certain judicial practices (such as the practice of cash endowments) with the power of law, even though they contradicted established juristic discourse, by arguing that they represented 'custom'. See Miriam Hoexter, '*Qāḍī*, *Muftī* and Ruler: Their Roles in the Development of Islamic Law' in Ron Shaham (ed), *Law, Custom, and Statute in the Muslim World* (Brill 2006).

64 On the history of practice (*'amal*) in the Maliki school, see Yasin Dutton, *The Origins of Islamic Law: The Qur'an, the Muwaṭṭa' and Madinan 'Amal* (Curzon 1999); on the utilization of judicial practice in a way similar to case law, see Hoexter (n 63) 71–72.

65 One example of jurists justifying court practice in order to remove the tension between the discourse and practice of law comes from procedural law. Many jurists valorized the practice of forum selection by employing various arguments and modes of reasoning. Ibrahim, *Pragmatism in Islamic Law* (n 22); Hoexter (n 63) 67–85.

66 Talal Asad clearly considers *'urf* as part of the Islamic tradition. Talal Asad, 'Thinking About Tradition, Religion, and Politics in Egypt Today' (2015) 42 *Critical Inquiry* 166, 179, fn 28.

67 Ibrahim, 'Child Custody in Islamic Law' (n 51).

The common law offers a point of comparison. Defenders of the common law against the encroachment of codification often argued that the law reflected the values of society since social customs were one of its main sources. According to Mark Lieberman, however, it was the custom of the courts and lawyers, not folkways, that defined what constituted custom. It was the activities of legal authorities in selection and interpretation that pronounced custom as law. Deploying the terminology of German law, Carleton Kemp Allen, according to Lieberman, argued that what is really meant by custom is the custom of the courts rather than of the people, *Gerichtsrecht* rather than *Volksrecht*.[68] In other words, the exclusive association of custom with community, rather than the class of jurists, is no more than a legal fiction.[69]

In premodern Islamic law, the adjudication of judges carried no normative value unless approved by author-jurists functioning outside of the court. Can Ottoman judicial practices, which were often rooted in local customs, be invoked by modern reformers as part of the contemporary discursive tradition of Islamic law even if they were never valorized by premodern author-jurists? For most Muslim jurists and legal scholars, the answer is in the negative and Islamic law is simply the discourse of author-jurists, not of judges. Contrary to this view, I contend that, in the same way social and judicial customs were often valorized by premodern author-jurists even when they were in tension or contradiction with juristic discourse, judicial customs that were never valorized by premodern author-jurists may also be invoked as part of the contemporary discursive tradition of Islamic law on the authority of premodern judges. What justifies my incorporation of custom into the normative doctrines of Islamic law is that premodern author-jurists, the setters of legal normativity, themselves utilized ʿ**amal** and ʿ**urf** to normalize court practices that were in tension, and sometimes in outright contradiction, with the law.

Furthermore, many of the practices of Ottoman courts, though left unjustified by author-jurists in legal manuals, were valorized by the stable practice of judges and scribes. Early modern Egyptian women, for instance, signed private separation deeds to gain greater custody and guardianship rights, even though these deeds contained stipulations in tension or contradiction with juristic discourse. These contracts were routinized through scribal practices and formularies that continued unchanged for centuries. Thus, a private separation deed containing controversial stipulations from 1520 Cairo used almost the same scribal formularies as one from 1640.[70] In other

68 Mark Lieberman, 'Law/Custom/Tradition: Perspectives from the Common Law' in Phillips and Schochet (n 4).

69 Lieberman argues that Blackstone's famous categorization of the common law into 'general customs', 'particular customs', and 'particular laws' can shed light on the 'judicially constituted nature of common law custom'. These particular laws include Roman and canon law adopted in some English courts and becoming part of the 'common law', though they were neither common social practice nor even English. Ibid, 240–41; Bl Comm 1–8.

70 Ibrahim, *Pragmatism in Islamic Law* (n 22) 146; Ibrahim, 'Best Interests of the Child' (n 50); Ibrahim, 'Child Custody in Islamic Law' (n 51).

words, these judicial practices were not isolated deformities of the discourse of author-jurists, but rather the mainstream discourse and practice of judges and scribes. The institutional consciousness inherent in these scribal practices represents an act of valorization on the part of the Ottoman judiciary, despite the lack of explicit support from author-jurists. Though in tension or contradiction with juristic discourse, these judicial practices should be considered part of the normative discourse of Islamic law due to their normalization and norm formation, that is, their inscription into judicial norms by consistent scribal formularies over time. However, these premodern Ottoman judicial practices, which may be seen as unspoiled by the cultural onslaught of modernity, do not represent a magic recipe for reform, since the pragmatic solutions of Ottoman judges do not always correspond to our own modern sensibilities.

CONCLUSION

The Islamic legal tradition is characterized by extensive legal pluralism, which was driven by the diversity of legal cultures with which Islam came into contact as well as the practices of the early caliphs and the nascent legal methodologies in the different regions of the Umayyad and Abbasid dynasties. This legal pluralism was not controlled by the state, due to the history of the relationship between the state and legal scholars in Islam, which was shaped by the events of the early Islamic period. A rejection of the pragmatic legal decisions of the early period, and of the ensuing legal pluralism, was launched by traditionalists who advanced the thesis that the Prophet's legacy could only be accessed through prophetic reports (*hadiths*) containing a chain of transmission. They argued that it is only through *hadiths* and the Qur'an, rather than human reasoning, that the law of Islam should be constructed. The ensuing synthesis between rationalism and traditionalism, coupled with a flexible system of hermeneutics and of *hadith* criticism, meant that the memory of the Prophet, as well as the manner in which jurists understood that memory, was malleable enough to allow for the retention of the legal pluralism characteristic of the first two hundred years of Islam. Through this flexible hermeneutic, jurists engaged in processes of justification of existing doctrines, many of which were pragmatic solutions offered in the formative period, as well as created new doctrines to deal with issues unaddressed by the ancestors.

The purist tradition, which generally opposed legal pluralism, based its approach on the deconstruction of the tradition through a process of constant reinterpretation and a rejection of the traditionality of schools. But even they could not escape the prison-house of tradition. Purists, who remained on the margins of the legal tradition, continued to exercise *ijtihad*, or, more accurately, verification of existing doctrine. However, since they could not operate outside of the tradition's lexicon, and the legacy of *hadith* criticism and qur'anic commentary, their verifications rarely posed a threat to the heritage of the Hanbali school.

In other words, this supposedly tradition-less methodology was itself traditionalized. In the final tally, the Islamic legal tradition tamed the traditionalist attack against legal pragmatism and its concomitant pluralism.

In the face of this pluralism, how does one define the Sunni legal tradition? I have argued that there are two types of formalism in Islamic legal studies. One of them is that the authoritative laws of author-jurists in the four Sunni schools are applied unchanged in the courts, and the second is that legal theory is always productive of legal rules. Both of these formalisms have been challenged by historians. I have suggested that Posner's famous reference to the mix of formalism and pragmatism in the context of American law applies perfectly to Islamic law. Muslim judges of the Ottoman period used formalist rules to adjudicate most cases, but they used pragmatic solutions in limited areas of the law to achieve a social good. To avoid formalism, one should conceptualize Islamic law as the interaction between the formal rules of author-jurists and the adjudication of judges – a conceptualization that could prove useful for Islamic legal reform.

Islamic legal reformers such as Muhammad Abduh and Rashid Rida relied on legal pluralism to bring Islamic law into closer compatibility with modernity. Others proposed a holistic hermeneutic approach to locate general values in the qur'anic text that can trump rulings considered specific to the historical context of seventh-century Arabia. Both of these approaches, whether based on legal pluralism or hermeneutic engagement, centred on the juristic discourse produced by jurists outside of the courtroom. If we conceptualize the Sunni legal tradition as both the discourse of author-jurists and the discursive practices of judges and scribes in dialogic interaction with one another, it follows that modern reform should draw upon court practice, utilizing the concepts of ʿamal and ʿurf in addition to the juristic discourse of author-jurists.

Finally, in order to ascertain whether a given judicial practice is part of the Sunni Islamic legal tradition, the legal historian should look at whether this practice was the *norm* in the court records in a particular region and period, as opposed to a practice observed in a few isolated registers and disappearing into oblivion soon after, by observing scribal practices over many years. The habituation and routinization of certain practices is what makes them judicial customs worthy of setting legal norms. These judicial practices can then be placed in dialogue with the doctrines of author-jurists, who are commonly considered the norm setters in Islamic legal historiography, through an analysis of books of high repute for different regions and historical periods. This holistic understanding of the premodern Sunni legal tradition can inform the discursive tradition of Sunni Islamic law today by allowing modern reformers to draw upon a larger pool of Sunni legal practices. To be sure, this reform process can be highly selective and subjective, but this is the promise of non-formalism, nay, the nature of law.

10

Commensurability, Comparative Law, and Confucian Legal Tradition

Marie Seong-Hak Kim[*]

INTRODUCTION

I met Professor H Patrick Glenn for the first time in Leiden in December 2012. It was at a conference held under the themes of the state and the rule of law in Asia, and Glenn was one of the keynote speakers. Few in the audience expected what he had to say in his talk. To the consternation of the organizers, he started by questioning the soundness of the conceptual framework of the conference: Is it helpful to talk about the rule of law in an Asian context when legal traditions there 'had no concept of the nation-state'? Awkward silence filled the room. Unfazed, he declared that we should 'abandon discussion of the rule of law in Asia' because it was a notion 'not appropriate for export', used mainly 'as a self-congratulatory measure' in the West. Glenn suggested that one focus the discussion not on the rule of law but on the rule of laws, directing attention to the multiplicity of law and the non-normative notion of law in Asia. Later that day, I had the good fortune of sitting next to him during a bus ride to a restaurant. I teased him that he did an excellent job ingratiating himself with those who had invited him, and he had a good chuckle.

Glenn's remark that morning was grounded on his fundamental understanding of law and legal tradition. He approached comparative law through legal history, using 'tradition' as the core concept of analysis. Tradition, as defined by Glenn, is 'information', 'a loose conglomeration of data, organized around a basic theme or themes'.[1] A common criticism directed against the individual chapters of his *Legal Traditions of the World* was that he did not explain clearly what 'legal tradition' was and how it was different from other elements of a tradition, such as morality, politics, and religion.[2]

* The writing of this chapter was completed during the author's stay as a Fellow at the Käte Hamburger Kolleg 'Recht als Kultur' in Bonn.

1 H Patrick Glenn, *Legal Traditions of the World: Sustainable Diversity in Law* (5th edn, OUP 2014) 15–16 (hereafter Glenn, *LTW*).

2 As many as fourteen specialists participated in a collective review of *Legal Traditions of the World*, each focusing on the particular chapter of his or her expertise. See Nicholas HD Foster (ed), 'A Fresh Start for Comparative Legal Studies? A Collective Review of Patrick Glenn's *Legal Traditions of the World*, 2nd Edition' (2006) 1 *J Comp L* 100. This unusual format is a testimony to the breadth and depth of

For Glenn, this sort of critique missed the point, as purported separation of law from all else was something particular to the Western legal tradition.[3] Each tradition differed in answering the question of what was legal, he argued. In this view, the amorphous and polysemic nature of law in certain traditions of the world would amount to a virtue not a vice. A blithe disregard for this fact and trying to explain laws in Asia and elsewhere with Western models would simply obscure a search for underlying interdependence and interconnectedness among the world's traditions.

Glenn was duly mindful of the problems of coalescing legal traditions into an overriding category. He changed, in the fourth edition of *Legal Traditions of the World* in 2010, the title of chapter 9 from 'An Asian Legal Tradition' to 'A Confucian Legal Tradition'.[4] He explained that this change was prompted by his unhappiness with using a geographical designation for the classification of a legal tradition. More important, 'the return or revival of confucianism' convinced him to make the change.[5] His interest in Communist China's embracement of Confucianism was evident in the rhetorical subtitle of the chapter, 'A Confucian Legal Tradition: Make It New (with Marx?)'. He was intrigued by the Chinese government's effort, as it pursued a capitalist economy, to rebrand Confucianism, once denounced as a symbol of feudal decadence, into a force for change. The purported identification of Confucian virtue in traditional China with communist virtue may not have been too farfetched. The rule by the Party leadership, which derived its authority from its supposedly superior virtue, seemingly pointed not so much to the rule of law as to the rule of men. In Leiden, Glenn made it clear that state law was not always the best instrument for protecting people; the state could exercise control to establish uniformity but it could not eliminate diversity. In this consideration, acknowledgement of 'diversity in law' is crucial.

Reminiscing about that memorable talk, I aim to examine in this chapter Glenn's insights on commensurability of legal traditions by focusing on Confucian law. Glenn had engaged in extensive discussion against the so-called incommensurability of legal traditions. His stance could not have been clearer: 'On commensurability, my position is very simple. I believe that everything is commensurable; that there is no such thing as incommensurability.'[6] He famously wrote, 'incommensurability provides a means of defence – a kind of philosophical Great Wall – against what have been described as "monistic theories."'[7] Monism in comparative law is a normative assumption that Europe is the agent of universal history and the rest of world must converge or assimilate with it. Against monism, it has been claimed, incommensurability allows

Glenn's work. Glenn's wide-ranging reply is in H Patrick Glenn, 'Legal Traditions and *Legal Traditions*' (2007) 2 *J Comp L* 69.

3 H Patrick Glenn, 'A Concept of Legal Tradition' (2008) 34 *Queen's LJ* 427, 436.

4 H Patrick Glenn, *Legal Traditions of the World: Sustainable Diversity in Law* (4th edn, OUP 2010).

5 Ibid, xxiv ('Preface to the Fourth Edition').

6 Glenn, 'Legal Traditions and *Legal Traditions*' (n 2) 75.

7 H Patrick Glenn, 'Are Legal Traditions Incommensurable?' (2001) 49 *Am J Comp L* 133, 137. Monism presupposes an ultimate value against which other things must be measured.

us to consider some things as intrinsically good in themselves; it thus grants each of legal traditions immunity from the influence of the others and protection from shades of legal domination, imperialism, and homogenization. But, argued Glenn, this 'logic of separation' simply made us 'incapable of mutual understanding', effectively saying that 'the only relations that could possibly exist are conflictual in character'.[8] He flatly declared: Incommensurability is not 'compatible with efforts to improve our understanding of the world, or of the legal traditions within it'.[9]

Besides the Great Wall cue, Confucian law offers a fitting material for discussing Glenn's idea of incommensurability. His description of Confucian legal tradition was thoughtful and balanced, but did not seem to add much to existing literature. He highlighted 'persuasion and obligation' in Confucianism. He said there is 'little place for detailed Confucian regulation' of society because '[y]ou are supposed to understand its general teaching' and 'once you understand that you will no longer be concerned with the detail of formal law'.[10] Such rather breezy assessments of Confucianism, with an emphasis on family and moral injunctions, appear not very different from the traditional historiographic stance that characterizes law in traditional East Asia as a recitation of Confucian teachings centred on filial piety and ritual propriety. More recently, scholars have demonstrated that Chinese magistrates decided cases faithfully based on the written codes and that judicial administration was far from arbitrary. Instead of rehashing what Glenn touched on in his work, this chapter focuses on the following questions: How did the Confucian precept of ancestor worship shape clan organization and property relations and, more broadly, how did it affect law and society in East Asia before and after the East's encounter with the West?

Ancestor memorial rites were arguably the most important element of common identity in China, Korea, Japan, and part of Vietnam. Unlike in Europe where the rites were traditionally thought of only in terms of church dogma, in East Asia they were detached from clerical doctrine and instead linked to the veneration of deceased family members in individual households. They had implications not just for religion but for society and the economy.[11] The desire to ensure the continuity of the family and patrimonial integrity is a universal phenomenon, and history has witnessed various restrictive measures put into place in different societies on succession and the alienation of family property. In Europe, strategies devised to

[8] H Patrick Glenn, 'Com-paring' in Esin Örücü and David Nelken (eds), *Comparative Law: A Handbook* (Hart 2007) 94, 98. Glenn referred specifically to Samuel Huntington's 'clash of civilizations' thesis.

[9] H Patrick Glenn, 'Commensurability and Translatability' in J Nafziger and Symeon Symeonides (eds), *Law and Justice in a Multistate World: Essays in Honor of Arthur T von Mehren* (Transnational 2002) 678.

[10] Glenn, *LTW* (n 1).

[11] Robert Jacob, 'La Coutume, les moeurs et le rite: Regards croisés sur les catégories occidentales de la norme non écrite' in Jérôme Bourgon (ed), *La Coutume et la norme en Chine et au Japon* (Presses universitaires de Vincennes 2001) 152–54.

protect the estate, through the instruments of marriage contracts, wills and donations, and promises, constituted the cornerstone of private law. In East Asia, in contrast, families accumulated and managed lineage wealth without well-defined laws of property; the primacy of ritual obligation instead served as the nominal legal edifice.

Under the broad rubric of Confucian ancestral rituals, economic activities in traditional East Asia were shaped by different kinship values and social pressures. Historical Confucianism in China was not the same as historical Confucianism in Korea, and it is necessary to ascertain a vital strand of empirical evidence that would illumine how different East Asian societies developed their own distinct practices regarding lineage organization and clan property to provide for proper rites. The juxtaposition of divergent practices of ancestor rituals and asset organization in premodern China and Korea affirms Glenn's call for comparison both across different legal traditions and simultaneously within a given legal culture. Lineage property in the framework of Confucianism, East Asia's *ius commune*, also illustrates his central idea that legal traditions of the world are not only comparable and translatable, but also transplantable. In the late nineteenth and the early twentieth centuries, Meiji Japan introduced to East Asia Romano-German civil law; it was a law that had undergone a thorough and identifiable process of *Japanisierung*.[12] The concept of individual property rights enforceable at law emerged in East Asia at this time. The gradual displacement of Confucian legal tradition by Japanized law embodied the transmission of information through which the boundaries of major legal traditions became permeable.[13]

Legal traditions require comparison both within and without; the sources and the nature of differences and similarities matter. Developments in East Asia reflected a distinct national history and identity. It was not different from the reception of Roman law in late medieval and early modern Europe during which indigenous custom and tradition continued to underpin each nation's legal evolution. Undertaking a substantive comparison of Confucian legal tradition with outside legal traditions and also within the Confucian sphere of influence in East Asia can help 'open the range of available legal sources'.[14] It can be an ideal testing ground for the arguments of scholars in favour of the integration of comparative law and legal history.[15] I think – and I hope Professor Glenn would have agreed – that comparative law should be distinguished from an anaemic version of the more theoretical social sciences. He stated that 'the commensurability of concepts can be assured through an increase in the information relating to criteria of commensuration, or

[12] H Patrick Glenn, 'The Grounding of Codification' (1998) 31 *UC Davis LR* 765, 772. See Helmut Coing and others, *Die Japaniesierung des westlichen Rechts* (JCB Mohr Paul Siebeck 1990).

[13] Marie Seong-Hak Kim, *Law and Custom in Korea: Comparative Legal History* (CUP 2012).

[14] H Patrick Glenn, 'Mixing It Up' (2003) 78 *Tulane LR* 79.

[15] Thomas Duve, 'Legal Traditions: A Dialogue between Comparative Law and Comparative Legal History' (2018) 6 *Comp Leg Hist* 15; Heikki Pihlajamaki, 'Merging Comparative Law and Legal History: Towards an Integrated Discipline' (2018) 66 *Am J Comp L* 733.

comparison, and to the objects of comparison'.[16] Comparative law as legal history can thrive with more imparting of information and less theorizing.

The first section following this Introduction summarizes Glenn's views of commensurability of legal traditions, put in his own words as much as possible. The second section discusses lineage property in China and Korea. The third section examines the legacy of Confucianism in modern Korea, a country which arguably was, and still is, the most orthodox in its Confucian precepts and practices. Together, this chapter aims to illumine the spirit of Glenn's world legal traditions, which 'both permits commensuration and ensures particularity, avoiding imposition of a single, uniformizing value'.[17]

I COMMENSURABILITY OF LEGAL TRADITIONS

'There is a tradition in the western world of being untraditional', observed Glenn, which 'is sometimes referred to as modernism and sometimes as postmodernism'.[18] This tradition of modernity posits that '[t]he independent, modern individual' is 'free of the attachments – to others, to the environment, to the past – that would characterize other, contextual, "traditional" societies'.[19] Western thought's 'ongoing denial of its own historical roots' spurred intellectual apathy, for which the idea of the incommensurability of different legal traditions was one glaring example. The supposed lack of commonality was, deplored Glenn, the result of the ubiquity of 'culture', a broad, catch-all term ('everyone talks about culture these days, though no-one knows what it really is'), and its reification.[20]

1 *The Reification of Culture*

Glenn ascribed the objectification of culture to sociology and anthropology. In the nineteenth century, anthropologists tried to find normativity in primitive society in the way of Western thinking, by abstracting culture in terms of the evolutionary ideas of custom. But such concepts of culture soon became 'major liabilities' for the social science disciplines, prompting the scholarly cultural shift 'by way of apology' for previous Western attitudes. As Glenn noted, '[t]he reluctance of much contemporary anthropology to engage in comparative endeavours would be by way of reaction to earlier, comparative, "universal history", which placed Western civilization at the pinnacle of a long process of development taken as progressive.'[21] As a result,

16 Glenn, 'Commensurability and Translatability' (n 9) 677.

17 Ibid.

18 H Patrick Glenn, 'Doin' the Transsystemic: Legal Systems and Legal Traditions' (2005) 50 *McGill LJ* 863, 871.

19 Ibid, 872.

20 Glenn, 'Com-paring' (n 8) 97.

21 Glenn, 'Are Legal Traditions Incommensurable?' (n 7) 139–40. See Brian Z Tamanaha, 'The Folly of the "Social Scientific" Concept of Legal Pluralism' (1993) 20 *JL & Soc'y* 192. For comparisons of

however, these scholars 'have themselves become victims of the process of reification, notably in the development of the idea of culture':

> Since a culture had to be internally consistent to be recognisable as a culture, diversity within one's own culture became inherently problematical, and diversity within other cultures (of which less was necessarily known) became essentially inconceivable. This is now known as essentialism, and is criticized, yet it was inevitable, given the large and homogenising concept of culture which was deployed.[22]

The deficiencies of this development were palpable. 'Arguments which reify concepts of legal culture, or legal systems, or legal civilizations, and urge their necessary preservation, are philosophically untenable, self-defeating, and incompatible with the underlying character of human organization.'[23] The prevalence of 'boundary-tracing endeavours which both homogenise (within) and differentiate (without)' has made comparing impossible.[24] More serious, the 'amazing tendency to objectify or reify human groupings' has been such that 'they appear almost certain to be constantly colliding with one another. War is the obvious example, but we are now finding ways of colliding, and killing, short of actually declaring war'.[25] Glenn's assessment in 2007 resonates today:

> The notion of the 'multi-cultural' (many conflicting entities) is now being sought to be replaced by a notion of the 'inter-cultural' which would be more compatible with com-paring. This involves, however, re-educating the general public, which now thinks in terms of culture wars.[26]

Glenn equated adherence to incommensurability with perpetuating ignorance.[27] Put briefly, incommensurability is the idea that the absence of a single scale of measure prevents comparison or translation of subjects.[28] For Glenn, the presumed absence of commonality was simply the result of the reification of cultures alluded to above, an

colonial law in Africa and Asia, including Dutch East India and Korea, see Kim, *Law and Custom in Korea* (n 13).

22 Glenn, 'Com-paring' (n 8) 97–98.
23 Glenn, 'Mixing It Up' (n 14) 79.
24 Glenn, 'Com-paring' (n 8) 98.
25 Ibid, 95.
26 Ibid, 98.
27 Glenn, 'Are Legal Traditions Incommensurable?' (n 7) 144.
28 Glenn, *LTW* (n 1) 45–49; ibid, 49. Briefly, Glenn's own rendition of the notion of incommensurability is as follows:

> [I]ts origins would lie well back in time, probably to the Greek mathematicians who thought in terms of numerical discontinuity. They accepted the existence of integers and fractions clearly distinct from one another, but refused to contemplate real numbers, expressed in decimals, or irrational numbers, such as the square root of 2. Real or irrational numbers would extend infinitely and destroy the sharp edges necessary for calculation. We owe the notion of incommensurability to this type of thinking.

Glenn, 'Doin' the Transsystemic' (n 18) 863.

ill-conceived effort to attach a defining element to particular groups of people.[29] Highlighting the internal unity of groups while emphasizing external separation led to an illusion that 'people, or concepts, or things, can be kept apart'. Between incommensurable values, one cannot, by definition, compare them; nor are there any rational, external criteria that would justify a choice between them. People resort to endless reasons and arguments available in law for choosing one option as opposed to another but, when denied the possibility of comparison – in the sense of drawing useful information from them – they are unable to make a choice, with a result that 'one of the [most important] objectives of the legal enterprise' becomes irrelevant.[30]

Incommensurability not only rejects the interdependence of legal traditions but also negates 'our considered judgments about how . . . goods are best characterized'.[31] It is used 'as a means of isolating or separating certain values, treated as fundamental and autonomous, from evaluation in terms of other, often utilitarian, criteria'.[32] Its danger is obvious when we consider that 'we are essentially dealing with highly developed bodies of normative information, of long standing, which tell us how to live and how to solve our disputes'.[33] The 'objects of comparison contain within themselves the resources to resolve conflict between them into a judgment of relative importance or into choice'.[34] The lack of comparison prevents us from making reasoned decisions. 'Absent information to evaluate, we thus effect acts of will; given information, we evaluate it in order to reach a more justifiable decision.'[35]

According to Glenn, legal culture, along with a legal system, is not a desirable analytical concept in comparative law because it allows us to understand only contemporary and momentary reactions to prior information, not its origins. Obscuring origins, culture and system tend to minimize the meanings of comparative legal history. Glenn was critical of the prevailing view that comparative law scholarship must serve as a guide for resolving contemporary problems, seen as important at the time. Does understanding the past on its own terms not already have enough justification? The normative survival of the past depends on the persuasive authority of tradition; in many cases it is not the same as the needs to be addressed by contemporary society or present politics.

2 *Tradition and Persuasion*

As Glenn saw it, '[t]he great and powerful traditions are those that offer great and powerful, even eternal and ultimately true, reasons for adherence.'[36] The legitimacy of

29 Glenn, 'Com-paring' (n 8) 95.
30 Glenn, 'Are Legal Traditions Incommensurable?' (n 7) 143.
31 Ibid, 138–39.
32 Glenn, 'Commensurability and Translatability' (n 9) 675.
33 Glenn, 'Concept of Legal Tradition' (n 3) 444.
34 Glenn, 'Are Legal Traditions Incommensurable?' (n 7) 144.
35 Ibid, 143.
36 Glenn, *LTW* (n 1) 42.

custom came from the fact that it contained 'something of great value, commanding respect'. Traditional law obtained spontaneous adherence because it was persuasive; because it was persuasive, no one needed think in terms of 'binding law'.[37] When one attempts to explain tradition, therefore, discussion of the merits is necessary, beyond the mere description of separate characteristics: 'The information presented by one side to the other is comparable or commensurable with information known to the other side, and debate on the merits of respective positions is possible.'[38]

Traditions create obligations. Glenn elaborated:

> The obligations of a tradition may be said to be binding when they are morally imperative or at least justifiable. It is more generally the case, however, that the obligations of a tradition may be seen as simply persuasive, since the authority of tradition is simply persuasive. They are obligations to which we bind ourselves. We are not forced to do so, and there are no guaranteed sanctions that will punish our failure to do so. So the world of tradition is an inherently normative world. There are no brute facts, social or otherwise.[39]

It followed that 'the relations between traditions are thus in principle relations of influence and persuasion, as opposed to conflict and dominance'.[40]

The idea that, in the long term, transfer of a tradition depends more on persuasion than domination or repression supports the validity of the concept of legal transplants. The spread of Western legal ideas during the last two centuries has invariably been viewed in terms of colonization, imperialism, and domination by hegemonic traditions. According to Glenn, however, the idea of imposed reception was overstated. Just as adherence to a tradition is more a matter of belief than coercion, legal transmission takes place more on the basis of choice than force. All reception that occurs is necessarily voluntary.[41] A successful legal reception takes place only when it is internally accepted by those who are subject to it, no matter whether it had been imposed by force by an outside power.[42]

The main argument against comparison or commensuration is that one becomes 'vulnerable to imposition of the large, single value', that is, exposed to a danger of monism.[43] An example of a monistic approach and the resulting misunderstanding

[37] In non-Western laws, '[t]here is no presumption of original and ongoing sin on the part of most of the population justifying clear prohibitions and major institutions of sanction. Law and other forms of persuasive information are all spontaneously adhered to.' Glenn, 'Concept of Legal Tradition' (n 3) 436.

[38] Glenn, 'Mixing It Up' (n 14) 80. See also H Patrick Glenn, 'Persuasive Authority' (1987) 32 *McGill LJ* 261.

[39] Glenn, 'Doin' the Transsystemic' (n 18) 881–82.

[40] Ibid, 897.

[41] Glenn, 'Persuasive Authority' (n 38) 265.

[42] See Alan Watson, *Legal Transplants: An Approach to Comparative Law* (2nd edn, University of Georgia Press 1993); Alan Watson, *The Evolution of Western Private Law* (Johns Hopkins University Press 2000).

[43] Glenn, 'Are Legal Traditions Incommensurable?' (n 7) 144–45.

was, it has been claimed, the use of the Weberian ideal types of the rationalization of legal systems, grounded on the nineteenth-century German civil law model. Max Weber famously classified Western European law as formally rational, and Chinese law as substantively irrational. The administration of justice in China was 'a transposition of the intrafamilial mode of settling conflicts into the political body'.[44] Weber theorized in *Protestant Ethic and the Spirit of Capitalism* that bourgeois capitalism emerged in Europe with the presence of the unique Protestant ethic, which became the foundation of the rational spirit of modern law.[45] Ten years after the writing of *Protestant Ethic*, Weber penned *Die Wirtschaftsethik der Weltreligionen: Konfuzianismus und Taoismus*.[46] In the latter, he contended that Confucianism, without the idea of a transcendental god, lacked 'the Puritan ethic which amounts to an objectification of man's duties as a creature of God' and the Confucian therefore was 'unsuitable for the rise of a rational spirit'.[47] In consequence, '[t]he legal and societal foundations for capitalist "enterprise" were absent' in traditional China.[48] He identified the kinship organization as the 'sib-fetter' of its economy.

Weber's China theory began to take a beating in the late twentieth century. How does his theorization of Confucianism as unchanging 'sacred tradition' fare in the sphere of family economy, and what are its implications for the commensurability of legal traditions?

II CONFUCIAN LEGAL TRADITION: PROPRIETY AND PROPERTY

Weber's Protestant bias was little disguised when he observed of Confucianism that its 'ethic of unconditional affirmation of and adjustment to the world presupposed the unbroken and continued existence of purely magical religion'.[49] His declarative juxtaposition of 'modern' Western spirit and 'traditional' Chinese spirit has since been challenged by many.[50] Since the 1980s, whether Confucianism was an impediment or a stimulus to the development of capitalism in East Asia became a burning question among scholars. The limitations in his cultural analysis notwithstanding, Weber's diagnosis of the all-comprising and all-pervading Confucian tenet of family

44 Max Rheinstein (ed), *Max Weber on Law in Economy and Society* (Edward Shils and Max Rheinstein trs, Harvard University Press 1954) 263.

45 Max Weber, *The Protestant Ethic and the Spirit of Capitalism* (Talcott Parsons tr, 2nd edn, Roxbury 1998) 21 ('[T]he Occident has developed . . . a very different form of capitalism which has appeared nowhere else: the rationalistic organization of (formally) free labour.').

46 Max Weber, *Gesammelte Aufsätze zur Religionssoziologie*, vol 1 (JCB Mohr 1963), translated as *The Religion of China: Confucianism and Taoism* (Hans H Gerth tr and ed, Free Press 1951).

47 Ibid, 236.

48 Ibid, 85.

49 Ibid, 229.

50 Kenneth Pomeranz, '"Traditional" Chinese Business Forms Revisited: Family, Firm, and Financing in the History of the Yutang Company of Jining, 1779–1956' (1997) 18 *Late Imperial China* 1; Robert M Marsh, 'Weber's Misunderstanding of Traditional Chinese Law' (2000) 106 *Am J Soc* 281.

piety is hard to dispute. He wrote that 'the duties of a Chinese Confucian always consisted of piety toward concrete people whether living or dead, and toward those who were close to him through their position in life',[51] and that this 'adherence to unconditional discipline' discouraged the rise of individual rights.[52] The main problem in Weber's formulation, for the purposes of the present discussion, is that he assessed the economic associations and business organizations in China solely in terms of European corporate models and dismissed them as 'family businesses' lacking entrepreneurial spirit.[53] He was reluctant to recognize the formation of 'capital' under the Confucian ritual framework. He did not entertain the idea that China, deep in ancestor worship ideology, might have been able to develop a capitalist economy before the rise of the ideology of capitalism.

Ancestor veneration was thoroughly interwoven with the kinship system, and the organization of lineage and clan property reflected the interplay among law, religion, philosophy, society, and economy. From the 1950s, scholars of China began to view the relationship between ancestor rituals and economic activities from a radically dynamic perspective. Maurice Freedman explained that many lineages under the Ming dynasty (1368–1644) were bound by patrilineal kinship and that they consolidated a certain portion of the family estate from the sixteenth century (the era of the Protestant Reformation in Europe).[54] They developed complex posthumous lineage trusts to meet ritual responsibilities and to make investments together. These ancestor trusts, holding property jointly, eventually evolved into clan corporations, something comparable to Western corporate bodies.[55] These findings raise questions of a deterministic cultural analysis that essentializes particular aspects of Confucianism, relegating important historical and social forces to obscurity.

1 *China: Lineage Property and Clan Corporation*

Around the world, the ultimate function of lineage wealth is status assertion. In Europe, lineage property was normally set up by passing property complexes in the same family or clan, prospectively, through generations to prevent their disintegration and dispersal. In East Asia, in contrast, clan estates were created retrospectively by pooling assets in the name of a distant ancestor, with the goal of meeting the expenses of conducting annual ceremonies in his memory. Some of the communal land might have been donated by a few prominent ancestors in their lifetime, but in

51 Weber, *Religion of China* (n 46) 236.

52 Ibid, 158.

53 Weber stated, 'this underdeveloped state of the Chinese of private associations and business organizations was caused by the continuing significance of the kinship group, within which all economic association is taking place'. Rheinstein, *Max Weber on Law in Economy and Society* (n 44) 184–85.

54 Maurice Freeman, *Lineage Organization in Southeastern China* (Athlone Press 1958).

55 Teemu Ruskola, 'Conceptualizing Corporations and Kinship: Comparative Law and Development Theory in a Chinese Perspective' (2000) 52 *Stan LR* 1599.

most cases it was collected by the offspring of the lineage for the purpose of ritual cooperation.

In both Europe and East Asia, lineage property in principle was owned in perpetuity, beyond the lives of any individual members. The French customs of *substitutions fidéicommissaires* (also known as trust entails) and *retrait lignager*, not to mention the feudal rule of primogeniture, were measures to keep properties within the family and to prevent fragmentation.[56] In East Asia, ancestor worship served as an additional organizing principle of lineage plots. Clan properties included the graveyard of the ancestors, monuments or buildings for ritual performance, or arable land for income generation.

During the Chinese Song dynasty (960–1279), Neo-Confucianism reconstructed the ancient family system along the principle of descent through male heirs. But the reinvigorated Confucian agnatic patriarchy was not in concurrence with the traditional inheritance system. In China, equal division of property among the heirs had been deeply grounded. The law codes expressly mandated equal inheritance among all heirs of each generation. The rule of partible inheritance had the effect of dissolving even the largest fortunes relatively quickly. In this situation, the creation of ancestral trusts became a lineage survival strategy against succession practices. Scholars have shown that, although many clan corporations portrayed themselves as ancestral trusts, they were in reality organizations created by contractual arrangements among the kin members. They had rights to partake in asset distributions although they could not dispose of them without the consent of the lineage segments.

The significance of shared ritual commitments was critical. Ritual cooperation in performing ceremonies for common ancestors remained a key element in collectively owned ancestral estates for recruiting kin group members and mobilizing investment resources.[57] It has been argued that the Confucian household was an ideal model for clan corporation. The patrilineal descent served to unite the members together and kept capital together; its hierarchical social structure provided an incipient separation of ownership and management found in a corporation.[58] Scholars now agree that late imperial Chinese kinfolk organizations were commercial enterprises grounded on the sociological foundation of the family. They were voluntary associations in pursuit of financial profit, although they formally preserved the Confucian principle of

56 Equivalent to *Familienfideikommiss* in Germany and *mayorazgo* in Spain. Under *substitutions*, the 'encumbered' was charged with preserving the property he inherited and bequeathing it intact to the new beneficiary substituted for him. The estate was meant to be kept within the family over generations, lasting beyond the lives of any individual members; the lineage members had the right to partake in asset distributions but could not dispose of them. *Retrait lignager* referred to the rule of redemptive rights of the kinsfolk who objected to the alienation of the ancestral lands to strangers. See Marie Seong-Hak Kim, *Custom, Law, and Monarchy: A Legal History of Early Modern France* (Oxford University Press 2021).

57 David Faure, *Emperor and Ancestor: State and Lineage in South China* (Stanford University Press 2007).

58 Ruskola (n 55) 1623.

patrilineal kinship. It was a specimen of a capitalist Confucianism, no matter how counterintuitive it might sound given the anticommercial spirit of Confucian teaching.

While ancestral property gradually lost its religious meaning in China, the situation seemed different in the neighbouring Confucian country. In Korea, lineage property was tightly attached to the clan's ritual purposes and material foundation, well beyond the purpose of ensuring family solidarity. In many respects, Korean people were far more conservative in their interpretation of Confucian precepts than the Chinese, a fact often *manqué* in comparative law and legal history scholarship.

2 *Korea: An Orthodox Variant*

Clans in Korea were patriarchal family groups dedicated to ancestral ritual duties. The purely religious – ritual – orientation of lineage property holding remained predominant. Kinship was always an integral aspect of Korean society but the importance of unilineal descent was dramatically reinforced by the introduction of the Neo-Confucian philosophy in the late fourteenth century. The governing elite of the new Chosŏn dynasty (1392–1910) embraced Neo-Confucianism as the state ideology.[59] The orthodox tenets of moralism led to a unique Confucianization of the country, in which Korea's indigenous kinship system was acculturated to dominant ritual creed.

As in the Chinese Ming code, *Kyŏngguk Taejŏn*, the Korean law code compiled in 1471, provided for equal distribution of property, setting aside additional allowance for the ritual presider.[60] Strictly speaking, succession meant succeeding the status as the presider of ancestor ritual, and the transfer of property took place only as incidental to ritual succession. A difference from China was that in Korea seniority in line of descent, through which genealogical headship passed, was given much more emphasis. The duty of performing ancestral sacrifices was exclusively incumbent upon the eldest male in the family of the most senior line. The orthodox Confucian teaching prescribed domestic ritual cooperation for as many as four-generational ancestor worship, and soon concerns arose that the equal partible distribution of slaves and land would threaten the maintenance of the main descent line. Ritual allowance given in law to the eldest son was considered insufficient, jeopardizing proper ritual observance. The religious understanding of common property accorded a special economic privilege to the primogenitary heir of

59 During the Song dynasty, Zhu Xi (1130–1200)'s interpretation became an authoritative view of Confucianism.

60 The Chosŏn *Kyŏngguk Taejŏn* provided that the children receive the property of the deceased equally, with the one who presided over the ritual receiving one-fifth in addition. For *Kyŏngguk Taejŏn*, see Jérôme Bourgon and Pierre-Emmanuel Roux , 'The Chosŏn Law Codes in an East Asian Perspective' in Marie Seong-Hak Kim (ed), *The Spirit of Korean Law: Korean Legal History in Context* (Brill Nijhoff 2016).

a particular segment of the lineage.[61] Ritual primogeniture engendered property primogeniture by necessity.[62]

By the seventeenth century, the Korean family system had attained its full agnatic and patrilineal structure, and the passing of property as a whole to the firstborn son in the main descent line became the standard inheritance practice. Solidarity within the direct descent group rendered statutory requirements of partible inheritance a dead letter. Strict primogeniture prevented, or rather suppressed the need for, the development of joint property-holding corporate estates as in China. The result was that economic relations between lineage members and the common property diverged in the two countries. The management of common property in Korea was by and large not a main concern of its members because their economic dependence on the corporate organization was minimal. Tracts of land were, in general, smaller in size than those of southeastern China. In short, the Korean lineage system remained a classic system of ancestor-centred agnatic classification. A corporate kin group organization functioned exclusively for the sake of faithful ritual cooperation of common ancestor worship.

What explains this divergence between China and Korea? Among various reasons, one can refer to the social importance attached to ancestral eminence and pedigrees in Korea. At issue was the 'uniquely Korean values about sources of prestige'.[63] Because of the deeply entrenched hereditary estate system, an individual's social position and status were determined foremost by his lineage affiliation and descent lines from the ancestors. A prominent ancestor, deserving distinction in genealogy, was one who gained a post in the imperial bureaucracy by passing the rigorous civil service examinations, which tested the mastery of texts of Neo-Confucian orthodoxy. Familial dignity derived from him. Genealogy recording descent lines exuded tremendous legitimacy in Korea.[64] This social obsession of ancestral prestige explains, in part, why the Chinese model of setting up a new ritual trust through segmentation, with the endowment of the separate fund of property, was rare.[65] The expansive notion of social responsibility internalized by aristocratic elders appeared to be an important element that distinguished Korean Neo-Confucian lineage from its Chinese counterpart.[66]

61 Yongwhan Kim, 'A Study of Korean Lineage Organization from a Regional Perspective: A Comparison with the Chinese System' (PhD Thesis, Rutgers, State University of New Jersey 1989).

62 Ibid, 303. For succession rules in Korea, see Marie Seong-Hak Kim, 'Rites and Rights: Lineage Property and Law in Korea' (2020) 22 *L'Atelier du Centre de recherches historiques* <http://journals.openedition.org/acrh/11667>.

63 Roger L Janelli and Dawnhee Yim Janelli, 'Lineage Organisation and Social Differentiation in Korea' (1978) 13 *Man* 272, 274.

64 All Korean lineages are equipped with written genealogies, which demonstrate the legitimacy of lineage membership. Koreans keep much more detailed genealogical records than the Chinese or the Japanese.

65 Janelli and Janelli (n 63).

66 This point is illustrated in the comparison of community compacts (community agreements initiated by local elites to spread Confucian ideals and standards) in China (*xiangyue*) and Korea (*hyangyak*): see Marie Seong-Hak Kim, 'Comparing the Incomparable: Local Custom and Law in Sixteenth-Century Korea and France' (2008) 12 *J Early Mod Hist* 507.

A symbolic meaning attached to ancestor rituals should not be underestimated. Ritual observance was a way for social elites to set them apart from the rest. Performing four-generation ancestor worship, as required in Confucian classics, could project 'a descent group's image as a coherent and ritually conscious social unit toward the outside world'.[67] Annual rites observed at gravesites served as a rallying point for the solidarity of a preeminent lineage group. Ritual performance costs in honour of key ancestors were what Pierre Bourdieu called 'demonstrative expenditures', that is, a cost justified for transforming economic capital into vital symbolic capital.[68] Ancestors lived among the descendants not only spiritually but also socially.

Overall, the Korean case closely corroborates Weber's characterization of Confucian sacred tradition. The value orientation of filial piety and ancestral social prestige played a more central motivational role than economic capitalist logic.[69] Weber did not mention Korea in his writings; it does not seem he was aware of differences between China and Korea. If he had based his discussion on 'Confucianism in Korea', his view of Confucianism as 'a religious barrier' to capitalism might have had more credibility. Ancestor rituals inculcated their own sense of 'calling', that is, to preserve the good name for both ascendants and descendants by fulfilling personal and social responsibility. Granted, it would be a bit of stretch to find in it sprouts of capitalism. Yet, the cases of China and Korea each showed that capital accumulation existed side-by-side with Confucian classicism. Confucian tradition in East Asia was carried on in many different facets of society.

Glenn said that 'if it can be established that there is commensurability and comparability across cultures, notably across legal traditions, then this does serious damage to the claim for incommensurability within a given culture'.[70] The examination of Confucianism affirms his opinion. As he put it, each legal tradition has a particular nature, an underlying justification, a concept of change, and a way of relating to other traditions.[71] East Asian patterns of lineage organization and property, with their particular characteristics and justifications fully on display, prevailed to the modern times. It raises the questions of change and relativeness to other traditions.

III LEGAL TRADITION AND CHANGE

Glenn observed that the reception of Western law in East Asia took place in two realms: 'The first was the making-over ("*Japanisierung*") of western models in their

67 Martina Deuchler, *Under the Ancestors' Eyes: Kinship, Status, and Locality in Premodern Korea* (Harvard University Asia Center 2015).

68 Pierre Bourdieu, *The Logic of Practice* (Richard Nice tr, Stanford University Press 1990) 131.

69 Kim, 'Study of Korean Lineage Organization' (n 61) 292.

70 Glenn, 'Are Legal Traditions Incommensurable?' (n 7) 139.

71 Glenn, *LTW* (n 1) 27.

actual operation; the second was the nesting of the entire concept of formal, civil law in the larger context of informal Japanese normativity.'[72] For him, the Japanization of European law became successful because the reception was done by choice. The fact that legal diffusion took place in East Asia where the countries belonged to the same cultural sphere of the Sinicized Confucian civilization was of critical importance. It has been noted that Korea (and Taiwan) suffered relatively little from the 'transplant effect', problems that normally beset a country that received law via colonization.[73] When the people – including the colonized – saw persuasiveness in the transferred law, its reception was much facilitated.

The courts in colonial Korea (1910–1945) and in republican China (1912–1949) had to negotiate between the Confucian legacy and European civil law to replace ritual authority with legal authority. Jurisprudence of clan ownership of land was often inconsistent, as the courts struggled with the customary status of kin organizations and their legal capacities.

1 *Rites and Rights*

The concept of a legal person did not exist in Qing China, but the Beijing Dali Yuan (Supreme Court) recognized that clan organizations could sue and be sued and dispose of property in a corporate capacity.[74] The situation was similar in colonial Korea. The colonial Chōsen Kōtō Hōin (High Court) recognized lineage property and the undivided corporate nature of the patrilineage. Ritual succession as a jural act was abolished in 1932, but the courts continued to implement Korean custom of exclusive inheritance by the eldest son.[75] The courts consistently treated property disputes among Koreans as factual questions: property acquired in the name of the family head (ritual heir) was considered his property, not common property of the clan members, in the absence of proof otherwise. Ancestral trusts were in principle indivisible but could be dissolved by consensus among clan members. Much of the colonial jurisprudence of customary law was adopted by the Supreme Court of South Korea following the nation's independence in 1945.

One can attempt brief, rudimentary comparisons of the lineage systems in China, Korea, and Japan. In China the principle of bloodlines defined family members, but kin group organizations showed a wider range of morphological and structural variation than that of Korean equivalents. Korea adhered to the rigid ideas of consanguinity and patrilineality. As seen earlier, the enduring bond among the family units was equated with the corporate basis of ritual land set up for the

72 Ibid, 345 (citations omitted).

73 Kim, *Law and Custom in Korea* (n 13).

74 Ruskola (n 55) 1652.

75 Marie Seong-Hak Kim, 'Custom as a Source of Law in European and East Asian Legal History' in Kjell A Modeer, Aniceto Masferrer, and Olivier Moreteau (eds), *Comparative Legal History Handbook* (Edward Elgar 2019).

common ancestors. Lineages as descent groups were the weakest in Japan.[76] Its corporate house (known as *ie*) membership emphasized the effective management of the house's collective goal, rather than the preservation of patrilineal lines or bloodline purity.[77] This structure served Japan well in the post-war years, as it implemented a powerful contractual kinship (also known as 'kintract'), highlighting loyalty and hierarchy, in the employment environment. While their corporate identity was weaker than Japanese business organizations, big Korean family firms known as *chaebol* have also resorted to a blending of modern business organization and traditional Confucian kinship values and work ethic. Some criticized it as a method for controlling the work force, but regardless it boosted productivity during Korea's industrialization. The vestiges of family organization and the idea of indivisible patrilineage may be seen in the management of state-owned enterprises in contemporary China.

How does Confucian legal tradition compare with Western legal tradition in terms of individual rights? Glenn provided a perceptive insight regarding the sense of presentism, or contingent time. In Europe, presentism – 'dead people are dead and gone, and those not yet born are not yet countable' – led to the diminishment of 'inter-generational equity', the kind powerfully in existence in East Asia.[78] Confucian teaching endowed the present and the individual with no special privileges; instead, the immutable principles of morality, extracted from the Confucian texts and executed in rituals, were regarded as sufficient to regulate private relations. One can conclude that the Confucian ideals of self-cultivation and filial piety as the basis of the polity represented a distinct direction of managing and improving human conditions, but its concern for one's own family and ancestors – family egoism – and 'refusal to conceptualize individuals in any way other than relational' suppressed the development of individual rights and private law. Glenn aptly summed up:

> There were of course obligations in east Asian society, but it is important that they were conceptualized from the perspective of the debtor, never from that of the creditor as an abstract, subjective advantage. So it is beside the point to say there must have been rights since there were obligations; development of the notion of rights and a subjective view of legal relations is precisely what is being rejected by the ongoing insistence in obligations rooted in human relations.[79]

[76] The division of landed property during the Tokugawa period was predominantly equal. See Akira Hayami, 'The Myth of Primogeniture and Impartible Inheritance in Tokugawa Japan' (1983) 8 *J Fam Hist* 3.

[77] Hong Yung Lee, 'A Comparative Study of Korean, Chinese, and Japanese Traditional Family and Contemporary Business Organizations' (2008) 14 *E Asia Inst Working Paper Series* 1.

[78] H Patrick Glenn, 'The Capture, Reconstruction and Marginalization of "Custom"' (1997) 45 *Am J Comp L* 613, 617. This 'presentism' is otherwise known as 'thinking like a lawyer', a virtue for the lawyer but 'anathema' for the historian. Martin Krygier, 'Law as Tradition' (1986) 5 *Law & Phil* 237, 249.

[79] Glenn, *LTW* (n 1) 353.

Glenn viewed Confucianism as 'a tradition of persuasion': 'pure tradition – not present positivism and not revealed truth – and tradition which seeks primarily to persuade and not oblige'.[80] He tended, perhaps not unknowingly, to overstate the transformative force of the informal rhetoric of persuasion. According to him, one would need to approach an Eastern legal tradition like Confucianism through an 'easternized' mindset in which, unlike a Western one, 'dominance, over persons or things, is either uninteresting, or unreal, or both'. 'You will be easternized neither by force nor by insidious and persistent efforts of acculturation.' How, then? 'You can be easternized', he quipped, 'if you think about it.'

Glenn's helpful advice aside, one notes that line between instruction and indoctrination became 'paper thin' in the Confucian tradition.[81] Both the Chinese and Korean codes were penal laws that included scattered provisions meting out specific punishment for civil wrongdoings – moral deviancies – as public offences. Confucian injunctions for moral rectification and regeneration and formal coercive commands incorporated into state codes should be seen in tandem. It was the centralizing effect of the state codes, not Neo-Confucianism per se, that led to the rigidity of Confucian law.[82] Emphasis on the existing order and hierarchical relations precluded a concept of universal human rights and conflicted with individual rights.[83] Should it come as surprise if one would find the resurrection of Confucian emphasis on obedience, once directed to the emperor, in the assertion of authority by the party leadership?[84]

2 *Piety and Proportionality*

This chapter has noted that orthodox rituals grew rigid over time in Chosŏn Korea. The uniquely Korean sensibility of filial piety has a powerful presence in modern law as well. Korea is the sole country in the world today of which a significant number of private citizens perform ancestor memorial services in their households several times a year. Ritual succession has had no legal meaning for nearly one hundred years, but it nevertheless remains a profound moral obligation among many Koreans.[85] In criminal law, Korean codes prohibit the filing of a criminal complaint against one's lineal ascendants (parents and grandparents), and also impose enhanced punishment for crimes (such as murder and assault) committed

80 Ibid, 320.

81 James B Palais, *Confucian Statecraft and Korean Institutions: Yu Hyŏn gwŏn and the Late Chosŏn Dynasty* (University of Washington Press 1996) 706.

82 William Shaw, 'Traditional Korean Law and Its Relation to China' in Jerome Alan Cohen, R Randle Edwards, and Fu-mei Chang Chen (eds), *Essays on China's Legal Tradition* (Princeton University Press 1980) 317.

83 Roger T Ames, 'Rites as Rights: The Confucian Alternative' in Leroy Rouner (ed), *Human Rights and the World's Religion* (University of Notre Dame Press 1988).

84 Ibid, 206.

85 Marie Seong-Hak Kim, 'In the Name of Custom, Culture, and the Constitution: Korean Customary Law in Flux' (2013) 48 *Texas Int'l LJ* 357.

against them.[86] These are provisions that have their origins in the Chinese Tang code of the seventh century. Neither the current Chinese nor Japanese penal codes have analogous laws. Taiwan has aggravated penalty provisions similar to those in Korea, but the latter is the only country in East Asia today that comprehensively prohibits criminal suits against lineal ascendants. These laws, viewed as the expression of the nation's identity, have so far survived constitutional challenges of equality and proportionality.

The continuing existence of these laws may have been part of a nationalist agenda to distinguish Korean law from Japanese law.[87] It shows that, the danger of reifying national stereotypes notwithstanding, one cannot downplay the fact that law is a product of historical contingencies that unfold at the national level. How legal culture and tradition of a country are modified by other factors is an empirical question.[88] A national legal tradition still matters in East Asia as much as in Europe under the overarching structures of the EU. Discussion of the commensurability of different cultures and traditions does not need to be beholden to a set frame, whether nationalist or imperialist. After all, doing comparative law 'is not a zero-sum game'.[89]

CONCLUSION

Glenn's key message is that legal traditions are externally open and internally accommodating. His optimistic belief in the receptivity and responsiveness of traditions has raised, not unreasonably, certain scepticism among scholars. Glenn's response was that the flow of information provided the grounds for ongoing choice and decision, which allowed the continuous transmission of traditions: one legal tradition deserves emulation and a successful reappropriation, another tradition may be less persuasive to the point of being rejected; either decision is made 'within a previously defined cadre of normative information'.[90] He stated: '[O]ld law speaks to us with *some* measure of normative force,' which (other than religious law) comes from a series of commitments that human beings make to their community.[91] What is this normativity exactly, is up for debate, but at least one can agree that ascertaining those commitments – ideas, merits, and values – in respectful detail, in all their complexity, is a worthwhile enterprise. Comparative legal history provides us with information regarding the specific forms of human experience that religions, politics, or philosophies may assume wherever they are found. Through them we

86 Marie Seong-Hak Kim, 'Confucianism that Confounds: Constitutional Jurisprudence on Filial Piety in Korea' in Sungmoon Kim (ed), *Confucianism, Law and Democracy in Contemporary Korea* (Rowman and Littlefield 2015).

87 Kim, *Law and Custom in Korea* (n 13).

88 David Nelken, 'Using the Concept of Legal Culture' (2004) 29 *Austl J Leg Phil* 1, 5.

89 Glenn, 'Concept of Legal Tradition' (n 3) 440.

90 Ibid, 437.

91 Ibid.

can grasp the complexity in humanity's efforts to respond to the various challenges it faced.

Acknowledging divergence among legal traditions does not mean that differences between legal traditions are irreducible. Seeking a global harmonization of the laws of the world entails neither subscription to nor rejection of cultural essentialism. One can compare legal traditions and allow for borrowings from one another without resorting to 'external, universal criteria'.[92] As Glenn noted, 'increasing the information available to us, for purposes of evaluation and comparison' is different from embracing functionalism.[93]

Just as we look for a plausible way of thinking and talking about the interconnectedness of the autonomous dimensions of life, the idea of commensurability of legal traditions has heuristic value. Main problems emerge not so much from information overload as from the apathy of incommensurability that threatens, inadvertently, to bring about conflicts among cultures. Glenn cautioned: 'There is an extremely high cost to incommensurability, since if it exists within cultures it is certain to exist across cultures and there would then be a kind of massive communication failure in the world, an inherent clash of civilizations.'[94] We 'must remain open to the notion of difference and to the need for commensuration to comprehend it'.[95] Commensurability can serve as a strategy for achieving diversity of traditions in harmonious coexistence. When traditions are presented as information and each of them interpreted on its own terms, 'they build real bridges', not just through toleration but through acceptance.[96]

Ever gracious, Professor Glenn asked me, during the bus ride in Leiden back in 2012, to send him my thoughts on *Legal Traditions of the World*, in particular the chapter on Confucianism. He left us not long after that, but not before he managed to persuade us that there were different perspectives in legal traditions in history and that there can be different interpretations in law. Perhaps we should 'think about it', as a good Confucian would.

92 Glenn, 'Commensurability and Translatability' (n 9) 677.
93 Ibid, 681.
94 Glenn, 'Are Legal Traditions Incommensurable?' (n 7) 139.
95 Glenn, 'Commensurability and Translatability' (n 9) 681.
96 Glenn, *LTW* (n 1) 372.

PART III

Crossing Boundaries

Cultural Transfer, Legal Cosmopolitanism, and the Dissolution of the State

11

The School of Salamanca: A Common Law?

Thomas Duve

INTRODUCTION

H Patrick Glenn's reflections on 'legal traditions', 'common laws', and the 'cosmopolitan state' are grounded in an impressively thorough acquaintance with the findings of legal history research on practically all regions of the world and all epochs. It is, therefore, hardly surprising that he has been criticized for certain overstatements and distortions. Nonetheless, some legal historians are also discovering the potential his thinking offers.[1] In particular, his thoughts on 'legal tradition' as normative information and on 'common laws' can provide the emerging field of global legal history with an important and in some regards liberating perspective.[2] Legal history addressing the transnationalization of law is in need of models for analysing the development of normativity as a continuous process of translation of normative information into new realities on a global scale, and for investigating the opening and closing of systems beyond nation state.[3] Glenn's works provides elementary components for such a model.

In the following, I want to illustrate this with a small example taken from early modern legal history, which Glenn mentions only in passing as part of a 'Hispanic common law'[4]: the so-called School of Salamanca. Despite its theological provenance, this intellectual current of the sixteenth and early seventeenth centuries is an important part of legal history. It had its cradle in Salamanca, the dynamically expanding Iberian empires were its context, but it has left enduring traces far beyond confessional and continental boundaries. Most famous were Francisco de Vitoria's lectures on the legitimacy of Iberian colonial rule overseas dating from 1539. They have remained controversial to this day, and not only in international law. More the

[1] See on this, Thomas Duve, 'Legal Traditions: A Dialogue between Comparative Law and Comparative Legal History' (2018) 6 *CLH* 15.

[2] See, on this emerging field, Thomas Duve, 'Global Legal History – A Methodological Approach' in Markus Dubber (ed), *Oxford Handbooks Online in Law* (OUP 2017).

[3] Thomas Duve, 'German Legal History: National Traditions and Transnational Perspectives' (2014) 22 *Rechtsgeschichte/Legal Hist* 16.

[4] H Patrick Glenn, *On Common Laws* (OUP 2005) 105 (hereafter Glen, *OCL*).

preserve of specialists, but perhaps no less important, is the fundamental impetus the School of Salamanca gave to contract law, restitution theory, and property law, as well as to criminal law, constitutional theory, and political thought.[5] The writings of the theologians, jurists, and canonists considered to be part of the School of Salamanca, as well as their practice, have provided an important additional layer of normativity to the discourse about questions of justice, traditionally built upon the *ius commune* (*ius civile* and *ius canonicum* and other parts) as well as the *ius particulare*, by their arguments about justice, based on (moral) philosophy and theology.

Interestingly, both critics and admirers of the school agree that the school produced a legal-political language in which the world has, to this day, communicated on matters of law and justice, especially at the international level. They concur that it reconfigured the relation between the secular and the religious spheres, was used to justify revolutions and juridical modernity, and that it shaped the language of empires, not only for the West. Some see in it a welcome diffusion of European Christian values, others an act of European Christian imperialism and later legal colonization of the world by the west.[6] Both views have their justification, and both are probably too rigid in the defence of their positions. The same can be said of competing claims that the school is either a 'Spanish', a 'European', or more recently, an 'American' or 'colonial' phenomenon. Such assertions, too, fail to do justice to the complex processes of global knowledge creation in the field of normativity, and to what Glenn regarded as the practically inevitable and desired emergence of *cosmopolitan law*.[7]

5 There is a vast and fast-growing literature on the School of Salamanca. Two fairly recent bibliographies together listed more than 8,000 titles. See Miguel Anxo Pena González, *Aproximación bibliográfica a la(s) 'Escuela(s) de Salamanca'* (Universidad Pontificia de Salamanca 2008); Luis E Rodríguez-San Pedro Bezares and Juan Luis Polo Rodríguez (eds), *Historia de la Universidad de Salamanca: Vestigios y entramados*, vol 4 (Ediciones Universidad de Salamanca 2009). In this chapter, I limit myself to mentioning some general bibliography, as well as select and important recent works. For a general overview, see eg, Anthony Pagden, 'The School of Salamanca' in George Klosko (ed), *The Oxford Handbook of the History of Political Philosophy* (OUP 2011). On the school's contribution to legal history, eg, with further references, see James Gordley, *The Jurists: A Critical History* (OUP 2013) 82–110; Wim Decock, *Theologians and Contract Law: The Moral Transformation of the Ius Commune, ca. 1500–1650* (Nijhoff 2013); Nils Jansen, *Theologie, Philosophie und Jurisprudenz in der spätscholastischen Lehre von der Restitution: Außervertragliche Ausgleichsansprüche im frühneuzeitlichen Naturrechtsdiskurs* (Mohr Siebeck 2013). The best summary of the development, content, and main representatives of the school is Juan Belda Plans, *La Escuela de Salamanca y la renovación de la teología en el siglo XVI* (Biblioteca de Autores Cristianos 2000).

6 Martti Koskenniemi, 'Empire and International Law: The Real Spanish Contribution' (2011) 61 *UTLJ* 1. For a survey with further references, see eg, Andrew Fitzmaurice, 'The Problem of Eurocentrism in the Thought of Francisco de Vitoria' in José María Beneyto and Corti Varela (eds), *At the Origins of Modernity* (Springer International 2017); Pablo Zapatero Miguel, 'Francisco de Vitoria and the Postmodern Grand Critique of International Law' in Beneyto and Varela (n 6).

7 See on legal history as a process of translation and global knowledge production Thomas Duve, 'Pragmatic Normative Literature and the Formation of Normative Orders in Early Modern Ibero America' in Thomas Duve and Otto Danwerth (eds), *Knowledge of the Pragmatici: Legal and Moral Theological Literature and the Formation of Early Modern Ibero-America* (Brill 2020).

We can doubtless better understand the language of the School of Salamanca, its impact, how it changed over time, and its importance for the development of our normative orders, if we see the school's normative reflection as a contribution to a common law, understood as 'a *contradictory* field of legal meaning, in which differences are resolved in an ongoing manner without prejudice to survival of the sources of both particular and common law', as normative information and thus a legal tradition in Glenn's sense.[8] This perspective is unlikely to resolve all problems, especially that of defining what belongs to the school and what does not, a question discussed extensively in the scholarship on the School of Salamanca. Legal historians will probably see in this an analytical weakness, related to Glenn's explicit rejection of taxonomy, because historians need to classify and structure their observations of the seemingly chaotic past.[9] The practical dimension, too – nothing short of constitutive for the School of Salamanca – escapes Glenn's analytic approach, which is hardly surprising since he explicitly distanced himself from taking into account every form of practice, creating an artificial and for me not convincing boundary between 'law' and 'practice'. But if the School of Salamanca is seen as a 'common law' or a special case of a legal tradition, it allows us to understand it not only as a historical formation tied to one place, but as the denomination for epistemic communities and communities of practice that produced normative information in a characteristic way and that influenced the worldwide discourse on law, becoming part of the huge process of looping or feedback Glenn described.[10] But before mapping out the common law produced in Salamanca and elsewhere, including not least the highly consequential historiographical reconstruction in the nineteenth and early twentieth centuries, some general characteristics of the school require at least brief consideration.

I PRAGMATIC REFLECTION ON THE ORDER OF THE WORLD

What made 'Salamanca' so special? In the turbulent years following Francisco de Vitoria's arrival in Salamanca, the leading University in the Iberian empire of its time, in 1526 – generally taken to be the founding date of the school – scholars at the University of Salamanca as well as in the Dominican monastery of San Esteban were occupied with no less a task than to reflect on the world order, both in its metaphysical and in its secular or scientific aspects. The theologians could conceive of this

8 The definition of common law is taken from Glenn, *OCL* (n 4) preface, pt VII. In the following, I am using the term 'normative information' just as Glenn used it, although in general terms I prefer to distinguish 'normative information' from 'normative knowledge', see on this Duve, 'Pragmatic Normative Literature' (n 7).

9 See his critique of the taxonomic project in H Patrick Glenn, 'Comparative Legal Families and Comparative Legal Traditions' in Mathias Reimann and Reinhard Zimmermann (eds), *The Oxford Handbook of Comparative Law* (OUP 2006); on categories of comparison, see H Patrick Glenn, 'A Western Legal Tradition?' (2010) 49 *Sup Ct L Rev* 601.

10 Glenn, 'Comparative Legal Families' (n 9) 428: 'A living tradition thus functions by way of the continual reflexive process, through looping or feedback.'

world order only as a divine order of being from which all else derives – the natural order, the economic order, the legal order. After a long tradition of organizing their reflections around the so-called sentences of Peter Lombard, since Vitoria came to Salamanca, the Dominicans started to take the *Summa Theologiae* of the Dominican and Doctor of the Church St Thomas Aquinas, as their principle reference for the teaching of theology and thus their reflection about the constitution of the world and its eternal principles.

Of course, when Vitoria came to Salamanca, the *Summa* was everything but unknown. There were classes dedicated to Aquinas's *Summa* before that, just as Francisco de Vitoria had already studied its content in Paris, where he collaborated on the preparation of a printed edition of the *Summa*. However, as the new holder of the Chair for the most important class of theology, the *prima*, in Salamanca he now based his entire lectures of theology in Aquinas. From then on, the *Summa* provided the architecture for all deliberations in class, where the teachers resolved all kind of questions drawing on the *auctoritates* that early modern massive book production had made increasingly available. Not least through this activity in the classroom, the preparation of the classes and the deliberations that were held in Salamanca, a huge number of voluminous treatises were composed and printed, many of them in the flourishing printing press of Salamanca. Especially important for legal history was a literary genre specialized in questions of justice and law: *De justitia et jure* and *De legibus*, grouping together the comments on certain questions of the *Summa* of Aquinas related to justice. The titles alone show that not theology but theologically grounded law was at the centre of this genre, and subsequent generations of theologians, canonists and lawyers would work with these texts, draw upon them, fight against them, reread and reinterpret them, with different intensity and attitudes well until the twentieth century.

Alongside their systematic work, however, the theologians in Salamanca were deeply engaged with real life. In the turbulent decades of sixteenth-century expansions, reformations, wars, financial speculation, and inflation, people were assailed by moral doubts, and they searched for advice. The Dominicans had to deal with problems of everyday life concerning just price, financial transactions, and fasting rules. With regard to the Americas, merchants and soldiers were insecure as to whether the use of force against insurgent indigenous peoples was justified, whether prisoners taken in the conquests could be enslaved, and whether there was a legitimate right to take booty, to buy and sell what had been obtained under the use of force. It was this need for moral advice, the enormous eschatological hopes and fears, together with a renewal of theology as well as the impact of personalities such as Francisco de Vitoria, Domingo de Soto, and Melchior Cano, that set the stage for the emergence of Salamanca as one of the centres of a new moral theology that had an eminently pragmatic character.[11]

[11] For an overview of the history of moral theology, see Jean-Louis Quantin, 'Catholic Moral Theology, 1550–1800' in Ulrich L Lehner, Richard A Muller, and AG Roeber (eds), *The Oxford Handbook of Early Modern Theology, 1600–1800* (OUP 2016).

Precisely because of this pragmatic orientation, in their classes, but also in their practice as consultants, everyday practices of Church authorities were examined in the light of the systematic principles laid out in the big treatises. In many cases, the theologians did not fear to draw conclusions probably not desired by the Crown or the Curia. In his classes, for example, Vitoria called the possibility of freeing oneself in certain cases from the duty of restitution by paying a fraction of the amount owed by acquiring a so-called crusade indulgence (the *compositio*, part of the *Bula de la Cruzada*) from the Church as 'the biggest joke in the world'. This *compositio* was highly important in times of war, sudden death, speculation, and systematic exploitation, and provided important income for both the Church and the Crown. However, Vitoria rejected it after analysing the *potestas* and *dominium* of the Pope, reaching the conclusion that the Pope was not entitled to do what he did with his *Bula de la Cruzada*. From a letter, we know that he did also put in practice what his teachings advocated: 'I do not preach against it (meaning: the indulgence, TD), but I grant no-one absolution.'[12]

However, since not only merchants and soldiers, but also the Emperor Charles, kings, and cardinals sought advice, Salamanca also addressed the major political issues of the period. Teachers from Salamanca took part in the sessions of the Council of Trent and the many so-called *juntas*, consultations on particular problems. They wrote opinions on the doctrine of justification, on the marriage of Henry VIII, on Erasmism, and not least on the legitimacy of the Castilian presence in America, on the just war, on the baptism of indigenous peoples, on slavery. It was, above all, the positions adopted on the 'New World' that made Francisco de Vitoria and with him Salamanca famous. Here, too, the *conquista* presented not so much an intellectual challenge, but a practical case that entailed risks to the salvation of the souls of all involved, not least of the emperor and his advisors.[13] This is why the theologians in Salamanca felt obliged and empowered to give their opinion on this like on so many other legal questions – despite not being jurists. As Vitoria had already expressed earlier, 'the task and office of the theologian are so far-reaching that no proof, no consideration, and no topic appears to lie beyond the purview of the theological profession and office'.[14] Theologians were the experts who knew how to relate universal principles of justice with particular situations, and how to resolve the fundamental dialogical tensions between the universal law in a wide sense and

[12] See on this Thomas Duve, '"La mayor burla del mundo"? Francisco de Vitoria y el dominium del Papa sobre los bienes de los pobres' in Juan Cruz (ed), *Ley y dominio en Francisco de Vitoria* (Ediciones Universidad de Navarra 2008).

[13] For a general introduction to this moral reasoning in the times of Trent Paolo Prodi, see Paolo Prodi, *Una storia della giustizia: Dal pluralismo dei fori al moderno dualismo tra coscienza e diritto* (Società Editrice il Mulino 2000).

[14] Francisco de Vitoria, 'Relectio . . . de potestate civili' in Francisco de Vitoria, *Relectiones Theologicae XII* (2018) [1557] in Thomas Duve and Matthias Lutz-Bachmann (eds), *Die Schule von Salamanca. Eine Digitale Quellensammlung*, vol 1.3.1, 174 <https://id.salamanca.school/texts/W0013> ('OFFICIVM, ac munus Theologi tam latè patet, ut nullum argumentum, nulla disputatio, nullus locus alienus uideatur à theologica professione, & instituto.').

the *ius particulare*, a key function of common law, according to Glenn. Vitoria was not the only one who saw it like that – but it was he who became famous for it. Why?

II FRANCISCO DE VITORIA AND INTERNATIONAL LAW

It was this conviction that the theologians had to give their opinion on all significant matters of justice that probably moved Vitoria to dedicate two of his extraordinary lectures – *Relectiones* – to the problem of the justification of the Castilian presence in the Caribbean and the Americas: the lecture *De indis*, continued with *De jure belli*. The question of the legitimacy of the Castilian presence overseas as such was not new, even if Vitoria himself made it seem like that. As early as 1512, a *junta* in Burgos had debated the issue also under the impression of violence and catastrophic conditions after the invasion in the Caribbean. However, it had become a burning issue again. Following the capture of Tenochtitlan, today Mexico City, in 1521, and again in 1532 after the bloody attack on the Inca Empire in Peru, reports multiplied of massacres and exploitation. In 1536, thousands died during the siege of Cuzco. Not least due to former students, but also because they were intimately connected with the imperial elite, the theologians in Salamanca were fully informed about the situation, and Vitoria was shattered.

Naturally, the question arose whether the Crown bore blame for these events. The papal donation under bulls issued by Alexander VI (1493) was still cited as the basis for legitimation, supplemented by a treaty with the Portuguese (the Treaty of Tordesillas of 1494) and its later confirmation by the Pope. But these, along with other titles mentioned in the debate, failed to convince Vitoria. Already in 1532 in his first *Relectio* on political power, he stated that 'the Pope is not lord of the earth', thus calling into question the theocratic arguments of many theologians and jurists – and hence the basis for the papal donation. Already at this point, with his reflections on *dominium* and *potestas*, he introduced a vocabulary from canon and civil law, theological and philosophical traditions into a new universe of discourse for deliberation on the world order. In his *Relectio de indis*, he expanded this and refuted other titles that were, in his view, just as unconvincing. He then set out a number of grounds on which the Spanish presence could be justified. The focus was on a *ius communicandi*, that is to say, a right of free movement and community formation grounded in natural law. This, and the right to proselytize peacefully, but also the struggle against tyranny, resistance, or other violations of divine law could legitimate violence – the just war. He did not state whether these prerequisites were actually given in specific cases. But, since the colonial endeavour had begun, there were also legitimate reasons for continuing it.

As one can imagine, Emperor Charles was not amused about the conclusions of the *Relectio*, despite the – weak – legitimation that emerged from the argument. In November 1539, the prior of the Dominican monastery in Salamanca received a letter in which the Emperor demanded clarification and apologies. Probably for this reason, too, Vitoria's *Relectiones* were printed only in 1557 in Lyon and in 1565 in Salamanca – after the death of Emperor Charles. Vitoria's students and colleagues, too, did not agree with everything he had said. Discussion continued, not least in the context of the renowned *junta* of Valladolid. With Cano and Soto, leading theologians from Salamanca were to rule on the arguments of Bartolomé de las Casas and Juan Ginés de Sepúlveda. However, it was Vitoria, the acknowledged central figure of the school, whose deliberations became a point of reference for all later writers on this issue until, not least due to the confessional divide, authors like Grotius put forward their ideas about international law.

Vitoria's fame grew again with the reconstruction of his argumentation in the context of the formation of international law as an academic discipline in late nineteenth century. In line with their attempts to highlight the Spanish contribution to European intellectual thought, in the last quarter of nineteenth century, Spanish jurists like Eduardo Hinojosa y Naveros presented Francisco de Vitoria as the founder of international law.[15] Influential Catholic international lawyers like James Brown Scott or Carl Schmitt emphasized the importance of Vitoria, and even contemporary critical legal studies and postcolonial critique by scholars like Martti Koskenniemi, Antony Anghie, third-world approaches to international law (TWAIL), and so on, have been contributing to a renewed and highly contested reading of the School of Salamanca's thought.

In the light of these different appropriations, it is not surprising that to this day Vitoria's arguments have been variously assessed. For many observers, the combination of *ius communicandi* and *jus ad bellum* appeared to justify expansion, mission, and violence. Many scholars draw a line between Vitoria's thinking and the colonialism of modernity. Others point out that his *Relectio* also set out the limits of power, recognized the legitimacy of exercising power beyond the *orbis christianus*, turned against the occupation, imposed conditions on the exercise of force, and placed the Emperor and Pope under the law. The frequently used labelling of Vitoria as the 'father of international law' is hence ambivalent: for some, it makes him the founder of a system for keeping the peace and protecting human rights, for others a proponent of imperialism. Interestingly, whether one regards him as the inventor of human rights or an architect of the persisting asymmetrical imperial structure of our world order, Vitoria and with him the School of Salamanca are usually seen as a European phenomenon that spread across the world. For some, it is a fruit of European legal culture that spread out over the continents, and for others, it is simply one more tool of European imperialism. Is this really an adequate understanding of the School of Salamanca? Or was Salamanca not, much more, one important place of production of normative information that can be considered as

[15] See on the 'first renaissance', Ignacio de la Rasilla del Moral, *In the Shadow of Vitoria: A History of International Law in Spain (1770–1953)* (Brill 2017) 80ff; Juan Pablo Scarfi, *The Hidden History of International Law in the Americas: Empire and Legal Networks* (OUP 2017).

'common law', part of a huge network of global norm production happening all over the globe?

III THE SCHOOL OF SALAMANCA AS COMMON LAW?

There is much to be said for this view.[16] In Salamanca the future elite for service in the Church and under the Crown were educated. Many who studied there would spend at least some of their careers in America or Asia. In the overseas territories of the empire, dioceses and ecclesiastical provinces were founded and the first printing presses and universities were established. Important positions were filled with students of the school, the statutes of the University of Salamanca were copied, and books from Salamanca were imported.

This meant that the normative information that had been produced in Salamanca was now reproduced, concretized, and 'translated' into new realities in many places around the world. In universities, monastery schools, and ecclesiastical and secular courts in many places beyond Salamanca, theologians and jurists read and wrote texts, held lectures, and passed judgement on mortal and venial sins and on political issues according to what they had learned from their books, in their seminars, or in the classroom. They did this on the basis of a stable knowledge architecture, the *Summa*, with scholarly practices taken from topic and dialectic, learned in Salamanca and elsewhere. Vitoria's *Relectiones* were known in Mexico, Manila, or seventeenth-century Taiwan, when the Spanish asked themselves about the rights of the indigenous peoples on the island. In doing so, they were naturally not acting in a vacuum. On the contrary, they found themselves obliged to take account of vested interests, the politics of religious orders and the Church, Christianization, and the economy. As taking the concrete case with all its specificities into consideration was precisely what casuistry was about, and what they were obliged to do, according to the rules of good practice, they produced new normative knowledge, drawing on the normative information they had received from tradition.

Thus, less than a 'reception' of models, what happened was a huge process of creation of new norms for special cases, a proliferation of norms that emerged from practical reasoning, inspired by authorities, but produced in a dialectical reasoning *in situ* by what can be called epistemic communities and communities of practice.[17] With this, the available normative information multiplied, texts written elsewhere circulated and enriched the normative options available, and the acts of finding just solutions for new cases added to this treasure of collectively shared knowledge that was, with every act of producing a new normative statement, itself modified. More

16 See on these aspects with further references, Thomas Duve, 'Salamanca in Amerika' (2015) 132 *Zeitschrift der Savigny–Stiftung für Rechtsgeschichte, Germanistische Abteilung* 116, as well as the contributions in Thomas Duve, José Luis Egío, and Christiane Birr (eds), *The School of Salamanca: A Case of Global Knowledge Production?* (Brill 2021).

17 See on these terms and the distinction Duve, 'Pragmatic Normative Literature' (n 7).

and more often, not only members of the elite sent from Europe but also locally born people of European descent, the Creoles, occupied positions in universities and the Church. And representatives of indigenous elites rapidly learned the language of the conquerors. In other words: many newly emerged and perhaps slightly different, but intimately interrelated epistemic communities produced new normative information, based on their (cultural) translation of the normative information they had at their disposal; and many new communities of practice did the same, when they exercised their office of giving advice, of judging as a *iudex animarum* in the confessional or of producing solutions for concrete cases in the Synods or Provincial Councils in Mexico, Manila or elsewhere in the Spanish and the Portuguese monarchy.

For all these epistemic communities and these communities of practice, Salamanca naturally remained an important point of reference. Books and expert opinions continued to be produced there. But at other universities, too – Coimbra, as well as Leuven and Rome, Lima and Mexico – there was teaching and writing, and above all there was everyday law-finding in many places around the globe. In the *forum externum* and the *forum internum*, principally in confession, which resembled a legal procedure – *ad instar judicium* was the formulation in Trent – decisions were made on what was right and wrong. It was precisely in this practice that the language of moral theology found its way into people's everyday lives, into political practice, and became part of what Patrick Glenn called the 'bran-tub', the common law, part of a legal tradition.

Looking at some of the remaining results of this process, the books and manuscripts that survived, we often do not know whether these texts ought to be ascribed to the European territories of the empire or to America, to Salamanca or Mexico, or the Asian parts. One well-known example is Alonso de la Veracruz, who, by narrow definition, did not belong to the School of Salamanca, which counted only teachers who had studied there; usually, he was seen only as a 'disciple of the school', whereas others now consider him to be the founder of Latin American philosophy. He had studied in Salamanca, came to Mexico City, and taught there at the university. Some of his works were printed in Mexico: in 1554 a *Dialectica resolutio cum textu Aristotelis* appeared, in 1556 his *Speculum coniugiorum*, a treatise on marriage law, which dealt not least with the particularities of matrimonial law with regard to indigenous peoples. The second edition of this book appeared in 1562 when he spent a number of years in Salamanca. Looking at the content, and the form, there are likely to be good reasons for attributing a text like the *Speculum* to the School of Salamanca, even though it was authored thousands of kilometres away, and contained some specific parts on indigenous peoples' marriages. The same can be said for the manual on contract law by Tomás de Mercado, who had lived in New Spain, studied later in Salamanca, and had his book published there – written at the urging of merchants from Seville and based on his experience in Mexico. It seems quite impossible, as well as quite pointless, to assign these authors to a particular continent or place. The territory they moved within was a far-flung empire, and the intellectual space they helped develop reached far beyond the imperial borders.

If we look not at individual authors but at processes of lawmaking, the extent of influence exercised by Salamanca, as well as the presence of a pattern of legal rationality as it was practised in Salamanca in other areas of the world becomes even clearer. One good example is the Third Mexican Provincial Council of 1585, of outstanding importance for the legal and ecclesiastical history of northern Latin America.[18] Seven of nine bishops of the gigantic ecclesiastical province had studied or taught in Salamanca; then there were the theological advisor and the secretary of the council, two key figures in the deliberations. The archbishop, also educated in Salamanca, held the office of viceroy, as well, and was thus the highest authority in New Spain, before he became president of the Council of the Indies. He could, therefore, be described as one of the most powerful men in America. The problems dealt with at the church assembly ranged from complaints about the conduct of the clergy, the treatment of indigenous people, their rights and duties, the acceptance of creole women in convents, the legitimacy of the war against the Chichimeca Indians, the so-called *repartimientos*, and trade and loan practices under suspicion of *usura*. At the same time, the bishops worked on provisions for the council canons and a confession manual. As we know from recent studies, in this month-long process of lawmaking, the literature from the School of Salamanca was repeatedly consulted: Domingo de Soto, Martín de Azpilcueta, and Juan de Medina were among the most often cited authors. When the Council fathers discussed over the legitimacy of the use of force against the resurgent indigenous peoples, they drew on Vitoria's *relectiones*. As far as we can reconstruct the process, they argued with the texts, using methods and practices resembling those in Salamanca and considered to be typical for Salamanca. Comparable situations have occurred in a wide range of places around the world, notably in Latin America, but also in the Pacific, for instance in the Philippines or in present-day Taiwan, where, during the brief Spanish presence, the arguments of Francisco de Vitoria were cited with respect to the legitimacy of the Spanish presence and the position of the local indigenous population.[19]

Priests and missionaries, theologians and jurists, servants of the Crown, and merchants had become members of a discourse community consisting of many smaller epistemic communities and communities of practice that could not be limited to certain cities, regions, or continents – for books, correspondence, and reports as well as the people themselves, circulated within a vast expanse of territory. They all helped translate the legal-political language whose production had one

[18] See on this, Duve, Egío, and Birr (n 16); on the Council and its procedures, see Osvaldo Moutin, *Legislar en la América hispánica en la temprana edad moderna: Procesos y caraterísticas de la producción de los Decretos del Tercer Concilio Provincial Mexicano (1585)* (Max Planck Institute for European Legal History 2016).

[19] See the case studies in Duve, Egío, and Birr (n 16).

important centre in Salamanca into similar and sometimes widely differing contexts, and their translations were also read and received and again translated in Salamanca, Coimbra, and elsewhere. They accordingly contributed to developing a language of theologically grounded law of a particular nature. Meanings naturally shifted. It was soon no longer a pure vocabulary as had perhaps been developed in Salamanca at the beginning. The more people were involved, the more diversified the language might have become. A highly diverse *common law*, in Glenn's sense of the term, had developed, to some extent very similar to the medieval and early modern *ius commune*, but also markedly different.

IV NORMATIVE INFORMATION AND PRACTICE

It might have become clear that Glenn's vision of legal history as a long enduring process of continuous looping and feedback of normative information can serve to develop a more adequate perspective on the School of Salamanca. It helps to show that the School cannot be restricted to Salamanca, nor to Iberia, Europe, and not even to the Spanish Empire. It seems much more adequate to understand it as a 'common law' in Glenn's sense, or as a case of global knowledge production. For many reasons, Glenn's view is an eye-opening perspective for further research and coincides with recent tendencies in the study of legal history as a phenomenon of legal knowledge creation.[20] It can help situate the School's thought into a wider horizon of similar phenomena in times of expansion, confessionalization, and media revolution, all of these factors contributing to an acceleration of communication and pluralization of normative thought and practices.

However, there is one important aspect of this historical moment where Glenn's perspective on legal traditions as normative information and the School of Salamanca as common law seems to lack explanatory force. As shown, the normative reasoning developed in Salamanca drew its vitality not least from its pragmatic character. It was meant to be used in resolving disputes and cases of conscience, and it was profoundly practical, an *ars*, due to its roots in topic and dialectic. Thus, the normative information that people found in the books as well as the same rules of rationality they took from topic and dialectic had to be translated by theologians and jurists working under very different conditions, in the light of different realities, in a casuist world. It is not least this pragmatic orientation of the School of Salamanca, but also the general characteristics of the historical regime of knowledge creation it was part of that gave an enormous importance to those parts of the 'legal knowledge' that can only be understood performatively, as practice. As James Boyd White has famously put it, legal knowledge is 'an activity of mind, a way of doing something with the rules and cases and other materials of law, an activity that is itself not

[20] I develop this further in Duve, 'Pragmatic Normative Literature' (n 7).

reducible to a set of directions or any fixed description. It is a species of cultural competence, like learning a language.'[21]

These practical dimensions of casuistic lawmaking are impossible to reconstruct with Glenn's terminology, especially as he explicitly rejects including 'practice' into his thinking (which he rejected to be called a 'theory', also).[22] Thus, from a legal historian's perspective, Glenn's model – not to say theory – needs supplementation by praxeological approaches and a wider understanding of 'normative knowledge'. These also offer the opportunity to develop a set of criteria that might help to distinguish the School of Salamanca from similar phenomena like, for example, Lutheran or Calvinist natural law. As legal historians, we need this to construct the objects of our research. Due to this, a legal historian necessarily ventures close to the taxonomy abhorred by Glenn.

Epilogue

Many of the problems addressed by the School of Salamanca still essentially preoccupy us today – some are among the ethically most demanding issues of our time. The justification of the legitimate use of force in international law is discussed under the label *responsibility to protect*. There is no consensus about the legal theoretical foundation and thus the extent of human rights. We seek to contain avarice, greed, and other phenomena previously called vice with *compliance* or techniques of self-optimization; *nudging* replaces what virtue discourse tried to do, in preaching, with music or visual means. Unlike in the Salamanca of the sixteenth century, today we can see exploitation and modern forms of slavery on the screen and in real time. We negotiate our view of humankind not with reference to aboriginal populations, but in debates about the rights of embryos, animals, and robots.

The language in which we can think about these questions was substantially shaped in Salamanca and in other places, as I tried to show. It is naturally no longer the same as in the sixteenth century, it changed in the continuous process of translation that is at the core of legal traditions. The 'looping or feedback process' Glenn describes so impressively took place in more and more locations. And it did not remain the language of the victors. Wherever kings occupied land, merchants and gunboats imposed free trade, protesters, victims, collaborators adopted the vocabulary of the invaders, sometimes allies: the language of a Vitoria, later a Grotius, a Locke. The legal experts in the struggle for power of the sixteenth

[21] James Boyd White, 'Legal Knowledge' (2002) 115 *Harv L Rev* 1396, 1399.

[22] When asked in a 2006 interview about the difference between tradition and culture, Glenn emphasized that the concept of tradition 'separate[s] the normative information that precedes us from what we actually do in life and the decisions we actually make, faced with the normative information of the tradition'. Mireille Hildebrandt, 'The Precision of Vagueness, Interview with H Patrick Glenn' (2006) 35 *Neth J Legal Phil* 346, 356.

century were makers and doers with interests of their own, lobbying for their institutions and beliefs, sometimes critical, opportunistic, often in search of justice. Their contribution to developing a global language of law and politics can better be captured if, with Glenn, we treat it as a common law. As such it became part of a major process of opening and closing of legal systems, and perhaps a sort of universal code of legality on which the law of the twenty-first century might be built. A small part of a cosmopolitan law, as Patrick Glenn envisioned it in his writings.

12

The Un-Common Law

*Vivian Grosswald Curran**

I realized then to what an extent the entire world is unified. It seemed to me as though a network of which I was a part performed some function in a single, world-wide organism – an organism from which no member, not even the most powerful, could separate itself.

Jan Karski[1]

INTRODUCTION

It is a privilege to contribute to this work in honour of Patrick Glenn, a dear colleague whose death came as a shock. It occurred just weeks after we had seen each other in Vienna at the International Academy of Comparative Law, where he seemed in excellent health and spirits. We discussed his talk for the following spring at the *Conseil constitutionnel* in France on a panel we never were to share and where his presence would be sorely missed. He died just days after the last, typically cheery, energetic-sounding email I received from him about American Society of Comparative Law business.

Patrick served as the Society's President with enthusiasm, grace, and talent. He was universally beloved as a leader of that organization, which he had served for decades. I am grateful to Helge Dedek and William Twining for organizing this volume in Patrick's memory, and I am grateful to be part of it.

Patrick was a great believer in the potentials of legal cross-fertilization, the inevitably changing needs wrought by transnationalization, and the technologies that have been part and parcel of that phenomenon.[2] Western nations now seem tempted to take up the cudgels of renationalization, both politically and legally. The forces of international commerce that have been transnationalizing law continue

* For feedback on previous and ongoing work in this area, I am particularly grateful to Professor Mireille Delmas-Marty and the other members of the *Ius Commune* project. Unless otherwise noted, all translations are mine.

1 Jan Karski, *Story of a Secret State: My Report to the World* (rev edn, Georgetown University Press 2014) 364.

2 See eg, H Patrick Glenn, *Legal Traditions of the World: Sustainable Diversity in Law* (2nd edn, OUP 2004) xxiii.

unabated, however, if not enhanced, and domestic courts, often reluctantly, have become players on an ever more internationalized stage, as their decisions increasingly affect parties from other sovereign states, laws in other sovereign states, and as they find themselves applying the laws of other nations.

Endless issues are regional and international without being governed by international law. Justice Stephen Breyer has pointed out that harmonious national solutions are called for to the extent that territorial borders cease to be significant in practical terms for the functioning of transnational actors.[3] Commerce has been efficient in adapting to, and finding advantage in global opportunities,[4] but commerce implies more than business and trade in its global reach. It is also linked to the conduct of its representatives, and the latter has given rise to worldwide issues concerning international human rights that engage actors connected to numerous nations with varying laws and legal practices, and complex legal structures whose origins in a pre-transnationalized world often seem inapposite and ill-suited to cope with current issues.

It has been said that 'wisdom consists of trying to see the signs of time'.[5] This chapter tries to do this by looking at the past. It contributes some remarks on the evolution of the common law as part of a larger project organized by Professor Delmas-Marty at the Collège de France to consider the possibility of a new and different *jus commune* for the future based on attempting to gauge signs from the past and present. It would be a *jus commune* that should address a larger swath of national domestic systems than that encompassed by the two supranational courts affecting European Union member states today. The project's purpose is to explore how harmonious, rather than uniform, legal results across national borders might be realized, if they are realizable.[6] It supposes a continuation of our present systemic makeup in the sense of national and cultural differences in *Legal Traditions* and perceptions in a world facing a growing set of problems whose solutions stand to benefit from transnational harmony.[7]

In the debates about comparative legal methodology, and even in the debates about the identity of the field of comparative law,[8] it has been emphasized that what seems like an identical issue is not identical in two different places precisely due to

3 Stephen Breyer, *The Court and the World: American Law and the New Global Realities* (Alfred A Knopf 2015) 4 ('[A] measure of coordination will become increasingly necessary', referring to 'judicial awareness [that] can no longer stop at the border.').

4 Mireille Delmas-Marty, *Globalisation économique et universalisme des droits de l'homme* (Thémis 2004) 9.

5 Father Bruno Hussar, *quoted in* Dan Vittorio Segre, *Memoirs of a Failed Diplomat* (Halban 2005) 70.

6 While the name of *jus commune* is taken from the system of mutual consultation that preceded national codifications in Continental Europe, the idea would be a process that could encompass the common law and Asian and African systems of law.

7 H Patrick Glenn, *Legal Traditions of the World* (5th edn, OUP 2014) xxiv (evoking 'the necessity of collaboration amongst jurists of all traditions in the resolution of many problems of the world').

8 For an interesting overview of these debates, see Robert Leckey, 'Review of Comparative Law' (2017) 26 *S & LS* 3.

differences in legal understandings and the untranslatables persisting among legal orders.[9] Any *jus commune* must be prepared to suppose both continuing limits of communication and an intersection of issue understandings at some level of mutual usefulness. The 'judgment arbitrage' that has gained preeminence as commerce has transnationalized is alone an impetus to see if there is not such intersectionality sufficient to justify cross-consultation and harmonization.[10] Another impetus is the desperate need to address the international human rights issues created by foreign subsidiaries of multinational corporations in a more harmonious manner than is presently possible under domestic jurisdictional constraints.[11] From the perspective of globalized business, there also are numerous reasons to increase harmonious judicial responses, such as consistency and coherence; they have their corporate disadvantages but also benefit companies by reinforcing security in outcome predictability.[12]

I THE ROOTS OF THE COMMON LAW

The common law, which has come to define a conception of law standing in stark contrast to that of the Continental European civilian legal orders, including none more so than France's, has been an irony of fate in its evolution, consolidated and strengthened as it was through the efforts of a Norman French king[13]: 'a system based on French feudal law, administered in French, became the pride of the English nation.'[14] It seems that the *how it got there* rather than the profounder *why* behind the differences between the common and civil law may turn out to be the more fruitful question of the two. In his illustrative work, *The Birth of the English Common Law*,[15] RC Van Caenegem has come to this conclusion. He disputes the issue of the national spirit of the English as contrasted with that of the Continental European, returning

[9] On the pitfall of considering legal issues to be globalized, see ibid, 13.

[10] See Gregory H Shill, 'Ending Judgment Arbitrage: Jurisdictional Competition and the Enforcement of Foreign Money Judgments in the United States' (2013) 54 *Harv Int'l LJ* 459. My thanks to Ted Folkman for introducing me to this article.

[11] See Vivian Grosswald Curran, 'Harmonizing Multinational Parent Company Liability for Foreign Subsidiary Human Rights Violations' (2017) 17 *Chi J Int'l L* 403.

[12] These are two of Justice Breyer's central points in Breyer (n 3).

[13] An analysis of the substantive distinctions is not the subject of this contribution. For my effort to analyse them elsewhere, see Vivian Grosswald Curran, 'Romantic Common Law, Enlightened Civil Law: Legal Uniformity and the Homogenization of the European Union' (2001) 7 *Colum J Eur L* 63.

[14] RC Van Caenegem, *The Birth of the English Common Law* (2nd edn, CUP 1988) 98. It has been pointed out, however, that William the Conqueror arrived with some six thousand men in England, a country of between two and three million in population, and that because of this numerical weakness, despite military conquest, he wisely decided to adopt the traditions and legal system he found in place. See Austin Lane Poole, *From Domesday Book to Magna Carta: 1087–1216* (2nd edn, OUP 1955) 37. According to Theodore Plucknett, it was, rather, five thousand men and two thousand horses. Theodore Frank Thomas Plucknett, A *Concise History of the Common Law* (5th edn, Liberty Fund 2012) 11.

[15] Van Caenegem (n 14) 86, 93.

ever again to the conclusion that the common law owes its existence not to a distinctive common spirit, but to the vagaries of historical happenstance. He disputes, in particular, the theory of the German–British scholar Fritz Pringsheim[16] who promoted the *Volksgeist* idea that the common law reflected the English people's spirit in a profound manner.

Van Caenegem points out throughout his analysis not only the historical coincidences and contingencies that resulted in the common law system, but also underscores that there was no such thing as an English people:

> Twelfth-century England had a very mixed population and was keenly aware of it – the amalgamation of the *Franci* and the *Anglici* did not take place until the turn of the century. . . . There were Normans, called 'French' in the documents, and Englishmen. There were also Flemings and Welshmen . . . and there were the descendants of the Danes.[17]

Blackstone also emphasizes the common law's multitude of origins in his *Commentaries*, noting also the importance of linguistic wealth: 'Our laws, saith lord Bacon, are mixed as our language: and as our language is so much the richer, the laws are more complete.'[18] To this multiculturalist admixture, Van Caenegem adds that, contrary to Pringsheim's assertion, the common law was not the law of an entire country, but only 'the law of a class' within it.[19]

1 A *Sketch of Common Law Traditions*

One might point to the first common law tradition as being its unwritten form.[20] Despite the infinite texts of court opinions and ever-increasing statutory and regulatory texts in common law countries today, one might venture to argue that the *unwritten* nevertheless continues to characterize the common law to this day, at least inasmuch as legal reasoning does not assume a beginning in textual law, as it does in civilian thinking, but, rather, in the intermingling of human events, present and past, brought before a court by litigants, and matched up for legal importance against the narratives of past litigants, as recounted in precedents.

When William the Conqueror became the King of England, he ascended to rule the best organized country in Europe.[21] There was incomparably more unity

[16] The cousin of Katia Mann (wife of Thomas Mann), Fritz Robert Pringsheim, was a Romanist jurist forced to leave Germany during the Second World War, whose work figured in Sir Jack Beaton and Reinhold Zimmerman (eds), *Jurists Uprooted: German Speaking Émigré Lawyers in Twentieth-Century Britain* (OUP 2004) (essay on Pringsheim by Tony Honoré).

[17] Van Caenegem (n 14) 93, 95.

[18] 'Blackstone's Commentaries as the Laws of England' 164 § 3 (*The Avalon Project*) <www.avalon.law.yale.edu/18th_century/blackstone_intro.asp>.

[19] Van Caenegem (n 14) 96.

[20] Van Caenegem, for instance, refers to unrecorded customs that were laws and that eventually gave way to unease due to this lack of written form. Ibid, 1–2.

[21] Ibid, 9.

throughout the English shires than in contemporaneous France, with England already possessing a system of direct, national taxation.[22] Whereas the Church was needed to maintain order on the continent due to disaggregating power, in England, the kings consolidated a national power.[23] As John Hunter has pointed out, England's centralization was a relative matter.[24] By today's standards, it would not be considered centralized, but it was in comparison to Continental Europe, and it was England's organization that spawned the common law.[25]

It is a well-known proposition that Roman law was not received in England as it was on the continent because at the time the scholars from Bologna brought it back to the four corners of Europe, the common law was a well-entrenched and developed system in England, which consequently resisted various repeated attempts by English scholars to reform English law into Roman-inspired codification.[26] While some have argued that the common law and classical Roman law share a basis in reliance on case law and in their lack of codification, Roscoe Pound argued persuasively that this was only a superficial resemblance.[27] Even in its pre-codified form, he maintained, Roman law was based on the application of a general principle to a particular instance through deductive reasoning, the hallmark of civilian legal reasoning, and the inverse of common law reasoning. The common law to this day is a law of the particular, the individual.[28] According to Pound, the Romans 'were not striving to realize individual freedom as an idea'.[29] To Pound, the common law has always focused on 'relation'[30] and on 'incidents in the way of reciprocal rights and duties'.[31]

English common law was fortified as strong kings accrued more power through the widening reach of their courts throughout the entire nation.[32] The legal system, which was working so well in practice that it resisted codification and which was

22 Ibid.

23 Ibid, 11.

24 John Hunter, *The Formation of the English Common Law: Law and Society in England from the Norman Conquest to Magna Carta* (Longman 1999) 2.

25 Ibid.

26 On the influences of Roman law by one who concludes that, although it was not received, its influence in England was considerable, see Edward D Re, 'The Roman Contribution to the Common Law' (1961) 29 *Fordham L Rev* 447; and, more generally, Frédéric Zenati-Castaing, 'Transystémisme et droit commun' (2017) 4 *RIDC* 733, 745.

27 Roscoe Pound, *Interpretations of Legal History* (Harvard University Press 1946) 56.

28 See Curran, 'Romantic Common Law' (n 13) 78. Isaiah Berlin has explained the phenomenon admirably in his contrast between Anglo-Saxon romanticism and empiricism and the Continental European, epitomized by the French traditions of the Enlightenment and deduction. See ibid (much of the article being an application to law of Berlin's exposé of Romanticism and the Enlightenment).

29 Pound (n 27) 56.

30 Ibid.

31 Ibid, 57. Pound then proceeds to analyse how Anglo-American law does not conceive in terms 'of transactions [as does the civil law] but of relations' (ibid).

32 See Janelle Greenberg and Michael J Sechler, 'Constitutionalism Ancient and Early Modern: The Contributions of Roman Law, Canon Law, and English Common Law' (2013) 34 *Cardozo L Rev* 1021, 1024.

transmitted mostly by means of studying precedents from the king's courts,[33] owed much to the jury institution[34] and was the oldest national legal system in existence in Europe. On the continent, by way of contrast, laws might be common throughout Continental Europe through the *jus commune* brought back by the glossators from Bologna, or they might be applicable to smaller localities, rather than national ones.

Ironically, the divergence of English and Continental European law began at a time when the two were undergoing the same influences through their common attention to canon law and the fact that the Norman and Angevin kings of England had property in Normandy.[35] At that time, however, the rest of Europe was only starting a process of modernization, beginning to form nation states, and to discard old methods and organizing principles, such as feudalism,[36] while that process of modernization and centralization had occurred in England in the preceding century. As Continental Europe was developing new approaches to law, among other innovations, England continued her well-entrenched customs. The generalized abstractions that formed the axioms of law from which case solutions were derived in civilian law were, from the beginning, more scholarly, while the practice of law in England was taught as a trade in the Inns of Court: Van Caenegem compares this legal training for English lawyers based on past cases decided in the Kings' courts to lawyers 'learn[ing] their craft like every [other] medieval craftsman, in contact with practicing masters . . . .'[37]

By virtue of England's more rapid modernization, it also held on to traditions that some might say the civil law later eclipsed when the latter adopted Roman legal organization. For instance, the old English law divisions that were based on historical developments persisted until recently, such as courts with jurisdiction in either equity or law, but not both. These court divisions lasted into the late nineteenth century in England until the Judicature Act of 1875, and until almost the mid-twentieth century in the United States, where they ended only with the 1936 enactment of the Federal Rules of Civil Procedure. Even today, remedies differ depending on whether they stem from law or equity. The significance of these separate concepts has been studied by civilians, perhaps most of all in terms of the Anglo-Saxon trust, which cannot be reproduced in the civilian world for want of the ability to divide the trustee's powers between law and equity in the same way. As Frederic Maitland expressed it, speaking of the eighteenth century, '[t]he main illustration of a purely equitable obligation is the duty of a trustee and person who

33 Ibid.

34 See Marianne Constable, *The Law of the Other: The Mixed Jury and Changing Conceptions of Citizenships, Law and Knowledge* (University of Chicago Press 1994) (tracing the English jury system from the Middle Ages to the nineteenth century).

35 Van Caenegem (n 14) 85. Plucknett notes that William the Conqueror had created separate canon courts after the conquest that eliminated the bishops' participation in the hundreds' courts, separation which persisted through the centuries. See Plucknett (n 14) 12.

36 Van Caenegem (n 14) 89.

37 Ibid, 88–89.

holds property upon trust for another. Of any such obligation the courts of common law knew nothing.'[38]

2 *Early Institutions*

In the early twelfth century, English courts were meeting places of many sorts, including for social and business purposes, as well as legal.[39] Legal decisions of minor matters were made principally by 'suitors', those who attended court.[40] It is interesting to note that in the United States in the early decades of the twentieth century, Justice Jackson, who was to become Supreme Court Justice and US prosecutor at the post-World War II Nuremberg Trials, started practising law in the state of New York in an atmosphere that seems to bear some resemblance to these twelfth century antecedents: 'Trials were held not only in the courthouse, but in barns and taverns, where lawyers and judges gathered in the evening to swap law and lore.'[41]

King Henry I or his representatives settled disputes in the king's court concerning a broad range of matters, including serious crimes, and anything considered a breach of the king's peace.[42] 'Eyres', visitations by the king or his representatives throughout the land to resolve disputes, were called circuit courts by the time of the reign of Henry II. They are the model for the travelling federal appellate circuit courts which continue to exist in the United States.[43]

The ancient English criminal trial was one by 'ordeal', a species of which was subjecting the hand of the accused to a hot iron, bandaging it, and seeing a few days later if it was clean or infected, the former to be taken as a sign of the accused person's innocence and the latter of his guilt.[44] By the thirteenth century, the Church had forbidden such trials, and King Henry III then forbade them by writ to his 'Justices itinerant' in 1219.[45] His royal writ did not suggest guidelines for replacing the ordeals, thus allowing the judges to develop them as they saw fit. This opportunity for judicial creation of legal standards seems part and parcel of

38 FW Maitland, *The Constitutional History of England* (7th edn, CUP 1931) 471.

39 See Hunter (n 24) 25.

40 Ibid.

41 Robert E Conot, *Justice at Nuremberg* (Harper & Row 1983) 58.

42 See Hunter (n 24) 27.

43 England and Wales continue to have judges who retain the name of 'circuit'. According to Plucknett, Philippe Auguste imitated this system which effected control by the king as well as royal income through charges to parties.

44 The other was trial by water. See Plucknett (n 14) 114; Maitland (n 38) 115–16, noting the possibility of judgment by oath to the ordeals (remarking that '[t]o reverence an oath as an oath is now a sign of low morality. Not so in old time: the appeal to God made all the difference; mean will not forswear themselves though they will freely lie . . . .'). For the Germanic and Scandinavian panoply of legally probative 'gestures', see Bernard J Hibbitts, 'Making Motions: The Embodiment of Law in Gestures' (1995) 6 *J Contemp Legal Issues* 51.

45 Plucknett (n 14) 119 (quoting 'Eyre Rolls' in GO Sayles (ed), *Select Cases in the Court of the King's Bench Under Edward I Vol III* (Selden Society 1939) vol 58, no 1239).

common law methodology, yet is also reminiscent of the civilian judicial standard of *intime conviction* in French law. According to Plucknett, in thirteenth-century England, 'the judges were to be guided entirely by suspicion, and were to reach their conclusions as to the reasonableness of that suspicion entirely from their discretion.'[46] What seems undeniably common law in methodology is that the justices felt their way by proceeding from one case to the next case until a viable, satisfactory system had emerged from their trials and errors. That system was the English jury.

At first, the jury was a non-physical form of trial by ordeal inasmuch as it was not conceived as a way based upon reason to assess guilt or innocence, but as another manner of determining God's will. Some maintain that the common law to this day is bound up in structures similar to those of magic:

> [L]ike case law, magic spells contain both archaic language and contemporary phrases added in more recent usage. Thus, like a common-law rule, a spell is being constantly remoulded as it passes through the chain of magicians, each probably leaving his mark, however small, upon it. Nevertheless, such spells – and common law – are regarded as timeless and authorized by the ancestors who originated them.[47]

In 1275, the jury became compulsory throughout England.[48] By then, it also had been reduced from larger numbers to twelve, with the rational goal of consisting of men who could give information about the defendant relevant to his guilt or innocence.[49] Its use in both criminal and civil trials has been a hallmark of the common law, of the development of evidence law around concepts of allowing laymen to hear only such evidence as will not prejudice them, of the legal importance of the judicial jury instruction, and of the common law civil trial as a concentrated oral hearing before a judge, with facts not to be retried at the appellate, non-jury levels. The first jurors were witnesses, however, and could be sued for perjury, in a proceeding known as 'attaint'.[50] As time passed, the eyres slowly became obsolete, their revenue-producing role replaced by royal taxation, and the itinerant courts by the King's Bench, later known as the Court of Common Pleas, a name still in use in some state courts of the United States, such as Delaware, Ohio, and Pennsylvania, although now defunct in England.

46 Ibid.

47 Jessie Allen, 'A Theory of Adjudication: Law as Magic' (2008) 41 *Suffolk U L Rev* 773, 788 (quoting in part Bronislaw Malinowski, *Argonauts of the Western Pacific* (Routledge 1961) 428–29). Allen underscores the performative aspects of common law trials, an aspect of trials to which Benoît Frydman has drawn attention without distinguishing between civilian and common law system. See Benoît Frydman, 'Les juges dans la démocratie' (2016) Centre Perelman de Philosophie du Droit Working Paper 1 <www.philodroit.be/Les-juges-dans-la-democratie?lang=fr>.

48 Plucknett (n 14) 126.

49 See Constable (n 34) 16–18; ibid, 126–27. John Langbein, 'The Criminal Trial before the Lawyers' (1978) 45 *U Chi L Rev* 263; John Marshal Mitnick, 'From Neighbor-Witness to Judge of Proofs: The Transformation of the English Juror' (1988) 34 *Am J Leg Hist* 201, 203.

50 Maitland (n 38) 131.

Another institution basic to the common law is the writ, around which pleadings and access to justice were organized in a highly formalistic manner.[51] The writs caused the King's Bench to become less of a discretionary body.[52] During the time of Edward I (1272–1307), Parliament assumed a judicial role, with the discretionary powers no longer attributable to the King's Bench.[53] Parliament's origins were both judicial and administrative in nature, with the early Parliament adjudicating petitions from landed subjects ('commons' or '*communes*') as well as clergymen.[54]

While the flourishing of writs narrowed judicial discretion, according to Maitland, it had the advantage to the king of consolidating royal power:

> By the beginning of Edward's reign we may, I think, say that all serious obstacles to the royal jurisdiction had been removed. The royal courts had in one way and another become courts of first instance for almost all litigation. . . . There were a certain number of writs in the royal Chancery; these were at the disposal of every subject; they were to be had on payment of the customary fees; they could not be denied; by these writs actions were begun, were originated; they were *brevia originalia*, original writs.[55]

In Maitland's view, in summary, while the writs constrained the development of the common law, their great popular appeal drew litigants to the king's court.[56]

3 A *Short Excursus into the Modern Common Law Age*

The early institutions echo still today, but they have become faint sounds in a system that bears little overt resemblance to its past. An excavation of early common law roots has been suggested as holding the meaning for interpreting the 2017 case of *Philipp v Federal Republic of Germany*.[57] The case arose under the US Foreign Sovereign Immunities Act's exception to state immunity for expropriations in violation of international law,[58] in the context of artistic treasure, the plaintiff claimed had been expropriated from his family under the Nazi regime. The court dismissed claims it categorized as tortious in nature (fraud in the inducement, breach of fiduciary duty, breach of covenant of good faith and fair dealing, civil conspiracy, tortious interference) and held it had jurisdiction over those related directly to the

51 According to Plucknett (n 14) 148, relying on Maitland, the writ dates to the mid-twelfth century.

52 Plucknett adds to the writs the King's Bench's own procedure as another cause of the court's loss of discretionary power. Ibid, 153.

53 Ibid.

54 Ibid, 153–55.

55 Maitland (n 38) 114.

56 Ibid.

57 248 F Supp 3d 59 (D.D.C. 2017), *aff'd*, 894 F.3d 406 (2018). The district court decision was analysed in Ted Folkman, 'Case of the Day: Philipp v. Germany' (*Letters Blogatory: The Blog of International Judicial Assistance*, 6 April 2017) <https://lettersblogatory.com/2017/04/06/case-of-the-day-philipp-v-germany/#more-24610>.

58 28 USC § 1605(a)(3).

plaintiff's title to property, namely replevin, conversion, unjust enrichment, and claim for declaration of ownership.[59] Under today's pleading standards, the court's categorization seemed dubious:

> In the olden days there were the real actions (eg writs of right) and the personal actions (eg trespass). At first you tried title to land in the real actions, but as the law developed, you could try title to land in an ordinary tort case, eg, a trespass claim. With this as background, is there a real reason, in principle, that the issue of ownership of the [property at issue in this case] cannot arise in what looks like an ordinary tort claim? Is this an example of the forms of action ruling us from the grave?[60]

In earlier times, when courts were divided into multiple different institutions, reforms united them. Jurisdictional unification did not suppress the legal concepts that prevailed in the various earlier courts, however. Thus, for example, where almost all courts have jurisdiction over both equity and common law today, those legal concepts remain substantively distinct and operative even today. In the United States, moreover, some, albeit very few, probate courts still have no power of equity.[61] Other areas of law remain separated by specialized courts, such as tax and admiralty, although their decisions are appealable ultimately to the United States Supreme Court, whose opinions often are cited in and applied to other areas of law.[62]

The civil jury was abolished in England but persists as a constitutional right of the US plaintiff in civil as well as criminal trials.[63] Significantly in England, vast differences persist between British and civilian evidentiary laws due to the civil jury's original presence. On the other hand, one sees modifications of a civilian nature in Britain that are not occurring in the United States in terms of evidentiary standards, as British courts grow less wary of what might be called the impurities or dangers of non-probative evidence submitted to the court.[64] Another overwhelmingly common law trait that has persisted on both sides of the Atlantic Ocean is the power of the legal professional, lawyer, and judge alike. We saw earlier that the

59 See above text accompanying note 55. About a month after *Philipp* was decided, the US Supreme Court altered the distinction in jurisdictional standards still applicable to *Philipp*. See *Venezuela v Helmerich & Payne International Drilling Co*, 137 S Ct 1312 (2017).

60 Folkman (n 57).

61 One such state is Alabama, where probate courts in only four counties have the potential to have equity jurisdiction; all others do not. See Sidney C Summey, *Litigating the Case in Probate Court* (Birmingham Bar Association 2016) 1.

62 See, for example, the rapid and profound influence on non-admiralty cases of *The Bremen v Zapata Off-Shore Co*, 407 US 1 (1972), with respect to forum selection clauses.

63 US Const, amend VII. The civil jury was repealed in England and Wales by the Administration of Justice (Miscellaneous Provisions) Act 1933, *repealed by* Supreme Court Act 1981, s 152(4), sch 7.

64 Equally interesting was the ongoing presence of civil law ideas in England. Jeremy Bentham both translated Pothier's *Traité des preuves judiciaires* of 1823, and argued against judge-made law and exclusionary rules of evidence, two profound hallmarks of common law legal systems. CJW Allen, *The Law of Evidence in Victorian England* (CUP 1997) 18.

conquering Norman king did not disrupt the English legal system he found upon arrival, and that the glossators returning from Bologna tried in vain to Romanize British legal practice. The legislator in common law countries also responds to the practitioner, rather than vice versa, by enacting reforms in the manner of highly specific, detailed solutions to problems judges are not solving as the citizenry sees fit, rather than by initiating principles for the citizenry to adopt in its conduct, as civilian legislators do.[65]

A more indirect reflection of common law culture and the society in which it developed in a dynamic of mutual interaction with that society, might be gleaned from the competitive manner in which the court system developed in England.[66] The Courts of Common Pleas and the King's Bench struggled and vied for business, for customers, and each developed more efficient systems of pleading and rapid adjudication in order to gain in clientele,[67] until the Judicature Act eventually put an end to duplicative courts with similar jurisdiction.[68] In the United States to this day, prospective judges in many states compete against each other for the favour of their clientele in elections for their positions, as do prosecutors. Thus, the idea of the state at the service of the citizenry takes on a meaning enmeshed with private competition, heightened by seeking campaign funding for judicial and prosecutorial positions, at odds with that of the civilian, Rousseauistic concept of the social contract by means of which the individual sheds his particular personhood when becoming a citizen, yielding to the view of legislators who embody the citizenry, but thereby command their loyalty and obedience.[69]

CONCLUSION

If we think of matters calling most urgently for transnational solutions, do the origins of the common law suggest differences of a nature that would create insuperable obstacles to a new *jus commune*? In *Bulmer Ltd v Bollinger* SA, Lord Denning reflected on the difficulties which membership in the European Union posed to the British judge in analysing treaties and statutes that were of civilian origin.[70] Methodologically, the civil and common law systems continue to clash, like vehicles moving in opposite directions on the same lane, one the converse of the other. Yet the questions their courts face today are increasingly issues of jurisdiction, of the reach of domestic courts beyond the territories that define national sovereignty, where the tables of old-fashioned legal imperialism may be turned on their heads

65 CJW Allen has concluded that the British legislator reflects the power of the legal professional due to the fact that many lawyers sit in Parliament and ensure that it enacts such reforms as the profession deems desirable. Ibid, 183.

66 See JH Baker, *An Introduction to English Legal History* (4th edn, OUP 2007) 39–41.

67 Ibid.

68 Judicature Act of 1875.

69 Jean-Jacques Rousseau, *Du contrat social ou principes du droit politique* (Librio Philosophie 2013).

70 [1974] 2 All ER 1226.

into arguments to abandon victims of transnational economic power to their native, unresponsive domestic courts. These questions are well beyond the problems raised by a supranational court telling them how to adjudicate or an institution in Brussels what to legislate.

We already have seen innovative strides by courts in Great Britain as well as the Netherlands and France in recent years to meet the needs of transnationalizing law.[71] Legal concepts such as *forum necessitatis* have been adopted by some but not all common law countries, as well as most civil law ones. Procedural issues are deeply substantive in common law jurisdictions, where common-law constitutional law in many ways is a law of procedure, based on the dual pillars of due process and equality of treatment. Procedural questions are considered far more mechanical in civilian states, and yet today courts of both stripes are able to consider the procedural stances of their 'other'. For instance, the French Parliament referred to the US law known as the Alien Tort Statute (ATS)[72] in its debates over the recently enacted French law conferring duties and liability on parent corporations and contractors with respect to foreign subsidiary and subcontractor conduct, the *Loi relative au devoir de vigilance des sociétés mères et des entreprises donneuses d'ordre*.[73] Both of those statutes are laws of extraterritorial jurisdiction, the ATS for some decades applicable to, and the French one's origin owing to, the complex situation that has mushroomed in recent decades of multilayered, multi-structured, multinational parent corporations in Western home states legally separated and immunized by corporate veils from the acts of foreign subsidiaries accused of grave human rights violations in non-Western host states that offer no realistic tort compensation avenues to victims.[74]

Writing about his theory of property law, Pierre-Joseph Proudhon concluded that '[t]he moral as well as the physical world is founded on a plurality of irreducible and antagonistic elements and it is from the contradiction of these elements that life and the movement of the universe result.'[75] As we comparatists go about our task of translating the irreducibles confronting each other in our national courts every day,

[71] See Curran, 'Romantic Common Law' (n 13) 415–23, 434–46. Since that article was published (in 2017), the French proposal for a law on multinational liability mentioned earlier was enacted into law, and subsequently partially struck down by the Constitutional Council; and the *Kiobel* case appears to be resurfacing in the Netherlands, as reflected by a successful 28 USC § 1782 motion brought by plaintiffs in New York in aid of discovery. See *In re Kiobel*, No. 16 Civ 7992 (AKH), 2017 WL 354183 (2nd Cir 24 Jan 2017).

[72] 28 USC § 1350.

[73] Loi 2017-399 du 27 mars 2017, *Journal Officiel de la République Française* [JO], 28 March 2017, n°0074; Conseil constitutionnel [CC] Decision No. 2017-750DC, 23 March 2017 (holding the law only partially in conformity with the French Constitution).

[74] See Curran, 'Harmonizing Multinational Parent Company Liability' (n 11) and sources cited therein.

[75] Pierre-Joseph Proudhon, *Théorie de la propriété* (first published 1862, A Lacroix, Verboeckhover et Cie 1866) 111 <http://dx.doi.org/doi:10.1522/cla.prp.the> ('Le monde moral comme le monde physique repose sur une pluralité d'éléments irréductibles et antagonistes et c'est de la contradiction de ces éléments que résultent la vie et le mouvement dans l'univers.').

perhaps we also can contribute ideas for harmonizing them in the continuously shrinking legal world we now inhabit. It was also Proudhon who said that humanity proceeds towards its goals only by approximations.[76] The irreducible in differences need not signify, one hopes, an absolute limit to comprehension. With increasing comprehension can come harmony and fruitful mutual consultation, if humanity decides that it wishes to proceed towards this goal in order, as Rousseau put it, 'that justice and utility not be divided'.[77]

[76] Proudhon (n 75) 125 ('L'humanité procède par des approximations.').

[77] Rousseau (n 69) preamble ('[A]fin que la justice et l'utilité ne se trouvent point divisées.').

13

The Fabric of Normative Translation in Law

Ko Hasegawa[*]

INTRODUCTION: NORMATIVE TRANSLATION AND ITS TWO PHASES

In the process of the transmigration of various laws in the world, there are many points of connection between the different laws interacting with each other. These connecting points are the sites for the mutual contacts between them. One such form of mutual contact is the translational process between different, or sometimes even heterogeneous, legal ideas. This is what I call 'normative translation'. When legal ideas cross borders, it is possible to differentiate between the incorporation of foreign legal ideas into a domestic legal practice and the internalization of those ideas. The corresponding phases of normative translation, I call, respectively, external normative translation and internal normative translation (in short, *eNT* and *iNT*).[1] Although this translational process is constitutive of the significant and unique features of the receiving law, there have only been a few theoretical enquiries into the transformative features of this process. My exploration in this chapter explicates those features from a perspective of philosophical hermeneutics that emphasizes the interpretive nature of our intellectual activities and the significance

* I wish to express my special gratitude to Professor Helge Dedek for his kind invitation to participate in a commemorative collection of essays for the late Professor H Patrick Glenn. Patrick had been kind enough to give insightful suggestions for my work on normative translation. I am also grateful to Professors Annelise Riles and Xingzhong Yu at Cornell University Law School and Professor Andrew Halpin at the National University of Singapore for their encouragement of my work. I also wish to express thanks both to Tsinghua University Law School in China for inviting me to the comparative law symposium in June 2013, where I presented the first draft of this chapter, and to Mr Naruhito Cho, a former JD fellow at Hokkaido University, for his stylistic advice and clarifying comments. This chapter is a sequel exploration to my article 'Normative Translation in the Heterogeneity of Law', discussed below at note 4.

1 This is also concerned with 'law as translation' in terms of the mutual interaction between different legal practices in different societies and cultures. 'Law as translation' considers that the formation and change of law in a society are the successive transformation of the meaning of normative concepts and institutions. Normative translations by various translators of thoughts and languages are its principal connecting points. This chapter may be taken not simply for the understanding of normative translation but also for a step towards the grasp of the multifaceted aspects of 'law as translation'. On the significant relationship between law and translation, the following chapters in this volume are also relevant: Esin Örücü, Chapter 4, pt V; Michele Graziadei, Chapter 5, pt VI.

of a legal philosophy focusing on the interpretive structure of our legal thinking.[2] In so doing, I also point out the critical elements necessary to a deeper understanding of the complexity in the diffusion of law.[3]

I wish to begin by confirming my basic understanding of normative translation in *eNT*. I have, in previous publications, discussed the pragmatic and circumstantial conditions of *eNT* and also its logical conditions in the heterogeneity of law; I started from the point that in a certain stage of its development, some legal practice incorporates foreign legal ideas into its own and that normative translation helps bridge different legal ideas.[4] Various factors, such as the accumulation of prerequisite materials, the isomorphic conversion, and the ideational expectation, form the pragmatic and circumstantial conditions of *eNT*.[5] These conditions are further bounded by the 'creole' of the translational diffusion of normative ideas.[6] This 'creole' situation is bounded finally by the macro flow of normative ideas through the *Legal Traditions* of the entire world.[7]

Normative translation in an *eNT* setting has some logical features.[8] While ordinary translation aims at attaining the equivalence of meaning between the original and the target language, the important task for normative translation is the *practical accommodation* of normative meaning between the original idea and the novel conceptualization thereof in a different sociocultural context. As philosophical hermeneutics reveals, translation, in general, is a perspectival activity in which the translator transforms the meaning and implication of the original idea.[9] Still, while ordinary circumstances call for a relative emphasis on the cognitive aspect of translation, practical situations emphasize the evaluative aspect. Normative

2 On philosophical hermeneutics, cf Hans Georg Gadamer, *Truth and Method* (2nd edn, Sheed & Ward 1989) pt II; Hans Georg Gadamer, *Philosophical Hermeneutics* (University of California Press 1976) pt I; Wolfgang Iser, *The Range of Interpretation* (Columbia University Press 2000) chs 1–4.

3 On the diffusion of law, in general, cf William Twining, *General Jurisprudence* (CUP 2009) pt B; Werner Menski, *Comparative Law in a Global Context* (2nd edn, CUP 2006) pt 1. Also, as to the transformation of Japanese law, cf Tsuyoshi Kinoshita, 'Legal System and Legal Culture in Japanese Law' (2010) 44 *Comp L Rev* 25, esp 78ff, 112ff.

4 Ko Hasegawa, 'Normative Translation in the Heterogeneity of Law' (2015) 6 *Trans LT* 501. Compare also Ichiro Kitamura, 'Problems of the Translation of Law in Japan' (1993) 23 *VUWLR* 1, esp pts III, IV.

5 Ko Hasegawa, 'Incorporating Foreign Legal Ideas Through Translation' in Andrew Halpin and Volker Roeben (eds), *Theorizing the Global Legal Order* (Hart 2009) esp 98ff. See also, more specifically, Ko Hasegawa, 'Between Rights and "Kenri"' in Eleanor Cashin-Ritaine (ed), *Legal Engineering and Comparative Law* (Schulthess 2009) esp 92ff.

6 Ko Hasegawa, 'Hou no Kureouru no Gainen ni tsuite no Kisoteki Kousatsu' ['Fundamental Considerations on the Concept of the Creole of Law'] (2007) 58 *Hokkaido L Rev* 244, 259ff.

7 In this regard, we need to take a holistic view of normative translation, which is ultimately connected to the transformations of law around the world. Cf H Patrick Glenn, *Legal Traditions of the World* (5th edn, OUP 2014) ch 2 (hereafter Glenn, *LTW*); Hasegawa, 'Normative Translation in the Heterogeneity of Law' (n 4) 513ff. Also, this nexus may constitute a fundamental part of the rule of law in human society. Cf Brian Tamanaha, *On the Rule of Law* (CUP 2004) chs 1–6.

8 Hasegawa, 'Normative Translation in the Heterogeneity of Law' (n 4) 506ff.

9 Eg, Lydia H Liu, *Translingual Practice* (Stanford University Press 1995) ch 1; Anthony Pym, *Exploring Translation Theories* (Routledge 2010) ch 6.

translation includes, along with the cognitive stance for understanding the original idea, the moral adaptation of the original to a different sociocultural context. This cannot be strictly cognitive; it is something 'in between' that helps us finally reach a meaningful accommodation of the original idea in a different society.[10]

Also relevant here is the *contextual substantiation* in normative translation. This is the process of translational twisting of the meaning of the original idea. The local process here is non-monotonic; certain analytical elements of a Western normative idea are newly configured by the intervening morality in a local context. While this logical transformation includes a substantial change to the meaning of a foreign idea, the skeletal relationship between the logical factors of that idea are analogically maintained. The result of the contextual substantiation is the *semantic twist* of the original idea to its newer conceptualization.[11]

In such a case, if some law has to accord certain translational ideas such a key role, then the next question is, what may occur within a law *after* the translational incorporation of foreign ideas? This is the problem of *iNT*.

This question is obvious in the sense that as a historical process, the initial circumstance is followed by some consequences, but also in the sense that even if such translational incorporation of foreign legal ideas occurs, a distinctively justificatory structure of law, which is independent of its generative process, will emerge. The translational incorporation of some foreign legal ideas from, say, the West to East Asia may be unique, and yet the consecutive interpretive process of those ideas in East Asian law might cause such translational features to be lost within the autonomous legal setting. Those legal ideas may experience their own developments over time in a distinctive space of East Asian legal practice, as the mode of this space is different from the original setting in the West. In this respect, the theoretical question now becomes, how or to what extent do the translational features of the incorporated legal ideas impact the change of law's problem-contexts? To answer this question, we should try extending the perspective of our initial view of *eNT* to the explication of *iNT*. This will allow us to suggest that a theory of *eNT* is a continuation of the theory of *iNT*, if we take *eNT* as the limiting case of *iNT*.

To tackle the above-mentioned problem, there are several stages in the spiral that I wish to discuss in the following sections:

(i) The process of the translational extension of legal ideas in the shaping of the interpretive recapitulations between relevant ideas.
(ii) The ways in which other foreign legal ideas are newly incorporated into new translations of the original translation.
(iii) The gradual expansion of normative translations over time.

[10] In this sense, normative translation is itself a challenge for shaping a newer societal order; the translational nexus of norms can be also an important aspect of moral nexus of worldwide values.

[11] Hasegawa, 'Normative Translation in the Heterogeneity of Law' (n 4) 509.

And I should add stage (iv), wherein the process returns to stage (i) with possibly introducing newer foreign ideas via further *eNT*.[12]

However, stage (iv) enters into the domain of historical developments in the translational normative spiral, and thus requires a thorough investigation of various historical events and courses concerning law, which I am unable to explore in this chapter. Rather, I will concentrate on the philosophical elements in stages (i), (ii), and (iii) to provide some suggestions for stage (iv). I will deal with stage (i) as the *extension* of normative translation, discuss stage (ii) as the *reprise* of normative translation, and consider a part of stage (iii) as *weaving* of normative translation.[13]

I THE EXTENSION OF NORMATIVE TRANSLATION

When key ideas in law are translationally incorporated, two kinds of problems in legal thinking arise. One is to formally construct the logical relationship with other key ideas; the other is to use the semantic field substantively for the working of relevant concepts. We need this distinction to understand the working of legal concepts in translational context, because, as I have previously argued,[14] a translationally introduced concept holds two combinatory dimensions of meaning – the skeletal isomorphism and the substantive accommodation between the original and the translating concept. If a translated foreign concept must have these two dimensions of meaning, that is, if the interrelationship between such two concepts must be twofold (twofold characterized as formal and substantive), and if we can say that, while the contents of the main concepts in law are contextual and particular, and that the forms of such concepts can be universal to a certain extent, then the working of normative translation may remain the same as nested in *iNT*.[15]

As for the formal part of the translational relationship between the two concepts in question, the relationship between the isomorphic aspects of concepts stays skeletally the same, as is the case in the context of *eNT*. To refer to the idea of rights, for example, the extension of the idea of rights in law, in the context of *iNT*, meets the idea of duty, no-right, liability, or disability in that practice, if we understand the typical conceptual functions of rights as 'jural correlatives' that Wesley Hohfeld

12 As a matter of fact, when we take into account later in the text some translational example in East Asia, the entire process of *eNT* and *iNT* proceeds with incessant translational introductions of newer ideas. In particular, the works of Japanese law scholars make this process actual since the time of modernization from the late nineteenth century until even today. Cf Part III below. Also, very interesting in this regard is the case of Taiwan. Cf Tay-shen Wang, 'Translation, Codification, and Transplantation of Foreign Laws in Taiwan' (2016) 25 *Wash Int'l LJ* 307, esp 312ff. Here, as I see it, Professor Wang focuses on the political functions of normative translation. In this regard, cf also Kinoshita (n 3) 96ff.

13 Another part of stage (iii) is the integrity of normative translation, the substantive consistency of normative translation in all relevant stages. I will discuss it in the near future. As to the possibility that normative translation forms and develops a kind of intellectual space, cf Catherine Valcke, Chapter 7 in this volume, pts IIIA, IIIB.

14 Hasegawa, 'Incorporating Foreign Legal Ideas Through Translation' (n 5) 98ff.

15 This is the key thought in this chapter. Cf Iser (n 2) chs 3 and 4.

famously analysed.[16] When the idea of rights indicates legitimate claims against others, others must hold certain duties to realize the content of such claims; when the idea of rights indicates a privilege towards others, they cannot hold any entitlements about the matter in question; when the idea of rights indicates certain normative power over others, they must hold liability to obey the order in question; and when the idea of rights indicates some immunity from others, they must be disabled from doing anything relevant to the matter in question. If we take these correlatives as the skeletal relationship between the idea of rights and other related concepts significant in law, these are one of the axes of the extension of the translation of the idea of rights in law.

As for the substantive part of the translational relationship between the two concepts in question, we can say the following. When the contextual substantiation for some foreign legal idea occurs, the semantic twist of that idea may also occur. In the case of the translation of 'rights' from the West to Japan, there was a shift from 'the legitimate claim of an individual against others' to 'the ordered power to demand one's due along with others'. Here, as the replacement of the Western point and postulates of rights-relationship occurs through normative translation, the Japanese idea of rights begins to hold such postulates as the principle of an allowed claim, the principle of bounded personhood and his long-term merit, and the standard of groupistic intercourse.[17] Here rights are translated to '権利', which could be understood as *diluted rights*. Then this idea of diluted rights meets such jural correlatives as duty, no-right, liability, or disability in a diluted way, and the corresponding correlatives appear in such forms as '*Giri* (義理)' or long-term mutuality instead of duty; no-say instead of no-right; subjection instead of liability; or neglect instead of disability. Even if these correspondences can be termed in the same way as the Hohfeldian correlatives of rights, their real substances reflect the dilutedness of '権利'.

This double character of the translational extension of the idea of rights can be also applied in a similar way to other related concepts such as responsibility for the infringements or the abuse of rights. *Diluted responsibility* may indicate that responsibility for the infringements or the abuse of '権利' is unclear and dispersed. The interrelationships of translated concepts hold these double translational aspects and

[16] For a suggestive theoretical interpretation of the Hohfeldian distinction, see Andrew Halpin, *Rights and Law – Analysis and Theory* (Hart 1997) ch II.

[17] Hasegawa, 'Normative Translation in the Heterogeneity of Law' (n 4) 508ff. The idea of rights in the West can hold such factors as (a) the presupposed elements for the sustenance of individualized rights-relationship, (b) the individualist moral postulates for the significance of rights-relationship, and (c) the point of the background of the idea of rights that morally yields the presupposed elements via the moral postulates described above. In the normative translation of the idea of rights from the West to, say, Japan, (a) above is dislocated by the Japanese view of social relation between parties in terms of each due in a group; (b) above is replaced by the locally Japanese moral postulates such as seniority and long-term mutual relationship; and (c) above is also curbed by the importance of the proper due of each in a group. As to the significance of communality in Japanese law, cf also John O Haley, *The Spirit of Japanese Law* (University of Georgia Press 1998) esp chs 6 and 8.

yield a type of systematization of those concepts at the pivotal part of law. And, the legal thinking there has the pivotal elements in its conceptual resources, which give some gravitational force for judgments. Also, through this force, the translational character of rights may pull the contents of relevant concepts to the initial mode determined by the initial translation of rights as '権利'. Of course, if a translator holds a different moral orientation for his translational hypothesis, the substance of those diluted correlatives may be different. In some cases, when the idea of rights is translated into Japanese as '権理', as once perceptively proposed by Yukichi Fukuzawa in the late nineteenth century, the substance might become simply the same as the correlatives in the very Hohfeldian sense.[18] Here, the idea of '権理' is not considered diluted because it tries to correctly transfer the genuine (ie, Western) meaning of rights.[19]

The extension of normative translation has another important aspect. That is, the idea of '権利' may be influenced by other translations of pivotal legal concepts. The most typical Japanese example that gives impact to the meaning of '権利' might be the idea of public welfare translated as '公共の福祉' introduced to Japan through Article 13 of the Constitution of Japan in 1946. Public welfare means basically the well-being or the good of people in society.[20] Yet, '公共の福祉' also instantiates the problem of the semantic twist in the Japanese context.

Interpretive debates about the meaning of '公共の福祉' have shown that there can be different understandings of this idea.[21] One is the authoritarian or paternalistic understanding, according to which public welfare is what expresses the ruler's concern about his subjects as dependents. The ruler, as the subjects' guardian, has to care for them while the interests of the entire nation to be cared for are public welfare. This interpretation sometimes makes it possible to realize a certain standard of life in a nation, but often justifies the maintenance of a status quo and the victimization of individuals who have their own urgent interests. In this sense, this interpretation sees public welfare as *external* to the system of rights. Another possibility is the libertarian interpretation, which conceives of public welfare as a negative

18 Hasegawa, 'Incorporating Foreign Legal Ideas Through Translation' (n 5) 89ff; Hasegawa, 'Between Rights and "Kenri"' (n 5) 89ff.

19 It is natural to suspect if the substance of the idea of rights, whether diluted or not in Japan, really shifts under the conditions of practical accommodation and contextual substantiation. This is a difficult problem; probably the degree of dilution is different between '権利' and '権理'. Here we might need the distinction between the *semantic character* and the *semantic core* of the concept in question: even if the semantic character of translation is the same, its semantic core may be different. In case of rights, we might say that, while the semantic character is the same between '権利' and '権理', the semantic core of rights can yet be apparently different between them. Also, if the translation of rights is only '権利', the semantic core may be different from the *semantic force* of it by context. Still, this problem is related to the reprise of normative translation to be discussed later. We have to take into account the types of political morality that tie the moral perspectives and critical distances of translators to the original concepts and its initial translations.

20 On the idea of welfare in general, see Mary Daly, *Welfare* (Polity Press 2011) chs 1 and 3.

21 Cf Hiroshi Oda, *Japanese Law* (3rd edn, OUP 2009) 90ff; Shigenori Matsui, *The Constitution of Japan* (Hart 2011) ch 6, pt III.

principle for the minimal arrangement of conflicts of rights. We need a certain arrangement in conflicts between, say, free speech and privacy, or between competing property rights. To protect such freedom rights from possible infringement by government or others, we need principles that establish certain conditions that forbid such infringement or provide compensation. These negative conditions can be called public welfare and, in this interpretation, it is internal to the system of rights. The working of rights comes first, and, when necessary and in exceptional cases, public welfare comes next. Another possibility is the liberal interpretation, which also shares with the libertarian view the internality of public welfare, but differs in its positive character. Public welfare here includes two kinds of restriction for the system of rights. One restriction limits rights to freedom through welfare rights or social rights, a situation sometimes referred to as the inherent limitation of rights. The other is the restriction of rights from the viewpoint of welfare policy-making. For example, when we restrict property rights for the sake of economic stabilization, public welfare means certain governmental concern for individual lives from a democratic standpoint rather than a paternalistic one.[22]

Even today, there are potential conflicts and tensions among the three views concerning '公共の福祉'. While the two democratic views tend to imply that '公共の福祉' should be understood as some well-balanced arrangement among various claims of individuals in society, the authoritarian view tends to imply that '公共の福祉' should be understood as the communal interest and order in society. In this thematic context, to the extent that the latter authoritarian understanding of '公共の福祉' is still strong, if not dominant in Japan, this idea has constraining effects on the Japanese understanding of '権利' through the constitutional interpretation of the above-mentioned Article 13. Here, as '公共の福祉' is basically regarded as creating external limits to the realization of individual rights, the authoritarian reading reinforces the limitation of their scope. And this is likely to reinforce the diluted understanding of '権利'. Whether this situation is good or bad for Japanese society, I characterize it as the *contraction* of normative translation, which is a reverse form of the extension of normative translation.

To note a related aspect of this translational extension of the concept of rights, we first need to understand the structure of legal reasoning which may also deepen the concrete contents of the translated idea of rights. Logically speaking, although legal reasoning basically holds the form of syllogism – one, *modus ponens*, and the other, teleological reasoning,[23] certain intervening premises work to interrelate the basic premises in syllogism as well. The simple logical form of syllogism is backed by other evaluative, factual, and auxiliary propositions. As these are, in a complex fashion,

22 On different understandings of the idea of welfare in general, cf Daly (n 20) chs 3 and 4, esp 70ff, 90ff. Also, as to the constitutional interpretation of public welfare in Japan, cf Oda (n 21) 91ff; Matsui (n 21) 165ff.

23 Logically, the former is $p(x) \rightarrow Lq(x)$, $p(a)$, therefore $Lq(a)$; the latter is, $Lr(x)$, $\sim s(x) \rightarrow \sim r(x)$, therefore $Ls(x)$.

combined to yield logical conclusions, the intervening premises establish various focal points for the introduction of translational concepts in judging particular cases.[24]

In this regard, we must not ignore the elaborative work of legal interpretation. Through the so-called subsumption, and also by bridging the factual and the normative in those two syllogistic forms, legal interpretation explicates the general predicative content of law to clarify the general conditions for the factual satisfaction of legal conditions and to intake particularities of the facts in an individual case.[25] In this process, especially when the general predicative content of law is explicated, the legal concept in question is interpretively analysed by utilizing other key legal concepts. As such, through this process, the significance of various legal concepts in the translational setting in question is fine-tuned gradually.[26] For example, when the given problem is the freedom of assembly in a particular case, the scope of the protection of such '権利' is limited by some concrete conditions. If it is demanded by some democratic association, the understanding of the scope of '権利' in this context may be limited by some communal considerations for the peace of the site of assembly, and a view for this limitation can imply a notoriously reductive understanding of '権利' that regards '権利' as mere 'reflex interest' mirroring communal considerations on the stability of the societal order.[27] It is apparent that this sort of concretization is a type of the contraction of the idea of rights mentioned earlier.

To add, various substantive factors of normative considerations hide behind the surface structure of those logical forms and accompanying interpretive propositions. Deep normative considerations work to orient the setting of premises for legal reasoning. This means that there are the points of entry for deeper normative considerations in accordance with the making of various premises and that, among those considerations, some directional force works to achieve the moral objective of legal judgment in the case in question. All of these considerations must be related in some evaluative way, though which part is decisive may be indeterminate.[28]

24 Recognizing this complexity of legal reasoning is important as there have already appeared many significant studies about the complicated logic of legal reasoning or legal justification. These logical forms are important frames to connect various legal concepts, propositions, and arguments in constructing legal reasoning. Cf Ko Hasegawa, 'Legal Reasoning and Interpretation of Justice' (1998) 48 *Hokkaido L Rev* 330.

25 Logically, in *modus ponens*, $p(x) \rightarrow Lq(x), <m(x) \cdot n(x) \cdot o(x) \rightarrow p(x), [a \in x] \cdot m(a) \cdot n(a) \cdot o(a), \therefore p(a)>, \therefore Lq(a)$; in teleological reasoning, $Lr(x), <\sim s(x) \rightarrow \sim r(x), [a \in x] \cdot \sim s(a), \therefore \sim r(a)>, \therefore Ls(a)$. The < > parts are the parts of legal interpretation, which indicate the concretizations of legal norms, in particular, problem contexts.

26 This is the process of the legal discussion among relevant parties, scholars, and lawyers. While the fine-tuning is to be done in contextual details, what I concentrate here is some general level of the meaning of legal ideas.

27 This is the so-called reflex interest theory of rights; which was once dominant particularly in the context of Japanese administrative law. Cf Carl F Goodman, *The Rule of Law in Japan* (Kluwer Law International 2003) 326ff.

28 In these deeper considerations, we may identify at least three points of entry in the structure of legal reasoning: legal interpretation, the very logical connection of various premises in reasoning, and the evaluative orientation of reasoning.

Lastly, the extension of normative translation may be followed by some communicative extension among various societal actors, including the translators themselves. As I have discussed this elsewhere in terms of what I call the attuned dispersal of connected critique,[29] a group dynamic exists between divergent legal actors while the initiative of intellectual leaders works in society. Still, as the effectuation of this communicative process is another philosophical task, it suffices here to note that this process is also an aspect of the further stage of translational expansion with the contest among various proposals, which will be discussed in the next Part: the *reprise* of normative translation.

II THE REPRISE OF NORMATIVE TRANSLATION

The reprise of normative translation starts from the preceding translation. Thus, the theory of normative translation makes possible an analogical understanding of *eNT* for *iNT*. That is, the latter translation depends on certain mirroring conditions of the ones in the former translation such as creole situations, accumulative pre-learning, isomorphic recognition and conceptual conversion, and ideational expectation. Indeed, there are differences between the problem-context of *eNT* and the one of reprise in *iNT*. While the former is the very beginning of translational efforts in law, the latter is the further revision of previous translations as *a translation of translation*. Thus, the reprise of normative translation requires the translator's evaluation with respect to the previous translation. In *eNT*, a foreign idea is already recognized as worth introducing and then evaluated for an ideational expectation afterwards. Conversely, in the reprise of normative translation, the preceding translated idea is recognized as already rooted in the society in question, but is morally re-evaluated for another, perhaps different, ideational expectation.[30]

This basic view leads us to the following suppositions for the reprise of normative translation. As several important problems in the reprise appear in the analogue of creole situations, it is important to clarify in what modes those situations appear in the encounter of different cultures. There are three patterns in this regard whose modalities indicate the problem-field for a translator who makes a moral push for his translational efforts. In *eNT*, first, the problem-field may hold the 'dominance-protest' relation between two given societies, whose nature is to be characterized as 'suppressing'. And, if so, translators face their task within the modality where translators' subjectivity becomes 'inverting', normative transformation 'resisting', normative mixture 'relativizing', and translators' moral agency 'repulsive'. Second,

[29] Hasegawa, 'Incorporating Foreign Legal Ideas Through Translation' (n 5) 94ff.

[30] Relevant here is the distinction made before in footnote 19 between the semantic character and the semantic core of translated concepts. In *eNT*, the semantic character is set first for leading to the nature of the semantic content of it. Yet in the reprise of normative translation, semantic character is already acknowledged and this is examined by the newer semantic core of the newer understanding of the concept in question.

the problem-field may hold the 'invasion-countering' relation between relevant societies, whose nature is to be characterized as 'pressing'. And, if so, translators face their task within the modality where translators' subjectivity becomes 'countering', normative transformation 'overlaying', normative mixture 'hybridizing', and the translators' moral agency 'repellent'. And third, the problem-field may hold the 'expansion-accepting' relation between relevant societies, whose nature is to be characterized as 'inflowing'. And, if so, translators face their task within the modality where their subjectivity becomes 'conforming', normative transformation 'receiving', normative mixture 'extending', and their moral agency 'receptive'.[31]

Following these patterns, we can distinguish first the patterns in the context of the reprise of normative translation such as 'dominance-protesting', 'invasion-countering', and 'expansion-accepting' as including the evaluative modes in moral agency of a translator such as being 'repulsive', 'repellent', and 'receptive' towards the initial translation. Second, as to the pre-accumulation of the reprise of normative translation, it is evident that this condition is already satisfied to a certain extent, because this is in itself an inherent trigger of internal normative translation. Third, as to the isomorphic conversion of the initial translation and its ideational expectation, this process is the nerve of the reprise of normative translation, which is to be discussed in detail later. Yet, for now, we can identify the moral orientation of the translator as conservative, moderate, and critical towards the initial translation. As the result of these distinctions, we may distinguish the following nine cases: (1a) repulsive cum conservative; (1b) repulsive cum moderate; (1c) repulsive cum critical; (2a) repellent cum conservative; (2b) repellent cum moderate; (2c) repellent cum critical; (3a) receptive cum conservative; (3b) receptive cum moderate; and (3c) receptive cum critical. Yet, *ex hypothesi*, as 'receptive' is always conservative, we shall disregard (3a). Similarly, as 'receptive' cannot be critical of the initial translation, we shall also disregard (3c). In contrast to these two, (3b) shall remain since some slight elaboration of the initial translation is possible.

Thus:

1(a) is the case where the translator *utilizes* the existing normative resources in a society to *upset* the initial translation;

1(b) is the case where the translator *accommodates* the ideal normative resources in a society to *upset* the initial translation;

[31] As examples of these three creole situations, we may raise, first, a typical problem scene in some colonial situation in a society such as India or Taiwan, second, the problem situation of modern Japan experienced when facing with Western powers in the late nineteenth century, and third, the case of the influence of Roman Empire and Roman law to the medieval France and Germany. Also, legally speaking, we may add the situations such as, first, law under colonial governance in India or Taiwan; second, the situation of modern Japan to catch up to Western law; and third, the so-called reception of Roman law in France and Germany. Cf Glenn, *LTW* (n 7) 342ff; Twining (n 3) 275ff; Menski (n 3) 37ff; Kinoshita (n 3) 95ff; Wang (n 12) pt II.

1(c) is the case that the translator *exploits* the ideal normative resources in a society to *upset* the initial translation;
2(a) is the case where the translator *utilizes* the existing normative resources in a society to *amend* the initial translation;
2(b) is the case where the translator *accommodates* the ideal normative resources in a society to *amend* the initial translation;
2(c) is the case where the translator *exploits* the ideal normative resources in a society to *amend* the initial translation; and
3(b) is the case where the translator *accommodates* the ideal normative resources in a society to *elaborate* the initial translation.

We should consider the reprise of normative translation in accordance with these seven cases.

By way of example, I examine the possibility of the reprise of normative translation on the concept of rights in Japan. Let me note the starting assumption that the Western idea of rights is first translated into the idea of '権利' by twisting its meaning from 'the legitimate claim of an individual against others' to 'the ordered power to demand one's due along with others'.[32] To capture the general characteristics of this reprise of normative translation corresponding to the nature of the seven cases outlined earlier, we can state the following. In (1a), the Japanese idea of '権利' is repulsively secured by the existing idea of traditional morality for the 'reflex interest' of legal regulations. In (1b), it is repulsively moderated by the idea of liberalism for one's due with others in limited spherical exceptions of fundamental liberty. In (1c), it is repulsively criticized by some radical ideal for the individualist or by the Marxist view of genuine rights. In (2a), it is repellently secured by the existing idea of traditional morality for legitimate interest of an individual against others in spherical exceptions of social welfare. In (2b), it is repellently moderated by the ideal of liberalism for the legitimate claim of an individual against others in limited spherical exceptions of social welfare. In (2c), it is repellently criticized by some radical ideal for the strong individualist or the strong Marxist view of genuine rights. And, in (3b), it is receptively moderated by some ideal for one's due with others in a slight elaboration for some spherical exceptions of legitimate interest of an individual.

With these seven possible situations, I wish to deal with at least two different, but connected, aspects of the reprise of normative translation by referring to the recent situation of the Japanese rights consciousness. One is the replacement of '権利' by another translation such as '権理'; the other is the renovation of '権利' with some more qualifications.

First, a Japanese word '権理' for rights, as was proposed by Fukuzawa, can be an expression of the right interest for an individual citizen in a democratic community even today. One can rely here on a view of political morality which deploys the importance of liberal equality and tries to reorient the idea of rights. This implies

32 Hasegawa, 'Normative Translation in the Heterogeneity of Law' (n 4) 508ff.

that to overwrite '権利' with '権理' is to correct, from some morally better position, the diluted features of the former translation.[33] In this case, we face the larger question of whether Japanese law has been adequately modernized. Some people tend to praise the recent development of Japanese civil society, which also implies the strength of rights among enlightened citizens. Others might think, however, that we have also been experiencing various drawbacks of public ethics in the political, economic, and cultural domains recently.[34] Thus, what one can wish to propose by a new translation of rights is some revision of the concept in search of a better, more just understanding for directing the culturally complex practice of rights in today's Japan; which can itself be an indication of (2b) as explained earlier. I call this sort of situation of the reprise of normative translation the *transpositional* reprise. Here, newer translations try to replace preceding ones to the end of a better orientation of those translations. Incidentally, this sort of process once happened in the Meiji period in the late nineteenth century when Fukuzawa and others competed with each other to propose new translations for the idea of rights. It was Fukuzawa himself who tried to confront the translation of '権利' with his own translation of '権義' or '権理'; the latter two emphasized the importance of the justness of individual claims in contrast to '権利' that focused on benefits.

In the transpositional reprise of normative translation, the question is mainly concerned with the replacement of the old translation by a new one. This is a somewhat direct sort of reprise. Still, very often, the reprise may occur in some indirect way. While (or even if) the initial translation is conventionally stable, the introduction of a newer understanding of that translation may change its

33 This variation depends on the moral and political orientation of the person who carries *iNT*. Its moral orientation determines the substantial direction of the *iNT*'s working; yet it is to be discussed in the judgement and evaluation of specific legal cases. Also, as discussed later, this point must be related to theories of justice and other political morality: conservative, libertarian, liberal, communitarian, dialogist, marketist, leftist, feminist, critical race theorist, postmodern sceptic and critic, and the like. I myself am basically an egalitarian liberal; my trial for this extension would be moderately critical of Japanese law, say, on its understanding of rights, while emphasizing the importance of broader interpretation and the expansion of equality rights. Ko Hasegawa, 'Human Well-Being and Public Provision' (2004) 54 *Hokkaido L Rev* 432, 428ff.

34 This position, with which I am sympathetic, maintains that Japanese legal practice is now faced with a novel problem situation characterized as postmodern and postdemocratic. Our politics and law are facing some crisis caused by globalization after the so-called Bubble Burst in the mid-1990s, by social fragmentation of values around the turn of the century, and by the so-called structural reform by the Koizumi administration from 2000 to 2006 and its subsequence in recent years by the Abe administration. Cf Elise K Tipton, *Modern Japan* (2nd edn, Routledge 2008) ch 14. I think its essence is concerned with what I call *the digression of freedom* which includes a multifaceted problem concerning rights – (i) various drawbacks of public ethics in the domains of the political (eg, the arrogance and conceit of government), of the economic (eg, the excess of business freedom), and of the cultural (eg, the fragmentation of values and the weakening of social bonds) and (ii) various failures of necessary attention in the domains of the political (eg, the respect and concern for identities and citizenship), of the economic (eg, the moderation of the market forces), and of the cultural (eg, the recovery of family and education and the acknowledgement of multiculturality). Yet, whether the translation of '権理' can respond to this situation adequately or not is another issue to be discussed elsewhere. Cf Gavan McCormack, *Client State* (Verso 2007) ch 9.

implications. This situation is another facet of the reprise of normative translation. For, in Japanese translational practice in law, we can find some broader way to incorporate newer ideas into the initial translational idea which may substantially impact the initial translation. This is the second case of the reprise – the *implicational* reprise of normative translation.

As a matter of fact, the famous debate on the rights-insensitivity of Japanese people is a significant example. The late Civil Law Professor Takeyoshi Kawashima, in his modern classic *Nihonjin no Hoishiki* (*Legal Consciousness of the Japanese People*) in 1967, maintained that the Japanese people did not fully understand the significance of the modern Western legal perspective, especially the importance of individual rights and obligations, and that this ignorance led the Japanese people to become averse to lawsuits. Such a tendency is due to that fact that Japanese legal consciousness is held back and disrupted by the traditional culture of communal harmony, particularly in rural areas. Kawashima's analysis was very influential for the self-criticism of the Japanese, especially of intellectuals, towards more effective modernization of rights.[35]

After Kawashima sparked much debate about the nature of Japanese rights consciousness, the following five kinds of revisionary or critical responses have appeared as of today[36]: (α) Kawashima is wrong in underestimating the real capability of the Japanese people in legal exchanges: even if they are reluctant to use official litigation, they can deploy unofficial procedures, or, they have certain abilities to make legal claims without relying on the language of rights;[37] (β) Kawashima is wrong in attributing the causes of the aversion to litigation to Japanese culture, because the real problem lie in the institutional structure of Japanese law that makes litigation prohibitive;[38] (γ) Kawashima is wrong because the aversion in question is actually the result of the economically rational behaviour the Japanese people show when faced with a given institutional structure;[39] (δ) Kawashima is wrong in taking seriously the Western ideals that are themselves biased by the patriarchal and male-centred model of law and society;[40] and (ε) While Kawashima is basically correct in

35 Takeyoshi Kawashima, *Nihonjin no Hoishiki* [*Legal Consciousness of the Japanese People*] (Iwanami Shoten 1967). Also, Takeyoshi Kawashima, 'Dispute Resolution in Contemporary Japan' in Curtis J Millhaupt and others (eds), *Japanese Law in Context* (Harvard University Asia Center 2001) 115ff. Although this might seem a reprise of (1c), it is actually a form of (2b). For Kawashima was not such a radical Western individualist as he also affirmed limiting rights-claims in some collectivity in Japan.

36 Here we can find the stage of the communicative extension of normative translation that includes some reprises. See text accompanying notes 23–27. Also, as an overview of this debate, cf Eric A Feldman, *The Ritual of Rights in Japan* (CUP 2000) ch 7, esp 148ff; Eric A Feldman, 'Law, Culture, and Conflict' in Daniel H Foote (ed), *Law in Japan* (University of Washington Press 2007) esp 58ff.

37 Cf Takao Tanase, 'The Empty Space of the Modern in Japanese Law Discourse' in David Nelken and Johannes Feest (eds), *Adapting Legal Cultures* (Hart 2001) 193ff.

38 John O Haley, 'The Myth of the Reluctant Litigant' in Millhaupt and others (n 35) 118ff.

39 J Mark Ramseyer and Minoru Nakazato, 'The Rational Litigant' in Millhaupt and others (n 35) 122ff.

40 Cf Sachiko Kaneko, 'The Struggle for Legal Rights and Reforms: A Historical View' in Kumiko Fujimura Fanselow (ed), *Transforming Japan* (Feminist Press at CUNY 2011) 7ff; Vera Mackie, *Feminism in Modern Japan* (CUP 2003) 4ff, ch 6.

paying attention to the cultural factors concerning rights in Japan, he is wrong in totally denouncing them from an 'occidentalistic' stance, because there are some historical cases that show that rights consciousness exists in Japan.[41]

These responses to Kawashima's claim are interpretive reactions to the Japanese idea of rights, which reflect corresponding moral attitudes about the significance of rights in the modernization of Japanese law and politics. Kawashima's claim was a typical result of the modernist perspective in Japan after WWII that tends to emphasize the Western ideal of rights as implying justice between dignified individual persons, and that the Japanese legal consciousness lacks this important condition due to cultural obstacles. Thus we can say that the position (α) is still against a Westernized reading of the situation of rights in Japan and tends to emphasize the working of traditional legal consciousness in Japan. This position belongs to the case of (1a) discussed earlier; the positions (β) and (γ) share some democratic understanding of Japanese legal consciousness and denounce the political-structural obstacles for the expression of it (1b); the position (δ) is critical of all the modernist or gendered tendencies (1c); and the position (ε) is an intermediate one which tends to still be critical of the Japanese practice of rights (2a).

Incidentally, we might also say that there are some other possible claims[42]: (ζ) Kawashima is basically correct in focusing on to the cultural factors concerning rights in Japan, but is wrong in thinking that simply accepting the Western idea of rights into Japanese society is an effective solution – we should try to find some gradual strategy to adapt the idea of rights to Japanese society (2b); we should create a more universal idea of rights by exploiting some universal ideal of human agency (2c); or (θ) we should pursue a more flexible understanding of the idea of rights by accommodating the contextual parameters of societal culture in different societies (3b).

All of these claims are to be grasped as the contested understandings of rights in the reprise of normative translation concerning the idea of rights in Japan. Although these claims are not concerned with the direct translations of the idea of rights, they include the modal qualifications for the idea of rights, even if the translation itself is the same as '権利', the typical translation of 'rights'.[43] Also, it is very important to note that the rights culture in Japan is to be considered dynamic mosaic as opposed to static and monolithic. It is a blend of various translational claims regarding the idea of rights, thereby people interpret Japanese and foreign legal culture. And, those claims themselves constitute significant elements of the multiplicity of the rights culture in Japan today. Still, which interpretation one wishes to endorse depends on

[41] Feldman, *Ritual of Rights* (n 36) 157ff.

[42] These possible claims are imaginary ones, except for (η), a form of the case of (2c), that is my own suggestion.

[43] Here normative translation is to be understood not as one-to-one relation for a concept but rather as the interrelation between possible implications of a concept.

one's ideational perspective on Japanese legal culture, particularly on one's own view on political morality for or against the significance of rights.

Lastly, the two kinds of reprise discussed so far are non-exclusive and may be complexly intertwined. In other words, there are at least two axes in the reprise of normative translation that tie together various possible dimensions in the reprise.[44] The combination of the two reprises makes the web of normative translation wide and dense. As the constitution of this web seems so complex and rich, it might be difficult to fully explicate it. It would suffice for the moment that my exploration could make clear some uniqueness of this web for the dynamic making of law.

III THE WEAVING OF NORMATIVE TRANSLATION

The problem that remains is, how all of what has been discussed so far about the generative expansion of normative translation is related to lawmaking in a condition of heterogeneity of law. In this regard, the generative features of *iNT* discussed so far, namely, the formal and substantive translational relationship between different concepts in the extension of normative translation and the open conditions of legal reasoning, as well as the transpositional and implicational reprise of normative translation, are themselves the interpretive constituents for the integral making of law, which bring together in an organic whole of how people think about law. These features also indicate the driving force for the dynamic development of law.

Particularly important operations of those constituents for lawmaking are of course concerned with the substantial consistency of various ideas and arguments in law. When we recognize the translational starting points and the subsequent process as discussed, we may consider such workings as the fine-tuning of those ideas and arguments; fine-tuning that is performed by the considerations of the general predicative conditions, the specific factual limitations, the evaluative requirements, and the logical arrangements of law. These workings incessantly operate together to shape and change the law in question. Of course, this does not mean that these workings operate negatively to maintain the earlier shape of law and its starting translational circumstances, but rather that they operate to transform the existing law by often leaving behind its initial circumstances. I call this entire operation the *weaving* of normative translation.

I wish to add in this regard some notes on the problem of the confluence of *Legal Traditions* in the sense expounded by H Patrick Glenn.[45] My discussion so far on the extension and reprise of normative translation in law may help explain the confluence of *Legal Traditions*. What Glenn coined 'confluence' is the interaction between *Legal Traditions* and the driving force in the making of hybrid law.

44 Of course, this includes the simple reiteration of the original translation of rights.

45 H Patrick Glenn, *Common Laws* (OUP 2005) 118ff.

Glenn mentioned only macroscopically the modernization of East Asian law.[46] However, from the viewpoint of the weaving process explicated above, it is normative translation that is central to the activity of mixing different legal resources to establish legal practice. From this viewpoint, the case of the translation of rights discussed in this chapter can be seen as a typical case of confluence as well: the idea of rights in Japan is a product of the confluence of several legal perspectives that originated in different societies such as Anglo-Saxon, French, Dutch, German, Chinese, and Japanese. The nature of confluence may get more complicated if we include economic or feminist understandings of rights.[47] Various legal views and ideas are translationally contested here, though the result of which cannot be ensured.

The important problem in the weaving of normative translation is concerned with the *reconfiguration* of normative translation. This is the problem in which various normative translations in a legal practice are to be integrated at some point in time. Here we need to discuss the conditions of reconfiguration, as well as the further introduction of novel ideas and the deeper involvements of them in some cyclic shaping of law in its entirety. As far as law continues to develop itself, further introduction of novel ideas occur incessantly as new problems are posed against the initial ideas; the deeper involvement indicates that, if the introduction of novel concepts is inevitable, law almost always use them somehow to develop itself. The important problem here is concerned with the deeper reconfiguration which leads to a positive cycle of normative translation in law.

I think the question of the reconfiguration of normative translation is a problem of commensuration of divergent legal views from a justificatory standpoint. This thought indicates that divergent views of law can be integrated through certain communicative manners, as suggested in the previous section; it is the contest of *models of law* that carries this communicative integration of normative translation. Each of us tries to interpretively work out a better model of law that can reconcile different permutations of legal views by erasing, omitting, or skipping the radical views that each of us cannot reasonably hold in the model. In this better model of law, various forces of normative translation spark the formation, maintenance, and transformation of various key legal ideas and arguments, as well as creating new legal perspectives to handle new problems. Here, law becomes the product of the *weaving* of normative translation and thus reformulates itself by adapting to new settings through its own features in the model of law in question. This is also related to what

46 In his *Legal Traditions of the World*, Glenn did not explicitly make this point, but rather suggested it. See Glenn, *LTW* (n 7) esp 342ff, 365ff. Still, I think that Glenn anticipated this point before he explicitly thematized it in his *Common Laws*. On the meaning of 'macroscopic', compare, John Bell, Chapter 3 in this volume.

47 The drafting of Article 416 of Japanese Civil Code in 1890 is a prime example of confluence. It is the product of the scholarly discussion about the significance of Western legal materials for combining or revising them to make legal rules which could be effective in Japanese society. See Ko Hasegawa, 'A Glance at the Dynamics of "Confluence" in a Legal System – Notes on H Patrick Glenn's Insights Concerning Legal Traditions of the World' (2016) 7 *TLT* 1, 4ff.

I have once called the metamorphosis of norms,[48] in which law is continually tested by accommodating various possible legal views from within through an adequate model of itself.

Of course, when the significance of a model of law is widely contested, the moral orientation underlying that model is to be seriously debated. In the case of rights translations mentioned before, there work some moral principles for leading the idea of rights in question. In this regard, possible legal views get reconfigured as the *parameters* of our own thinking and doing concerning the matter of rights. And each of these parameters claims its priority in a different way.[49] In the example of rights discussed before, a conservative reconfiguration of normative translation might place a stronger version of (α) at the integral centre and replace the earlier translation that is initially perceived as wrong, while regarding (β) and (γ) as the compromising or derivative applications of (α) and disregarding (δ) and (ε) as the mistaken cases of (α). A moderate reconfiguration might place (ε) at the integral centre and replace the initial translation as incorrect, while partially recognizing the adequacy of (β) and (γ), but excluding (α) and (δ) as exceptional cases of (ε). Or some other critical reconfiguration might place (δ) at the integral centre and replace the initial translation as wrong, while resolving all other cases as surface cases of (δ). Of course, these are simple possibilities of reconfiguration, and what to choose from these possibilities is itself a problem of interpretive justification in the cluster of normative translations of ideas of rights. In establishing the entire space of rights with the reprise of normative translation, we proceed in and out of the reprise and seek its entirety through locating the parameters of various normative translations under a moral perspective of rights.[50] The weaving of normative translation is generally the incessant contest among moral views that leads to the realization of important legal ideas in society.

Incidentally, this process of reconfiguration is to be characterized as the *constructive* reconfiguration of normative translation. This process is repeated to positively adapt normative translation to a new situation. Meanwhile, when we are not fully aware of the possibility of this adaptation, we might analyse and refute normative translation in some critical way. This can be called the *therapeutic* reconfiguration of normative translation, which is negative in the sense that it aims at the critical deconstruction of normative translation. Yet the two reconfigurations may be complementary, although priority is placed on the constructive one. The therapeutic reconfiguration matters after the constructive one is completed, simply because the former needs the latter as its target. This does not diminish the significance of the

48 Ko Hasegawa, 'How Can Law Hold Hope in Cultural Complexity? Critical Comments on Prof. Annelise Riles' View of Law and Culture' (2011) <https://papers.ssrn.com/sol3/papers.cfm?abstract_id=2472538>.

49 This means that the contest of the priority of parameters is itself a commensuration problem.

50 Simple analyses of legal justification or grounding of law is to be understood as capturing the surface structure of this interpretive reconfiguration; the deeper structure needs to be formed with substantive moral views for the direction of law.

therapeutic reconfiguration by making it a secondary reflection; it helps *ex post facto* revisions or corrections of the orientation of the constructive reconfiguration.

CONCLUDING REMARKS

It is easy for us to assume that law is a normative system that displays a unity, especially in the form of modern national law. However, as the globalization of law and the complexities of national laws develop rapidly, the assumption discussed earlier becomes untenable and has to be reconsidered. Meanwhile, we also know that all laws in the world, especially those in East Asia, have to cope with translational and interpretive complexities as well as divergent cultural circumstances. We need a better, dynamic view of law that takes into account these fluid situations. This is the grand theme that I have tried to explore through a theory of normative translation in law. The task is just begun; we have to continue further to attain a more thorough understanding of this dynamism.

As I suggested at the outset of this chapter, the leading thought of my theorizing of normative translation is a philosophical-hermeneutic view of human thinkings and doings. This view is guided by the idea that the interpretive process of shaping law works in a nested way. Thus, normative translation in law, both external and internal, operates in this way as well. This is *a* hypothesis. Yet, we might have to beware that this thought may lead to some autopoietic perspective of the complex nature of law in terms of normative translation. If normative translation works in multiple dimensions in law, we will arrive at the result that the complexity of normative translation is itself a necessary driving force and framework for the transformation of law.[51] This view seems invaluable as the next step for the theory of normative translation in law in order to better understand today's transnational movement of law.

[51] Gadamer, *Truth and Method* (n 2) ch 2; Iser (n 2) ch 6.

14

Statehood as Process: The Modern State Between Closure and Openness

Gunnar Folke Schuppert[*]

In his well-received book *The Cosmopolitan State*, Patrick Glenn vividly described the development of the modern state as a yin/yang process: on one side, 'elements of closure' as instruments of strategy, and on the other, the 'cosmopolitan way'.[1] With regard to the 'elements of closure', he identified three of them: 'boundaries' (the most obvious one), 'hierarchy', understood as 'governance capacity', and – perhaps surprising at first – 'writing'. As for the 'cosmopolitan way', in Glenn's view, it can be approached in three ways, namely, through 'common laws', 'constitutionalism', and, last but not least, through 'institutional cosmopolitism'. It is not my goal in this chapter to comment on Glenn's lines of argumentation or to test their plausibility,[2] but rather, to proceed further along the path proposed by Patrick Glenn and illustrate through three concepts the sequence of processes that limit opening up. I have chosen the following three concepts, which seem especially apt for visualizing these processes of yin and yang:

(i) Knowledge,
(ii) Sovereignty, and
(iii) Citizenship.

Let us begin with the nationalization and trans-nationalization of knowledge.

I KNOWLEDGE

The generation and dissemination of knowledge – and this is particularly true for judicial knowledge – was largely enabled and favoured by the invention of writing[3] and the triumphal march of printing.[4] The textualization of knowledge led – to echo

[*] The English translation of this Chapter is courtesy of Sandra Pontow.

[1] H Patrick Glenn, *The Cosmopolitan State* (OUP 2013) (hereafter Glenn, *TCS*).

[2] Compare my review of Glenn's book with the same title, Gunnar Folke Schuppert, 'The Cosmopolitan State' (2014) 22 *Rechtsgeschichte/Leg Hist* 294.

[3] See Thomas Vesting, *Die Medien des Rechts*, vol 2 [*The Media of the Law*] (Velbrück Wissenschaft 2011).

[4] Regarding printing as a 'fire accelerant' for the Reformation, see Thomas Kaufmann's compelling description of the history of the Reformation as a history of communication in Thomas Kaufmann,

Peter Burke – to an 'explosion of knowledge'.[5] Given this uncontested fact, we should turn our attention to the reasons why Glenn begins his presentation of 'elements of closure' with, of all things, 'writing'. As Glenn explains, textualization is not inherently associated with closure. However, in relation to drawing boundaries and as a component of 'governance capacity', the written word can take on the character of excluding the other:

> Arguably, in itself writing is not a form of closure, since anything can be written and, in principle at least, anything can be read. Yet writing has played a significant role in the closure that has been brought about in contemporary states because of its combination with the other elements of closure discussed in this section. Writing is open, but writing as an instrument of hierarchy within fixed boundaries becomes an instrument of closure.[6]

This argument by Glenn, which he relates primarily to the writing of legal texts, becomes even more plausible if we now replace 'writing' with 'knowledge', and at the same time consider how it makes sense or could even be appealing[7] to reserve knowledge primarily for one's own use and to keep others from ready access to this knowledge; in seeking the reasons for applying such a strategy of 'closure', I have come up with the following three.

The first compelling reason is that of 'secrecy', which is practised by states especially when it promises an advantage in the competition for power with other states, for example, keeping military knowledge to itself at all costs, in order to keep a possibly decisive advance in knowledge to itself. In her fascinating book *The Secret*

Erlöste und Verdammte: Eine Geschichte der Reformation [The Saved and the Damned: A History of the Reformation] (CH Beck 2016).

5 Peter Burke, *Die Explosion des Wissens: Von der Enzyclopédie bis Wikipedia* (Wagenbach 2014). An English version is Peter Burke, *A Social History of Knowledge: From the Encyclopédie to Wikipedia*, vol 2 (Polity Press 2012).

6 Glenn, *TCS* (n 1) 52.

7 An attractiveness of this kind may be derived from the property of knowledge as goods: an instructive example of this is the portrayal of the journey of Gotha's Prince Friedrich I, always in financial difficulty, who visited Amsterdam in 1688 in search of a formula for manufacturing gold, as told in Martin Mulsow, 'Das Geheimnis von Amsterdam, Politik, Alchemie und die Kommodifizierung von Wissen im 17. Jahrhundert' ['The Secret of Amsterdam: Politics, Alchemy, and the Commodification of Knowledge in the 17th Century'] (2017) Max-Weber-Kolleg Erfurt Workshop Report. Martin Mulsow described the contours of such a market for secret knowledge for us as follows:

> There had been a market for common knowledge well before the 17th century. However, it was in the late 17th century and in cosmopolitan places such as Amsterdam that it took on a new dimension and was increasingly interwoven with other financial activities and force fields. Research is still needed on the exact configuration of the knowledge market in alchemy here, and the nature of its unwritten laws. It was a transnational market, with providers from England, Holland, Italy, and Germany, and also with customers from the greatest variety of countries, who stood in competition with each other, without any of this being expressed openly. Such closure made the market delicate and inscrutable, even for its actors. No one around Friedrich was allowed to know about it. Nobody in Gotha ever discovered the secret of Amsterdam.

Ibid, 25.

War, Eva Horn clearly described this strategy of concealing scientific knowledge with extreme military relevance, using as an example the research essential to the development of an operational atomic bomb. Contrary to normal scientific principles, nothing was published, the research had to be compartmentalized internally, in order to provide nobody within the research apparatus with full knowledge; at the same time, the constant fear of external 'leaks' had to be met.[8]

It is not a long road from this example of an arcane science of military technology to an *arcane knowledge* of, for example, at least in Germany, the way of managing the whole *science of administration*, in this case not for the primary goal of shutting out other states – though this was also a part of it – but rather, to shut out its own citizenry, who were granted only general rights to information about public administration as a result of the influence of the European Union (eg the Federal Environmental Information Act). Other examples of rights of access include the Scandinavian model and the United States' approach,[9] ultimately through the Freedom of Information Act.[10] This *bureaucratic arcane tradition* has been compellingly described by Michael Stolleis[11] and Arno Scherzberg.[12]

Today, by contrast, the prevailing notion is one of a 'right to know' – as an expression of a truly fundamental shift – to which Pierre Rosanvallon, in his book, *The Good Government*,[13] attributes central importance, both with respect to the concept of 'open government' and with respect to what he calls the 'legible society':

> Attempts to realize open government and a legible society are two complementary methods of citizen reappropriation. Alongside exercises in participatory democracy that seek to diversify, and thereby enrich, opportunities for individual expression and involvement in order to correct the shortcomings of the electoral-representative system, the idea behind both these methods is to reduce the distance between the governed and their governors, as well as the distance separating the governed from one another, through greater knowledge. Under both methods, the right to know also has the property of going beyond the traditional division between human rights (which protect the individual) and civil rights (which organize participation in a political body). It creates a right of personhood, allowing individuals greater control over the world in which they live, while at the same time giving tangible effect to citizenship, so that the reality of social ties will be immediately apparent.[14]

8 Eva Horn, *Der geheime Krieg. Verrat, Spionage und moderne Fiktion* [*The Secret War: Betrayal, Espionage, and Modern Fiction*] (Fischer 2007) 387.

9 Freedom of Information Act 1966, 5 USC § 552.

10 See Matthias Rossi, *Informationszugangsfreiheit und Verfassungsrecht* [*Free Access to Information and Constitutional Law*] (Duncker & Humblot 2004).

11 Michael Stolleis, *Staat und Staatsräson in der frühen Neuzeit* [*State and State Reason in the Early Modern Era*] (Suhrkamp 1990).

12 Arno Scherzberg, *Die Öffentlichkeit der Verwaltung* [*Public Access to Administration*] (Nomos 2000).

13 Pierre Rosanvallon, *The Good Government* (Harvard University Press 2018).

14 Ibid, 167–68.

The third reason I cite here can be characterized as the deliberate *profiling of one's own national statehood*. One aspect of this phenomenon is the process, which accelerated in the nineteenth century, of the *nationalization of knowledge*, which Peter Burke termed a pursuit of politics by other means, and, in this regard, referenced a statement by the prominent scientist Herrmann von Helmholtz that men of science constituted a kind of organized army, as their endeavour to enhance knowledge was in the best interest of the whole state.[15] Regarding the forms of expression of the nationalization of knowledge, Burke writes that projects such as the foundation of museums and galleries were marked by the idea of *nation building* or *national pride*. Examples he gives include the National Art Gallery of the Hague (1800), the Danish National Museum (1809), the Prague National Museum (1819), the National Gallery in London (1824), and the German National Museum in Nürnberg (1852). Most of these initiatives were undertaken by the respective governments, but there were also major private undertakings, as in the case of the National Historical Museum in Hillerød (1878), financially supported by Jacob Christian Jacobsen, the owner of the Carlsberg Brewery, who possibly saw this as a response to Denmark's defeat in the German–Danish War of 1864. Founding libraries and archives also reflected nation building. The former Royal Library in Paris was turned into the Bibliothèque nationale de France in 1793. The Royal Library in the Hague was founded in 1798 as the National Library, followed by the Hungarian National Library (1803), Spain's Biblioteca Nacional (1836, formerly the Biblioteca Real), Italy's Biblioteca Nazionale (1861, the year of Italian unification), and the Bulgarian National Library (1879).[16]

This political focus on nationalizing knowledge in the interests of raising national prestige became obsolete. Today, it is essentially uncontested that beyond a 'denationalization'[17] of knowledge, one must speak of a *globalization of knowledge*,[18] a development that is virtually irreversible given the progress of *digitization*, including in science. Google Book Search, Creative Commons, and Open Access are the new forms of knowledge transmission in the digital world;[19] at the moment that Google's plans as a global player in the digital age proves successful, the classical National Library will have been replaced by a digital world library.

So much for the first of the three concepts.

15 Burke, *Explosion des Wissens* (n 5) 227.

16 Ibid, 230.

17 See ibid, 251ff.

18 See the essays in Jürgen Renn (ed), *The Globalization of Knowledge in History* (Max Planck Research Library for the History and Development of Knowledge Studies 2012).

19 Olaf Sosnitza, 'Google Book Search, Creative Commons und Open Access – Neue Formen der Wissensvermittlung in der digitalen Welt?' ['Google Book Search, Creative Commons and Open Access – New Forms of Knowledge Transmission in the Digital World?'] (2010) 3 *Rechtswissenschaft. Zeitschrift für rechtswissenschaftliche Forschung* 225.

II SOVEREIGNTY

Sovereignty is, without a doubt, the legal-political concept that best illustrates the interplay between 'closure' and the 'cosmopolitan way'.[20] In the early modern territorial state, sovereignty was seen as having the character of a protective outer skin, but over time, this characterization has been overtaken by the concept of 'cosmopolitan sovereignty'.[21] Let us consider the sequence in which this occurred.

1 *On the Twofold Exclusion Function of the Concept of Sovereignty*

As so-called internal sovereignty, the notion of sovereignty refers to the removal of power from the major intermediary forces so important to the medieval political order, such as nobility and clergy, which concentrated all power solely in the person of the sovereign:

> The historical function of the notion of sovereignty consists of the establishment of a binding critical centre of power and emancipation from the claims of co-governance by supra- and sub-national actors. Simultaneously, this signalled the modern autonomy of politics from other functional areas of society. In addition, the political system claimed for itself the regulation of all other areas of societal function, such as religion, science, and economy – even if it did not necessarily interfere in them. At the same time, it shifted from the polycratic structures of the Middle Ages to a new, strictly hierarchical mode of control.[22]

Of greater importance for our ongoing dialogue with Patrick Glenn, however, is 'external sovereignty', whose nature is aptly captured by the term, the 'state's sovereignty armour' (*staatlicher Souveränitätspanzer*).[23] By traditional understanding, this refers to the independence of the state from other powers, especially from those of another state:

> The reason that independence, above all else . . . became a major criterion for external sovereignty . . . is that by virtue of their territorial character, states by definition can only be thought of in the plural, as a plurality. Since they are all

20 On sovereignty as a basic legal and political concept, see Dieter Grimm, 'Souveränität – zur aktuellen Leistungsfähigkeit eines rechtlich-politischen Grundbegriffs' ['Sovereignty – On the Current Efficacy of a Basic Legal-Political Concept'] in Tine Stein, Hubertus Buchstein, and Claus Offe (eds), *Souveränität, Recht, Moral. Die Grundlagen politischer Gemeinschaft* [*Sovereignty, Law, Morality: Foundations of Political Community*] (Campus 2007).

21 Term in Ulrich Beck and Edgar Grande, *Das kosmopolitische Europa* [*Cosmopolitan Europe*] (Suhrkamp 2004); positively adopted in Christine Landfried, 'Kosmopolitische Souveränität' ['Cosmopolitan Sovereignty'] in Stein, Buchstein, and Offe (n 20).

22 Peter Niesen, 'Souveränität' ['Sovereignty'] in Stefan Gosepath, Wilfried Hinsch, and Beate Rössler (eds), *Handbuch der Politischen Philosophie und Sozialphilosophie* [*Handbook of Political Philosophy and Social Philosophy*], vol 2 (de Gruyter 2008) 1206.

23 Concept in Ulrich K Preuß, 'Souveränität – Zwischenbemerkungen zu einem Schlüsselbegriff des Politischen' ['Sovereignty – Incidental Remarks on a Key Concept in Politics'] in Stein, Buchstein, and Offe (n 20) 319.

> equally characterized by the consistent feature of the highest sovereignty over their respective territory, they are all legally equal. However, in order to be able to effectively operate as lord of their own house, this claim to power must also be respected externally and protected from interference.[24]

I find the reflections by Ulrich K Preuß on the constructive parallels between the concept of sovereignty and the concept of property relevant and instructive, in that they are both 'legal institutions with an exclusive character'.[25]

> Over the course of time, this classical, somewhat 'introverted'[26] understanding of sovereignty – similar to the attempts to nationalize knowledge just described – has been transcended, and, indeed, because of a fundamental change in understanding the function of international law, in a twofold way. For one thing, there is a general agreement that sovereignty has been transmuted from an exclusive right of rule and disposition into a *communicative and interactive right of participation*. The understanding of sovereignty has thus been 'adjusted' to fit the new conditions of international politics, even while maintaining the original function of sovereignty to protect state self-determination.[27] At the same time, there is broad consensus that we are dealing with a *process of constitutionalization of international law*,[28] one that is progressively implementing the insight, in part under the influence of the Charter of the United Nations and its legal principles, that one should conceive of the international order as a *constitutional order* sui generis.

It seems questionable to me, however, whether it is justifiable to speak, with Ulrich Beck and Edgar Grande, of a 'cosmopolitan sovereignty';[29] certainly, this term sounds appealing and would also have served well as a title for the book by Patrick Glenn that is the focus of this chapter, but I think that overall, it pushes the

24 Ibid, 317.

25 Ibid, 317–18.

26 See Stephan Hobe, *Der offene Verfassungsstaat zwischen Souveränität und Interdependenz. Eine Studie zur Wandlung des Staatsbegriffs der deutschsprachigen Staatslehre im Kontext internationaler institutionalisierter Kooperation* [*The Open Constitutional State between Sovereignty and Interdependency: A Study on the Change of the Notion of the State in German Political Science in the Context of International Institutionalized Cooperation*] (Duncker & Humblot 1998) 49ff.

27 Preuß (n 23) 324.

28 Jochen A Frowein, 'Konstitutionalisierung des Völkerrechts' ['The Constitutionalization of International Law'] in Klaus Dicke (ed), *Völkerrecht und Internationales Privatrecht in einem sich globalisierenden internationalen System* [*International Law and International Private Law in a Globalizing International System*] (CF Müller 2000); Bardo Fassbender, 'The Meaning of International Constitutional Law: Towards World Constitutionalism' in Nicholas Tsagourias (ed), *Transnational Constitutionalism: International and European Perspectives* (CUP 2005); Ronald St J Macdonald and Douglas M Johnston (eds), *Towards World Constitutionalism: Issues in the Legal Ordering of the World Community* (Nijhoff 2005); Anne Peters, 'Global Constitutionalism in a Nutshell' in Klaus Dicke and others (eds), *Liber Amicorum Jost Delbrück* (Duncker & Humblot 2005).

29 Christine Landfried expresses great certainty about this point. See Landfried (n 21) 296 ('Souveränität kann im Zeitalter von Entgrenzung, Internationalisierung und Globalisierung nur kosmopolitische Souveränität sein.') ('In an age of vanishing boundaries, internationalization, and globalization, sovereignty can only be cosmopolitan sovereignty.').

pendulum too far from yin to yang. At this point, I would want to join neither the chorus of those who, with determined radicalism, declare the notion of sovereignty as obsolete,[30] nor the chorus of those who – in completely the opposite direction – predict a shining future in the beautiful world of cosmopolitanism. Instead, I would return once more to the parallels to the concept of property enunciated by Ulrich K Preuß, and to further pursue this duality – to introduce the *idea of responsibility*, which is immanent to both the concepts of property and sovereignty.

2 *On the Concept of Responsible Sovereignty*

What is meant by the concept of 'responsible sovereignty' becomes apparent if we first take a quick look at what is called the 'social responsibility' of property.

i On the Social Responsibility of Property

The social responsibility of property is a familiar trope in the (German) legal system at the level of constitutional law, as highlighted in Article 14(2) of the Basic Law, based on the model of Article 153(3) of the Weimar Constitution. As the notion of sustainability, which is so popular today, is derived from forestry management,[31] so the notion of a responsibility regarding property has long been associated with the realm of real estate property. Neighbourly considerations and multifaceted integration of the requirements of community (the need for local recreation areas, for example) have always been characteristic of real estate property. A just legal and social order – as Peter Badura states in his presentation of property law[32] – requires that general public interest in land be brought to bear much more broadly than for other classes of property: 'Land is not simply equivalent either economically or in its societal meaning as other assets: it cannot be treated the same way in legal exchange as a mobile asset.'[33]

In other words, the extent of responsibility in property varies according to the type of property and its social function and can therefore be flexibly prescribed by the legislator:

> The law that shapes the content and bounds of property limits property rights and their exercise, for example in the interests of orderly urban development . . . for the

30 For an overview discussion, see Gunnar F Schuppert, 'Souveränität – überholter Begriff, wandlungsfähiges Konzept or "Born in 1576, but Still Going Strong?"' ['Sovereignty – An Obsolete Term, Transformable Concept or "Born in 1576, but Still Going Strong?"'] in Stein, Buchstein, and Offe (n 20) 251–69.

31 On the history of the notion of sustainability, see Michael Rödel, 'Die Invasion der "Nachhaltigkeit": Eine linguistische Analyse eines politischen und ökonomischen Modeworts' ['The Invasion of "Sustainability": A Linguistic Analysis of a Political and Economic Buzzword'] (2013) 2 *Deutsche Sprache* 115.

32 Peter Badura, *Staatsrecht. Systematische Erläuterung des Grundgesetzes* [*Constitutional Law: A Systematic Explanation of the Basic Law*] (6th edn, CH Beck 2015) 286.

33 BVerfGE 52, 1/32.

> protection of nature and the environment and for art and culture, through legislation concerning water rights and mining rights. It also restricts property owners through responsibilities, such as for protecting land and forest industry production or in the interests of historical preservation.[34]

From this, one can learn that the character of a legal position, such as that property as a primary and exclusive right for private use in no way rules out that this right is phrased in such absolute terms, contains from the outset, *responsibilities*, which becomes actualized under certain circumstances. If one formulates this idea generally, then it is transferrable to any structurally comparable legal position.

ii On the Obligations of Sovereignty

The transformation of the notion of sovereignty is most clearly expressed in the 'discovery' of the 'responsibility to protect', as has been documented in the influential Report of the International Commission on Intervention and State Sovereignty.[35] The parallels between the interpretations of responsibility in the civil and constitutional concepts of property, on the one hand, and the concept of sovereignty in international law, on the other, seem fully evident: while the emphasis of social responsibility in property significantly limits the 'sovereign' prerogative of the property owner to 'deal with the object as he wishes',[36] and 'to forbid the influence of another on the object',[37] the emphasis on the responsibility of states to protect their population significantly limits state sovereignty. In both

[34] Badura (n 32) 236.

[35] International Commission on Intervention and State Sovereignty (ICISS), *The Responsibility to Protect* (IDRC 2001). The *Report* formulates the basic principles as follows:

> (1) BASIC PRINCIPLES
>
> A. State sovereignty implies responsibility, and the primary responsibility for the protection of its people lies with the state itself.
> B. Where a population is suffering serious harm, as a result of internal war, insurgency, repression or state failure, and the state in question is unwilling or unable to halt or avert it, the principle of non-intervention yields to the international responsibility to protect.
>
> (2) FOUNDATIONS
>
> The foundations of the responsibility to protect, as a guiding principle for the international community of states, lie in:
>
> A. obligations inherent in the concept of sovereignty;
> B. the responsibility of the Security Council, under Article 24 of the UN Charter, for the maintenance of international peace and security;
> C. specific legal obligations under human rights and human protection declarations, covenants and treaties, international humanitarian law, and national law;
> D. the developing practice of states, regional organizations, and the Security Council itself.

Ibid, xi.

[36] Bürgerliches Gesetzbuch [BGB] [Civil Code] para 903.

[37] Ibid, para 904.

instances, the restriction on property or sovereignty does not come from the outside, but rather is conceived of as an inherent responsibility.

The Report cited earlier refers to – as we might call it – the 'doctrine of inherent responsibility' in the clearest terms:

> The defence of state sovereignty, by even its strongest supporters, does not include any claim of the unlimited power of a state to do what it wants to its own people. The Commission heard no such claim at any stage during our worldwide consultations. It is acknowledged that sovereignty implies a dual responsibility: externally – to respect the sovereignty of other states, and internally, to respect the dignity and basic rights of all the people within the state. In international human rights covenants, in UN practice, and in state practice itself, sovereignty is now understood as embracing this dual responsibility. Sovereignty as responsibility has become the minimum content of good international citizenship.[38]

The important practical consequence of such 'thinking of sovereignty as responsibility' is that the state and its administrators are responsible to its citizens and to the international community for their behaviour, and if necessary, can be held to account. The Report states this as follows:

> Thinking of sovereignty as responsibility, in a way that is being increasingly recognized in state practice, has a threefold significance. First, it implies that the state authorities are responsible for the functions of protecting the safety and lives of citizens and promotion of their welfare. Secondly, it suggests that the national political authorities are responsible to the citizens internally and to the international community through the UN. And thirdly, it means that the agents of state are responsible for their actions; that is to say, they are accountable for their acts of commission and omission. The case for thinking of sovereignty in these terms is strengthened by the ever-increasing impact of international human rights norms, and the increasing impact in international discourse of the concept of human security.[39]

In his 'brief history of the present',[40] Andreas Rödder discussed the 'responsibility to protect' under the heading 'between the imperialism of human rights and indifference: the responsibility to protect and humanitarian intervention', writing as follows:

> The sovereignty of the state and universal human rights were repeatedly called upon as the foundation and ideals of the international order, especially since 1990 – and often stand in competition with each other. A theoretical way out is the concept of responsibility to protect, formulated in 2005 by the United Nations and accepted by 192 nations .... When a state fails to meet its responsibility to protect its population,

38 ICISS (n 35) 8.

39 Ibid, 13.

40 Andreas Rödder, *Eine kurze Geschichte der Gegenwart* [*A Brief History of the Present*] (CH Beck 2015).

protection of humans from severe violations of human rights justifies the right of armed outside intervention, even against the sovereignty of this state.[41]

In other words, the notion of sovereignty that established its global position as a constant partner of the 'nationalization of the world', and which seemed unassailable as a cornerstone of the Westphalian world order, finds its function as the protective outer skin of statehood usurped by another concept with global position, namely the idea of human rights, to the extent that the claim of human rights to global validity lends it the particular function of permeating or penetrating this skin. One could refer in this instance to an internal conflict in the global language of law as a 'language of politics'.[42]

So much for the second concept to be discussed in this chapter.

III CITIZENSHIP

The third concept I discuss in this chapter is that of *citizenship*. In this context, citizenship refers to a status of membership, which 'is set up to constitute an inside and an outside, an *inclusion* as well as an *exclusion*'.[43] The legal institution of citizenship, therefore, seems to me to be especially well suited to illustrate and concretize the basic theme of Glenn's book, the complex polarity of 'elements of closure' and the 'cosmopolitan way'. Let us begin with ancient Rome.

1 *The Granting of Citizenship as an Integration Strategy of the Roman Empire*

In their book *Empires in World History*, Jane Burbank and Frederick Cooper deal extensively with the repertoire of imperial power[44] and assigned special significance to law.[45] In their view, the granting of Roman citizenship was an integral component of Rome's expansion strategy: the expansion of citizenship was both a reward for fulfilment of duties and an instrument for expanding the area of loyalty.[46] Leaving the Roman Empire behind and – crossing the Alps – one can take a huge leap into the last years of the nineteenth and the early twentieth centuries.

41 Ibid, 346.

42 Details on the language of the law as a 'language of politics' may be found in Gunnar F Schuppert, *A Global History of Ideas in the Language of Law* (Max Planck Institute for Legal History and Legal Theory 2021) <https://library.oapen.org/handle/20.500.12657/47096>.

43 Dieter Gosewinkel, *Schutz und Freiheit? Staatsbürgerschaft in Europa im 20. und 21. Jahrhundert* [Protection and Freedom? Citizenship in Europe in the 20th and 21st Century] (Suhrkamp 2016) 633 (emphasis added).

44 Jane Burbank and Frederick Cooper, *Empires in World History: Power and the Politics of Difference* (Princeton University Press 2010).

45 On the law as a unifying bond of imperial rule, see also Peter Heather, *The Fall of the Roman Empire: A New History of Rome and the Barbarians* (OUP 2007).

46 Burbank and Cooper (n 44) 54ff.

2 *An Institution of Closed Statehood: Citizenship in the German Reich*[47]

The legal institution of citizenship can be strategically deployed to further imperial integration policy, but much more often, it has been used to exclude 'undesirable' groups of people from belonging to a state entity.[48] For example, the Prussian Citizenship Act was primarily an *exclusion policy* directed at Poles, Danes, and Francophile groups in Alsace-Lorraine:

> Here, the binary logic of the nation state was in effect, based out of a hegemonic titular nation, which subjected the divergent minorities to the pressure of national homogenisation. This policy directed special severity against the efforts for political autonomy and secession, which the national groups threatened to increase through cross-border contacts and immigration from the neighbouring territories of France, Denmark, and the Polish settled areas of Russia and Austro-Hungary. These tensions became further aggravated when national minorities – such as the Danish and French minorities – sometimes obtained support from a bordering national state or, specifically, when the largest and politically best organised minority – the Poles – grew especially strong through immigration.[49]

In 1913, a new citizenship act was passed at the Reich level, the spirit of which was characterized by a policy of targeted exclusion. Dieter Gosewinkel described this situation in the following words:

> In particular . . . – against parliamentary resistance by groups from the political left and the national minorities – the 'right of blood' (*ius sanguinis*) was implemented as the exclusive principle for granting initial citizenship. This was not merely a continuation of a Prussian bureaucratic tradition from the 19th century, but rather, a political decision made under changed national political and economic conditions. By excluding every element of territorial affiliation, citizenship became a central *instrument for the targeted exclusion of certain immigrant and foreign groups*, especially those immigrants 'from the East' regarded as ethnically and culturally foreign and inferior as well as dangerous to the national state. The 'right of blood' principle for citizenship and the naturalisation procedures created a new system of regulation, on the one hand enabling economically useful immigration, but at the same time being able to suppress it at any time for ethnic-cultural reasons: *Citizenship in the German national state became an institution of potentially closed statehood.*[50]

In fact, citizenship has always been associated with a particular 'image of the citizen', which ultimately forms the basis for the regulatory system for citizenship – as evidenced, for example, in the designation of the Prussian citizenship law as an 'Untertanengesetz'

47 Heading in Gosewinkel, *Protection and Freedom?* (n 43) 42.

48 More details can be found in Dieter Gosewinkel, *Einbürgern und Ausschließen. Die Nationalisierung der Staatsangehörigkeit im Deutschen Bund bis zu Bundesrepublik Deutschland* [*Naturalization and Exclusion: The Nationalization of Citizenship in the German Bund up to the Federal Republic of Germany*] (2nd edn, Vandenhoeck & Ruprecht 2003).

49 Gosewinkel, *Protection and Freedom?* (n 43) 45.

50 Ibid, 48 (emphasis added).

('Subjects Law').[51] This image of the citizen is typically the image of the 'ideal citizen' – which automatically means that those who fall outside this image are not allowed to belong. In her book *The Citizen in Administrative Law*, Susanne Baer associated this exclusionary effect of membership status of the citizen with the 'notion of hierarchy' and, in terminological accord with Patrick Glenn, wrote the following:

> The focus thus turns to who does *not* fit into an image, a mould or model, and, due to recourse to the 'citizen', will be generally marginalized or excluded, put into a hierarchical, socially unequal, disadvantageous relationship to the normal citizen. This approach, which takes on both the historical development of the notion of the citizen and the identity-conferring process of exclusion, may be understood as a hierarchization perspective. . . . Hierarchization indicates the active, social differentiation implemented and enforced by social actors, which works to the disadvantage of one side. It may be manifested as exclusion, marginalization, paternalism, or homogenization. . . . it is not differences that are of interest, but rather, the social categories that mark such hierarchies as social disadvantages.[52]

The use of the exclusion strategy was by no means – as it might appear – an exclusively German matter; it also applied in the entire structure of the British Empire, in which, as Gosewinkel has presented in detail, the right of citizenship was *territorially segmented*, as the following example of Canada makes clear:

> Canada, for example, attempted, through the Immigration Act of 1910, to prevent the entry of immigrants whose 'race' did not match 'Canada's climate or requirements'. In doing so, the nation was trying to shield itself primarily from Asian immigrants, especially from India, and in fact, regardless of whether they were 'British subjects'. . . . With the exclusion, for example, of 'British subjects' of Indian origin from entry into Canada, this group was not only excluded from residence in Canada, but at the same time, from the expanding social and political rights in this portion of the British Empire at the end of the 19th century. Thus, nationality, or the status of 'British subject', not only failed to guarantee freedom of movement within the Empire. It also remained a required but insufficient condition for enjoying citizenships rights in the various portions of the Empire. Both components of citizen status, nationality and citizenship rights, were *territorially segmented* around the Empire – and therefore not equally guaranteed.[53]

3 *From Nationalization to the Denationalization of Citizenship Rights*

If we call yet again upon the catchword of sovereignty, it is to recall that the power of the idea of human rights was that it was poised, in the name of the 'responsibility to

[51] More details can be found in Gosewinkel, *Naturalization and Exclusion* (n 48).

[52] Susanne Baer, *'Der Bürger' im Verwaltungsrecht. Subjektkonstruktion durch Leitbilder vom Staat* ['The Citizen' in Administrative Law: Construction of the Subject Through Guiding Principles from the State] (Tübingen Mohr Siebeck 2006) 50–51.

[53] Gosewinkel, *Naturalization and Exclusion* (n 48) 92–93.

protect', to perforate the protective outer skin of sovereignty. We can observe a surprisingly similar parallel development in the area of citizenship rights. Starting from around 1989, rights understood and formulated as human rights gradually displaced earlier, mostly nation state conceptions of individual rights. Dieter Gosewinkel wrote an insightful description of this process, with which I would like to conclude these remarks on citizenship:

> With the European changes in 1989 . . . an alignment of the constitutional situation in the two hemispheres of Europe took place. A mixture of citizenship rights and human rights prevailed, whereby the universalistic guarantees of human rights gained in importance against national citizenship rights. . . . Overall, at the beginning of the 21st century, there developed a corpus of guarantees of individual rights in Europe, significantly influenced by the international codification of human rights and the growth of European law, which represented a significant change when compared to the start of the 20th century. *The process of nationalization* during the first half of the 20th century *reversed itself starting in 1989*, first in the region of Western Europe, and then *throughout Europe as a whole*. Citizenship in the European Union solidified a growing set of individual rights for EU citizens, which established transnationally effective, genuinely European rights alongside national citizenship rights. As a result, the legal boundaries of membership became permeable between the states of the European Union, and to some extent, between the Union and the rest of the world. . . . In the first quarter of the 21st century, member status as citizen was still recognizable and relevant in Europe, but less prominent, and it lost significance compared to transnationally formulated guarantees of individual rights.[54]

A Few Concluding Remarks

In *The Cosmopolitan State* by Patrick Glenn, the reciprocal relationship between 'elements of closure' and the 'cosmopolitan way' plays a central role. My goal in this chapter was to adopt this perspective in order to illustrate and concretize this reciprocal relationship in three areas. In all three examples, the actual 'driving forces' of 'elements of closure' were *nationalization processes*, whether this involved the nationalization of knowledge or the legal notions of sovereignty and citizenship, which function as indispensable requisites for the self-interested life of the nation state. With the processes of progressive economic interdependency, along with the increased mobility as a result of the development of transport and communication technology and transnational migration on a massive scale, these protective walls of national statehood have come under ever-increasing pressure. But, if I am correct, it ultimately took the idea of human rights as a globally valid legal concept to bring down this bastion.

54 Gosewinkel, *Protection and Freedom?* (n 43) 635–36 (emphasis added).

15

Cosmopolitan Attachments

Neil Walker

I BEYOND COMPARATIVE LAW

I would not be the first[1] to find it remarkable that in *The Cosmopolitan State*[2] – his last and arguably most important book – the famous comparative lawyer Patrick Glenn had hardly a word to say about the discipline that had made him famous.[3] Remarkable, but, for reasons both personal and intellectual, perhaps not surprising.

I had fewer opportunities than I would have wished to meet and get to know Patrick Glenn. But from the occasions I did have the privilege of spending time with him, I vividly recall someone who wore lightly and with playful good humour the extraordinary erudition that marked his writings. He took his subject matter seriously without ever taking himself too seriously, always more interested in exploring the new issues in front of him than in looking back to and refining his own undoubtedly impressive corpus. He was driven by intellectual curiosity, and also a strong, if typically understated, social and political conscience, rather than any need to nurture his intellectual reputation. He understood the academic endeavour not as a competition for accolades and awards but as a collaborative exercise – happy to view himself as part of a large and mutually enriching conversation. And even though, as we shall see, there are a number of powerful and important continuities in his work, I suspect he was temperamentally inclined to see himself as fox rather than hedgehog – as the accumulator of knowledge about many disparate things rather than the sponsor of one big idea.

All these factors help explain why comparative law and his singular contribution to the subject over many years figure so little in his subsequent study of the cosmopolitan state. But another part of the explanation lies at the level of ideas. For Patrick Glenn, comparative law was always a subject in part defined *against*

[1] See, in particular, the insightful biographical essay by Richard Janda, 'Cosmopolitan Normative Information: Patrick Glenn's Legal Theory' (*Intergentes*, 2016) <http://intergentes.com/es/tag/richard-janda-es/>.

[2] H Patrick Glenn, *The Cosmopolitan State* (OUP 2013) (hereafter Glenn, *TCS*).

[3] In particular, through five editions of H Patrick Glenn, *Legal Traditions of the World: Sustainable Development in Law* (5th edn, OUP 2014) (hereafter Glenn, *LTW*).

itself. It was as much an examination of what connects different legal doctrinal streams and systems as of what divides them. Emerging in the age of the modern state, comparative law contained and exhibited a fundamental tension. On the one hand, it had from the outset an inherent state-centred bias. Comparative law's very existence as a discipline presupposed the state as the unit most amenable to comparison, and many of the studies carried out under its name were concerned both to sustain the idea of the state as a distinctive and self-contained normative order and to provide an external resource for the improvement of its internal normative order. On the other hand, the idea of comparative law also required a common spectrum of normative possibilities in terms of which the exercise in comparison could be meaningfully pursued. And any such pursuit, if carried out with due attention to actual patterns of normativity over time and space, was bound to expose the fragility and contingency of the forms of normative closure associated with autonomous statehood, reveal the extent of common normativity across states, and exhibit the range of forms of normative movement between states.

Glenn's own work as a comparativist did much to uncover and explain such transnational movements and commonalities, and it is precisely his appreciation of the insights thereby gained that provides the point of departure for his analysis of the tensions and complexities of the 'cosmopolitan state'. Comparative law was the ladder he climbed that allowed him to glimpse the outline of the cosmopolitan state, but it was a prop that he could then put to one side, along with that part of its legacy that tended to compartmentalize the world in strictly statist terms, as he embarked on his last great project. This was a project, as we shall see, which broadened and deepened Glenn's challenge to the statist tendency in the juristic mindset and in the broader political culture. But it is also a project which itself remains open to counterchallenge from a statist perspective, and one that to some minds may even *invite* such a reaction.

II ANCHORING THE COSMOPOLITAN STATE

Glenn may not have coined the term 'cosmopolitan state',[4] but he certainly adds much to our understanding of the notion. There is a provocative catchiness to the label, an oxymoronic suggestion in the idea that something as fenced-in and particularizing as the state could exist in the same conceptual space as the unbounded and all-encompassing cosmos. Glenn, of course, is alive to this provocation, but he does much to persuade us that the very viability and continuing justification of the modern state depends upon a rejection of any such oppositional understanding.

4 See eg, Ulrich Beck, 'The Cosmopolitan State: Redefining Power in a Global Age' (2005) 18 *Int'l J Pol Culture & Soc'y* 143; Mattias Kumm, 'Constitutionalism and the Cosmopolitan State' NYU School of Law Public Law Research Paper No. 13–68 <https://papers.ssrn.com/sol3/papers.cfm?abstract_id=2338547>.

Glenn's framing strategy is to situate himself between what he takes to be two extreme positions. On the one side, he rejects the very idea of a 'nation state', with its monocultural implication, as a mythical construct of both popular and academic discourse. There are no 'pure' nation states today; neither, he insists, have any such homogenous entities existed in history. Outside the romantic imaginary, there are always ethnic, linguistic, or religious minorities to be found alongside the dominant groups – minorities which, if they are not to be denied and repressed, as has often been the instinct of dominant groups, must somehow be accommodated.[5] On the other side, he dismisses 'strong cosmopolitanism',[6] with its assumption that we all belong to a single global community; with its conviction that this global community, rather than the state or any other sub-global unit, is the primary source of our legal and political rights and obligations; and with its notion that such primacy is due either (or both) to a profound ethical universalism or to the increasingly manifest and manifold global interdependence of our local actions.[7] Instead, he opts for an older and, he claims, more etymologically precise and more commonly recognizable understanding of the cosmopolitan condition. This consists of a harmonious bringing together of what is appropriate to the 'cosmos' on the one hand, namely those general 'characteristics which arise from, or are suited to, a range over many different countries',[8] and, on the other hand, that which is distinctive to the particular 'polis'; and, crucially, it is a bringing together that finds no universal form or articulation, but only takes place *within* the perspective of the particular 'polis'. Rather than a contradiction in terms, therefore, for Glenn, the idea of the cosmopolitan state is merely the default and dominant modern form through which the particular polity positions itself as part of an interdependent world of partly shared interests and common values and commits itself to an ethic of harmonious coexistence.

What is most distinctive – and arguably most original – in Glenn's approach, is the depth with which and the range of ways in which cosmopolitanism is claimed to be anchored in the structures of political modernity. For Glenn is keen to emphasize how cosmopolitan practices are the product of various interlocking attachments, and to stress how these attachments serve to normalize and stabilize the cosmopolitan tendency in the contemporary framework of global relations.

First and foremost then, for Glenn, cosmopolitanism is anchored in local experience and practice. As the 'cosmopolitan state' label suggests, the modern state, and the diverse interests, cultures, and practices that make up the modern state, are the primary source of the cosmopolitan way of being today. This state of affairs,

5 Glenn, *TCS* (n 2) ch 5.

6 Ibid, 173.

7 For a discussion of these different options, see Neil Walker, 'The Gap Between Global Law and Global Justice: A Preliminary Analysis' in Nicole Roughan and Andrew Halpin (eds), *In Pursuit of Pluralist Jurisprudence* (CUP 2017).

8 H Patrick Glenn, 'The Cosmopolitan State' (2013) 61 *Kan L Rev* 735, 742 (citing the *Oxford English Dictionary*).

moreover, can be seen as part of a longer historical pattern. For the modern state's various predecessors, the classical Greek *polis*, the early 'church as state',[9] the imperial state, the medieval city state, and the dynastic states that provided a bridge to the modern age, also provided the local wellsprings of cosmopolitanism in their own times. In some respects, this insistence on the local may be considered unexceptional. Glenn himself recognizes that most contemporary versions of cosmopolitanism that set themselves apart from the 'strong' variant stress the importance of the local, using adjectives such as 'rooted', 'situated', 'bottom up',[10] or indeed, 'anchored' itself.[11] Yet, in both normative and empirical terms, Glenn's commitment to the local goes deeper than most.

Normatively, Glenn's endorsement of the local roots of cosmopolitanism appears categorical. There is no sense in which, for him, a locally based cosmopolitanism, with its strong pre-modern heritage, is a 'second best' result, acceptable only in the absence of, and perhaps as a prelude and pathway, to a more robust framework of global morals and world government. Rather, an ethic of irreducible difference is central to Glenn's vision of social and political relations both within and between states. The different cultures we experience and the different traditions we inhabit and interpret are constitutive of our social selves and are the baseline from which we come to recognize both our diversity and our commonalities. In Glenn the comparative lawyer's celebrated discussion of the 'sustainable diversity' of legal systems in the world,[12] the emphasis was as much on the necessity of maintaining that diversity as on the quality of the relations through which the coexistence of these diverse entities should be negotiated and sustained. That same sense of valuing difference as much as urging its reconciliation is present in his wider cosmopolitan theory.

Various historically embedded local practices and institutions both corroborate and give flesh to the normative endorsement of a locally anchored approach towards the nurturing of cosmopolitanism. Glenn, of course, has a particular eye for legal practices and institutions. In *Common Laws*,[13] which I am surely not alone in considering his most brilliant book, he showed how all local and particular *Legal Traditions*, and not just those in the Anglo-American lineage that incorporate a nominal 'Common Law', are supplemented and enriched by an understanding of legal norms and principles held *in common* beyond the territorial jurisdiction in question. Common laws, then, are the permanent and necessary shadow of particular laws, their outward-looking ambition always available to moderate and complete the local vision. This theme is repeated and reinforced in *The Cosmopolitan State*,[14] but now Glenn is equally concerned to extoll the cosmopolitan credentials of some

[9] Glenn, *TCS* (n 2) 20–26.
[10] Glenn, 'Cosmopolitan State' (n 8) 176.
[11] See Fred Dallmayr, 'Cosmopolitanism: Moral and Political' (2003) 31 *Pol Theory* 421.
[12] Glenn, *LTW* (n 3).
[13] H Patrick Glenn, *Common Laws* (OUP 2007).
[14] Glenn, *TCS* (n 2) ch 6.

of the other familiar furniture of the modern state, including constitutionalism[15] and also what he terms 'institutional cosmopolitanism'.[16] He argues that modern state constitutionalism, with its internal checks and balances, its resistance to arbitrary or unilateral decision, its methods of second-order resolution of first-order differences, and its reference to the freedom and equality of *all* peoples as the basis of its appeal for the freedom and equality of *this* particular people, has always harboured the cosmopolitan gene. For its part, institutional cosmopolitanism refers to the fact that states, like their predecessors, were not born institutionally free, but always had to accommodate other institutional forms. These might be the church hierarchies with which state jurisdiction overlapped, or resilient indigenous structures at the local outposts of empire, or other sovereign states and the embryonic frameworks of public international law and private international law through which modern states' dealings with their own kind came to be mediated.

As this last example intimates, alongside this vertical anchoring in the local subsoil, there is for Glenn an additional and complementary horizontal anchoring of cosmopolitanism in a network of transnational mechanisms and practices that have intensified hand in hand with the latest and largest surge of globalization of economic relations and of forms of knowledge, communications, and mobility. This second type of anchoring, indeed, is significantly continuous with the first. Common laws, constitutional orientations, and patterns of institutional pluralism are not simply experienced and developed discretely in local sites. Because in all such sites they are a product of the same outward-looking sensibility, and since their success depends in some measure on the reciprocal coordination of trans-site practice, they tend to generate strong and self-reinforcing connections across jurisdictions. We see this process at work in the emergence or resurgence of many transnationally 'joined-up' forms of common law, from *lex mercatoria* to *lex digitalis*.[17] We also see it in the exponential increase in the use of non-national authorities, both foreign national and international, as sources for the interpretation of national constitutional texts.[18] And we see it more broadly in the proliferation of transnational institutions, both global and regional, jurisdictionally general and functionally specific,[19] and in the growth of a more multifaceted (if not necessarily 'multivalent'[20]) approach in the development of new streams of international jurisprudence.[21]

15 Ibid, ch 7.

16 Ibid, ch 8.

17 Ibid, ch 12.

18 Ibid, ch 11.

19 Ibid, ch 13.

20 It would need another article to discuss this properly, but I tend to side with Andrew Halpin against Glenn that at the point of resolution of legal disputes or otherwise reaching a legal decision, legal method is best understood as bivalent rather than multivalent, even if the sources and resources of such bivalent decisions may be described as multifaceted; see, in particular, Andrew Halpin, 'Rejoinder to Glenn' (2007) 2 *J Comp L* 88.

21 Glenn, *TCS* (n 2) ch 14.

Together, these vertical and horizontal elements supply contemporary cosmopolitanism with an impressive set of attachments. On Glenn's understanding, then, cosmopolitanism is not to be understood as working against the grain of, and in spite of, the global legal and political terrain, but as something that gains traction from and helps to shape that terrain. One might caution, however, that so far, the emphasis has been on structure rather than culture, on system rather than spirit. Besides the *objective attachments* that facilitate the cosmopolitan way, what of *subjective attachment*? Just who are the 'cosmopolitans' who choose, promote, or enjoy cosmopolitanism?

Glenn does address this matter, but less fully and systematically than he does the other dimensions of his enquiry. His discussion of citizenship is where he deals most directly with the ways in which the cosmopolitan approach has come to influence popular consciousness. He recounts how, over the last century, we have moved away from the idea of citizenship as a pattern of mutually exclusive national statuses.[22] As cosmopolitan citizens, we instead increasingly embrace dual or even multiple citizenship, 'denizenship', and other graduated forms of community membership, and even citizenship of entities other than states. The ideas of political belonging and entitlement associated with citizenship, therefore, are no longer so singular, so categorical, so rigidly compartmentalized. Yet, citizenship apart, his treatment of the affective dimension of cosmopolitan attachment is largely incidental to other themes, and in particular, to two themes that emphasize quite contrasting aspects of the cosmopolitan sensibility.

On the one hand, he is interested in the role of those 'cosmopolitan *officials*'[23] who are actively involved in making the structures of transnational common law, open constitutionalism, international organizational law, and the like, and who operate in a duly cosmopolitan-friendly manner. But here, we are talking about judges, lawyers, diplomats, and other high-ranking public servants and specialist functionaries, an essentially elite rather than a demotic constituency. On the other hand, it appears to be implicit in Glenn's argument about the extent to which our institutional landscape and embedded practices of recognition are already cosmopolitan apt, that a cosmopolitan openness has become part of what Pierre Bourdieu would call the *doxa* of everyday experience; namely, the frame through which 'the natural and social world appears as self-evident'[24] to us – where what 'goes without saying because it comes without saying'.[25] That is to say, everyday cosmopolitanism today in some ways runs even deeper and wider than popular culture, supplying a taken-for-granted feature of our common experience and practice. For example, for most of us most of the time, 'it goes without saying' that we do not live in one-nation states, and we do not normally differentiate, still

[22] Ibid, ch 10.

[23] Ibid, 743.

[24] Pierre Bourdieu, *Outline of a Theory of Practice* (Richard Nice tr, CUP 1972) 164.

[25] Ibid, 167.

less discriminate, in our personal dealings – legal, political, commercial, or social – on the basis of narrowly constructed national categories. Equally, many of the transnational regulations that govern our lives in matters as disparate as food safety, environmental protection, and product standards 'come without saying', and are accepted as the natural contours of our daily lives every bit as much as are more home-grown capacities and constraints.

III COSMOPOLITANISM ADRIFT?

There is much that I find insightful and persuasive in Glenn's general theory of the cosmopolitan state and very little with which I disagree. Even his account of the subjective dimension of cosmopolitan attachment, for all that it is preliminary, contains important insights. He is right to focus on the importance of officials, but also, at the other extreme, he is undoubtedly correct to stress how much of cosmopolitanism is so embedded in the objective structures to which we are all subjected, in particular, the legal and political structures he is so concerned to trace, as to seem banal – unremarked because unremarkable.

But we are left with two related concerns. The first has to do with the sheer inclusiveness of his theory, and whether and how that allows us to discriminate between different types of cosmopolitanism, and even between 'good' and 'bad' cosmopolitanism. The second returns us to the question of cosmopolitan attachment, and asks how we are to defend cosmopolitanism against its ever present and recently reinvigorated enemies.

As regards the question of inclusiveness, here it seems that the strength of Glenn's thesis is also its weakness. In making such a powerful case for the pervasiveness of cosmopolitan structures and dispositions, Glenn is very effective in marginalizing his chosen opposition. Who could be a unitary nation statist, or a strong cosmopolitan in the face of Glenn's meticulously constructed picture of actually existing cosmopolitanism then and now? Yet, even though the argument Glenn makes for anchored cosmopolitanism is quite compelling, and typically depends not on the aggressive construction of straw men but on the sober (and often gentle) exposure of the genuine inadequacies of other positions, he ends up occupying so much terrain that important distinctions and difficult choices remain. Does his inclusiveness not slip into over-inclusiveness? If the global tendency is towards cosmopolitanism, which of its many variants predominates, and which should predominate?

Glenn might reasonably retort that this is not his question to answer. His take-home message is already a powerful one, and indeed for many, an interestingly counter-intuitive one: in the age of late modernity, where the state form is more prevalent than at any time in human history, the state in question has, in fact, become the fundamental cornerstone of an essentially cosmopolitan system of global governance. And so strong is his belief in cosmopolitanism in principle that even if and when the cosmopolitan state wanes, his advice would be: 'Don't worry. Something will take its place. [Even if we] don't know what that will be.'[26]

Yet, the worry persists. For Glenn, the key variable of interest is that of identity and recognition. He seeks to make sense of the world in terms of how closed or open are our frameworks, in particular, our legal frameworks, for exchange with other people, and for making social bonds and political community. However, as others have noted,[27] this may sideline equally vital and cross-cutting questions, in particular, questions of economic power and distributive justice. A familiar argument against contemporary cosmopolitanism, as we shall see, is precisely that it favours the mobile elite, the 'frequent travelers'[28] who surf the wave of global economic liberalism or inhabit the more civil spaces of global administration, rather than the relatively immobile majority of the population from whom they become progressively detached.

This is where the first concern connects to the second. For even in the short time since Glenn published *The Cosmopolitan State*, and his untimely death the following year, there has been a marked resurgence in forms of populism, understood in one well-known formulation as a 'thin-centred ideology that considers society to be ultimately separated into two homogenous and antagonistic camps, "the pure people" versus "the corrupt elite" and which argues that politics should be an expression of the . . . general will of the people.'[29] And in the age of Trump and Orban, Putin and Erdogan, Maduro and Kaczynski, the forces of populism have assumed a transnational resonance that has intensified its appeal.

That may seem surprising. After all, populism is always concerned with the 'unitary collective particular',[30] with a specific populace, and with certain core characteristics and propensities that can plausibly be attributed to that populace. It tends, therefore, to be nativist in outlook, fronted by slogans such as 'America First' or 'Putting the Great Back into Britain'. The 'other' against whom the authentic people is defined includes not only elites and self-identifying internal minorities who disturb the sense of a unified whole, but also migrants and foreign influences more generally, not least those that take institutional form as international organizations mandated to 'interfere' in national affairs.

But there is the twist. While nativism would seem to offer fallow ground on which to build transnational alliances, opposition to forces that would deny the moral authority of such nativism *is* undoubtedly common across various strands of populism, and provides the basis for a kind of negative solidarity. Nativist populists can

26 Glenn, 'Cosmopolitan State' (n 8) 746.

27 See eg, Janda (n 1).

28 See eg, Craig Calhoun, 'The Class Consciousness of Frequent Travelers: Toward a Critique of Actually Existing Cosmopolitanism' (2002) 101 *S Atl Q* 869.

29 Cass Mudde and Cristobal Rovira Kasltwasser, *Populism: A Very Short Introduction* (OUP 2017) 6. See also Jan-Werner Muller, *What Is Populism?* (University of Pennsylvania Press 2016); Neil Walker, 'Populism and Constitutional Tension' (2019) 17(2) *Int'l J Const'l L*.

30 See Walker, 'Populism and Constitutional Tension' (n 29).

and do find common cause *against* a generic category of roles, interests, sensibilities, and practices for which their chosen pejorative label is often none other than *cosmopolitan*. Cosmopolitanism, through this sceptical lens, tends to be associated not only with the 'frequent traveller', but also with the 'dotcom Web' set, or any other epistocratic or other privileged communities that enjoy high mobility and communicability – in which, according to the nativist charge, national particularity does not register as an important human value.[31] One key unifying target in this oppositional politics is that of a disembedded universalism, which, in the populist imaginary, underpins forces hostile to populism, even if this kind of one-size-fits-all 'covering-law'[32] approach bears little relationship to the actual practices of anchored cosmopolitanism. And here the significance of the legal and constitutional themes in which Glenn takes such a close interest become clear. Nativist populists are opposed to all political values and interests that are 'foreign' to their peculiar conception of the national collective good, but they see a special and encompassing threat in those alien political values and interests that they are wont to accuse of wearing the cloak of universalism in so doing. As law itself, through many of the very historical forms and discourses of extended justification that Glenn celebrates, is well adapted to the making of claims that transcend particular jurisdictions, so populists can often find and pursue common cause against legal institutions that claim transnational normative force, as also against domestic legal institutions that recognize the legitimacy of such universally coded claims of transnational validity.

How stands the defence of cosmopolitan attachment in the face of these populist and nativist forces? Does not the confidence that Glenn expresses in the spread and solidity of cosmopolitan institutions seem overstated in light of these attacks? Does it not seem more urgent to distinguish within Glenn's highly inclusive category between those forms of cosmopolitanism that attend to global interests broadly conceived and those that are slanted towards mobile elites? And, perhaps most urgently of all, how do we develop a better understanding and practice of cosmopolitan attachment where this is exposed to the hostile rhetoric and blunt caricatures of nativism? The irony here is that the very embedded and taken-for-granted quality of cosmopolitanism that Glenn rightly hails as one of its strengths and as a measure of its success can also become a weakness in such an ideological maelstrom. It is not true that nativism always has the best stories – that is just a nativist story – but it *is* true that defenders of cosmopolitanism have to develop better vernaculars. The historical, yet often unsung achievements of cosmopolitanism can be too easily dismissed as unearned and covert privilege, as a conspiracy of the powerful, and as a prize list for the deracinated, rather than as the

[31] On the significance of the nativist/cosmopolitan opposition within populist discourse, see Pierre Ostiguy, 'Populism: A Socio-Cultural Approach' in Cristóbal Rovira Kaltwasser and others (eds), *The Oxford Handbook of Populism* (OUP 2017).

[32] Michael Walzer, *Thinking Politically: Essays in Political Theory* (David Miller ed, Yale University Press 2007) ch 12 ('Nation and Universe').

simultaneously inward-looking and outward-looking balance of interests, values, and priorities appropriate to the public culture of every modern cosmopolitan state.

Patrick Glenn makes a finely nuanced case for why we have long sought and developed cosmopolitan institutions and dispositions and should continue to nurture and treasure them. If he were still with us, I am sure he would have much to say about how, in such hostile circumstances, we defend and refine the cosmopolitan way and prevent it from coming adrift from its moorings while seeking to do justice to the real concerns on which such hostility feeds. We best honour his legacy by continuing to study his writings for insights into how we should approach this urgent task.

IMAGE 5 H Patrick Glenn, 1940–2014 (photo: Lysanne Larose)

H Patrick Glenn
Publications

ARTICLES

'Differential Cosmopolitanism' (2016) 7 Transnational Legal Theory 57

'The State as Legal Tradition' (2013) 2 Cambridge Journal of International and Comparative Law 704

'The Cosmopolitan State' (2013) 61 University Kansas Law Review 735

'A Western Legal Tradition?' (2010) 49 Supreme Court Law Review 601

'Tradition in Religion and Law' (2010) 25 Journal of Law & Religion 503

'A Concept of Legal Tradition' (2008) 34 Queen's Law Journal 427

'Continuity and Discontinuity of Aboriginal Entitlement' (2007) 7 Oxford University Commonwealth Law Journal 23

'Legal Traditions and Legal Traditions' (2007) 2 Journal of Comparative Law 69

'Legal Traditions and the Separation Thesis' (2006) 35 Nederlands Tijdschrift voor Rechtsfilosofie & Rechtstheorie 222

'On the Use of Biological Metaphors in Law: The Case of Legal Transplants' (2006) 1 Journal of Comparative Law 358

'Transnational Common Laws' (2006) 29 Fordham International Law Journal 457

'The Common Laws of Europe and Louisiana' (2005) 79 Tulane Law Review 1041

'Doin' the Transystemic: Legal Systems and Legal Traditions' (2005) 50 McGill Law Journal 863

'La Disposition préliminaire du Code civil du Québec, le droit commun et les principes généraux du droit' (2005) 46 Cahiers de Droit 339

'The ALI/UNIDROIT Principles of Transnational Civil Procedure as Global Standards for Adjudication?' (2004) 9 Uniform Law Review 829

With Dominic Desbiens, 'L'appartenance au Québec: Citoyenneté, domicile et résidence dans la masse législative québécoise' (2003) 48 McGill Law Journal 117

'La tradition juridique nationale' (2003) 55 Revue international de droit comparé 263

'Mixing It Up' (2003) 78 Tulane Law Review 79

'Prospects for Transnational Civil Procedure in the Americas' (2003) 8 Uniform Law Review 485

'Qu'est-ce que la common law en français?' (2003) 5 Revue de la common law en français 97

'Harmony of Laws in the Americas' [2003] University of Miami Inter-American Law Review 223

'North America as a Medieval Legal Construction' (2002) 2 Global Jurist Advances 1

'Integrating Civil and Common Law Teaching Throughout the Curriculum: The Canadian Experience' (2002) 21 Penn State International Law Review 69

'Are Legal Traditions Incommensurable?' (2001) 49 American Journal of Comparative Law 133
'Comparative Law and Legal Practice: On Removing the Borders' (2001) 75 Tulane Law Review 977
'Conflicting Laws in a Common Market? The NAFTA Experiment' (2001) 76 Chicago-Kent Law Review 1789
'La Cour suprême du Canada et la tradition du droit civil' (2001) 80 Canadian Bar Review 151
'Commensurabilité et traduisibilité' (2000) 3 Revue de la common law en français 53
'Conciliation of Laws in the NAFTA Countries' (2000) 60 Louisiana Law Review 1103
'Globalization and Dispute Resolution' (2000) 19 Civil Justice Quarterly 136
'Vers un droit comparé intégré?' (1999) 51 Revue international de droit comparé 841
'L'Affaire Bre-X et les recours collectifs transfrontaliers' (1999) 12 Revue québécoise de droit international 33
'Preface' (1999) 44 McGill Law Journal 255
'Reconciling Regimes: Legal Relations of States and Provinces in North America' (1998) 15 Arizona Journal of International & Comparative Law 255
'The Grounding of Codification' (1998) 31 UC Davis Law Review 765
'L'étranger et les Groupements d'États' (1998) 43 McGill Law Journal 165
'How to Think About Medical Secrecy' (1998) 19 Health Law in Canada 27
'The Capture, Reconstruction and Marginalization of "Custom"' (1997) 45 American Journal of Comparative Law 613
'Recognition of Foreign Judgments in Quebec' (1997) 28 Canadian Business Law Journal 404
'Codification of Private International Law in Quebec' (1996) 60 RabelsZ 231
'Une justice de masse – Reflexions sur la responsabilité civile en Amerique du Nord' (1996) 26 Victoria University of Wellington Law Review 313
'The Common Law in Canada' (1995) 74 Canadian Law Review 261
'Divided Justice – Judicial Structures in Federal and Confederal States' (1995) 46 South Carolina Law Review 819
With Mahmud Jamal, 'Selective Legality: The Common Law Jurisdictional Appeal' (1994) 73 Canadian Bar Review 142
'Sur l'impossibilité d'un principe de "stare decisis"' (1993) 4 Revue de la recherche juridique 1073
'Harmonization of Law, Foreign Law and Private International Law' (1993) 1 European Review of Private Law 47
'Foreign Judgements, the Common Law and the Constitution: De Savoye v Morguard Investments Ltd' (1992) 37 McGill Law Journal 537
'Comparative Law, Immigration and Human Rights' (1991) 3 African Journal of International and Comparative Law 668
'Droit comparé et droit québécois' (1990) 24 Revue juridique Thémis 341
'Law, Revolution and Rights' [1990] Archives for Philosophy of Law & Social Philosophy, Revolution & Human Rights 9
'Judicial Authority and the Liability of the Manufacturer, or Jusqu'ou Peut-on Aller Trop Loin' (1990) 38 American Journal of Comparative Law 555
'Professional Structures and Professional Ethics' (1990) 35 McGill Law Journal 424
'Pour une Cour d'Appel' (1990) 31 Cahiers de Droit 537
'À propos de la maxime "Nul ne plaide par procureur"' [1988] Revue trimestrielle de droit civil 59
'Droit Internationale Privé du Divorce et de la Filiation Adoptive: Un Renversement de la Methadologie Conflictuelle, Le' (1988) 19 Revue generale de droit 359

'Persuasive Authority' (1987) 32 McGill Law Journal 261
'The Dilemma of Class Action Reform' (1986) 6 Oxford Journal of Legal Studies 262
'Les nouveaux moyens de reproduction audio-visuelle et numérique et les droits de la personnalité: rapport general' (1986) 46 Revue du Barreau 693
'Class Actions and the Theory of Tort and Delict' (1985) 35 University of Toronto Law Journal 287
'Class Actions in Ontario and Quebec' (1984) 62 Canadian Bar Review 247
'La responsabilité des juges' (1983) 28 Revue de Droit de McGill 228
'Where Heavens Meet: The Compelling of Religious Divorces' (1980) 28 American Journal of Comparative Law 1
'Le droit au respect de la vie privée' (1979) 39 Revue du Barreau 879
'Secret de la vie privée en droit Québécois, Le' (1974) 5 Revue generale de droit 24
'The Local Law of Alsace-Lorraine: A Half-Century of Survival' (1974) 23 International & Comparative Law Quarterly 769

COMMENTS AND NOTES

'À l'appui du pouvoir' (2007) 52 McGill Law Journal 237
'Prospects for Transnational Civil Procedure in the Americas' (2003) 8 Uniform Law Review 485
'A North American Transformative Judgment' (2002) 81 Canadian Bar Review 469
'Conflicting Laws in a Common Market – The NAFTA Experiment' (2001) 76 Chicago-Kent Law Review 1789
'The Supreme Court, Judicial Comity and Anti-Suit Injunctions' (1994) 28 UBC Law Review 193
'Class Proceedings Act, 1992, S.O. 1992, c. 6 – Law Society Amendment Act (Class Proceedings Funding), 1992, S.O. 1992, c. 7' (1993) 72 Canadian Bar Review 568
'Lawyers – Legal Ethics – Change of Firm by Lawyer – Standard for Disqualification of Law Firm to Act in Litigation' (1991) 70 Canadian Bar Review 351
'Droit comparé et droit Québécois' (1990) 24 Revue juridique Thémis 341
'Professional Structures and Professional Ethics' (1990) 35 McGill Law Journal 424
'On Blackstone, California Divorces and the Retrospectivity of the Common and Civil Laws: *Edward v Edward*' (1989) 34 McGill Law Journal 186
'Conflicts of Laws – Tort Liability and Choice of Law – Role of Private International Law and of Constitutional Law' (1989) 68 Canadian Bar Review 586
'The Use of Computers: Qualitative Case Law Analysis in the Civil and Common Law' (1987) 36 International & Comparative Law Quarterly 362
'Le Droit en l'an 2000: L'envahissement des contrôles gouvernementaux et des technologies nouvelles dans la vie privée des citoyens' (1987) 18 Revue generale de droit 705
'Maritime Law – Federal Court Jurisdiction – Canadian Maritime Law – Relationship to Civil and Common Law' (1987) 66 Canadian Bar Review 360
'Civil Procedure and the Conflict of Laws – Pre-judgment Remedies in the Federal State' (1986) 64 Canadian Bar Review 382
'Limitations on Judicial Freedom of Speech in West Germany and Switzerland' (1985) 34 International & Comparative Law Quarterly 159
'Methodologie conflictuelle et protection de l'incapable étranger' (1985) 26 Cahiers de Droit 1031
'La compétence internationale et le fabricant étranger' (1985) 45 Revue du Barreau 567
'Conflict of Laws – Eviction of Proper Law of Contract by Legislation Creating Provincial Offence – Extraterritorial Effect of Provincial Legislation – Where Is an Omission?' (1981) 59 Canadian Bar Review 840

'Le droit au respect de la vie privée empêche-t-il la preuve en matière civile par enrégistrement clandestin?' (1980) 40 Revue du Barreau 827
'Propogation volontaire et competence international' (1977) 23 McGill Law Journal 125
'Capacity to Marry in the Conflict of Laws: Some Variations on a Theme' (1977) 4 Dalhousie Law Journal 157
'The Constitutional Validity of Abortion Legislation: A Comparative Note' (1975) 21 McGill Law Journal 673

BOOK REVIEWS

Philippe Jestaz and Christophe Jamin, *La Doctrine*; Alexandra Braun, *Giudici E Accademia Nell' Esperienza Inglese: Storia Di Un Dialogo*; Baudoin Dupret, *Droit et Sciences Sociales* (2007) 55 American Journal of Comparative Law 197
Susan G Drummond, *Mapping Marriage Law in Spanish Gitano Communities* (2007) 45 Osgoode Hall Law Journal 203
Symeon C Symeonides, *The American Choice-of-Law Revolution in the Court: Today and Tomorrow* (2006) 51 McGill Law Journal 211
Erik Jayne, *Lange et droit* (2001) 49 American Journal of Comparative Law 541
George Panagopoulos, *Restitution in Private International Law* (2001) 46 McGill Law Journal 1178
Kevin YL Tan, *The Singapore Legal System* (1999) 45 McGill Law Journal 339
Jan Kropholler, *Internationales Privatrecht* (1992) 40 American Journal of Comparative Law 272
César E Dubler, *Les clauses d'exception en droit international privé* (1985) 34 International & Comparative Law Quarterly 643
Lennart Palsson, *Marriage in Comparative Conflict of Laws: Substantive Conditions* (1983) 31 American Journal of Comparative Law 754
Paul Heinrich Neuhaus, *Die Grundbegriffe des Internationalen Privatrechts*; Leo Raape and Fritz Sturm, *Internationales Privatrecht Band I: Allgemeine Lehren* (1979) 27 American Journal of Comparative Law 120
RC van Caenegem, *The Birth of the English Common Law* (1974) 24 University of Toronto Law Journal 464

BOOKS AND MONOGRAPHS

Patrick H Glenn and Lionel D Smith (eds), *Law and the New Logics* (CUP 2017)
Legal Traditions of the World: Sustainable Diversity in Law (5th edn, OUP 2014)
The Cosmopolitan State (OUP 2013)
On Common Laws (OUP 2005)
Droit québécois et droit français: Communauté, autonomie, concordance (Éditions Yvon Blais 1993)
Strangers at the Gate: Refugees, Illegal Entrants, and Procedural Justice (Éditions Yvon Blais 1992)
La capacité de la personne en droit internationale privé français et anglaise, vol 19 (Dalloz 1975)

ARTICLES/CHAPTERS IN BOOKS AND MONOGRAPHS

With Aline Grenon and Helge Dedek, 'The Global Challenge in Common and Civil Law Contexts: A Canadian Perspective' in Christophe Jamin and William van Caenegem (eds), *The Internationalization of Legal Education* (Springer 2016)

'Against Method?' in Maurice Adams and Dirk Heirbaut (eds), *The Method and Culture of Comparative Law: Essays in Honour of Mark Van Hoecke* (Hart 2014)

'The Aims of Comparative Law' in JM Smits (ed), *Elgar Encyclopedia of Comparative Law* (2nd edn, Edward Elgar 2012)

'How to Think About Law in North America' in James McHugh (ed), *Toward a North American Legal System* (Palgrave Macmillan 2012)

'Sustainable Diversity in Law' in Brian Tamanaha and others (eds), *Legal Pluralism and Development: Scholars and Practitioners in Dialogue* (CUP 2012)

'The Ethic of International Law' in Donald Earl Childress (ed), *The Role of Ethics in International Law* (CUP 2012)

'The Irrelevance of Costs Rules to Litigation Rates: The Experience of Quebec and Common Law Canada' in Mathias Reimann (ed), *Cost and Fee Allocation in Civil Procedure*, vol 11 (Ius Gentium: Comparative Perspectives on Law and Justice, Springer 2012)

'The Three Ironies of the UN Declaration on the Rights of Indigenous Peoples into CERD Practice' in Steven Allen and Alexandra Xanthaki (eds), *Reflections on the UN Declaration on the Rights of Indigenous Peoples* (Hart 2011)

'Doin' the Transsystemic: Legal Systems and Legal Traditions' in Michael Giudice and others (eds), *The Methodology of Legal Theory* (Ashgate 2010)

'Cosmopolitan Legal Orders' in Andrew Halpin and Volker Roeben (eds), *Theorizing the Global Legal Order* (Hart 2009)

'L'arbitrage religieux au Canada: Un statut personnel qui n'ose pas dire son nom?' in Marc Aoun (ed), *Les statuts personnels en droit compare* (Peeters 2009)

'The Prospective Effect of Res Judicata' in National and Kapodistrian University of Athens (ed), *Essays in Honour of Konstantinos Kerameus* (Sakkoulas/Bruyland 2009)

'Globalization and Traditions' in Jürgen Schwarze (ed), *Globalisierung und Entstaatlichung des Rechts*, vol 1 (Mohr Siebeck 2008)

'Com-paring' in Esin Örücü and David Nelken (eds), *Comparative Law: A Handbook* (Hart 2007)

'Multivalent Logic and the Rome Convention' in Katharina Boele-Woelki and Willem Grosheide (eds), *The Future of European Contract Law: Essays in Honour of Ewoud Hondius* (Kluwer 2007)

'Judicial Enforcement of Lawyers' Ethics' in Mads Andenas and others (eds), *Liber Amicorum Guido Alpa: Private Law Beyond the National Systems* (BIICL 2007)

'The National Legal Tradition' in Katharina Boele-Woelki and Sjef van Erp (eds), *General Reports of the XVIIth Congress of the International Academy of Comparative Law* (Bruylant 2007)

'Comparative Legal Families and Comparative Legal Traditions' in Reinhard Zimmermann and Mathias Reimann (eds), *Oxford Handbook of Comparative Law* (OUP 2006)

'Professional Traditions: The Reciprocating Ethics of Jurist and Judge' in Johan Erauw and others (eds), *Liber Memorialis Petar Sarcevic: Universalism, Tradition and the Individual* (Sellier European Law 2006)

'Droit mondial, droit mondialisé ou droit du monde?' in Bénédicte Fauvarque-Cosson and others (eds), *De tous horizons: Mélanges Xavier Blanc-Jouvan* (Société de législation comparée 2005)

'Penser le plurijuridisme' in Jean-Louis Bergel (ed), *Le plurijuridisme* (Presses universitaires d'Aix-Marseille 2005)

'Teaching Comparative Law and Teaching Law Comparatively' in Leska Ogiegly and others (eds), *Mélanges Maksymiliana Pazdana* (Zakamycze 2005)

'Comparative Legal Reasoning and the Courts: A View from the Americas' in Guy Canivet and others (eds), *Comparative Law Before the Courts* (BIICL 2004)

'Conclusions générales: La codification à la française, une petite histoire d'une grande tradition' in Régine Beauthier and Isabella Rorive (eds), *Le Code Napoléon, un ancêtre vénéré? Mélanges offerts à Jacques Vanderlinden* (Bruylant 2004)

'Legal Cultures and Legal Traditions' in Mark Van Hoecke (ed), *Epistemology and Methodology of Comparative Law* (Hart 2004)

'Legal Education and Legal Hegemony' in Swiss Institute of Comparative Law (ed), *Imperialism and Chauvinism in the Law* (Schulthess 2004)

'A Transnational Concept of Law' in Peter Cane and Mark Tushnet (eds), *The Oxford Handbook of Legal Studies* (OUP 2003)

'L'echo double du champart. Y a-t-il des traces en droit civil québécois?' in Benoit Moore (ed), *Mélanges Jean Pineau* (Themis 2003)

'The Nationalist Heritage' in Roderick Munday and Pierre Legrand (eds), *Comparative Legal Studies: Traditions and Transitions* (CUP 2003)

'The Relations Between Parties, Judges and Lawyers in the Quebec Civil Procedure' in Marcel Storme and Cipriano Gómez Lara (eds), *La relación entre las partes, los jueces, y los abogados*, vol 3 (XII Congreso Mundial de Derecho Procesal Universidad Nacional Autónoma de México 2003)

'Commensurability and Translatability' in James Nafziger and Symeon Symeonides (eds), *Law and Justice in a Multistate World: Essays in Honor of Arthur T von Mehren* (Transnational 2002)

'North America as a Medieval Legal Construction' in Mauro Bussani and Ugo Mattei (eds), *The Common Core of European Private Law* (Kluwer Law International 2002)

'International Private Law of Contracts' in Patrick J Borches and Joachim Zekoll (eds), *International Conflict of Laws for the Third Millenium: Essays in Honor of Friedrich K Juenger* (Transnational 2001)

'The Historical Origins of the Trust' in Alfredo Mordechai Rabello (ed), *Aequitas and Equity: Equity in Civil Law and Mixed Jurisdictions* (The Harry and Michael Sacher Institute for Legislative Research and Comparative Law 1997)

'Quebec: Mixité and Monism' in Esin Örücü and others (eds), *Studies in Legal Systems: Mixed and Mixing* (Kluwer 1996)

'Du droit international privé' in Barreau du Québec and Chambre des notaires du Québec (eds), *La réforme du Code civil: Personnes, successions, biens* (Presses de l'Université Laval 1993)

'La civilisation de la common law' in Alain-François Bisson and others (eds), *Mélanges Germain Brière* (Wilson & Lafleur 1993)

'Le Trust et le ius commune' in Pierre Legrand (ed), *Common Law d'un siècle à l'autre* (Éditions Yvon Blais 1993)

'Private International Law and the New International Legal Professions' in *Mélanges von Overbeck* (Presses de l'Université Fribourg 1990)

'Le droit comparé et la Cour suprême du Canada' in Ernest Caparros and others (eds), *Mélanges Louis-Philippe Pigeon* (Wilson & Lafleur 1989)

'The Right to Privacy in Quebec Law' in Dale Gibson (ed), *Aspects of Privacy Law: essays in Honour of John M Sharp* (Butterworths 1980)

CONFERENCE PROCEEDINGS

'Transnational Legal Thought: Plato, Europe and Beyond' in Miguel Maduro and others (eds), *Transnational Law: Rethinking European Law and Legal Thinking* (CUP 2014)

'Accommodating Unity' in Sam Muller and Sidney Richards (eds), *Highest Courts and Globalisation* (Hague Academic Press 2010)
'Culture and the Common Law' in H Patrick Glenn and Monique Ouellete (eds), *Culture, Justice and Law* (Éditions Thémis 1994)
'Harmonization of Private Law Rules between Civil and Common Law Jurisdictions' in International Academy of Comparative Law, *XIIIth International Congress General Reports* (Éditions Yvons Blais 1992)

Index

Lightning Source UK Ltd.
Milton Keynes UK
UKHW020213101221
395414UK00002B/28